Supreme Courts Under Nazi Occupation

Supreme Courts Under Nazi Occupation

Edited by
Derk Venema

Routledge
Taylor & Francis Group
LONDON AND NEW YORK

First published in 2022 by Amsterdam University Press Ltd.

Published 2025 by Routledge
4 Park Square, Milton Park, Abingdon, Oxon OX14 4RN
605 Third Avenue, New York, NY 10158

Routledge is an imprint of the Taylor & Francis Group, an informa business

ISBN: 9789463720496 (hbk)
ISBN: 9781041186731 (pbk)
ISBN: 9781003704553 (ebk)
NUR 689

Cover photo: Processen tegen illegale werkers. Vermoedelijk het proces tegen leden van de verzetsgroep de Geuzen en de Oranjewacht in het gebouwvan de Hoge Raad. Beeldnr. 91043, Beeldbank WO2 – NIOD.

Cover design: Coördesign, Leiden

DOI: 10.5117/9789463720496

For Product Safety Concerns and Information please contact our EU representative:
GPSR@taylorandfrancis.com
Taylor & Francis Verlag GmbH, Kaufingerstraße 24, 80331 München, Germany

Table of Contents

List of Figures and Tables

Acknowledgements

This research project was initiated and organised without any special organisational embedding and largely without any special funding. The authors would like to thank Martin Löhnig, the University of Regensburg and the Deutsche Forschungsgemeinschaft for making possible the project symposium at that university in 2017. The University of Regensburg also graciously financed the proofreading of the text. The Open University's Library Commission and Law Faculty kindly sponsored the open access version of this book. The editor wishes to thank Alex Jettinghoff and Hans den Tonkelaar for their helpful comments on chapters 1, 9 and 13. Finally, the editor would like to express his gratitude to the reviewers for Amsterdam University Press, Wolfgang Form and an anonymous reviewer, for their appreciation and helpful suggestions.

Note on quotations: all translations of quotes are the authors' except where indicated otherwise.

Wijchen, 27 May 2022

Acknowledgments

1 War, Law, Society, and the Courts, 1939-1945: An Introduction

Derk Venema

Abstract

This chapter presents in brief the function of courts in a democratic rule of law state, the German ideas and strategies of occupation rule, the international and national laws regarding military occupation (the Hague Regulations for Land Warfare), and the relations between occupier and occupied. The reality of occupation is characterized in sociological and anthropological terms, as distinguished from a moral approach. The choice of cases and the structure of the book are explained, and the possibility of answering the question 'how did the courts do?' is addressed.

Keywords: Nazi occupation, World War II, supreme courts, judiciary, Hague Regulations

1 Introduction

'Some consider striving for expediency fundamentally wrong, others consider the principled standpoint unjustifiable', wrote P.A.J. Losecaat Vermeer, a member of the Dutch supreme court, on 11 November 1943 to Leiden University law professor R.P. Cleveringa.[1] This quote from their discussion of the supreme court's policy characterizes many of the difficulties judges across Europe faced under Nazi occupation. The court's dilemma was as follows: should we either assert our right to review the occupier's ordinances and thus assume the position of official evaluator of the occupation regime's policies, or deny Dutch courts that right, lie low, and apply the occupier's

1 Correspondence published in Venema 2008, 75-85, quote at 83. All translations from it are the author's.

Venema, D. (ed.), *Supreme Courts Under Nazi Occupation*. Taylor & Francis Group 2022
DOI: 10.5117/9789463720496_CH01

measures unchecked? This book will show that this and similar dilemmas are not easily solved.

In this first comparative study on all supreme courts of the democratic countries occupied by Nazi Germany,[2] the question is explored what the highest judicial body can do to defend democracy, the rule of law, and the population against an antidemocratic occupier. In the many studies on Nazi rule over Europe during the Second World War, the judiciaries have not usually had a very prominent place. This is hardly justified when their position is taken into account: when the executive and legislative powers often had to be shared with German officials, the courts, as highly specialized government organs, were left relatively intact. Therefore, the highest courts were looked to for guidance and moral support. Not only the lower judges, but also lawyers and the general public expected from their supreme courts a clear stance on the occupation regime and instructions on how to deal with the occupier's measures and policies. Irrespective of the extraordinary circumstances, courts play a crucial role in maintaining public order, which is in the interest of the people as well as the rulers, in normal times as much as in war.[3] But the Germans wanted to introduce a particular kind of totalitarian ethnocentric order called National Socialism, which went much further than merely preserving the existing social order and benefitted only a small minority, even in the 'racially similar' Germanic countries. This left the judiciaries, at least as much as other civil service institutions, caught between the powerful Nazi occupier and the interests of the population they served. The supreme courts, as the occupier's liaison for the judiciary, found themselves in a particularly precarious position. I shall first discuss further the necessary historical and socio-legal background, and say more about the choice of cases and the structure of the book at the end of this introduction.

Here, I will present in brief the function of courts in a democratic rule of law state, the German ideas and strategies of occupation rule, the international and national laws regarding military occupation, and the sociology of the relations between occupier and occupied. The country studies will present in detail the legal and other interactions between the courts and the German occupying authorities. They will discuss, as far as sources permit, the supreme courts' adjudication and other actions, their opinions on their role and their duty, the degree of

2 Joeri Michielsen wrote a comparative study of Belgium, the Netherlands and Luxembourg: Michielsen 2004. Another comparative study is Venema 2012.

3 Lammers 1995, 6.

their Nazification, the measure of their success in preserving what was left of democracy and rule of law, and what else they could do for their countries and their peoples. The last chapter will summarize the results of the country studies, and draw conclusions regarding the question of the defensibility of democracy, rule of law, and society under Nazi occupation. Finally, the inescapable question of 'judging the judges' will have to be addressed: what could be expected from them, as judges and as humans, and did they live up to it? And what could not be expected from the supreme courts and why?

2 Courts in a Democratic Rule-of-law State

For present purposes,[4] the rule of law, or German *Rechtsstaat*, is defined in the words of a leading German pre-war constitutional lawyer, Richard Thoma, as a principle that 'requires that the powers of the public authority and the rights and freedoms of citizens and their corporate bodies be as clearly and precisely delineated as possible, and above all that the legality of the life of the state be guaranteed by the right to invoke independent courts in legal disputes of all kinds.'[5] Democracy is, very generally, taken as a 'method or process by which a group or association of people makes collective decisions about their common affairs' based on and aimed at realizing the two fundamental democratic values: liberty and equality.[6] It belongs to any credible form of democracy, that it 'observes the rule of law, sustained by an independent judiciary.'[7]

Three elements of the democratic rule of law state are especially relevant here: first, the courts as independent and impartial appliers of the law; secondly, power balance: the courts as one branch of government checking the other two (executive and legislative);[8] thirdly, the democratic content of the law. Connecting these three elements are, on the one hand, legal guarantees for the independence of the judiciary and, on the other, the

4 The literature on the rule of law and democracy is vast. It is not attempted here to do it justice. A very brief characterisation of democracy and rule of law will have to suffice.

5 Thoma 1930-32, 186-200. Cited from the translation by Peter C. Caldwell in Jacobson & Schlink 2000, 168.

6 In the monumental study by Frederick G. Whelan, Whelan 2019, 1 & 36.

7 Whelan 2019, 622. Empirical support for the claim that an independent judiciary is a necessary condition for democracy and the development of political and civil liberties is delivered by Howard & Carey 2004 and Linzer & Staton 2015.

8 See the section 'The Separation of Powers' in Barak 2006, 35-51.

professional attitude, often equated with integrity, that is vital to the realization of the legal framework: 'the commitment of judges to exercise their powers in accordance with the law, and the corresponding willingness of politicians to accept their determinations.' This commitment and willingness are symbolically and ritually affirmed in the oath of office.[9] The public nature of the oath psychologically warrants the effect of the promise on the official's behaviour.[10]

In this context, judges support the rule of democratic law by their commitment to due process. A number of virtues and values, which are necessary to realise due process, have been attributed to the 'good judge.'[11] They have not changed much from ancient times to the democratic era.[12] Today, they can be found in many codes of professional ethics drafted by the profession itself. In the *Bangalore Principles of Judicial Conduct*,[13] drafted under the auspices of the United Nations, the following values or virtues are listed: *independence* (individual and psychological as well as institutional: from private, societal, and political pressures), *impartiality* (absence of bias or prejudice and appearance thereof in process and decision), *integrity* (exemplary behaviour and scrupulous respect for the law and community standards in professional and private conduct), *propriety* (never damage the dignity of the office in social relations and activities, misuse confidential information, nor abuse your judicial status), *equality* (never treat parties differently on irrelevant grounds, always hear both sides), and *competence and diligence* (maintain your expertise and skills, and good working relationships within the court; work efficiently).

In the concluding chapter, I will return to the functions and virtues of the supreme court judge in a rule-of-law democracy, and assess what the Nazi occupiers broke down and what supreme courts could preserve under the occupation.

9 Aroney 2018, 197.

10 Schwartz et al. 2019.

11 See on judicial ethics generally Soeharno 2009.

12 A series of prints from 1606 by Dutch artists Joachim Uytewael and Willem van Swanenburgh titled *Thronus Iustitiae* depicting court scenes has not ceased to inspire judges to this day, hence the subtitle of the 2014 edition: '400 years of inspiration for judges': Den Tonkelaar & Den Tonkelaar 2014. As most model judges in the pictures date from biblical times (like Salomon) and classical antiquity (like Roman jurist Papinian), it is fair to say that the inspiration for today's judges dates back even another 2500 years. Cf. also United Nations Office on Drugs and Crime 2007, 147-159.

13 The Bangalore Principles have been published in United Nations Office on Drugs and Crime 2007.

3 German Expansionism: Ideas and Strategies

As many wars before and after, the German war of expansion was justified by the initiating state with arguments historically appearing in many 'just war theories',[14] such as reclaiming rightful possessions (against the Treaties of Versailles, Verdun, even Westphalia (1648)[15]), securing peace and self-protection (against the British, Jews, Slavs, liberals, communists), and organizing the protection of others (the Germanic peoples). But there was also the ethnocentric argument: restoration of German greatness, for which *Lebensraum* (living space) was necessary, the only clear war aim Hitler had.[16] Some of these motives had already been developed into elaborate theories about the superiority of the German race, the deadly conspiracy of the Jews and the inferiority of other races in general, the mythical status of Hitler, and National Socialism as the magic road to eternal glory and bliss – for 'ethnic Germans.' According to German ideologues, the Second World War was no ordinary military conflict. The war was 'total', not primarily because of its extensive impact on every-day life in Europe, but, as Arthur Seyss-Inquart, the *Reichskommissar* in the Netherlands, put it: because it was the 'expression of the struggle [*Kampf*] for the spiritual [*geistliche*] foundations of human life on this continent.'[17] How exactly a Europe under German rule was to be organized politically, however, had not been thought through at all by Hitler and his leadership circle; the Führer did not have so much as a rough 'programme',[18] only his ideology of 'expansion without object' and eternal existential struggle.[19] The German conquerors made up their occupation policies as they went along.[20] Maybe Hitler's social-Darwinist idea of *Elitenauslese* (selection of the best functionaries by means of uncontrolled competition) also extended to occupation schemes.[21]

Nevertheless, there were German *theories* about ruling a large part of the European continent, meant to replace much of existing public international law, appearing under the moniker of '*Großraumverwaltung*' (administration of a large region). It was the 'Crown Jurist of the Third Reich', law professor

14 See for an overview: Walzer 1992.

15 Propaganda minister Joseph Goebbels in a speech on 12 July 1940, Mazower 2008, 108-109.

16 Kroener et al. 2000, 165.

17 Seyss-Inquart 1942, 9-10; cf. Krois 1942, 22, who speaks of the 'formation of a world section (*Erdteil*) in the sense of a new world view (*Weltanschauung*).'

18 Kroener et al. 2000, 152-153.

19 Kershaw 2000a, Ch. 6, esp. 158-159; Kershaw 2000c, 402-404.

20 Mazower 2008, Introduction.

21 Broszat 1983, 166-167; Hitler 1942, p. 577, 676.

Carl Schmitt, who in his April 1939 book had coined the term *'völkerrechtliche Großraumordnung'* (order of large regions under international law), serving as justification for Germany's expansionist desires.[22] These desires had become manifest reality in the *Anschluss* of Austria and the annexation of the Czech *Sudetenland* the year before, and in the partition of Czechoslovakia and the establishment of the *Protektorat Böhmen und Mähren* the previous month. A *Großraum* is a region where different states participate in an association in which the *Führungsvolk*, the people creating and leading the *Großraum*, has the leading role. Powers from one *Großraum* are forbidden to intervene in another. When Germany invaded Poland, going against international law, Schmitt's theory was considered outdated by some. Werner Best, who was one of them, constructed a new version called *'völkische Großraumordnung'*, replacing 'under international law' with 'of peoples'. This meant that all peoples – not 'states' – taking part in a certain *Großraumordnung* could organize themselves in their own way, within the limits set by the *Führungsvolk*. The rules organising the *Großraum* should, according to Best, be much more flexible than the outdated international legal rules, allowing the *Führungsvolk* to rule as it sees fit.[23]

Best himself became directly involved in the administration of occupied territories, first as *Kriegsverwaltungschef* (Chief of the Administration) under the Military Commander in France in 1940, before being appointed in 1942 as *Reichsbevollmächtigter* (the Reich's Plenipotentiary) in occupied Denmark. He interrupted his work in France for a research tour of all other occupied democracies except Luxembourg, and compiled his findings in a comparative study of the occupation administrations under the title *Die deutschen Aufsichtsverwaltungen* (the German supervisory administrations).[24] In this report, he expressed two maxims of *Großraumverwaltung* for the period of belligerent occupations: 'Kein Schema!' ('No scheme!'), referring to the importance of letting local and current circumstances determine the course of action,[25] and 'Wenig regieren' (minimal government), which was based on grounds of efficiency as well as the cultural diversity of the peoples under the *Großraumverwaltung*.[26] Building on this, he constructed a fourfold typology of *Großraumverwaltungen* meant for the thousand years after the war. The *Aufsichtsverwaltung* was one of the types, which he defined as consisting of

22 Schmitt 1939. See Stirk 1999; Herbert 1996, 271-275.

23 Herbert 1996, 275-279. See also Best 1941a, 35.

24 Best 1941b.

25 Best 1941b, 66; see also Best 1941a, 44-49.

26 Best 1941b, 67, 68; see also Best 1941a, 39-40;

a small staff supervising and guiding the loyally collaborating government agencies who themselves remain responsible for the administration.[27] Still, his theory was primarily an academic exercise, and no more than Schmitt's suited as a practical guide for ruling the occupied countries.[28] Nevertheless, one element of Best's theory was indeed executed, albeit not with reference to it: he explicitly mentioned the possibility of the 'total annihilation or removal' from the *Großraum* of 'weaker peoples' by the *Führungsvolk*, in a word: genocide – although he seemed to prefer their subordinate inclusion in the *Großraum*.[29]

Although the theories of Schmitt and especially Best give an insight into Nazi ideology about the future political situation of Europe,[30] they were never used to guide the administration of occupied territories. An obvious reason for that was the temporary nature of the 'Western' occupations as opposed to the millennial post-war *Großraumverwaltung*. Another reason was the constantly changing dynamics of the situation: increasing exploitation of the occupied countries for the German war efforts, and the corresponding levels of resistance on the part of the inhabitants. There was no opportunity to build a stable uniform regime structure. Add to that the difference in personalities of the occupation regimes' leaders and the power struggles between the German army, security and police forces, NSDAP, and administrative bodies, and it becomes clear that not theory but practical problems and racist prejudice determined the form of occupation administrations.[31]

The only things the 'western' occupations had in common, was how they differed from the 'eastern ones': the occupations of the democratic countries were not undertaken to wipe the soil clean for German resettlements. They functioned, first, as protection against possible British attacks, and, secondly, the Germanic peoples in Norway, Denmark, Flanders (Belgium's northern, Dutch-speaking half), Luxembourg, and the Netherlands were viewed as racially similar and therefore potential allies in a post-war *Großraum*. The Protectorate and Luxembourg were destined to be integrated in the Reich as soon as the war was over, while the future status of France, a 'mixed-race' country, remained somewhat vague.[32] There are, however, two other factors

27 Best 1941a, 54-58; cf. Best 1941b, 71-72; Röhr 1997, 13-14; Kroener et al. 2000, 123-124.

28 Moll & Wassermann 2017, 2124, on the journal by the same title appearing from 1941 to 1943, devoted to this subject, of which Werner Best was an editor.

29 Herbert 1996, 283, leaves out this last point; see Meyer 1992, 36; Quotes from Best 1941a, 42.

30 Herbert 1996, 290 on Best's prestige as *Großraum* ideologue.

31 Cf. the excellent explanation by Röhr 1997, 19-20, 45.

32 Mazower 2008, 109-111.

of influence on the occupation regimes and their attitudes towards the judiciaries: the international law of war, which the Germans did take into account to a certain extent, and the sociological intricacies of foreign occupation in general and the Nazi occupations in particular. The interactions of these factors with the local contexts determined the manoeuvring room and the actions of the supreme court judges in the occupied territories.

4 The Hague Regulations for Land Warfare

Hitler's distrust of law and lawyers is well documented.[33] Although he used laws himself to implement his policies, he did not like the idea of existing laws hindering the realization of his goals. This points towards the 'dual state'-character of Nazi rule: on the one hand there still existed the whole administrative system of laws and formalities, called the 'state of norms', which was necessary to maintain order in the administration and in society. On the other hand, simultaneously a 'state of measures' operated in the form of organizations like the SS, who could act in complete disregard of the law and legally competent authorities to persecute persons perceived as undesired or dangerous to the National Socialist order.[34] The German administrators in the occupied territories, many of whom had law degrees, knew very well they had to rely on the local legal system and other administrative institutions to maintain public order.[35] That is why in all occupied democratic countries they kept most of it intact. They also understood that any organization must be well oiled by rules to work. In the Netherlands, the official occupation gazette (*Verordnungsblatt*) published over 800 ordinances from May 1940 to March 1945. And there is another reason why Hitler's law and lawyers allergy was unnecessary: most German lawyers, including judges, were loyal to National Socialist Germany, and often found ways to interpret or bend existing law to produce desired outcomes in their 'working towards the Führer'.[36]

Not only were most laws of the occupied countries left in force, in the first years of the occupations German officials kept insisting that they respected international law as well. This primarily regarded the Hague Regulations of Land Warfare, which are annexed to the 1907 Hague Convention of Land

33 Kershaw 2000c, 506-508, 510-511, 522; Weinkauff 1968, 46-56. Cf. Mazower 2008, 5, 11.

34 Fraenkel 2017.

35 This is the case with many oppressive regimes: Graver 2015, 35-45.

36 Rüthers 1997; Kershaw 2000b, Ch. 13.

Warfare. The Hague Convention was signed and ratified by most independent countries in the world, including Germany. Although Germany had left the League of Nations in 1933, Hitler never withdrew from this treaty, which is applicable law to this day, supplemented by article 64 of the 4th Geneva Convention from 1949.[37] One single article of these Hague Regulations governed the relation between the courts of the occupied country and the legislative activity of the occupier: article 43. It defines the position of any occupational regime as follows:

> The authority of the legitimate power having in fact passed into the hands of the occupier, the latter shall take all the measures in his power to restore, and ensure, as far as possible, public order and civil life, while respecting, unless absolutely prevented, the laws in force in the country.[38]

The Hague Regulations were included in a German army manual containing the relevant international laws of war, issued 1 October 1939, one month *after* Germany had started the invasion of Poland.[39] Even inside the *Wehrmacht*, there were some advocates of international law.[40] In the occupations of the Netherlands, Denmark and Norway, Germanic *Brudervölker*, the Hague Regulations were, initially, to be strictly observed. Denmark was to be treated as a model occupation, and used as window-dressing in political propaganda.[41] For the other western occupations, the Hague Regulations were also treated as relevant, although not necessarily binding, by the occupation regimes.[42]

In the course of its history, occupiers and occupied have interpreted this article differently: the scope of 'public order and civil life' and the meaning of 'absolutely prevented' were especially contested. There has never been an independent inter- or supranational institution for the review of occupiers' ordinances, which leaves the privilege and burden of review to the courts

37 Dinstein 2009, 110-111 (No. 258). Regulations Concerning the Laws and Customs of war on Land, annexed to Hague Convention Hague Convention (IV) of 1907. The text of the Hague Regulations, as that of the Geneva Conventions, is available through the International Red Cross humanitarian law database: http://www.icrc.org/ihl.nsf.

38 For 'civil life', the French text reads 'vie public'. This is often misleadingly translated as 'public life', which has a much narrower scope.

39 Heeresdruckvorschrift 231, *Kriegsvölkerrecht: Sammlung zwischenstaatlicher Abkommen von allgemeiner Bedeutung für die Truppe* (1 Oct. 1939), see Kroener et al. 2000, 15, 18.

40 For example, Helmuth James Graf von Moltke: Luban 2021, esp. 640-654.

41 As was extensively proclaimed by 'X.' in the *Frankfurter Zeitung* of 4 July 1940 (X. 1940). See for Norway and Denmark specifically: Kroener et al. 2000, 63-64, 127.

42 Kroener et al. 2000, 15, 121; see also the country studies in this volume.

of the occupied countries. The fact that there were no international legal rules regarding judicial review by national courts, is probably explained by two factors: first, occupations were not expected to last longer than a few months, so legal changes were expected to be but few and the resolution of disputes over their necessity could wait until the *postliminium*, the post-war settlement of disputes concerning the war and occupation period.[43] Secondly, the larger and most influential signatory states in 1907 regarded themselves primarily as potential occupiers and had no interest in mechanisms restraining their legislating powers.[44] An authoritative opinion of the day was that the phrase 'unless absolutely prevented' actually meant 'unless military interests dictate otherwise', which was considered a much lower threshold.[45] This argument originated in the 19th-century Prussian invention of 'military necessity' as a blanket justification for breaking rules of war.[46]

Another problem for the interpretation of Hague Regulations article 43 was that it was almost literally copied from the Brussels Declaration from 1874: for the night-watchman state of the 19th century, 'public order and civil life' had a far more limited scope than it had in the mid-20th century developing social democracies.[47] And even this broader scope was not enough for Nazi ideologues like Holland's *Reichskommissar* Seyss-Inquart, who viewed the task of his occupational regime as exceeding the duties of a 'regular' occupier. Not only should the German occupier ensure mere 'public order and civil life', but he should also engage in the political task of *Menschenführung*, the comprehensive guiding of people in all their actions and planning, which included unifying all religious and political creeds in order to take part in the epic historical struggle of the Germanic peoples.[48] State practices and court opinions regarding Hague Regulations 43 since 1907 have been, as we shall see, ambiguous.

Important to note is that, while article 43 of the Hague Regulations limits the right to formally change the law, it says nothing about disrespecting it. Some parts of the law of an occupied country, notably its constitution, are necessarily breeched by the mere fact of the occupation.[49] This state of affairs is taken as the point of departure for the international law of occupation and

43 Best 1999, 619-634.

44 Hull 1908, 216; Cassese 2000, 193-198.

45 Baxter 1950, 243-244.

46 Nabulsi 2007, 29-31.

47 Benvenisti 2004, 10-11, 29-31.

48 Seyss-Inquart 1942, 9-10.

49 Stirk 2009, 178.

is not regulated by it. The country studies will show what role international law played in negotiations between occupier and occupied.

5 The Problems of Occupation: Reality and Morality

The word *war* derives from a Germanic verb meaning 'to bring into confusion',[50] which emphasizes an essential aspect of war: the obscurity and unpredictability of its course and outcome. Meticulous planning, ideological determination, military superiority nor supreme legal knowledge can ever fully prepare occupying forces for the complexities and exigencies of organizing the administration of the occupied territory, especially when it lasts longer than a few months.[51] Factors influencing the social dynamics of the occupied territory include the political situation, the economy, the treatment of the population by the occupier, the attitude of local elites, the reactions of other countries, etc.[52] After a closer look at some important aspects of these dynamics and their relevance for the supreme courts, we are in a position to discuss the possibilities of historical and moral judgement concerning the supreme courts' courses of action under Nazi occupation. I will call these aspects philosophical, sociological, and anthropological, without claiming total conceptual distinctness or absence of overlap.

5.1 Philosophy: Utilitarianism and Deontology

Occupation is not merely a rational technocratic problem of logistics and social control, the practicalities of which can be soberly negotiated between occupier and occupied. Between the two sides there will also be differences in cultural and linguistic identity, and above all: for the occupied the occupier is the enemy, the 'Other' dominating the 'Self',[53] which makes it an emotional and existential issue of *them* against *us*.[54] The two categories of concerns facing occupied countries – practical-material versus existential-spiritual concerns – correspond to two ethical approaches to the assessment of officials' behaviour under dictatorship. The first is utilitarianism, which looks at the best foreseeable outcomes in terms of practical consequences

50 https://www.etymonline.com/search?q=war.

51 Cf. Stirk 2009, Chapter 1. This became clear already in the 19th century, Nabulsi 2007, 63-65.

52 A study of the continuous adaptation of an occupation regime is reported by Majerus 2006, 131-145.

53 Brüggenmann 2006, 155-162, at 155; Lammers 1995, 8-10, 26-27.

54 Cf. Venema 2016; Lammers 1995, 4.

for aggregate social wellbeing.[55] This may amount to choosing the 'lesser evil', making non-heroic pragmatic decisions, not taking a principled stand, but cooperating to prevent worse – which may feel very unsatisfactory, but nevertheless be the safer option that better serves the material interests of the people. The other perspective is a moral or deontological one, arguing from the strict observance of principles. I will call it *moral hygiene*, which is the practice of keeping one's own identity distinct from that of the enemy, as well as the assessment by others of the successfulness of that practice. What matters in this perspective is the expression or rejection of (affiliation with) identities, irrespective of material costs, because the identities in question are of existential importance: good and evil. In this vein, for example, Hannah Arendt argues that under a totalitarian, and thus evil, regime, anyone who 'participates in public life at all, regardless of party membership or membership in the elite formations of the regime, is implicated in one way or another in the deeds of the regime as a whole.'[56] The 'nonparticipators' on the other hand, are the ones 'who have refused their support by shunning those places of "responsibility" where such support, under the name of obedience, is required.'[57] From this perspective, utilitarian justifications for not resigning under an evil regime like Hitler's sound 'rather absurd and indeed usually were not much more than hypocritical rationalizations of an ardent desire to pursue one's career.'[58] The correspondence from which I quoted at the start of this introduction shows the two aspects of the problem of occupation: the supreme court judge Losecaat Vermeer, still in office, stresses the need to keep the judiciary in Dutch hands for the material benefit of the people by keeping relations with the occupiers friendly, while professor Cleveringa, whose university had been closed by the occupier, points to the vital need to preserve Dutch legal and cultural values, even at the cost of material wellbeing. The judge was looking out for the best technical (and tactical) solution for keeping daily life for the Dutch people as normal as possible, arguing as a utilitarian. The professor, however, feared the possible loss of national identity and pride, demanding that judges practice strict moral hygiene. A sociological view of foreign occupation shows how these two concerns are inextricably entwined. It will prove equally difficult to keep their justification methods, utilitarianism and deontology, clearly separated.

55 A classic text is John Stuart Mill's *Utilitarianism* from 1861.

56 Arendt 2003a, 33.

57 Arendt 2003a, 47.

58 Arendt 2003b, 147-158, at 156.

5.2 Sociology: Cooperation and Legitimation

Sociologist C.J. Lammers has made several analyses of occupation regimes.[59] Every occupation regime can be analysed as a system of 'control organizations':[60] some of them newly erected by the occupier, such as the office of *Reichskommissar* or police organizations, others indigenous, such as municipal councils or the judiciary. When running an occupied country, it is wise to involve existing administrative organs, called by Lammers 'representative organizations', and use them as control organizations, simply because they already organize society and enjoy a certain amount of legitimacy. In the occupied country, there will be 'loyal elites', loyally cooperating with the occupier, and therefore 'legitimized from above', and 'native elites' who are 'legitimized from below' and whose loyalty lies with the part of the population less enthusiastic about the new rulers.[61] What legitimacy the Nazi occupiers had, rested chiefly on charisma and shared values, as opposed to the legitimacy of the domestic administration, which derived mainly from tradition and legal-rational procedures.[62] Of course, people always have pragmatic reasons to obey current rulers as well, but that is different from recognizing them as legitimate. The Nazis also realized that working with collaborating native elites not only had more legitimate authority, but could also save a great deal of administrative staff. France is a case in point: a partial occupation was also much cheaper and less complicated, and collaborationist president Pétain had more standing with the French than the German army.

Largely confirming Lammers' analysis, renowned fascism expert Philip Morgan in his recent study of the Western occupations emphasizes that functionaries of the occupied country, in turn, will be inclined to cooperate with an occupier, instead of resigning or rebelling, because they see themselves as impartial and objective 'representatives and defenders of the national interest,' and wish to continue their important work.[63] Their idea was, that the occupier's measures and policies could be handled and mitigated better when the administrative, legislative and adjudicative institutions

59 Lammers 2005, which is a monograph in Dutch. I will reference some of the chapters in their earlier English versions.

60 Lammers 1988, 446.

61 Lammers 1995, 7-10; Lammers 2003, 1379-1403.

62 See for these types of political legitimacy: Weber 1922, 124 & Teil 1, Kapitel 3; Conway & Romijn 2008, 8-11; Hechter 2009, 298; Lammers 2005, 66.

63 Morgan 2018, 155, 159.

remained in national hands.[64] They saw working with the enemy not as collaborationism, but as their duty to their country and their compatriots. And because the occupiers knew they needed local institutions, Morgan points out that for both sides, 'collaboration was the preferred outcome of collaboration.'[65] Note that Morgan uses the term *collaboration* in a neutral sense meaning cooperation, as distinct from *collaborationism*, which means cooperating on the basis of a shared ideology or for selfish reasons.

When an occupation starts, some functionaries of representative-turned-control organizations will turn out to be or become part of the loyal elite, while others will remain local elite. Mixed loyalties are a potential problem for any control organization. An occupier may try to improve loyalty by appointing more members of the loyal elite in control organizations or install new control organizations primarily staffed with loyal elite. A case in point are the courts. Some options were: pack the courts with more loyal elite, strengthen their control function, add new courts, or suspend the functioning of the courts. The last option would obviously be very costly and inefficient, and thus unattractive for both sides. Nevertheless, it could be useful as a threat or a last resort, again for both sides. The first three options were used in most occupied countries.

5.3 Anthropology: Purity and Contamination

As I have explained, an important and complicating factor is cultural and national identity.[66] When occupation is perceived as 'foreign', which in most cases it will be, the identity difference is emphasized and the inhabitants of the occupied country experience their identity as being under stress or threat, which boosts the group dynamical process producing and maintaining a national group identity and pride, in a word: nationalism.[67] These feelings are apparent in professor Cleveringa's letters, where he calls it a 'duty of every citizen to his people' to 'protect its spiritual values (morals, language, law) to the best of his ability'.[68] In his famous November 1940 protest speech as law faculty dean against the dismissal of Jewish professors by the occupier, Cleveringa called his Jewish colleague and friend Eduard Meijers a 'noble and true son of our people', as opposed to the 'foreigner, who

64 Morgan 2018, 174-175, 330. From this argument, David Luban coined the term 'desk mitigator' as the counterpart to 'desk perpetrator.' See Luban 2021, 615.

65 Morgan 2018, 189.

66 See for an overview: Gellner 1983.

67 Brown 2000, 132-133; Venema 2011, 93-94, 96-8; Mach 1993, Ch. 1 and 102-103.

68 Venema et al. 2008, 76, cf. 84.

at present hostilely reigns over us.'[69] These quotes heavily emphasize shared values, tradition, and group loyalty as the principal grounds for legitimacy. In this light, it is not surprising that making and maintaining distinctions between 'us' and 'them', or 'friend' and 'enemy' has been identified as the most fundamental function of politics.[70] The fact that these distinctions between friend and enemy, compatriot and foreigner, victim and perpetrator, us and them, right and wrong are so ingrained in occupied peoples' vocabulary during and after an occupation, points to the normative and moral character of an occupation.[71]

As a consequence, the blurring or transgression of the boundaries between those categories is highly problematic – another way in which war 'brings into confusion'. In anthropological terms this is called 'pollution'. It endangers not only the purity of the categories, but also social order in general.[72] A key aspect of pollution is that it is contagious. That is why, for example, women who had been romantically involved with members of the occupying forces were subjected to purging[73] (=purifying) rituals after liberation: they had overstepped the identity line, got themselves contaminated, and the contagiousness of their stained identity was considered a threat to social order. The purging rituals (for example, shaving the women's heads) identified, publicized and cleansed the potential sources of disorder, so as to symbolically disarm them. Contamination can occur irrespective of intentional or causal links between the contaminated individual and (actions of) the contaminating party.[74]

We can apply this to the subject at hand as follows. In the eyes of the general public, a supreme court judge who remains in office under an enemy occupier, may therefore be considered contaminated with the enemy's identity, even when he never meets a member of the occupation forces nor applies any of their laws. Another supreme court judge may choose to 'dirty his hands'[75] on purpose, for example by advising the occupier on a draft ordinance with the aim of making it less repressive than it would likely have

69 Protestrede Rudolph Cleveringa, 6, available at: https://www.universiteitleiden.nl/dossiers/de-universiteit-en-de-oorlog/cleveringas-biografie.

70 The classic text is Schmitt 2002 (orig. 1932). A contemporary version is presented in Mouffe 2000, Ch. 2.

71 Cf. Stirk 2009, 2-3.

72 Key texts are Douglas 1984, esp. 39-40, 128, 138; Ricoeur 1960; Oudemans & Lardinois 1987, esp. section 3.1, Ch. 4 and section 8.2.

73 Etymologically, 'purge' comes from Latin *purus* (pure), and thus means literally to purify.

74 Douglas 1984, Ch. 6, esp. 99, 113; Ricoeur 1960, first chapter.

75 Cf. Coady 2018.

been without his advice. Both judges can avert or cure the contamination by reaffirming the difference of the categories of 'us' and 'them' and showing that they still belong unequivocally to the 'us' side, for example, by a public protest against occupation policies or by their resignation. This is exactly what Cleveringa demanded of the supreme court judges: to reaffirm the difference between the national legal system (us) and the occupier's policies (them) either by reviewing of the occupier's ordinances, or by stepping down.[76] Or in the words of Hannah Arendt: only those who 'withdrew from public life altogether' – practising strict moral hygiene – could avoid legal and moral responsibility, by keeping their identity pure.[77] It has been noted by historians, that the way the Nazi ideology was forced upon the peoples of occupied democracies was counterproductive in the light of their interest in cooperation by the people, because it overemphasized the identity difference instead of trying to build more on common ground.[78]

Supreme courts have an especially significant place in occupation regimes.[79] As mentioned, the highly specialized judicial organs are usually left relatively intact. This makes their highest instances of great importance for both sides: for the occupier, being able to rely for its rule on the highest state organs is the most efficient way to govern. For the non-loyal native elites and their supporters, the highest judicial organ is seen as a very significant protector of their material interests as well as their national identity against the occupier's attempts to undermine those. Being so important and useful for both sides renders the position of a supreme court precarious. When it cooperates with the occupier it makes dirty hands, risks contamination with the occupier's identity, and thus loss of legitimacy. This in turn might make the occupier's use of the court less efficient, because he may need to resort to other means to ensure that the lower courts and other control organizations keep recognizing the court's authority. Those means will be more repressive and less efficient. When the court succeeds in retaining its authority with lower officials and the people by being critical of the occupier's actions and not cooperating automatically and wholesale, the occupier might be tempted to try and tip the scales in its favour by appointing loyal elite jurists in the court. This, however, would also contaminate the court and might compromise its authority. Again, this may cause lower courts and other legal officials to comply less, and, from the occupier's perspective, in turn make

76 Venema et al. 2008, 78.

77 Arendt 2003a, 34.

78 E.g. Mazower 2008, 7; Carlton 1992, 178.

79 For this paragraph cf. Lammers 1995, 25-27.

more repressive measures necessary. The struggle for material well-being and identity obviously is a power struggle, requiring many subtle tactics.

Judge Losecaat Vermeer tried to put professor Cleveringa's insistence on national values and moral hygiene into perspective by calling it the attitude of '*fiat iustitia, pereat mundus*' (let justice be done, though the world perish).[80] He himself was thinking along strategic lines and insisted on the legitimacy of rational and utilitarian considerations by weighing the material consequences of Cleveringa's position against those of his own. The dilemmas of remaining in or leaving office, cooperating or protesting, are part and parcel of the proverbial 'predicament of the wartime mayor,'[81] which characterizes the position of civil and public servants under enemy occupation. How this played out for Losecaat Vermeer and his colleagues in the Dutch and other supreme courts will be unveiled in the following chapters.

6 The Choice of Cases, the Structure of the Book, and the Big Question

The question we aim to answer in this study is: what can supreme courts do to defend democracy, the rule of law, and the population against an antidemocratic occupier? Therefore, all the countries that were democracies before they were occupied by Germany are included in this study. It might be argued that Slovakia should be included as part of the former democratic state of Czechoslovakia. Apart from the formal reason that it was not occupied, but formed by Nazi Germany as a satellite state, in the relevant respects the Protectorate of Bohemia and Moravia was the real successor of Czechoslovakia, and its supreme courts were the continuation of the Czechoslovakian institutions of the same name. Three other cases not fitting the description of Nazi-occupied democracy are included in this book to provide necessary and helpful context.

The opening chapter on the Belgian *Cour de Cassation* during the German occupation in the First World War presents the most important precedent of a recent and prolonged, and therefore comparable, military occupation. Besides being the experience the Belgian institutions had drawn lessons from, it was the most recent and relevant case other judges and lawyers in

80 Venema et al. 2008, 83.

81 Romijn 2006, 33-66; See also Morgan 2018, 208-209 on 'the classic and oft-repeated defence or justification of the collaborating official across occupied Europe in 1940.'

Europe could have been familiar with and would have looked to for guidance in the second wave of German occupations.[82] The next chapter presents a short history of the German *Reichsgericht* during Nazi rule. It serves two purposes: it shows how a supreme court functioned in a state under Nazi home rule, where it cooperated in the destruction of democracy and rule of law. It also shows what the occupiers were familiar with, and what they, as a consequence, may have expected and demanded from supreme courts in the occupied countries, regarding the level and methods of cooperation.

The central cases are then loosely ordered from the lightest occupation regime in Denmark to the most extensive in *de facto* annexed Luxembourg. This order presents the methods of oppression and incorporation in increasing measures of intensity. Before the concluding chapter, we present a very different case: the Italian *Corte di cassazione* in the puppet state of the Italian Social Republic (1943-1945) set up by the German occupiers and headed by *il Duce* Benito Mussolini. This brief look at the supreme court of an occupied, (partly) friendly and formerly allied nation will show what was different in a fellow fascist country, and, more interestingly, what was not.

Finally, how to answer the Big Question: how did the courts do? If we, living in the 21st century, want to draw evaluative conclusions on the behaviour of the supreme court judges under Nazi occupation, we have to keep three aspects of the German expansionist project in mind. First, the principal war aim was *Lebensraum* in the east, which necessitated strategic occupations to ward off British and French military threats. Secondly, although a German *Großraum* was a more distant goal to pursue properly after the war would be won, cultural and racist Nazification policies, including the persecution of the Jews, had started already. Thirdly, the ongoing war against Russia (among other factors) demanded ever-increasing exploitation of the occupied western countries, which included the dispossession of the Jews. The gradually intensifying nature of these three factors took its toll on the occupied societies, especially when Russia started to push back the German army in 1943, and made keeping public order a growing problem.

In the midst of these forces, the supreme courts had to take account of the two types of interests of the people, which have been discussed above. On the one hand, *material interests* were at stake: citizens' lives, freedoms, possessions, and what was left of the normality of everyday life. These

82 It was well known in the literature. For example, the two-volume study *International Law and the World War* by the American scholar James Wilford Garner (Garner 1920) discusses in detail the occupation of Belgium, including its judiciary's conflict with the German occupier.

are strongly dependent on a well-functioning legal system, which is the backbone of every society and economy.[83] Preserving it would therefore seem an obvious priority. On the other hand, *national identity interests* were at stake: the demarcation of the 'us' as opposed to the 'them', democracy versus Nazism, especially in those countries where cultural Nazification was being attempted. And because a national legal system is an important part of national identity, its preservation serves identity interests as well. But as law is an instrument in the hands of inventive and interpreting creatures called humans, it can be used to promote very different, indeed opposing goals: in many cases, national law can be invoked against the occupier's policies as well as employed to promote them. The fact that some interests were shared by both parties, like public order, made the use of the law potentially ambiguous. Ambiguity is precarious,[84] especially in a volatile and tense situation where the distinction between morally right and wrong persons and actions becomes all-important.

The sources do not permit complete and detailed comparisons of every imaginable aspect of supreme court judging under Nazi occupation, as reflected in the difference in length and content of the country studies. Moreover, the different situations of the occupied countries – size, location, accessibility, resources, politics, law, ethnic make-up, history, etc. – present many different forms and aspects of occupier-supreme court relations, their interactions and power struggles. Taken together with the many relevant factors in each separate country, however, this plethora of possibilities makes any 'what if…' scenario very unconvincing – an academic thought experiment at most. Taking into account also the *burden* of hindsight, passing moral judgement over the supreme courts' decisions appears somewhat presumptuous. So what *can* we learn from this research? If not an answer to the question what the judges *should* have done, it does provide an answer to the question what the supreme courts deemed necessary or optimal courses of action to promote material wellbeing and/or national identity and which results they produced. It also sheds light on the possibilities and limits of the legal system and the courts in the protection of democracy and rule of law. Therefore, what we can learn from the studies in this book, is not only what might be expected from the courts under an oppressive regime, but also, not unimportantly, what *cannot* be expected from them.

83 In a very different case of foreign rule, Paddy Ashdown experienced this first hand as High Representative in Bosnia, after his predecessors had failed to make the establishment of the rule of law their first priority. Stirk 2009, 192.

84 Douglas 1984, 39-40.

References

Arendt, Hannah, 'Personal Responsibility Under Dictatorship', in: Hannah Arendt & Jerome Kohn (Ed), *Responsibility and Judgment*, New York: Schocken Books 2003a, 17-48.

Arendt, Hannah, 'Collective Responsibility', in: Hannah Arendt & Jerome Kohn (Ed), *Responsibility and Judgment*, New York: Schocken Books 2003b, 147-158.

Aroney, N., 'The rule of law, religious authority, and oaths of office', *Journal of Law, Religion and State* (6) 2018-2-3, 195-212.

Barak, Aharon, *The Judge in a Democracy*, Princeton University Press 2006.

Baxter, Richard R., 'The Duty of Obedience to the Belligerent Occupant', *The British Yearbook of International Law* 1950, 235-266.

Benvenisti, Eyal, *The International Law of Occupation*, Princeton: Princeton University Press (2nd Ed) 2004.

Best, G., 'Peace conferences and the century of total war: the 1899 Hague Conference and what came after', *International affairs* (75) 1999, p. 619-634.

Best, Werner, 'Grundfragen einer deutschen Großraum-Verwaltung', in: *Festgabe für Heinrich Himmler*, Darmstadt: L.C. Wittig Verlag 1941a, 33-60.

Best, Werner, *Die deutschen Aufsichtsverwaltungen in Frankreich, Belgien, den Niederlanden, Norwegen, Dänemark und im Protektorat Böhmen und Mähren, vergleichende Übersicht*, Typescript 1941b, https://www.delpher.nl/nl/boeken/view?coll=boeken&identifier=MMKB18B:056057000.

Broszat, Martin, 'Das weltanschauliche und gesellschaftliche Kräftefeld', in: Martin Broszat & Norbert Frei (Eds), *Das Dritte Reich, Ursprünge, Ereignisse, Wirkungen*, Freiburg: Ploetz 1983, 158-168.

Brown, R., *Group Processes. Dynamics within and between groups*, (2nd Ed) Malden: Blackwell Publishers 2000.

Brüggenmann, K., 'Foreign Rule and Collaboration in the Baltic Countries, 1860-1920. New Directions in Research', *Journal of Baltic Studies* (37) 2006-2, 155-162.

Carlton, Eric, *Occupation. The Policies and Practices of Military Conquerors*, London: Routledge 1992.

Cassese, A., 'The Martens Clause. Half a Loaf or Simply Pie in the Sky?', *European Journal of International Law* (11) 2000/1, 187-216.

Cleveringa, R.P., [Protestrede], https://www.universiteitleiden.nl/dossiers/de-universiteit-en-de-oorlog/cleveringas-biografie.

Coady, C.A.J., 'The Problem of Dirty Hands', in: Edward N. Zalta (Ed), *The Stanford Encyclopedia of Philosophy* (Fall 2018 Edition), https://plato.stanford.edu/archives/fall2018/entries/dirty-hands/.

Conway, Martin & Peter Romijn, 'Political Legitimacy in Mid-Twentieth-Century Europe. An Introduction, in: Martin Conway & Peter Romijn (Eds), *The War for Legitimacy in Politics and Culture 1936-1946*, Oxford: Berg 2008, 1-27.

Den Tonkelaar J.D.A. & E.S.F. den Tonkelaar (Eds), *Thronus Iustitiae. 400 jaar inspiratie voor rechters*, Deventer: Kluwer, 2nd Ed. 2014.

Dinstein, Yoram, *The International Law of Belligerent Occupation*, Cambridge: Cambridge University Press 2009.

Douglas, M., *Purity and Danger. An Analysis of the Concepts of Pollution and Taboo*, London, ARK Paperbacks, 1984 (orig. 1966).

Fraenkel, Ernst, *The Dual State. A Contribution to the Theory of Dictatorship*, New York: Oxford University Press 2017 (orig. 1941).

Garner, James Wilford, *International Law and the World War*, London: Longmans, Green and Co. 1920.

Gellner, Ernest, *Nations and Nationalism*, Oxford, Blackwell, 1983.

Graver, Hans Petter, *Judges Against Justice. On Judges When the Rule of Law is Under Attack*, Heidelberg: Springer 2015.

Hechter, M., 'Alien Rule and Its Discontents'. *American Behavioral Scientist* (53) 2009-3, 289-310.

Herbert, Ulrich, *Best. Biographische Studien über Radikalismus, Weltanschauung und Vernunft*, Bonn: Dietz 1996.

Hitler, Adolf, *Mein Kampf*, München: Zentralverlag der NSDAP 1942.

Howard, R. M., & Carey, H. F., 'Is an independent judiciary necessary for democracy?', *Judicature* (87) 2004-6, 284-291.

Hull, William I., *The Two Hague Conferences and their Contributions to International Law*, Boston: Ginn & Company 1908.

Jacobson, Arthur J. and Bernhard Schlink (Eds), *Weimar A Jurisprudence of Crisis*, University of California Press Berkeley 2000.

Kershaw, Ian, *The Nazi Dictatorship. Problems & Perspectives of Interpretation* (4th Ed), London: Arnold 2000a.

Kershaw, Ian, *Hitler 1889-1936: Hubris*, New York: W.W. Norton 2000b

Kershaw, Ian, *Hitler 1936-1945: Nemesis*, New York: W.W. Norton 2000c.

Kroener, Bernhard R., Rolf-Dieter Müller & Hans Umbreit (Eds), *Germany and the Second World War, Vol. V/1 Organization and Mobilization of the German Sphere of Power*, Oxford: Clarendon Press 2000.

Krois, 'Die Verwaltung des Reichskommissars', *Reich – Volksordnung – Lebensraum* (II) 1942, 15-52.

Lammers, C.J., 'The Interorganizational Control of an Occupied Country', *Administrative Science Quarterly* (33) 1988, 438-457.

Lammers, Cornelis J., 'Levels of collaboration: A comparative study of German occupation regimes during the Second World War', *The Netherlands' Journal of Social Sciences* (31) 1995, 3-31.

Lammers, C.J., 'Occupation Regimes Alike and Unlike: British, Dutch and French Patterns of Inter-Organisational Control of Foreign Territories', *Organisation Studies*, 2003, 24(9), 1379-1403.

Lammers, C.J., *Vreemde overheersing, Bezetten en bezetting in sociologisch perspectief*, Amsterdam: Bakker 2005.

Linzer, D. A., & Staton, J. K., 'Global measure of judicial independence, 1948-2012' *Journal of Law and Courts* (3) 2015-2, 223-256.

Luban, David, 'Complicity and Lesser Evils: A Tale of Two Lawyers', *Georgetown Journal of Legal Ethics* (34) 2021-3, 613-664. https://papers.ssrn.com/sol3/papers.cfm?abstract_id=3817495

Mach, Zdzisław, *Symbols, Conflict, and Identity. Essays in Political Anthropology*, Albany: State University of New York Press 1993.

Majerus, Benoît: 'Von Falkenhausen zu Falkenhausen. Die deutsche Verwaltung Belgiens in den zwei Weltkriegen', in: Günther Kronenbitter, Markus Pöhlmann & Dierk Walter (Eds), *Besatzung. Funktion und Gestalt militärischer Fremdherrschaft von der Antike bis zum 20. Jahrhundert*, Paderborn: Ferdinand Schöningh 2006, 131-145.

Mazower, Mark, *Hitler's Empire. How the Nazi's Rules Europe*, New York: The Penguin Press 2008.

Meyer, Ahlrich, 'Großraumpolitik und Kollaboration im Westen Werner Best, die Zeitschrift 'Reich-Volksordnung-Lebensraum' und die deutsche Militärverwaltung in Frankreich', *Beiträge zur nationalsozialistischen Gesundheits- und Sozialpolitik* (10) 1992, 29-76.

Michielsen, J.N.M.E., *The 'Nazification' and 'Denazification' of the courts in Belgium, Luxembourg and the Netherlands, The Belgian, Luxembourg and Netherlands. Courts and their Reactions to Occupation Measures and Measures from their Governments Returning from Exile* (PhD Diss Maastricht), Maastricht: Universitaire Pers Maastricht 2004.

Mill, John Stuart, *Utilitarianism*, orig. 1861, many editions.

Moll, Martin & Heinz P. Wassermann: 'Reich, Volksordnung, Lebensraum', in: Michael Fahlbusch, Ingo Haar & Alexander Pinwinkler (Eds.), *Handbuch der völkischen Wissenschaften: Akteure, Netzwerke, Forschungsprogramme*, De Gruyter 2017, 2118–2124.

Morgan, Philip, *Hitler's Collaborators. Choosing between bad and worse in Nazi-occupied Western Europe*, Oxford: Oxford University Press 2018.

Mouffe, Chantal, *The Democratic Paradox*, London: Verso, 2000.

Nabulsi, Karma, *Traditions of war, Occupation, resistance, and the law*, Oxford: Oxford University Press 2007.

Oudemans, Th.C.W. & A.P.M.H. Lardinois, *Tragic Ambiguity. Anthropology, Philosophy and Sophocles' Antigone*. Leiden, E.J. Brill, 1987.

Ricoeur, P., *La Symbolique du mal* (*Finitude et culpabilité*, Vol.2), Paris, Aubier, 1960.

Röhr, Werner, 'System oder organisiertes Chaos? Fragen einer Typologie der deutschen Okkupationsregime im zweiten Weltkrieg', in: Robert Bohn, *Die deutsche Herrschaft in den „germanischen" Ländern 1940-1945*, Stuttgart: Franz Steiner Verlag 1997, 11-45.

Romijn, P., 'Ambitions and dilemmas of local authorities in the German-occupied Netherlands, 1940-1945', in: H. van Goethem, B. De Wever & N. Wouters (eds.) *Local Government in Occupied Europe*, Antwerp, University Press, 2006, 33-36.

Rüthers, B., *Die unbegrenzte Auslegung, Wandel der Privatrechtsordnung im Nationalsozialismus*, Heidelberg: C.F. Müller Verlag (5th Ed), 1997.

Schmitt, Carl, *Völkerrechtliche Großraumordnung: mit Interventionsverbot für raumfremde Mächte. Ein Beitrag zum Reichsbegriff im Völkerrecht*, Berlin: deutscher Rechtsverlag 1939.

Schmitt, Carl, *Der Begriff des Politischen*, Berlin, Duncker und Humblot, 2002 (orig. 1932).

Schwartz, S., Spires, E. & Young, R., 'Why do people keep their promises? A further investigation', *Experimental Economics* (22) 2019, 530–551.

Seyss-Inquart, A., 'Die politische Aufgabe des Reichskommissars', *Reich – Volksordnung – Lebensraum* (II) 1942, 9-14.

Soeharno, Jonathan, *The Integrity of the Judge. A Philosophical Inquiry*, Ashgate 2009.

Stirk, P., 'Carl Schmitt's "Völkerrechtliche Grossraumordnung"', *History of Political Thought* (20) 1999-2, 357-374.

Stirk, Peter, *The Politics of Military Occupation*, Edinburgh: Edinburgh University Press 2009.

Thoma, Richard, 'Das Reich als Demokratie', in Richard Thoma & Gerhard Anschütz (Eds) *Handbuch des deutschen Staatsrechts*, Vol 1, Tübingen: Mohr 1930-32, 186-200.

United Nations Office on Drugs and Crime (Ed), *Commentary on The Bangalore Principles of Judicial Conduct*, 2007, 147-159. https://www.unodc.org/documents/nigeria/publications/Otherpublications/Commentry_on_the_Bangalore_principles_of_Judicial_Conduct.pdf.

Venema, D., 'Transitional Shortcuts to Justice and National Identity', *Ratio Juris* (24) 2011-1, 88-108.

Venema, Derk, 'The Judge, the Occupier, His Laws, and Their Validity. Judicial review by the Supreme Courts of occupied Belgium, Norway, and the Netherlands 1940-1945 in the context of their professional conduct and the consequences for their public image', in: Margo De Koster, Hervé Leuwers, Dirk Luyten & Xavier

Rousseaux (Ed), *Justice in Wartime and Revolutions*, Brussels: State Archives 2012, 193-213.

Venema, Derk, 'Judiciaries and Foreign Rule. Legal anthropological reflections on three Belgian cases', in: Annie Hondeghem, Xavier Rousseaux & Frédéric Schoenaers, (Eds.), *Modernisation of the Criminal Justice Chain and the Judicial System. New Insights on Trust, Cooperation and Human Capital*, Dordrecht: Springer 2016 (*Ius Gentium: Comparative Perspectives on Law and Justice*, Vol. 50), 266-275.

Venema, Derk, Leny de Groot-van Leeuwen & Thomas Mertens (Eds), *Onder de huidige omstandigheden, De Hoge Raad en het Toetsingsarrest 1942*, Den Haag: Boom Juridische uitgevers 2008.

Walzer, Michael, *Just and Unjust Wars*, New York: Basic Books 1992.

Weber, M., *Wirtschaft und Gesellschaft*, Tübingen, Mohr, 1922.

Weinkauff, H., 'Die deutsche Justiz und der Nationalsozialismus. Ein Überblick', in: *Die deutsche Justiz und der Nationalsozialismus*, Vol. 1, Stuttgart: Deutsche Verlags-Anstalt 1968, 17-188.

Whelan, Frederick G., *Democracy in Theory and Practice*, Routledge 2019.

About the Author

Derk Venema is assistant professor at the Law Faculty of the Open University in the Netherlands. He has published on the Dutch judiciary in WWII and transitional justice theory, amongst other subjects. He teaches professional ethics at the Training Centre for the Judiciary SSR, and is an associated researcher at CegeSoma, Brussels.

2 Prelude: The Belgian Judiciary's First Experience of German Occupation, 1914-18

Mélanie Bost

Abstract

This chapter discusses the role of the Belgian Cour de Cassation during the German occupation in the First World War. It introduces the national and international rules regarding enemy occupation, and explains the controversy between the occupier and the court regarding the latter's legislative powers. The significance of Flemish activism and the internal struggles of the court are addressed. As the culmination point of occupier-court relations, the strike of 1918 is highlighted, which resulted in the introduction of German courts but also secured the court's post-war reputation.

Keywords: German occupation of Belgium in WWI; International law of occupation; Belgian Cour de Cassation; strategy of lesser evil; judicial strike.

1 Introduction

Between 1914 and 1918, most parts of Belgium were occupied by the German army. While the King and the army were struggling in the Flanders Fields, and the government was exiled in France and parliament was suspended, the magistracy, alone amongst the three state powers, kept on working as the guarantor of the permanence and continuity of the State.[1]

1 For a general overview of the history of occupied Belgium in 1914-18, see De Schaepdrijver 1997.

Venema, D. (ed.), *Supreme Courts Under Nazi Occupation*. Taylor & Francis Group 2022
DOI: 10.5117/9789463720496_CH02

With quite sketchy instructions, confidentially received from the government, and a recent body of international law of occupation that, still under construction in 1914, had rarely been applied, the magistracy found itself in a difficult position. It had to preserve the functioning of the judicial system and resist German interferences. Numerous *modi vivendi* had to be worked out in challenging political and military circumstances. The development of these circumstances would lead, in February 1918, to a severe crisis: a judicial strike that lasted ten months.

At the top of the judicial pyramid, the Supreme Court – the *Cour de Cassation* – was particularly exposed, even if, at the same time, it exerted an unprecedented influence. With the help of some key episodes of judicial 'cohabitation', this chapter focuses on the attitude of Belgium's highest-ranking magistracy during the country's first German occupation.[2] After an overview of the political and juridical resources available to the Court of Cassation, and a short description of the new judicial landscape shaped by the presence of an occupier, the following topics will be successively discussed: the role played by the Prosecutor General of the Court of Cassation during the first months of the military occupation; the official position of the Court regarding the issue of the legislative power of the occupier; the main sources of internal division within the Court, namely the support of magistrates who fell victim to the German repression and the administrative splitting of the country in 1917; and, finally, the events that led to the 1918 judicial strike.

2 How to Behave during the Military Occupation: Political and Juridical Guidelines

The continuity of the judicial service was prescribed by the Belgian government, which, on 1 August 1914, just before the German invasion, had left confidential instructions to the magistrates.[3] These instructions outlined the general principles that must guide the magistrates in the context of an occupation.

According to this document, all magistrates should continue in their functions, as long as the occupier did not impose obligations on them prejudicial

2 This chapter was written in the framework of the Interuniversity attraction pole P7/22 "Justice & Populations", Federal Public Service Scientific Policy Planning.

3 *Principes à observer par les magistrats de l'ordre judiciaire résidant en pays occupé*, Brussels Courthouse, Archives of the Court of Cassation Prosecutor Office, Occupation 1914-1918, 14 (XI).

to their honour or inconsistent with their patriotic duties, such as an oath of loyalty. This was the general principle that was to be observed. More precisely, the instructions provided, amongst other things, that all courts and tribunals should continue to apply the Belgian Constitution and Belgian laws, except those that were in conflict with the prerogatives of the occupier as recognized by international law. The government admitted in advance some consequences of an eventual military occupation, like the setting up of military tribunals by the occupier and the proclamation of martial law. It acknowledged to the occupier the exercise of a limited legislative power and even considered that an oath of loyalty could be required from the magistrates. In short, far from encouraging any civil resistance, these instructions given to the judiciary favoured a neutral and loyal cooperation with the occupying forces. In this regard, the guidelines complied with the legalistic attitude that the government had adopted since August 1914. The country entered the war in the name of international law, the treaties ensuring its perpetual neutrality having been violated by Germany; during its occupation, Belgian citizens were instructed to behave in accordance with international law. Facing German force, calling upon the protection of international law and its guarantors seemed the only possible strategy.[4]

The directives were directly influenced by international law: the legal texts (the Hague Convention IV, 1907) and the legal doctrine of *occupatio bellica* (war occupation), which gives an occupier provisional administrative tasks within the territories having fallen under its control.

International law, though still young and under construction, had developed considerably since 1870, in reaction to the brutal Franco-Prussian War. The three fundamental steps of the movement towards codification of the customs of war were the Brussels Conference of 1874, and the Hague Conferences of 1899 and 1907, called 'Peace Conferences'. Whereas the first, in the absence of a consensus, only resulted in a Declaration, the texts produced by the latter two constituted formal treaties for the states that had ratified them.[5] Throughout the three conventions, the powers of belligerents were progressively limited. Regarding the occupation of a territory by an enemy army, international law evolved from the ancient right of conquest into the new concept of occupation law. The key idea of this new branch of international law was that an occupier only had the *administration* of an occupied territory. Transfer of sovereignty, as it was under the conquest

4 On the major role the Hague Convention played during the war for Belgium, see Graditzky 2018.

5 On the role Belgium played in the negotiations of the three texts see Verwaest 2011.

paradigm, was no longer accepted. The occupier's power was considered a *de facto* one, not a legal one. It is provisional.

In 1914, the Hague Convention (IV) Regarding the Laws and Customs of War on Land of 1907 and its Annex, the Hague Regulations (HR), provided the legal framework for military occupations. Germany and Belgium had both ratified the Convention; it was, therefore, applicable during the occupation of Belgium. Under Articles 42 and 43, the occupier was entrusted with the mission to provisionally administer the occupied territory. Within the framework of its mission, the occupying power had to respect local laws, unless absolutely prevented.

The Hague Convention did not specifically address the judicial issue. Yet, prescribing that domestic law be maintained, it fostered the continuity of the judicial system. If the 1907 Convention remains silent on the behaviour that must be adopted by the judiciary of an occupied country, some recommendations can be gleaned from authors of legal doctrine. The decision to maintain judicial authorities was also subject to a widespread consensus among the scholars specialised in international law, even the German ones. The maintenance of the criminal laws of the invaded state would have a more imperative nature than other laws.[6] For this purpose, the occupying power must preserve the autonomy of the judicial power: "Pour les tribunaux existants il n'y a aucun motif de suspendre leur action, aussi longtemps que le vainqueur ne viole pas leur indépendance. (...) La liberté du juge doit être garantie, le juge ne peut se faire l'instrument de l'ennemi."[7] The maintenance of the national magistrates must rest on the free will of the two parties and respect for individual freedom: magistrates may at any time leave their posts. Although, for its part, the occupier preserves its rights to suspend and replace them. The possibility of justice being dispensed on behalf of the legitimate ruler is also accepted by doctrinal authors.

Beyond these basic principles, the issue of the behaviour of local magistrates in occupied territories received little attention before the war. Yet Paul Pradier-Foderé, an eminent French lawyer and magistrate himself, wrote: "La prudence et les aspirations saines d'un patriotisme intelligent leur conseilleront de tenir compte de l'état de fait où se trouve leur pays et

6 Bonfils 1908, p. 711. "For the existing tribunals, there is no motive to suspend their activities, as long as the victor does not violate their independence. (...) The liberty of the judge must be guaranteed, the judge cannot turn himself into the instrument of the enemy."

7 Loening 1873, 94-99. "For the courts of the occupied country, there is no ground to suspend their action, as long as the occupier does not violate their independence. (...). The judge's freedom must be guaranteed. The judge cannot become the instrument of the enemy."

de ne point entrer dans une lutte inutile avec l'occupant".[8] Henry Bonfils, professor of Law at the University of Toulouse, expressed a similar view: "Les magistrats locaux doivent tenir compte de l'état de fait de l'occupation, et le souci de leur propre dignité comme l'intérêt des justiciables leur commandent d'éviter tout conflit comme toute faiblesse envers l'ennemi."[9]

Belgian magistrates had very few experiences upon which to build. Since its independence, the country had never lived under enemy occupation. In 1914, the judiciary had, therefore, to draw on experiences from other countries. Yet these experiences were not very helpful. The closest reference – by virtue of proximity in space and time, and because of the close relationship between the French and Belgian legal systems – is the German occupation of French territories during the Franco-Prussian war in 1870-71, a conflict that in many aspects prefigured the First World War. The judicial cohabitation in 1870 started under good auspices as, conforming to a German instruction, the civil jurisdiction had to be exercised in accordance with French laws.[10] However, the cohabitation quickly fell short. After only three months, most jurisdictions suspended their activities. The writ of execution of the judgments was the source of conflict; Germans would not allow the tribunals to judge in the name of the new French Republic.[11] The tribunal of Laon, for its part, had ceased to operate since the beginning of the war; it considered the coexistence of justice and a foreign administration as both potentially incompatible and unacceptable.[12] This decision was heavily criticized in legal doctrine as irresponsible. Contrary to this, in 1914-18, the Belgian government instructed the judiciary to stay in office, as long as the cohabitation was tolerable.

After the Peace Conventions had entered into force, there was no experience of military occupation that was really comparable to that faced by the Belgian magistrates in 1914-18. In 1877, during the Russian occupation of Turkish territories (Russo-Turkish War, 1877-78), the Ottoman judicial organization, considered archaic by the Russians, was completely reorganized.

8 Pradier-Fodéré 1897, 828. "Caution and cleaver patriotism will advise them to take into account the de facto situation experienced by their country and not to enter a useless struggle with the occupier."

9 Bonfils 1908, 713. "Local magistrates must take into account the *de facto* nature of the occupation; plus, the concern to preserve their dignity and the interest of the citizens order them to avoid any conflict or weakness towards the enemy."

10 See Berger 2011.

11 See Loening 1873, 95-99.

12 Deliberation of the general assembly of the Laon's civil tribunal, 15 October 1870 (*Dalloz* 1871, 39-40). *Dalloz* is the gazette that published commentary, cases and legislation.

During the first Sino-Japanese War (1894-95), the Chinese judiciary ran away from the enemy and the Japanese authority had to install provisory tribunals. Lastly, during the Second Boer War (1899-1902), the British, who generally refused the application of the 1899 Hague Convention and behaved more as conquerors than occupiers, from the outset installed their own tribunals.[13]

In short, to guide their conduct, Belgian magistrates had few precedents upon which to draw. Belgian case law during the first German occupation of 1914-18 is therefore particularly interesting to study, in that it constituted one of the first applications of the new international law by national tribunals and complemented a hitherto quite theoretical legal doctrine.

3 New Actors

In 1914-18, German authorities opted for maintaining Belgian administrative services and establishing a civil administration in charge of supervising them.[14] Belgian public services continued to deal with current affairs under the direct supervision of the Germans. Within the civil administration, the *Justiz Abteilung* (Justice Department), made up of a few legal practitioners, was in charge of supervising the Ministry of Justice and relations with the judiciary. Since the latter was an independent power, the relations with it were more complex.

All in all, the fact that national judicial authorities carried on their activities suited the occupiers, who were anxious to maintain order and to pacify the territory. The magistrates, to keep their salaries and positions, were compelled to sign a statement of loyalty, as anticipated by the Belgian government.[15] This statement established the basis of the compromise enabling the judicial cohabitation to work. Magistrates would keep their position and be free to deliver rulings, as long as they acknowledged German authority and its prerogatives according to international law, and – as an additional clause for the members of the Public Prosecutor's Office – refrained from perpetrating any hostile action against the occupier.

The German authorities intervened in judicial life in many ways. Acting as a substitute for the executive power, the civil administration occasionally sent circular letters to public prosecutors (*procureurs du Roi*), but these were

13 Freeman 1947, 583-584.

14 In fact, the German General Governor set up a double administration: a military one and a civil one, the latter devoted to the administration of the occupied country.

15 Meyers 1919, col. 542.

rare and the Belgian prosecution offices were in fact fairly autonomous when it came to defining their penal policy. The German Governor-General, who took over royal prerogatives, exerted the power of pardon, which allowed him to intervene in the carrying out of punishments.

Furthermore, the German military often interacted with Belgian judicial authorities through its courts, in charge of enforcing martial law and applying occupation decrees. The scope of action of German military justice was constantly extended throughout the occupation, as thousands of decrees were issued to organise control over the population and the exploitation of the occupied territory's resources.[16] Magistrates partly lost their authority in favour of German military justice. They lost their jurisdiction over all individuals, German or Belgian, related to the occupation authorities and their area of jurisdiction was gradually reduced.

4 The Leading Action of the Chief Prosecutor at the Court of Cassation

War broke out in August 1914, during the judicial recess. The Prosecutor General of the Court of Cassation, Georges Terlinden, remained at his post, meeting daily at his office with the members of the Supreme Court who were present in Brussels. He assumed the role of spokesman and principal negotiator on behalf of the magistracy with the occupier, with whom he discussed all matters of principle – even intervening in matters exceeding his competency, such as the judicial police conferred by law to Courts of Appeal. Besides this diplomatic mission, his legal expertise was sought out. Terlinden acted as a guide for lower ranking magistrates and other civil servants, especially mayors, who searched for some guidelines when, facing the occupier, they felt helpless with the new legal situation. With the help of international law, the high magistrate tried to define what was acceptable and what was not. The concept of 'mediator' developed by Dirk Luyten is particularly relevant in describing this position.[17]

In this double mission, Terlinden was omnipresent – at least, during the first months of the occupation, when attitudes and *modi vivendi* with the

16 On the German legislation in occupied Belgium, see Pirenne et Vauthier 1925.

17 "In situations of occupation and revolution, legal professionals acted foremost as mediators: mediators between different legal systems and between the judicial system and the individuals subject to legal proceedings." (Luyten 2012, 11).

occupier had to be defined.[18] Discussions with the latter were conducted in several fields: occupation of the courthouses, repatriation of magistrates that were refugees or hostages, procurement of *laissez-passer* for the different judicial actors, and so on. Terlinden's actions mainly consisted of trying to calm down conflicts between Belgian magistrates and German members of the occupying forces; conflicts that were, in most cases, the result of interferences of the latter in judicial life. If general attempts to control the judicial apparatus were few and essentially due to local military authorities, problems in proceedings were frequent, the occupier ordering the transmission of judicial files or arbitrarily releasing some detainees of Belgian justice.

In these delicate issues, the Prosecutor General was both firm and moderate. If, in line with the government instructions, he acknowledged the necessity of the imposition of martial law or tolerated some withdrawals of competencies from the Belgian judges, he denounced abuses of power and required that fundamental principles like the confidentiality of instructions or the independence of the magistrates were respected – sometimes successfully.

The Prosecutor General was in direct contact with the chief of the German civil administration, Maximilian von Sandt,[19] who recognized the authority of the Court of Cassation. Terlinden's position as high magistrate even conferred on him some negotiating capacity. Threats of collective action often seemed to have been successful in opposing the German interferences. The existence of a civil German administration, composed of numerous lawyers, certainly made things easier. However, when German interests were at stake, the protestations of the Belgian magistrates were unsuccessful. Terlinden's action certainly contributed to keeping the magistracy in office until the strike of February 1918.[20]

5 The Issue of the Legislative Power of the Occupier

A civil issue led the judges of the Supreme Court to take up a position on the tricky question of the occupier's legislative power. They had to discuss

18 See Terlinden 1919.

19 Maximilian von Sandt (1861-1918), lawyer by training (University of Bonn and Strasbourg), served, before the First World War, as *Regierungspräsident* of Aix-la-Chapelle (1907-14). In 1914, he was placed at the head of the civil administration of Belgium (*Zivilverwaltung*) (25 August 1914 – July 1917). After having left Brussels for political reasons in 1917, he fulfilled the same functions in Warsaw (1918).

20 Bost 2013.

the validity of the occupier's decrees with respect to international law and, no less importantly, their own right to assess the decrees. As we have seen above, international law on occupation and, in particular, Article 43 of the Regulations annexed to Hague Convention IV of 1907 is not very clear on this. During the first occupation of Belgium, it was the subject of multiple interpretations by local tribunals and courts, which finally led the Supreme Court to take a position officially.

The context of the Court's intervention was the assessment of the validity of a 1915 German decree that put into place arbitration tribunals in charge of rent cases. This creation took place in the context of the rental crisis.[21] Like several of the other European countries involved, Belgium faced significant difficulties with regard to housing during World War I. Widespread material destruction in war-torn areas, the need to address the refugee problem and also provide lodging for German soldiers or public servants, together with inactivity in the building sector, created a housing shortage. Moreover, the drop in household income caused the multiplication of rent disputes and the polarization of relations between two classes of citizens with conflicting interests: tenants and landlords.

Early on during the occupation period, the German occupier got involved in the rental crisis and its resolution by the Belgian justice system. The German Governor General's Decree of 20 November 1914 extended the conditions for the exemption or reduction of the price of the rent in favour of the tenant.[22] A second decree of the Governor General, dated 10 February 1915, put into place arbitration tribunals in charge of rent cases in municipalities of more than 20,000 people.[23] Justices of the peace, who had previously judged alone, were now assisted by two extrajudicial assessors – one representative of the tenants, one representative of the landlords. Furthermore, the parties involved had to appear in person; Belgians living abroad – hundreds of thousands of exiles were targeted by this provision[24] – could not protect their interests. Lawyers and other professional agents were no longer allowed to participate in the debates. Arbitration tribunals could provide for an extension to payment deadlines, forbid evictions, and take other measures favourable to tenants. In addition, the proceedings were more or less free of charge. This was not a small innovation: by implementing the decree, the occupier modified laws of judicial organization and competencies. It

21 Mélanie Bost 2021.

22 De Huberich and Nicol-Speyer 1915, 1, p. 46.

23 De Huberich and Nicol-Speyer 1915, Vol 2, 82–86.

24 On the situation of the Belgian refugees during the war, see Amara 2008.

set up new jurisdictions, which had not provided been for by Belgian law and which were even unconstitutional in some aspects.

Besides triggering a strong resistance from the Brussels Bar, which would provoke the deportation of its president, Leon Theodor,[25] the German rent decree raised before the Belgian justice system, for the first time, the issue of the occupier's decrees' legality. This issue caused a huge controversy in the judicial world, dividing it between supporters for and opponents against the legislative power of the occupying forces. What about the legality of the German decree on rents and of the legislative power of the occupier in general? Did the courts have, according to the 1907 Hague Convention, the right to assess this legality? Two of the three Belgian courts of appeal, seized of some rent affairs, ruled on the question and provided conflicting answers. The Brussels Court of Appeal, on 19 July 1915, considered that the German decree was opportune for Belgian public life.[26] According to this Court, the rent issue was becoming "as urgent as the issue of bread"; the arbitration tribunals would facilitate finding solutions more quickly and without expense for the citizens involved in rental cases. The absolute need for the occupier to legislate was demonstrated: solving the rent issue was a social emergency. This reasoning was not shared by the Court of Appeal of Liège. The Court had stated the opposite a few weeks before, on 31 May 1915, arguing that the occupying power was *never* entitled to legislate in civil matters.[27] This opposition between the two Courts fed the controversy and led to major legal uncertainty.

Nearly one year later, the Court of Cassation, seized of two appeals, settled the juridical dispute with its decision of 20 May 1916.[28] Prosecutor-General Terlinden, representing the Public Prosecutor's Office, in favour of the applicability of the German decrees, presented comprehensive conclusions. The question to be decided by the Court, in his words, "essentially belongs to international public law, which was given precedence over domestic law". In this regard, even the national constitution had to bow to international law. The Prosecutor General defended the Hague heritage: the legislative power of the occupier is necessary. In his eyes, the modernity of the juridical notion of 'occupation' – "one of the most beautiful conquests of contemporary international law" – consisted in this duty recognized towards the winner and

25 On the attitude of the Brussels Bar during the occupation, see Bost and De Brouwer 2018.

26 On the public prosecutor's opinion and the decision of the Court, see *Belgique judiciaire* 1919, 119–130.

27 *Belgique judiciaire* 1919, 130–138.

28 *Pasicrisie belge* 1915–1916, Vol I, 375–418.

in the acceptance by the defeated government that it temporarily cannot exercise its powers. Considering this, citizens – including magistrates – must apply the occupier's measures. Furthermore, the intervention of public international law made it impossible for the courts to interpret the occupier's decrees. Otherwise, they would be arrogating the right to impose their decisions on a foreign nation; in other words, to encroach upon a foreign state's sovereignty. Must the judicial power, therefore, totally submit itself to the occupier's rules? No, answered the Prosecutor General. Magistrates can always refuse to apply a decree. Under this scenario, the occupier should seek other judges.

The decision of the Court of Cassation was split into two sections. In the first part, the Court qualified the acts emanating from the occupier: if these acts served provisionally as laws, they were still orders from a military authority and not real laws, since national sovereignty had never been transferred to the occupier. The sitting judges rejected the Prosecutor General's idea that occupier's decrees belonged to national legislation and required, at the return of the national government, an express repeal. In its second part, the Court's decision followed the reasoning of the Public Prosecutor. Though they were only military orders, the occupier's decrees had to be observed by the magistrates. Their legal validity was derived from Article 43 of the Hague Regulations, which had been ratified by Belgium. Indeed, Article 43 required that, regarding public order and safety, the occupier could, when necessary, take measures that do not fit with national legislation. As regards the conditions limiting this power, such as the absolute necessity to derogate from national legislation, their assessment was forbidden to the Courts in occupied territory; such an assessment would encroach on the sovereignty of the Convention signatory States.

Being very controversial, the decision provoked a great deal of concern within the judicial world – and even outside. The occupier's decrees, eventually, were not subject to judicial review in occupied Belgium. By doing so, the highest Belgian jurisdiction, an institution highly representative of the national sovereignty, provided the occupier's actions with a welcomed legitimacy, to which the latter would not hesitate to refer.

How can we interpret the Court's position? Beyond legal interpretation, the stakes were eminently political: was it better to oppose the occupying forces and to be exposed to replacement by foreign judges? Would it not be better, in order to safeguard the protection of a national justice for the citizens, to submit to this legislative power, even if it went beyond the limits fixed by international law? Under cover of legalism, the reasons were probably essentially pragmatic. In 1914-18, the legal power was taken over by the occupier; it was a fact. The influence of the views of the Prosecutor General, Terlinden, on the Supreme Court is discernible. The high magistrate defined at the beginning of the military occupation what would remain his guideline during the four years of the war, prefiguring the policy of lesser evil generalized during the Second World War amongst Belgian authorities. Inspired by the French lawyer Pradier-Foedere (see *supra*), Terlinden considered that "patriotism is *not* insurrection against the occupying forces; it consists in keeping our fatherland and cities safe from evils that can be avoided".[29] Under exceptional circumstances, thought the magistrate, the magistrate's conscience could be a better guide than strict legalism. The rent case was not worth an open conflict with the occupier; consequences of the suspension of the national justice could have been much worse for the population.

6 Some Internal Divisions

Critics of the 20 May 1916 decision came essentially from the Brussels Bar Council that strived to transform the bar into a space of moral resistance against the occupier. Some underground newspapers, where lawyers were overrepresented (e.g. *Le Flambeau*, *L'Âme belge*), denounced the 'unpardonable failing' of the Court.[30] But what put the Court in a particularly difficult and unusual position was the fact that, in Belgium, judges deliberate in secret and the practice of separate opinions doesn't exist; nevertheless, some criticism emanated from within. One judge of the Supreme Court, Joseph de Haene, published a series of anonymous pamphlets – *Les lettres d'un provincial* – through which he publicly expressed his disagreement with the Court's decision; both its interpretation of international law and its attitude he considered a demonstration of weakness.[31] The judicial authorities, as long as they remain functional, having as their professional duty to say what the law is, do not, following de Haene, have to apply decrees foreign to the law.

Other dissensions arose within the Court. Offering support to magistrates who suffered German repression also constituted a source of division. More

29 Copy of the response letter from Prosecutor General Terlinden to the mayor of Saint-Josse-ten-Noode, 28 November 1914, Brussels Courthouse, Archives of the Court of Cassation Prosecutor Office, Occupation 1914-1918, 4(III). Emphasis in original.

30 Albert de Louvain [Émile Kebers, lawyer] 1917, 120-126.

31 [De Haene, J.] 1919, 7-22.

often than not, the violations of the magistrates' independence and the pressures that they had to deal with from the Germans resulted in reports and protestations that were addressed to German authorities by the Public Prosecutor's office. In the most serious cases, the Court of Cassation was asked by its prosecution office to contemplate whether issuing an official protestation was appropriate. Amongst the sitting judges, the decision as to whether or not to support prosecuted magistrates systematically gave rise to debates. The deliberations of the counsellors of the Court of Cassation showed the limits of the corporative solidarity that is supposed to be so strong among magistrates.

The fate of three magistrates who had been removed from office led to deliberations at the Court of Cassation.[32] The Court officially protested and demanded that a deported magistrate be sent back to Belgium in only one case; it decided not to intervene in the two other cases. This difference in the way that the cases were handled might be linked to a deontological conception of magistrates' behaviour in times of war, which probably did not differ much from that applied in peacetime. The rescued magistrate was considered a 'model' magistrate. Here are the facts: the deputy public prosecutor, Wouters, had prosecuted a Flemish activist in Ghent for an unauthorized raising of funds.[33] This judicial proceeding against a collaborator with the Germans earned the magistrate his deportation to Germany for 30 months.[34] For the Court of Cassation, Wouters had done nothing but impartially enforce the law. By contrast, the two other magistrates had given their judicial interventions a political character and they lacked moderation in the views they expressed. Benoidt, judge and vice-president of the Brussels tribunal, indeed, became famous during the occupation for his patriotic speeches. For example, in 1915, when judging a rent case pending before the tribunal, he refused to refer the case to the arbitration tribunal set up by the Germans: "le tribunal constate qu'il lui serait impossible d'appliquer l'arrêté du 10 février-27 mars 1915 sans heurter, dans ce qu'il a de plus sacré, le droit dont la justice est inséparable; que le juge trahirait ses devoirs, violerait le serment qu'il a prêté, qu'il faillirait à sa conscience en concourant à un acte qui méconnaît le droit; qu'il ne peut appartenir à personne de

32 Brussels Courthouse, Archives of the Court of Cassation Prosecutor Office, Occupation 1914-1918, 2 (I).

33 The term 'activist' referred to the minor fraction of the Flemish Movement that chose to collaborate with the occupant in the First World War to achieve its linguistic claims.

34 See Terlinden 1919, 12-14.

solliciter de lui une décision qui serait une preuve de forfaiture".[35] Benoidt spoke loudly against German laws and Belgian collaborators in other cases until his suspension *sine die* in April 1916 by the German authority. The investigating judge Waleffe (tribunal of Liège), for his part, investigated Belgian metal traffickers working for the occupier. Outraged by the facts discovered, Waleffe, during the suspects' interrogation, warned them that, after the war, they would be prosecuted for treason, a statement that caused him to be reported by the collaborators to the German police. Like Wouters, Waleffe was deported to Germany until the Armistice. The judge, Benoidt, and the investigating judge, Waleffe, had been punished on the basis of a German decree for their 'germanophobic' case law or speeches during court hearings.

For the Court, the two magistrates' recklessness endangered the judicial power as a whole. Neutrality, an *ordinary* virtue of the magistracy, henceforth played a strategic role in the context of the occupation. Besides, when the principle of a protestation was put to the vote, the result was almost always the same: eight counsellors voted in favour of a reaction, nine voted against. Therefore, our perception of a very prudent, even wait-and-see Supreme Court attitude does not perfectly reflect the reality. A faction more open to resistance actions existed in 1914-18, but was silenced by a narrow majority.

A second source of division between high magistrates was the administrative splitting of the country. On 21 March 1917, in the context of the *Flamenpolitik* – a policy of favour towards the Dutch-speaking population aimed at weakening the occupied country[36] – the Governor General von Bissing decided to divide the country into two unilingual administrative regions with their own institutions: one in Flanders, including Brussels; the other in Wallonia. The measure provoked strong public disapproval – not only in Belgium, but also abroad amongst the Belgian diaspora. There could be no doubt this time. The measure could not be justified by international law. Public order and safety were not at stake. How did the Court react? Prosecutor General Terlinden called a secret meeting. The words he used in addressing the counsellors and members of the Public Ministry of the Court of cassation showed an obvious change of mind. In Terlinden's

35 "The tribunal concludes that it cannot apply the 10 February-27 March decree without hurting – in its most sacred aspects – the law that is inseparable from justice. It concludes that the judge would betray his duties, violates the oath of office, fails in his conscience committing an act that ignores the law; no one can ask him for a decision that would be a proof of treachery." (Gille, Ooms and Delandsheere 1919, Vol 1, 322.)

36 On the *Flamenpolitik*, see the classic work: Wils 1974 and, on the administrative splitting, the more recent: Delforge 2008.

opinion, the Court could not participate in this political measure aimed to divide Belgians. It was a war act: to agree with it would be a treason. Now, magistrates must stop their activities in protest.

However, once again, the democratic decision-making process prevented effective action. The question 'should something be done?' was put to the vote. As an exception, the Public Prosecutor's Office was invited to vote alongside the counsellors. Once again, the wait-and-see camp won: eleven magistrates against ten answered the question in the negative. One of the few explanations provided by the 'no' side, coming from one Advocate General, is very instructive: "As far as the judicial organization is not affected by the German decree, we don't have to interfere in a political matter."[37]

Nevertheless, if silent in these cases, the Court of Cassation spoke loudly on other occasions. In November and December 1916, it protested publicly against the deportation of Belgian workers to Germany by addressing letters of protest to the German Chancellor in Berlin. The condemnation was severe: the German measure was criticized as disregarding international, natural, and positive law, and the Court denounced the reintroduction of slavery.[38] Later, in June 1917, 400 members of the legal profession – members of the judiciary and bars – signed another protest, this time against the deportation of the Belgian civil servants who had refused to assist in the administrative splitting of the country and were therefore deported to Germany.[39] The letter of protest explicitly referred to the law of nations, which states that a civil servant may always resign.

Finally, dissensions appeared in the case law. In January 1918, the Court – whose magistrates were different from those of May 1916 – overturned its previous jurisprudence. It had to examine an appeal against a decision in a tax matter.[40] The decision had been issued by a provincial administrative body, composed of Belgians but headed by a German high-ranking official. Advocate General Paul Leclercq presented the conclusions preceding the ruling. He concluded that the appeal was inadmissible. In his opinion, the decisions of an institution set up during the occupation by a German decree, with a hybrid and temporary nature, could not be assessed by the Supreme Court, this one having been installed to review the decisions of

37 Note from the Advocate General Pholien to the Prosecutor General Terlinden, 23 April 1917 (Brussels Courthouse, Archives of the Court of Cassation Prosecutor Office, Occupation 1914-1918, 2 (I).

38 Both letters of protest are reproduced in Terlinden 1919, 15-17.

39 Copy of a letter dated 15 June 1917, Brussels Courthouse, Archives of the Court of Cassation Prosecutor Office, Occupation 1914-1918, 34 (XXIIbis).

40 *Pasicrisie belge* 1918, Vol I, 177-197.

the national jurisdictions. The sitting judges followed Leclercq's new line and the Court declared the case inadmissible.

A general change of attitude was perceptible. Growing criticism within the judicial world and increasing violations of international law committed by the Germans made the neutral policy towards the occupier no longer possible to observe.

7 The 1918 Judicial Strike

Shortly after, the *Flamenpolitik* took a step forward. Some Flemish activists – who were political collaborators of the Germans – proclaimed the political autonomy of Flanders. The proclamation raised huge protests, both in the occupied country and in the Belgian diaspora. The Belgian elites feared that the proclamation of autonomy would be misinterpreted abroad as the willingness of the Flemish people to secede from Belgium. This fear was particularly vivid in the context of the debates around the right to self-determination of peoples.[41]

One of the strongest sources of opposition came from the judiciary. The Brussels's Court of Appeal, after an extraordinary assembly, urged the chief public prosecutor to prosecute the main activist leaders, as initiators of an attack against the form of government.[42] Following this demand, the Brussels Prosecutor's Office arrested two activist leaders, but these were set free by the Germans a few hours later. On orders of the latter, the Court of Appeal's first president and two presidents of the chambers were deported to Germany, while all the counsellors were suspended indefinitely for "having participated in a political manifestation". It did not take long before the Court of Cassation retorted and it did it with panache. On 11 February 1918, condemning this flagrant violation of the independence of the judiciary, it decided to symbolically suspend its functions.[43] Following this example, numerous other bodies went spontaneously on strike, with the support of the lawyers. This was a protest movement that would last until the Armistice, forcing the occupier to install German jurisdictions to ensure the security of its armies in the occupied territory.[44]

41 Gille, Ooms and Delandsheere, Vol IV, 1919, 35-36.

42 The decision of the Brussels Court of Appeal is published in Passelecq 1918, 42-44.

43 Bost and François 2009.

44 With no archives discovered so far, the setting up and the exercise of the German justice during the strike months is little known. See Wunderlich 1930.

8 Epilogue

After the war, the ten months' strike would be celebrated as a key act of national resistance during the occupation. The controversial judicial decision of 20 May 1916 was apparently forgotten. The stroke of genius of the Belgian magistracy was to have taken a sensational action at the right moment, which absolved it of the compromises of the previous years. The singular nature of the strike in the light of the previous behaviour of Belgium's highest magistracy also enables us to assess what constituted its point of no return. It was, ultimately, not so much the defence of the national institutions (the Court of Cassation did not protest at the moment of the administrative splitting of the country) as it was the defence of the essential attribute of the magistracy – its independence – that made it choose resistance over cooperation. It was only when the independence of the magistracy was disregarded, when the counsellors of the Court of Appeal of Brussels were suspended and their chiefs of staff deported, that the Court of Cassation unanimously decided to withdraw collectively.

Benefiting from the success of the strike episode, the magistracy embodied in 1918 the force of law against the law of force. The 'unanimous' resistance of the judicial body during the long months of the enemy occupation formed one of the topics of the patriotic literature. In this stronger position, and because the judiciary in Belgium formed a truly independent power, the judiciary was not subjected to an external purge.[45] It was allowed to conduct its own purification exercise in the context of 'ordinary' disciplinary proceedings. The high magistrates of the Court of Cassation did not suffer prosecutions; during the war, treasons had been predominantly local and, for a large part, linked to Flemish activism (as having accepted a promotion from the German occupier or having publicly supported the administrative splitting of the country). On the contrary, in 1918, the role of the high magistracy was exalted. In the post-war period, the judicial power was confirmed in its role of pillar of the State. It showed itself to be indispensable, and the government, despite four years of suspension of the relations between both powers and despite the criticisms of the Brussels's bar towards the judiciary, had kept faith in it. In return, and as usual, the judiciary was loyal to the political authority. The Court of Cassation delivered several rulings, sometimes in conflict with its own wartime case law, that contributed to restore the State's legitimacy.

45 On the judicial purge after both wars, see Bost and Zurné 2018.

The First World War experience prefigured in many respects the second German occupation of the country.[46] As experts of law and members of the establishment, magistrates' opinions would be again particularly solicited and commented upon. Yet again, magistrates would play an important political role. Once more, judicial crises would occur. The memory of the 1918 strike and its negative effects both for the Belgian population and for the occupier would inevitably influence the negotiations in 1940-44.

References

Amara, Michael, *Des Belges à l'épreuve de l'exil: les réfugiés de la Première Guerre mondiale: France, Grande-Bretagne, Pays-Bas*, Brussels: Éditions de l'Université de Bruxelles 2008.

Berger, Olivier, 'Des questions de justice dans l'occupation allemande de 1870-1871. Essai sur le fonctionnement particulier de la justice civile française et de la justice militaire allemande', in: Marie Houllemare and Philippe Nivet (Eds), *Justice et guerre de l'Antiquité à la Première Guerre mondiale. Actes du colloque (Amiens, 18-20 novembre 2009)*, Amiens: Encrage 2011, 173-182.

Bonfils, Henri, *Manuel de droit international public (droit des gens)*, 5ème éd., Paris: Rousseau, 1908.

Bost, Mélanie, *Traverser l'occupation 1914–1918. Du modus vivendi à la grève, la magistrature belge face aux occupants allemands*, unpublished PhD thesis, Louvain: Université catholique de Louvain, 2013.

Bost, Mélanie, 'Judges, Lawyers, "Vultures' and 'Butchers": Actors and Stakes of the Rental Crisis in Occupied Brussels, 1914–1918', in: Mélanie Bost and Toon Vrints (Eds), *Doing Justice In Wartime: Multiple Interplays between Justice and Populations during the Two World Wars*, Studies in the History of Law and Justice 19, Switzerland: Springer 2021, 11-24.

Bost, Mélanie, and Jérôme De Brouwer, 'Le Barreau de Bruxelles face à l'Occupant au cours du Premier conflit mondial', *SIHPA* 2018-13.

Bost, Mélanie, and Aurore François, 'La grève de la magistrature belge (février à novembre 1918). Un haut fait de la résistance nationale à l'épreuve des archives judiciaires', in: Dirk Heirbaut, Xavier Rousseaux and Alain Wijffels (Eds), *Histoire du droit et de la justice: une nouvelle génération de recherches/Justitie-en rechtsgeschiedenis: een nieuwe onderzoeksgeneratie*, Louvain-la-Neuve: Presses universitaires de Louvain 2009, 19-44.

46 See Muller and Peters's contribution in this volume.

Bost, Mélanie, and Jan Julia Zurné, 'Excluding the wrongdoers: the use of judicial discipline as a purging tool of the Belgian magistracy after the two German occupations', in: Marc Bergère et al. (Eds), *Pour une Histoire connectée et transnationale des épurations en Europe au sortir de la Seconde Guerre mondiale*, Brussels: Peter Lang 2019, 117-133.

[de Haene, Joseph], *Les lettres d'un provincial ou les propos du Conseiller Eudoxe. Nouvelle édition vendue au profit des mutilés de la guerre*, Bruxelles-Paris: J. Van Oest 1919.

De Huberich, Charles Henry, and Alexander Nicol-Speyer, *Législation allemande pour le territoire belge occupé (textes officiels)*, 21 Vols, La Haye: Martinus Nijhoff 1914-1918.

Delforge, Paul, *La Wallonie et la Première Guerre mondiale: pour une histoire de la séparation administrative*, Namur: Institut Destrée 2008.

de Louvain, Albert [Émile Kebers, lawyer], 'Lettre ouverte à Monsieur Edmond Picard', *L'Âme belge* 1917, 120-126.

De Schaepdrijver, Sophie, *De Groote Oorlog. Het Koninkrijk België tijdens de Eerste Wereldoorlog*, Antwerpen: Atlas 1997.

Freeman, Alwyn V., 'War crimes by Enemy Nationals Administering Justice in Occupied Territory', *The American Journal of International Law* XLI 1947-3, 579-610.

Gille, Louis, Alphonse Ooms and Paul Delandsheere, *Cinquante mois d'occupation allemande*, Brussels: Dewit, 1919.

Graditzky, Thomas, 'Les expériences d'occupation autour de la Grande Guerre: quelle mobilisation du Règlement de La Haye?', in: James Connolly, Emmanuel Debruyne, Élise Julien and Matthias Meirlaen (Eds), *En territoire ennemi 1914-1949. Expériences d'occupation, transferts, héritages*, ed. by, Villeneuve d'Ascq: Septentrion 2018, 153-164.

Loening, Edgar, 'L'administration du gouvernement-général de l'Alsace durant la guerre de 1870-1871. Deuxième article', *Revue de droit international et de législation comparée* V (1873), 94-99.

Luyten, Dirk, 'Introduction', in: Margo De Koster, Hervé Leuwers, Dirk Luyten and Xavier Rousseaux (Eds), *Justice in Wartime and Revolutions. Europe, 1795-1950, Justice and Society VI*, Brussels: AGR 2012, 5-13.

Meyers, Armand, 'La Magistrature et l'Occupation. Discours prononcé à l'audience solennelle de rentrée du 1er octobre 1919 de la cour d'appel de Liège', *Journal des Tribunaux*, 1919, col. 542.

Passelecq, Fernand, *La magistrature belge contre le despotisme allemand*, Paris – Nancy: Librairie militaire 1918.

Pirenne, Jacques, et Marcel Vauthier, *La législation et l'administration allemandes en Belgique*, Paris – New Haven: Presses universitaires de France 1925.

Pradier-Fodéré, Paul, *Traité de droit international public européen et américain suivant les progrès de la science et de la pratique contemporaines*, Paris: G. Pedine-Lauriel 1897.

Terlinden, Georges, *La magistrature belge sous l'occupation allemande: souvenirs de guerre, août 1914 – octobre 1918, discours prononcé devant la Cour de Cassation de Belgique*, Bruxelles: Bruylant 1919.

Verwaest, Rik, *Van Den Haag tot Genève: België en het internationale oorlogsrecht (1874-1950)*, Justice and Society II, Brugge: De Keure 2011.

Wils, Lode, *Flamenpolitik en aktivisme: Vlaanderen tegenover België in de Eerste Wereldoorlog*, Leuven: Davidsfonds 1974.

Wunderlich, Georg, *Der belgische Justizstreik, insbesondere die deutschen Staatsanwaltschaften in Belgien (Zugleich eine Studie zum Rechte der Okkupation)*, Berlin: Heymann 1930.

About the Author

Mélanie Bost holds a PhD in contemporary history and is an associated researcher at CegeSoma and the Royal Military Academy (Brussels). Her research focuses on the exercise of justice during the two world wars, daily life in occupied Belgium in 1914-1918 and military intelligence.

3 Germany: The *Reichsgericht* 1933-1945

Martin Löhnig

Abstract

This chapter presents an account of the German Reichsgericht under court president Bumke during Hitler's rule of Nazi Germany. It discusses the court's jurisdiction and the government's measures that adapted it, such as the introduction of special courts. It further describes the function of the de-formalization, or 'materialization', of adjudication in the implementation of National Socialist ideology and policy. In this context, the role of general clauses is highlighted, and it is shown how this method of adjudication could sometimes be turned against the system. Finally, post-war evaluations and the continuity from *Reichsgericht* to *Bundesgerichtshof* are explained.

Keywords: German Reichsgericht; Nazi Germany; Erwin Bumke; General clauses; Nazi ideology

1 Introduction

When the *Reichsgericht* started its work on 1st October 1879 in Leipzig, a new country-wide jurisdiction had been established, based on § 12 *Gerichtsverfassungsgesetz* (GVG).[1] As the country's highest civil and criminal court, the *Reichsgericht* ranked above all federal courts. This could not be taken for granted, as in Germany organizing jurisdiction has been – and still is – a matter of the federal states. This was one reason for basing the *Reichsgericht* in Leipzig rather than in the country's capital Berlin. There had been a broad political debate before about the court's purpose in general.[2]

1 Gerichtsverfassungsgesetz of 27 January 1877, *Reichsgesetzblatt* (*RGBl.*) 1877 p. 41 et seq., § 12 GVG: 'Local Courts, District Courts, Higher Regional Courts and the Reichsgericht exercise jurisdiction in Criminal and Civil law matters.'

2 On its development in general: Schubert 1981, 153 et seq.

Venema, D. (ed.), *Supreme Courts Under Nazi Occupation*. Taylor & Francis Group 2022
DOI: 10.5117/9789463720496_CH03

In fact, the *Reichsgericht* was entirely rejected by federalist political camps in opposition to a Prussian dominated state. They feared that Germany would become a new 'Eastern France', that a 'Code Bismarck' would come along with the Code Napoléon and the Parisian Court of Cassation would be followed by a Berlin one.[3]

Eduard v. Simson (1810-1899),[4] professor at the University of Königsberg, became the court's first president. He had been a member of the Frankfurt national parliament after the revolution of 1848 and its President from December 1848 to May 1849. He had also presided Erfurt's Union Parliament in the *Volkshaus* in 1850 and the parliaments (*Reichstag*) of the *Norddeutsche Bund* and the Empire from 1867 to 1873. To put it with some pathos: He became father of Germany's constitutional tradition, leading from Frankfurt (1848/49) to Weimar (1919) and Bonn (1949). Totally different was Erwin Bumke's (1874-1945)[5] legacy, the *Reichsgericht*'s last president from 1929 to 1945, who embodied the prevailing anti-republican and anti-liberal legal elite which submissively cooperated with the *Third Reich's* authorities. We will discuss his Criminal Senate's decisions later.

On the threshold of National Socialism, we are not faced with an undisputed *Reichsgericht*. Due to a substantial conflict between the government of the *Reich* and its Supreme Court, neither the President nor the Chancellor of the *Reich* showed up at the official ceremony[6] on the occasion of the Court's 50th anniversary in 1929.[7] Because of a dispute between the federal government and the states (Art. 19 sec. 1 WRV), the Public Supreme Court[8] had to decide on personal policy matters in the national railway's administrative council – by the way, the position of Administrative Court president came along with the presidency of the Supreme Court, and its judges were Supreme Court judges at the same time. Despite the upcoming trial date, the government unexpectedly took a decision regarding the council's personnel composition, thus thwarting the pending court proceedings. Reacting to this humiliation of the highest German Court, its president Walter Simons

3 Frantz 1873, 3.

4 Cf. Kern & Schroeder 2001.

5 Cf. for personal details: Kolbe 1975.

6 Cf. Lobe 1929.

7 Different from the faculties of law as they dedicated a commemorative publication to the Reichsgericht published in six volumes: Schreiber 1929.

8 The Public Supreme Court had been established at the Reichsgericht based on Art. 108 WRV by the Supreme Court Act of 9th of July 1921, *RGBl.* 1921 p. 905. Meetings and trials were only called if necessary.

(1861-1937)[9] stepped back from office and condemned the government's actions as unconstitutional interference with a pending case.[10] In his speech at the anniversary ceremony, the Court's new president Bumke addressed the judiciary's permanent crisis of confidence and the 'low level of law'. Remarkably, he did not hesitate to admit this crisis – not without suggesting a solution, of course: In his opinion, freedom and independence of the judiciary from written law were the answers to 'stormy and rapidly changing times'. Judges needed to be able to adapt the law to new developments.[11]

But keep in mind: In fact, one of the main reasons for this 'crisis of confidence' Bumke and others complained about was the generous way in which the Court handled general clauses.[12] On the one hand, since the day the *Bürgerliches Gesetzbuch* (BGB) came into force (1 January 1900), legal practice has been strictly bound by written law. On the other hand, in certain cases, positive law, which was considered unjust, had to be open for corrections, especially after World War I with its enormous social and political transformations and problems. The means, again, had to be provided by written law itself. For example, the *Reichsgericht* ranked norms such as § 138 BGB (immorality) or § 242 BGB (good faith) higher than others[13] and started using them as control and correction instruments, which they still are nowadays. As a consequence, judges finally took the legislature's role by closing normative gaps.[14] Philipp Heck[15], leading proponent of the doctrine of jurisprudence of interests, rightly defined § 242 BGB as a 'delegation norm'. In fact, the fathers of the German Civil Code had been aware of these consequences and the way general clauses were supposed to work, as they referred to § 138 BGB as a 'meaningful legislative step'. They further stated that judges now were granted wider discretion than ever before. But, with respect to the diligent and conscientious German judiciary, they did not expect any problems at all.[16] Notwithstanding all criticism, Arno Buschmann recently acknowledged the *Reichsgericht's* peak of recognition in 1929.[17]

9 Cf. Gründer 1975.
10 On this process Simons 1929; Kolbe 1975, 47 et seq.
11 Kolbe 1975, 75 et seq., here 81.
12 Wadle 2008, 285 and 286.
13 In detail: Schröder 2014, 151-174.
14 Cf. Rüthers 2012, 267.
15 Heck 1994, § 4.1.
16 *Motive* 1896, 211 et seq.
17 Buschmann 2006, 47.

2 Personnel Policy Measures by the NS Regime Affecting the *Reichsgericht* and the Self-image of its Judges

The 'law on restoration of the civil service' (*Gesetz zur Wiederherstellung des Berufsbeamtentums*; better: 'law on conformity of the civil service') was passed by the NS-Regime on the 7 April 1933.[18] It allowed the dismissal of officials who were not 'Aryan' (§ 3 sect 1) or whose 'full loyalty to the National Socialist state could not be guaranteed' because of their 'previous political activities' (§ 4). This also affected judges of the *Reichsgericht*. President Bumke's suggestion not to apply this law to members of the *Reichsgericht* was rejected by some members of the Court's council. They – NSDAP members at the same time – voted against it at a plenary assembly which had been initiated by Bumke himself in order to bring about a unanimous decision. Thus, Bumke's plan failed[19] and six members of the *Reichsgericht's* council and one Senate President were forced to retire based on § 3 sect. 1.[20] The Senate President in question was Dr. Alfons David (1866-1954), who had affirmed his strong national beliefs in a letter to Hitler before. Bumke himself tried to intervene in the ministry of justice in favour of David, but soon decided to let him down in order to prevent an SA attack on the *Reichsgericht*, planned for 20 of March 1933. And he not only acted opportunistically in this case: When David wanted to move to Luxembourg in 1938, Bumke refused his application: A Jew should not be allowed to 'enjoy his pensions abroad'.[21] Herrmann Grossmann (1878-1960), member of the 3rd Civil Senate, was the only *Reichsgerichtsrat* who could be considered 'politically unreliable': he had been the only SPD-Member in the Court's history so far. Grossmann was one of the founding members of the Republican Association of Judges, founded in 1921 in response to a judiciary which more or less rejected the newly born Weimar Republic.[22] But Grossmann had applied for retirement even before the new law could affect him, hoping to avoid his pensions being cut according to § 4 of the 'law on re-establishment of the Civil Service'. His pensions were cut anyway, but Grossmann's former Senate President Fritz Katluhn (1865-1942) successfully intervened at the ministry of justice.[23]

Apart from that, the political attitudes obviously were no reason for state interventions at all. On 20 August 1934, after Reich President Hindenburg

18 *RGBl.* 1933 I, p. 175.

19 Hartung 1971 p. 96.

20 See Kaul 1971, 54 et seq.; Miosge 2008.

21 See Miosge 2008, 226 et seq.

22 Cf. *Lüth & Wesel* 1988.

23 Cf. Kaul 1971, 56 et seq.

had died, all judges swore a new oath of allegiance to 'Hitler, the leader of the German people'.[24] The national-conservative, anti-liberal, anti-republican legal elite, centre of socialization also for *Reichsgerichtsräte*, seemed to affirm its self-image by serving the 'government of the national uprising' (how the government used to present itself). They consciously decided to make a new beginning, a revolution, a radical change, hoping for the re-establishment of the old order which seemed to have been broken in 1918. Without exaggerating, these terms describe that these people seemed to experience something magic, something ecstatic. According to Sebastian Haffner, the mood changed completely in spring 1933. It changed to a feeling of community, in other words: it felt like autumn 1914. 'It was – you can't describe it otherwise – a broad feeling of liberation from democracy'[25], which the *Reichsgerichtsräte* obviously did not want to defend.

The next big changes in staff took place after 1939. After the dissolution of the High Court in Vienna, two new Senates were established, most of them staffed by former High Court members. By contrast, the former High Court of shattered Czechoslovakia in Brno remained untouched.[26] The next changes took place in 1944, due to judges being drafted into the *Wehrmacht*.[27] Thus, beyond 1933 the staff remained stable over a long period, interrupted only by retirements due to old age.

There are only a few examples of one-sided National Socialist personnel policy at the *Reichsgericht*. Kirchner[28] mentions the appointment of three Senate Presidents, including the 'fanatic National Socialist'[29] Otto Georg Thierack (1889-1946), who became President of the *Volksgerichtshof* in 1936 and became Minister of the justice department in 1942. According to Kirchner, he had been appointed to the *Reichsgericht* as a watchdog and was called 'the folkish observer' ('*Völkischer Beobachter*', the NS daily newspaper). Besides, there was probably no need for such unilateral interventions, also because of the strong loyalty of the legal elite. Even if most of its members were not convinced National Socialists, they step by step agreed to bad compromises, ending up deeply involved in the National Socialist regime. Of course, there were also judges like the head of the IVth Civil Senate, Martin Jonas (1884-1945), who interpreted their authority highly politically from the beginning, serving racial ideology and population policy by even

24 Kaul 1971, 56 et seq.
25 Haffner 1993, 237.
26 See Jaromir Tauchen's chapter on this matter in this book.
27 Kaul 1971, 56.
28 Kirchner 1959, 107.
29 Schädler 2009, 87.

aggravating NS-law (see below for details). At the same time, 36-year-old Hans von Dohnanyi (1902-1945) became the youngest *Reichsgerichtsrat* ever. He was not a member of the NSDAP and had criticised NS racial policy before his appointment.[30]

Acts of resistance by *Reichsgericht* judges are barely known. Hans von Dohnanyi, a famous exception, was removed in November 1941 and, after taking part in Henning von Treschkow's attack on Hitler, detained in March 1943 and finally executed in April 1945.[31] But in fact, you did not have to become a hero in order to express resistance. For example, Wilhelm Bruner (1875-1939), Vice President of the *Reichsgericht*, resigned on April 1, 1939 and retired three years and nine months before reaching pensionable age. Despite the requirements of his rank, he did not want to become a member of the NSDAP and rather quit his job. Resigning at retirement age was not compulsory. President Bumke, for example, 're-signed' upon his death on April 20, 1945 shortly before his 71st birthday. He was followed by Dieprand von Richthofen (1875-1946), a *Reichsgerichtsrat* who had joined the party on 1 May 1933[32] and is quoted as follows (1933!): 'The *Reichsgericht* has always born in mind that its judicature has to serve the aims of the National Socialist uprising and in this sense to influence lower courts.'[33]

3 The Court's Powers and Measures of the NS Regime Regarding these Powers

Since 1879, the *Reichsgericht* had been competent for revisions and complaints against civil law decisions of the High Courts (§ 135 GVG) and for revisions against judgments of criminal divisions of first and second instance (§ 136 sect. 1 Nr. 2 GVG). In the first and last instance, the *Reichsgericht* was competent for high treason and treason against the emperor and the Reich, § 136 sect. 1 Nr. 1 GVG. In this first instance adjudication, the *Reichsgericht* also had to assess the substance of a case. Differently from the *Bundesgerichtshof* nowadays, the *Reichsgericht* was not a mere court of cassation, but as a revision court it was competent to actually decide the case if possible, § 528 *Zivilprozeßordnung* (ZPO)/§ 394 *Strafprozeßordnung* (StPO).

30 Gruchmann 2009, 253 et seq.

31 See Chowaniec 1991; Stern & Sifton 2013.

32 On this process Kolbe 1975, 291.

33 *Ein bißchen Bibel* 1979; *Hohle Nuß* 1992.

After 30 January 1933 there were significant changes regarding the Court's jurisdiction. Based on § 1 sect. 1 of the 'Government's order on establishing Special Courts' of 21 March 1933 (*Verordnung der Reichsregierung über die Bildung von Sondergerichten*),[34] each High Court district was provided with a 'Special Court' (*Sondergericht*). They were competent for criminal cases according to the 'President's order on protection of the people and the state' (*Verordnung des Reichspräsidenten zum Schutz von Volk und Staat*) of 28 February 1933[35] and the 'Order on the defence of insidious attacks against the government of the national uprising' (*Verordnung zur Abwehr heimtückischer Angriffe gegen die Regierung der nationalen Erhebung*) of 21 March 1933,[36] § 2. These Special Courts tended to restrict the *Reichsgericht*'s powers as their decisions could not be challenged, § 16 sect. 1 of the order. Special Courts were also meant to apply general criminal law to 'their' cases, § 3 of the order. Another restriction of power was the 'Amendment to criminal law and criminal law procedure of 24 April 1934'.[37] According to Art. III § 1 sect. 1 and § 3 sect. 1 of the amendment, the soon-to-be established *Volksgerichtshof*[38] ('People's Court') whose jurisdiction encompassed crimes of high treason and treason (radically changed by amendments to §§ 80 subs. *Strafgesetzbuch* (StGB)) from now on; before, these crimes were part of the *Reichsgericht's* first-instance jurisdiction. The *Volksgerichtshof* also was entitled to apply general criminal law, Art. III § 3 sect. 2 and 3 of the Amendment. The establishment of the *Volksgerichtshof* was obviously a political decision, as it correlated with the NS regime's dissatisfaction with the results of the 'Reichstag fire trial'[39], ending with some acquittals of communists.[40] According to §§ 5 and 10 of the 'order on Criminal Procedure for Military Crimes' from 17 August 1938[41], the *Reich's* Military Court and the *Reichsgericht* were no longer responsible for cases based on the order.

In addition, the jurisdiction of the Special Courts extended constantly. Since 21 February 1940, prosecutors could deliberately choose any court – general or special – for criminal charges, based on the 'order on the jurisdiction of criminal courts, Special Courts and other criminal law

34 *RGBl.* 1933 I, p. 136.

35 *RGBl.* 1933 I, p. 83 (*Reichstagsbrandverordnung*).

36 *RGBl.* 1933 I, p. 135.

37 *RGBl.* 1934 I, p. 341.

38 On law and 'the people' in the Third Reich see Chapoutot 2017, and in detail Chapoutot 2014.

39 See Deiseroth 2009.

40 See also Kaul 1971, 341 et seq.

41 *Kriegsstrafverfahrensverordnung*; published only under the 26 August 1939, *RGBl.* 1939 I, p. 1457.

norms'.[42] According to § 14 sect. 1 of the order, the prosecution was entitled to prosecute offences before Special Courts even if they were not competent in the first place. The only requirement was the prosecutor's belief in the necessity of a judgment by the Special Court, regarding the gravity of the case, public excitation or serious endangerment of public order and safety. Thus, the court's jurisdiction was dependent on the prosecutor's decision. And the number of Special Courts rose, § 10 sect. 1 of the order. Decisions of the Special Courts could not be challenged, § 26 sect. 1 of the order.

On the other hand, as part of the same act the nullity appeal[43] according to §§ 34 et seq. VO challenged the legal validity of final judgments and extended the *Reichsgericht*'s powers by implying possibilities of appeal against final decisions of the Special Courts, § 35 VO. This 'nullity appeal' was comparable to revisions as it was only allowed if 'a judgment, based on the assessed facts' was 'considered unjust', § 34 VO. But: this extraordinary appeal was provided only for the Senior Prosecutor, § 34 VO, not for the accused. Nevertheless, the term 'unjust' also expressed that the nullity appeal also allowed for the correction of final criminal judgments, based on considered criteria.[44] The 'Act on further simplification of criminal justice' (*Verordnung zur weiteren Vereinfachung der Strafrechtspflege*) of 13 August 1942[45] also permitted the nullity appeal against 'unfair decisions based on a mistake in application of the law or in case of considerable concerns about the truth of the facts or against the terms of punishment; for this purpose the Court takes evidence if necessary', Art 7 § 2 sect. 1 VO. Thus, the *Reichsgericht* became a court that had to assess the facts. Gerhard Pauli[46] estimates that about 2000 nullity appeals were lodged between 1940 and 1945 (indeed also in favour of the defendants).

Moreover, the *Reichsgericht*'s jurisdiction concerning civil law was restricted by the newly established Court of Appeal. According to § 40 sect. 1 *Reichserbhofgesetz*[47] ('Act on the inheritance of manors'), *Anerbengerichte*, *Erbhofgerichte* and a *Reichserbhofgericht* (all special courts for inheritance matters) had to be established in order to serve the special purposes of the Act. Further details were left to upcoming decrees which could also require a 'confirmation of the courts' decisions by the '*Reichsminister*'

42 *RGBl.* 1940 I, p. 405.
43 *RGBl.* 1940 I, p. 405.
44 Pauli 1992, 18.
45 *RGBl.* 1942 I, p. 508.
46 Pauli 1992, 19.
47 *Reichserbhofgesetz* of 29 September 1933, *RGBl.* I, p. 685.

for Nutrition and Agriculture', § 47 sent. 2 *Reichserbhofgesetz*; this meant exclusive rights of confirmation for the executive, which should better have remained legal history with respect to historical facts. Furthermore, the *Reichsgericht*'s jurisdiction considering matters of war damages[48] was affected by the *Reichsverwaltungsgericht*[49] ('Reich's Supreme Administrative Court'), established by the *Führer's* order of 3rd April 1941.[50] Anyway, it should not be forgotten that the *Reichsgericht's* powers had been restricted long before by Supreme Courts established during the Weimar years such as the *Reichsarbeitsgericht* ('Labour Court') 1926, the *Ehrengerichtshof* ('Disciplinary Court') for lawyers, the *Reichsschiedsgericht* ('Court of Arbitration'), the *Wahlprüfungsgericht* ('Electoral Court'), the *Reichsbahngericht* ('National Railway Court'), the *Reichswirtschaftsgericht* ('Economic Court') or the *Reichsversorgungsgericht* ('Court of Public Supplies').[51] At the end of the war, even more restriction orders affected the admissibility of legal remedies and as a consequence the Court's decisions.[52] But still: Between 1933 and 1945, the *Reichsgericht* remained the most important and influential German court for criminal and civil law matters.

4 Legal Sources and Court Decisions

In general, *Reichsgerichtsräte* had to base their decisions on norms that had come into force long before 1933. All major legislative projects of the Nazis failed; they only had partial proposals for a new Criminal Code[53] and a 'People's Code'[54] (*Volksgesetzbuch*) which was meant to replace the Civil Code. However, in the view of many party leaders these projects probably were not of high priority. In their opinion the desired goals of NS-ideology could probably also be achieved by selective interventions and changes in adjudication. Despite the vagueness of the NS-ideology, this at least entailed the implementation of race ideology, the leader principle and the concept of a national community in legal practice.

48 Cf. Vollprecht 1943.

49 In further detail Jasch 2005.

50 *RGBl.* 1941 I, p. 201.

51 Cf. Buschmann 2006, 59.

52 E.g. §§ 1 et seq. of 'Verordnung über außerordentliche Maßnahmen auf dem Gebiete des bürgerlichen Rechts, der bürgerlichen Rechtspflege und des Kostenrechts aus Anlaß des totalen Krieges' of 27 September 1944, *RGBl.* 1944 I, p. 229 et seq.

53 Programmatically Freisler et al. 1934; see also Schubert et al. 1989.

54 See Hattenhauer 1983; Schubert 1988.

4.1 Criminal Law

In his examination of the *Reichsgericht's* judgements on criminal matters between 1933 and 1945[55], Gerhard Pauli rightly states that this kind of adjudication can be characterized as 'materialization' of law. His point of reference is the successful fight for a formal constitutional state in the 19th century, which finally achieved the codification of law: Law protecting civil liberties and fighting despotism. In the late years of the German Empire, the formal procedure of decision-making began to change to a more and more 'materialized', result-oriented way. Ambitions to 'release the prosecution from formal obstacles' and to base decisions on external factors like purpose, justice and morality had been recognized long before 1933 and reach far beyond 1945. Obviously, the amendment of (supposed) injustice by materialization started before 1933. But: in the conflict between formal and material decision-making criteria, National Socialism explicitly took the 'material' side. Principles such as '*nulla poena sine lege*' ('No punishment without law'), the prohibition of analogies in criminal law adjudication or the authority of final decisions were criticized and abolished as anti-nationalist formalities, opposing the State's valid claim of punishment. On 1 September 1935, for example, the Amendment on the criminal code of 18 June 1935 came into force.[56] It formally repealed the prohibition of analogy and explicitly allowed 'judicial discretionary power by appropriate application of criminal law' according to Art. 1. It came along with the 'Amendment on criminal procedure'[57] which entailed another important change: Art. 2 was headlined 'dispensation of the *Reichsgericht* from the binding of earlier judgements'. It said: 'The *Reichsgericht* as German Supreme Court of Justice is appointed to ensure that changes in views and ideas and in legal opinions caused by the renewal of the state are observed when interpreting the law. In order to enable the *Reichsgericht* to do so without any obstacles caused by earlier decisions, the following is determined: When deciding a case, the *Reichsgericht* can differ from decisions made before this Amendment came into force.'

This evolution of 'materialization' was supported in an unexpected way by National Socialist ideology. One important factor was the growing unease about restrictions on criminal-law judges under a liberal constitution.

55 Pauli 1992.

56 Gesetz zur Änderung des Strafgesetzbuchs of 28 June 1935, *RGBl.* 1935 I, 839.

57 Gesetz zur Änderung von Vorschriften des Strafverfahrens und des Gerichtsverfassungsgesetzes of 28 June 1935, *RGBl.* 1935 I, 844.

This unease could be addressed openly now and was linked to other ideas of 'justice'. Based on a predominant anti-liberal attitude, the principle of subsidiarity of criminal law, its incompleteness and its character as a 'Magna Carta' of the accused were foreign to the judiciary.[58] This attitude had existed even before 1933 and did not just disappear after 1945. Against previous tradition[59] and before such law actually came into effect,[60] courts recognised the legal concept of alternative legal qualifications in case of uncertainty about the actual course of events (*Wahlfeststellung*),[61] due to the reluctance about perceived unjustified acquittals. Referring to 'the common sense of the people' (*gesundes Volksempfinden*), the right of self-defence was denied to members of minority-groups in case of disparity between means of attack and defence.[62] The legal concept of a prolonged single act (*fortgesetzte Handlung*) became diminished[63] in order to enable the courts to sentence 'dangerous habitual criminals' for multiple separate criminal acts. Procedures were driven by results, the judiciary became legislative. Thus, the regime did not need any criminal law reforms to pursue its aims.

As Pauli rightly states,[64] a special form of materialization was the evolving subjectivism of criminal law. Even in the emperor's era, the value and independence of the courts' decisions were emphasized as their judgements were considered 'more than mere mechanism'. In addition to the judges' growing self-confidence, their focus moved from criminal actions to the criminal as a person and to his or her motives and attitudes, as this implied a wide margin of discretion in deciding cases. After 1933, this strategy intensified rapidly.

We can observe this on two levels: Criminal law statutes enacted after 1933 emphasize the accused's motives and refer to them extensively. For example, § 2 of the Treachery Act of 20 December 1934[65] says: 'Who publicly speaks of leading personalities of the state or the NSDAP in a spiteful or heretical way

58 See Pauli 1992, 245.

59 *Reichsgericht in Strafsachen* (*RGSt*) 53, 231, 232; *RGSt* 56, 61.

60 Later this was brought into effect by Art. 1. Nr. 1 of the Amendment of the law on Criminal procedure and on the constitution of courts of 28 June 1935, *RGBl.* 1935 I, p. 844.

61 Full Court's decision *RGSt* 68, 257 ff.; in detail Pauli 1992, 49 et seq.

62 *RGSt* 71, 133 which against previous jurisdiction implemented ideas of a criminal law bill of 1936 that never came into effect. In detail Pauli 1992, 63 ff.

63 See Grand Criminal Panel in *RGSt* 70, 243 against *RGSt* 43, 134 in order to avoid inappropriate preferential treatment of offenders by ignoring the Act on dangerous habitual criminals and on security measures of 24 November 1933, *RGBl.* 1933 I, p. 995. In detail Pauli 1992, 91 ff.

64 Pauli 1992, 123 et seq.

65 Statute against malicious attacks on state and party and on protection of the party's uniforms of 20th December 1934, *RGBl.* 1934 I, p. 1269.

or with a despicable attitude (...)' can be punished. To distinguish murder from homicide (or better: the murderer from someone who committed homicide), § 211 StGB still refers to subjective elements relating to the attitude of the accused, such as 'base motivation'. This version of § 211 StGB is still in force and dates back to the amendment of 4 September 1941.[66] On the level of applicable law, the judiciary extended the criminal liability for attempt[67] and took increasingly into account whether the offender *assumed* he would cause danger for legally protected rights rather than whether there was indeed such danger.[68] Mere wrong aspirations rather than actual violations of rights were considered punishable. Within the field of perpetration and participation, this attribution of mental elements enabled judges to arbitrarily[69] make perpetrators accomplices and vice versa,[70] according to their (the judges') perceived need for punishment.

This course of materialization has to be distinguished from the enforcement of criminal law-related specific National Socialist aims by the *Reichsgericht's* adjudication.[71] In this context it should be mentioned that even though NS-ideology cannot be fixed, at least three aspects were of central importance: the 'leader principle', the Nazi race ideology and the ideal of the *Volksgemeinschaft*, or 'community of the people'. Certain terms became quite popular and were intentionally reinterpreted in a subtle or very vague way such as honour, loyalty, community, performance of duty and *Volksempfinden*, or 'common sense of the people,' or its counter term *Entartung*, namely 'degeneration'.[72] According to the guiding principles of National Socialist criminal law laid down by *Reichsrechtsführer* Hans Frank, for example, the violation of the principle of loyalty leads to a loss of honour, and National Socialist criminal law has to be based on the 'common sense of loyalty' (*völkische Treuepflicht*).[73] As Pauli[74] convincingly shows, these keywords serve to shorten or even replace legal arguments. Again, this development originates in the 19th century; but unlike before, competing views could not be represented and be publicly supported now.

66 Amendment of the Reich's penal code of 4 of September 1941, *RGBl.* 1941 I, 549.

67 First *RGSt* 54, 35.

68 In detail: Pauli 1992, 135 et seq.

69 Pauli 1992, 131.

70 In detail: Roxin's classic *Täterschaft und Tatherrschaft*, meanwhile published in its 10th ed., 2019.

71 See Pauli 1992, 177 et seq.

72 See especially Lepsius 1996, 72 et seq.

73 Frank 1935, 5 et seq.

74 Pauli 1992, 177 et. seq.

For example, the *Reichsgericht*[75] based the extension of the guarantor's obligation derived from domestic partnership on the 'spirit of sacrifice' within the 'community of the people' (*Volkgsgemeinschaft*) which 'for the widest group derives from the duty to Christian charity and for an inner circle from the comradeship of front-line soldiers and from national-socialism' [1935!]. Here, moral obligation became legal obligation. Terms such as 'community of the people' and 'spirit of sacrifice' helped to enforce the community-oriented National Socialist attitude, even though this attitude had earlier origins, of course. The same applies to the extension of the guarantor's obligation in terms of the guarantor's participation in the criminal offence of giving wrong evidence by omission,[76] as 'at least in general, the legal order must require that someone rather pleads guilty for his own wrongdoings than lets comrades (*Volksgenossen*) commit additional ones, especially because he caused those wrongdoings himself. The court here also recognized the capability of collectives to be insulted, because 'according to actual legal views which focus on the collective as the central concern of legal order' they (the collectives) also were endowed with honour ('honour of the collective').[77]

Supporting the fight against 'degenerate' citizens, the *Reichsgericht* extended the criminal liability according to § 175 StGB: All kinds of homosexual acts were penalized now,[78] even though – or maybe because – this section had been made harsher by legislation anyway.[79] The same can be observed for the *Blutschutzgesetz*[80] ('Act on the protection of Aryan blood'): Despite the fact that § 11 of the First implementation regulation[81] stated that 'extramarital intercourse only means sexual intercourse', the court[82] understood 'extramarital sexual intercourse between Jews and citizens of German or other Aryan blood' (§ 2) as 'all sexual acts with a member of the other sex apt to replace sexual intercourse or to serve the sexual satisfaction of at least one partner'.

75 *RGSt* 69, 321.

76 *RGSt* 72, 20.

77 *RGSt* 70, 140.

78 *RGSt* 71, 281: 'mutual masturbation'.

79 Art. 6 of the amendment of the penal code of 28 June 1935, *RGBl.* 1935 I, 839.

80 Act on the protection of German blood and German honour of 15 September 1935, *RGBl.* 1935 I, 1146.

81 First implementation order on the Act on the protection of German blood and German honour of 14 November 1935, *RGBl.* I, 1334.

82 Grand Criminal Panel, *RGSt* 70, 375.

4.2 Civil Law

According to Lobe,[83] the *Reichsgericht* established a prominent feature of civil law adjudication by increasingly using general clauses in order to replace the strict commitment to legal positivism. The court steadily continued 'using good morals and good faith as a benchmark for decisions', Lobe summarized in a commemorative publication on the occasion of the court's 50th anniversary in 1929. Thus, the court's decisions were characterized by materialization in the area of civil law as well. This materialization also originates in the later years of the empire and especially in the Weimar years, when the *Reichsgericht* tried to handle the devastating economic consequences of World War I by applying general clauses. For example, the court adapted a debt's numerical amount to changes of cash value even in the absence of any according contractual clauses; so-called 'adjudication of revaluation'.[84] The *Reichsgericht* progressively transformed general clauses into something they still are: superior control or correction norms, today, of course, in the light of a new constitution, the basic law (*Grundgesetz*).

Without changing their wording, general clauses can adapt laws to social transformation, to changes in needs and views as well as to changes in constitutional law. At the same time, they give considerable powers to individual judges: In a sense, they turn themselves into legislature by answering open questions, and evaluating norms, and in doing so, they take delayed legislative measures.[85] General clauses had first been discussed at the end of the 19th century, the BGB being the first great codification containing such regulations. Justus Wilhelm Hedemann condemned the 'flight into general clauses' as 'a threat to law and state' and made the treatment of this 'incomplete legislation'[86] a central point of interest in legal discussions. Nevertheless, against Hedemann's apprehension, arbitrariness, mildness, softness, and legal uncertainty ("Willkür, Milde, Weichheit und Rechtsunsicherheit") did not sneak into German civil law after 1933. To various authors, general clauses rather seemed helpful in reinterpreting the old 'liberalistic' codification. The number of contemporary publications on this issue is huge and almost unmanageable.[87] To a larger extent than before, the *Reichsgericht* made law subject to materialization under 'good

83 Lobe 1929, 244.

84 *Reichsgericht in Zivilsachen* (*RGZ*) 107, 78.

85 See, Rüthers 2012, 267; Because of this Heck 1994, § 4.1., refers to them as 'delegating norms' (*Delegationsnormen*).

86 Hedemann 1933, 58.

87 See Rüthers 2012, 214, footnote 6.

faith'. By the way, the same happened to Austrian law after the Annexation (*Anschluss*) of 1938, even if such delegating regulations were unknown to the Austrian legal system.[88] However: At first sight, a content-based analysis does not reveal any Nazi patterns: Rights to information, plea of malice, clausula rebus sic stantibus, protection of good faith, and plea of illegality.

In fact, the vague use of the *exceptio doli generalis* (the defence that the plaintiff has not acted in good faith) frequently allowed the court to conceal the true reasons for a decision and to replace legal arguments.[89] During the Weimar years, legal scholars tried to shape common doctrines on the abuse of law, whereas after 1933, Siebert's far-reaching doctrine on the abuse of law prevailed.[90] This doctrine submitted personal rights to the state's abuse-control, using National Socialist slogans and principles despite the fact that it initially had been designed to actually implement them into the law: As Bernd Rüthers has shown,[91] the concept of 'good faith' served as a dogmatic 'multi-purpose formula',[92] offering the courts legislation-like powers over all rights and claims. After 1945, this 'formula' continued under a different framework.[93] The *Reichsgericht* gratefully adopted this doctrine because Siebert designed a 'legislation-based instrument for re-interpretation', as Haferkamp rightly states: 'a law-related concept which legalizes the implementation of external legal views, unknown to the valid legal order'.[94]

A re-interpretation-instrument which significantly exceeded the original intention of the legislature resulted in the implementation of several 'delegating' provisions into the BGB. In 1936, this reads as follows: 'Since the historic transformation, 'violation of good morals' as used in § 138 and § 826 BGB must be interpreted in the light of the now prevailing common sense of the people (*gesundes Volksempfinden*), which is the National Socialist ideology.'[95] Or, in 1943: 'The basic attitude of national-socialism as laid down in national (*völkisch*) laws on life and morals is universal for the interpretation and evaluation of existing law and contracts and defines the concepts of 'good faith' (§§ 157, 242 BGB) as well as of 'good morals' (§ 138 BGB).'[96] But – and

88 Löhnig 2017.
89 Haferkamp 1995, p. 339.
90 Siebert 1934.
91 Rüthers 2012, 214 et seq.
92 Rüthers 2012, 231.
93 Haferkamp 1995, 183 et seq., 341 et seq.
94 Haferkamp 1995, 264.
95 *RGZ* 150, 1, 4; referring to this decision and its history of reception: Thiessen 2013, 187 et seq.; see also Rüthers 2012, 217 et seq. and Schmoeckel 1997, 9 et seq.
96 Decision of the *Reichsgericht* in the *Juristische Wochenschrift* (*RG JW*) 1943, 610.

this finding is due to Rüthers[97] as well – some judges also used the broad margin of discretion given by § 242 BGB in order to undermine the system under the cover of Nazi slogans, for example in securing pension claims of former Jewish employees or board members.[98]

As with its strategy in criminal law, the *Reichsgericht* submitted new civil law to NS ideology and thereby exceeded the legislature's original intentions. According to the 'Act on last will and testament' (*Testamentsgesetz*),[99] enacted 31st July 1938 in the 'Greater German Reich', a will was null and void 'to the extent that the testator violates legitimate interests of the family and the community of the people in a way that obviously affronts the common sense of the people'. The court applied this regulation to a far larger extent than actually required, not surprisingly clearly on the basis of National Socialist ideology. The court expressly named race ideology as well as the maxim of 'public welfare before self-interest' in determining responsibilities towards one's own family or clan (*Sippe*); in each case, the Senates seemed to have detailed knowledge about the right dimension of these responsibilities. In this way, the judges deliberately instrumentalized § 48 sect. 2 TestG in order to reduce the testator's freedom of testamentary disposition by creating a forced heirship and extending it in its personal and objective dimension.[100]

The Marriage Act (*Ehegesetz, EheG*) of 1938[101] not only excluded marriage law from the BGB, but also in some points changed its content. Now, divorce suits could be based on a new ground, i.e. 'if the domestic partnership of the spouses has ceased for at least three years and cannot be expected to be re-established in a reasonable way in accordance with the nature of marriage; due to deep, irretrievable disruption of the marital relation', § 55 sect. 1 EheG. But: if the plaintiff himself had predominantly or alone caused the disruption, the defendant could object to the divorce according to § 55 sect. 2 sent. 1 EheG. So in a way, the new disruption-based regulation still entailed the continuing principle of fault and liability. On the other hand, the contradiction itself could be ignored, 'if upholding the marriage with respect to the true nature of marriage and to the whole behaviour of the spouses' could not be justified morally, § 55 sect. 2 sent. 2 EheG. Consequently, the effect of the objection not only depended on the behaviour of the spouses, but on a superior legal understanding, required to define concepts like 'the

97 Rüthers 2012, 233 ff.

98 See for example RGZ 161, 301 (Juli 1939); Thiessen 2017, p. 214 et seq.

99 Act on drawing up last wills and inheritance contracts of 31st of July 1938, *RGBl.* 1938 I, p. 973.

100 Löhnig 2017, 181 et seq.

101 Act on the unification of marriage law and divorce law in Austrian and other areas of the Greater German Reich of 6 July of 1938, *RGBl.* 1938 I 807.

true nature of marriage' and 'moral justification'. The *Reichsgericht's* case law on § 55 EheG was based on the community-related National Socialist view on marriage and its according use for the state. Thus, individual contractual and religious aspects were of subordinate importance. As Dieter Niksch[102] has shown, the IVth Civil Senate under Martin Jonas actively pursued national population policies by generally deeming the § 55 sect. 2 – contradiction ineffective.[103] On its own initiative, the court examined all facts and circumstances that were required to assess the marriage as useful or useless for population policy aims. By contrast, the actual question whether the spouses had drifted apart irreversibly was not important to the court anymore. Thus, the *Reichsgericht* exceeded the legal structure accepted by the National Socialist legislature, namely a compromise between principle, exception and counter-exception in terms of disruption-based divorces. Because of its consistent implementation, this solution also found its way into the adjudication of lower courts. The crucial question was, if the marriage could still lead to 'hereditarily healthy' (*erbgesund*) offspring for the 'people's community' (*Volksgemeinschaft*). If it could not fulfil this essential function (any more), the marriage could be dissolved – at least, if the spouses (or one of them) had the opportunity to procreate in another relationship that already might have existed. Thus, 'morality' in § 55 sect. 2 EheG only meant fertility. At the time when marriages are brought before the court, they have usually lost this capacity – and, as a consequence, the contradiction used to be ignored. So, the once liberal idea of disruption-based divorces perfectly matched the National Socialist understanding of marriage. Once again, this shows the 'subtle ambivalence of the Civil Law of the Hitler-state'.[104] In addition, the first Civil Senate established the possibility of introducing an independent 'blood-line'[105] declaratory action,[106] based on the major significance of the bloodline (*blutsmäßige Abstammung*) for National Socialist ideology.[107]

5 Evaluation of the *Reichsgericht*'s Role from 1933 to 1945

The following aspect should not be missed in assessing the ideologisation of the *Reichsgericht*'s case law: Till the late 1930s, the court in

102 Niksch 1990; Nahmmacher 1999; for the development see Löhnig 2016.

103 Niksch 1990, 107 et seq.

104 Zarusky 2006, 420.

105 See Haferkamp 2012, 159 et seq.

106 RGZ 160, 293.

107 In detail see Löhnig 2007.

some cases explained that racial affiliation itself could not affect the decision-making process and the judgement.[108] Until 1942, Jewish parties and their counsel pursued their claims before the court. It seems as if they tried to hold on to 'normal life'-structures which already had been abolished brutally. Maybe the *Reichsgericht* as well as the whole judiciary in strongly confirming and ensuring the rule of law seemed to provide the greatest 'normality' possible. For example, in 1941 a Jewish plaintiff, the widow of a factory director whose husband had died in an accident, won her revision procedure against the German *Reich* after a well-founded decision of the court.[109] Of course, in many of the proceedings, the parties and their consultants sooner or later had 'new addresses unknown', according to the case-files. The *Doppelstaat*:[110] business as usual until persons were collected at their doors and the authoritarian state could show its deathly face – 'Orders of the Secret Service (*Gestapo*) cannot be challenged in front of Administrative Courts' (§ 7 of the Prussian Secret Service Act of 1936[111]). Courts early on decided not to be empowered to negate political actions and thereby restricted their power towards the authoritarian state.[112]

Wadle[113] rightly states that until the end of the Hitler regime, the regime's desire for full control had to face a tradition-based institution. For Bumke's 70th birthday on 7 July 1944, just like in 1929, he – the court's Presiding Judge – only received a telegram; this time from the *Führer* himself. This shows the aversion of National Socialist leaders against the judiciary. The court's members, despite their strong will to comply with the state's requirements, always emphasized their autonomy. Of course, this had nothing to do with resistance. The best example is probably Bumke himself: According to his biographer Kolbe, after some scepticism about enforced political conformity (*Gleichschaltung*), he rapidly became a 'willing servant', 'submissive', 'compliant', 'deeply devoted'.[114] This is revealed by – at first sight – minor details: in 1933, for example, Bumke removed the portrait of the first Presiding Judge, Simson.[115] He was not only a convinced liberal, but also, according to National Socialist race-ideology, a Jew.

108 Thiessen 2017.
109 RG 5 July 1941, VIII 64/41.
110 See Fraenkel 2012.
111 *Preußische Gesetzessammlung* (*PrGS*) 1936, 21/28.
112 Cf. Plum 1965, 191 et seq.
113 Wadle 2008, 289.
114 Kolbe 1975, 260-263.
115 Wadle 2008, 290.

By feigning a crisis in 1942, parts of the regime tried to weaken the judiciary, which in a sense still functioned in a traditional way. In a speech on 26 April 1942, Hitler threatened to remove judges from office without observing binding procedures if they still had 'not realized the order of the day'. The *Reichstag* 'unanimously supported' the *Führer's* speech in claiming these rights and, according to its resolution and amongst other statements, declared him to be the 'highest Presiding Judge'.[116] The ministry of justice tried to prevent the imminent removals by sending letters to the judges (*Richterbriefe*)[117] and taking other measures, because even judges who were dedicated to the party did not agree with these plans. By contrast, the SS-press kept on criticizing single judgements and insinuated that judges still adhered to liberal Weimar rules instead of new National Socialist values.[118] Content-related compliance of the courts was obviously not enough; binding procedures had to be abolished as well: National-socialist values had to overrule the rule of law. It was not the will of the law that judges had to execute, but the government's will as established by the NSDAP. The majority of the judges did not meet these expectations; most of them did not want to give up on principles such as the independence and irremovability of judges in favour of a new order or being bound to (materialized and thus 'soft') law, irrespective of its content. According to Schädler,[119] the driving forces behind the pretended crisis were Hitler's hatred of jurists, Himmler's and Heydrich's plans to strengthen their own power bases (police and SS) against a supposed slow and formalistic judiciary and a competition amongst the party's leading jurists. But nota bene: This cannot be labelled as 'breaking the resistance' of a non-collaborative judiciary and its Supreme Court.

6 Evaluating the *Reichsgericht* from a Post-war Perspective

The opening of the *Bundesgerichtshof* on 8 October 1950 raised the question, if, and if so, how one should adhere to the tradition of the *Reichsgericht*. In the commemorative publication in honour of the opening,[120] Georg Petersen as head of department in the ministry of justice explained that the *Reichsgericht*'s case law shows some 'dark spots', but also had excelled

116 Resolution of the Great German Reichstag of 26 April 1942, *RGBl.* 1942 I, p. 247.

117 See Boberach 1975.

118 For this and the following, cf. Schädler 2009, 24 ff.

119 Schädler 2009, 32 ff.

120 Petersen 1950.

in multiple other ways. He wanted 'to separate the wheat from the chaff' – a still pending task that might never be completed. On the occasion of the 75th anniversary of the *Reich*'s great judicial codifications in 1954, state secretary of the ministry of justice, Walter Strauß, strongly emphasized that the *Bundesgerichtshof* had to be classified as identical with the *Reichsgericht*, not as its mere follow-up institution. Thus, the ministry felt particularly obliged to elect members of the former *Reichsgericht* as judges of the *Bundesgerichtshof* again.[121] Indeed, the first president of the *Bundesgerichtshof* was Herrmann Weinkauff, a former judge of the *Reichsgericht*. Other former *Reichsgericht*'s members were elected as well. This continuity was not mere lip service but followed a personnel policy programme. It shows the retrospective high estimation of the *Reichsgericht* and its work during the post-war years.[122] This programme was continued by the *Bundesgerichtshof*, which still quotes the former *Reichsgericht's* decisions of 1933 to 1945; even those obviously referring to National Socialist ideology.[123]

Arno Buschmann[124] rightly states that this high praise of traditions reached its peak at the ceremony on the occasion of the Court's 100th anniversary at the *Bundesgerichtshof* in 1979. Presiding Judge Gerd Pfeiffer, the first SPD member who had managed to become head of the *Bundesgerichtshof* in a hundred years, discussed in detail the development of the *Reichsgericht's* case law in a widely observed commemorative speech. As a matter of priority, he wanted to examine the Court's history in a neutral way without judging it, simply in order to understand what had happened and to build upon lessons learned.[125]

For several decades, post-war jurists had ignored the possibility of 'learning lessons' by referring to positivist approaches: 'There was in fact no way of deciding differently'. It was Bernd Rüthers who put a stop to this self-serving declaration in 1968 by precisely examining and revealing working methods and margins of discretion in decision-making procedures applied by the *Reichsgericht* and other judges of the Third *Reich*. Particularly telling is the fact that Rüthers' – according to himself: caring – academic teachers tried to prevent him from working on this topic because they expected it to end his academic career.[126] Meanwhile, various studies show the many facets of the *Reichsgericht*'s judges and their work in the Third *Reich*. In fact,

121 Cf. Strauß 1954, 51 et seq.

122 Cf. Görtemaker & Safferling 2016, p. 267 et seq.

123 See one detailed example in Thiessen 2022.

124 Buschmann 2006, 50.

125 Pfeiffer 1979, esp. p. 329.

126 Rüthers 2012, preface and epilogue.

German Supreme Court adjudication still follows methodical lines, which originate in years long before 1933 and reach beyond the Bonn republic. Today's tendencies of materialization by constitutionalizing the law do not follow significantly different methods than during the Third *Reich* – of course against completely different backgrounds. Comparative work shows, as Haferkamp[127] rightly states, that tendencies of materialization still characterize German law.

References

Boberach, Heinz, *Richterbriefe. Dokumente zur Beeinflussung der deutschen Rechtsprechung 1942–1944*, Koblenz: Bundesarchiv 1975.

Buschmann, Arno, *Das Reichsgericht – Ein Höchstgericht im Wandel der Zeiten*, in: Bernd-Rüdiger Kern & Adrian Schmidt-Recla (Eds), *125 Jahre Reichsgericht*, Duncker & Humblot 2006, 41-76.

Chapoutot, Johann, *La loi du sang. Penser et agir en nazi*, Gallimard 2014.

Chapoutot, Johann, '"Volk" and "Justice" under the Third Reich', in: Émilie Delivré, Emmanuel Berger & Martin Löhnig (Eds), *Popular justice in times of transition (19th and 20th century Europe)*, 2017, 149-154.

Chowaniec, Elisabeth, *Der ‚Fall Dohnanyi' 1943–1945. Widerstand, Militärjustiz, SS-Willkür*, Oldenbourg Wissenschaftsverlag 1991.

Deiseroth, Dieter, 'Der Reichstagsbrand-Prozess – ein rechtsstaatliches Verfahren?', *Kritische Justiz* Vol. 42 2009, 303-316.

'Ein bißchen Bibel und viel Unrecht', *Der Spiegel* 40/1979.

Fraenkel, Ernst, *Der Doppelstaat* (2nd Ed), Europäische Verlagsanstalt 2012.

Freisler, Roland et al., *Grundzüge eines Allgemeinen Deutschen Strafrechts. Denkschrift des Zentralausschusses der Strafrechtsabteilung der Akademie für Deutsches Recht über die Grundzüge eines Allgemeinen Deutschen Strafrechts*, Berlin: R. v. Decker's Verlag 1934 (= *Schriften der Akademie für Deutsches Recht*, Heft 1).

Frank, Hans (Ed), *Nationalsozialistische Leitsätze für ein neues deutsches Strafrecht*, Teil 1, 3rd ed., Berlin: Deutsche Rechts- und Wirtschaftswissenschaft Verlags-Ges. 1935.

Frantz, Constantin, *Die Nationalliberale Rechtseinheit und das Reichsgericht*, Augsburg 1873.

Görtemaker, Manfred & Christoph Safferling (Eds), *Die Akte Rosenburg: Das Bundesministerium der Justiz und die NS-Zeit*, C.H. Beck 2016.

127 Haferkamp 1995.

Gruchmann, Lothar, *Justiz im Dritten Reich 1933-1940. Anpassung und Unterwerfung in der Ära Gürtner*, Oldenbourg Wissenschaftsverlag 2009.

Gründer, Horst, *Walter Simons als Staatsmann, Jurist und Kirchenpolitiker*, Mocker & Jahn, 1975.

Haferkamp, Hans-Peter, *Die heutige Rechtsmissbrauchslehre: Ergebnis nationalsozialistischen Rechtsdenkens?*, Berlin: Verlag Spitz, 1995.

Haferkamp, Hans-Peter, "Österreichisches', 'Deutsches' und 'Nationalsozialistisches' in der Rechtsprechung des Reichsgerichts zum ABGB zwischen 1939 und 1945', in: Barbara Dölemeyer & Heinz Mohnhaupt (Eds), *200 Jahre ABGB. (1811-2011) Die österreichische Kodifikation im internationalen Kontext*, 2012, 159-175.

Haffner, Sebastian, *Von Bismarck zu Hitler. En Rückblick*, Kindler Verlag 1993.

Hartung, Fritz, *Jurist unter vier Reichen*, Carl Heymanns Verlag 1971.

Hattenhauer, Hans, 'Das NS-Volksgesetzbuch', in: Arno Buschmann et al. (Eds), *Festschrift Rudolf Gmür zum 70. Geburtstag*, Bielefeld 1983, 255-297.

Heck, Philipp, *Grundriss des Schuldrechts*, Scientia Verlag 1994.

Hedemann, Justus Wilhelm, *Die Flucht in die Generalklauseln*, Tübingen: Mohr 1933.

'Hohle Nuß', *Der Spiegel* 05/1992.

Jasch, Hans-Christian, 'Das Ringen um die Verwaltungsgerichtsbarkeit. Verwaltungsgerichtsbarkeit als Instrument der Rechtsvereinheitlichung im Dritten Reich', *Die Verwaltung* (38) 2005, 546-576.

Kaul, Friedrich Karl, *Geschichte des Reichsgerichts*, Vol 4: *1933 – 1945*, Akademie 1971.

Kern, Bernd-Rüdiger & Klaus-Peter Schroeder (Eds), *Eduard von Simson (1810–1899): 'Chorführer der Deutschen' und erster Präsident des Reichsgerichts*, Baden-Baden: Nomos 2001.

Kirchner, Carl, 'Reichsgericht und Bundesgerichtshof. Berufsherkunft, Alterszusammensetzung und Schicksal seiner Mitglieder', *Deutsche Richterzeitung* 1959, 107.

Kolbe, Dieter, *Reichsgerichtspräsident Dr. Erwin Bumke: Studien zum Niedergang des Reichsgerichts und der deutschen Rechtspflege*, C.F. Müller 1975.

Lepsius, Oliver, 'Personengebundene oder strukturorientierte Bewertungskriterien für juristisches Verhalten im Nationalsozialismus', in: Hermann Nehlsen & Georg Brun (Eds), *Münchener rechtshistorische Studien zum Nationalsozialismus*, Frankfurt/Main: Peter Lang 1996, 63-102.

Lobe, Adolf, *50 Jahre Reichsgericht*, Berlin/Leipzig: Walter de Gruyter 1929.

Löhnig, Martin, 'Ehelichkeitsanfechtung durch den Staatsanwalt (1938 – 1961)', *Zeitschrift der Savigny Stiftung fur Rechtsgeschichte – Germanistische Abteilung* (124) 2007, 323-346.

Löhnig, Martin, *Neue Zeiten – Altes Recht. Die Anwendung von NS-Gesetzen durch deutsche Gerichte nach 1945*, Berlin: de Gruyter 2016.

Löhnig, Martin, 'Generalklauseln in der Rechtsprechung der österreichischen Senate des Reichsgerichts 1939-1945: Eine Studie auf Grundlage der Wiener

Reichsgerichtsakten', in: *Beiträge zur Rechtsgeschichte Österreichs* (7) 2017-2, 181-203.

Lüth & Wesel, 'Arnold Freymuth (1878–1933), Hermann Großmann (1878–1937(?)), Alfred Orgler (1876–1943(?)), Drei Richter für die Republik', in: Redaktion Kritische Justiz (Eds), *Streitbare Juristen. Eine andere Tradition*, Baden-Baden: Nomos 1988, 204-218.

Miosge, Dieter, 'So begann 1933 der Zugriff auf das Reichsgericht', *Recht und Politik* (44), 2008, 226-230.

Motive zu dem Entwurfe eines Bürgerlichen Gesetzbuches für das Deutsche Reich (Band 1, Allgemeiner Theil), Berlin/Leipzig: Guttentag 1896.

Nahmmacher, Kathrin, *Die Rechtsprechung des Reichsgerichts und der Hamburger Gerichte zum Scheidungsgrund des § 55 des EheG 1938 in den Jahren 1938 bis 1945*, Berlin: Peter Lang 1999.

Niksch, Dieter, *Die sittliche Rechtfertigung des Widerspruchs gegen die Scheidung der zerrütteten Ehe in den Jahren 1938-1944*, Köln 1990.

Pauli, Gerhard, *Die Rechtsprechung des Reichsgerichts in Strafsachen zwischen 1933 und 1945 und ihre Fortwirkung in der Rechtsprechung des Bundesgerichtshofes*, De Gruyter 1992.

Petersen, Georg, 'Die Tradition des Reichsgerichts', in: Albert Kistner (Ed), *Festschrift zur Eröffnung des Bundesgerichtshofes*, C.F. Müller 1950, 25-37.

Pfeiffer, Gerd, 'Das Reichsgericht und seine Rechtsprechung', in: *Deutsche Richterzeitung* 1979, 325-332.

Plum, Günter, 'Staatspolizei und Innere Verwaltung 1934-1936', *Vierteljahrshefte für Zeitgeschichte* 13 (1965), p. 191-224.

Roxin, Claus, *Täterschaft und Tatherrschaft*, 10th Ed, De Gruyter 2019.

Rüthers, Bernd, *Die unbegrenzte Auslegung*, Mohr Siebeck 2012.

Schädler, Sarah, *Justizkrise und Justizreform im Nationalsozialismus. Das Reichsjustizministerium unter Reichsjustizminister Thierack (1942-1945)*, Mohr Siebeck 2009.

Schmoeckel, Mathias, 'Der maßgebliche Zeitpunkt zur Bestimmung der Sittenwidrigkeit nach § 138 BGB', in: *Archiv für die civilistische Praxis* (197) 1997-1/2, 1-197.

Schreiber, Otto (Ed), *Die Reichsgerichtspraxis im deutschen Rechtsleben. Festgabe der juristischen Fakultäten zum 50jährigen Bestehen des Reichsgerichts (1. Oktober 1929)*, Berlin, de Gruyter 1929.

Schröder, Jan, 'Gab es eine (Privat-) Rechtstheorie der Weimarer Republik?', in: Martin Löhnig & Mareike Preisner (Eds), *Weimarer Zivilrechtswissenschaft*, Mohr Siebeck 2014, 151-174.

Schubert, Werner, Peter Rieß & Jürgen Regge (Eds), *Quellen zur Reform des Straf- und Strafprozeßrechts, Abt. II: NS-Zeit (1933-1939) Strafgesetzbuch, Vol 1 & 2*, De Gruyter 1989.

Schubert, Werner, *Die Deutsche Gerichtsverfassung 1869-1877*, Vittorio Klostermann 1981.

Schubert, Werner (Ed), *Volksgesetzbuch. Teilentwürfe, Arbeitsberichte und sonstige Materialien*, Berlin 1988.

Siebert, Wolfgang, *Verwirkung und unzulässige Rechtsausübung*, Marburg 1934.

Simons, Walter, '7 Jahre Reichsgerichtspräsident', in: *Deutsche Juristenzeitung* 1929, 1249ff.

Stern, Elisabeth & Sifton, Fritz, *Keine gewöhnlichen Männer, Dietrich Bonhoeffer und Hans von Dohnanyi im Widerstand gegen Hitler*, C.H. Beck 2013.

Strauß, Walter, 'Reichsgericht und Bundesgerichtshof', in: Bundesminister der Justiz (Ed), *Festgabe 75 Jahre Reichsjustizgesetze*, 1954, 51-55.

Thiessen, Jan, 'Gute Sitten und „gesundes Volksempfinden': Vor-, Miss- und Nachklänge in und um RGZ 150, 1', in: Arndt Kiehnle, Bernd Mertens & Gottfried Schiemann (Eds), *Festschrift für Jan Schröder zum 70. Geburtstag*, Tübingen: Mohr Siebeck 2013, 187-219.

Thiessen, Jan, '"Anschluss" an die "Arisierung": Drei wirtschaftsrechtliche Reichsgerichtsfälle aus Österreich', in: *Beiträge zur Rechtsgeschichte Österreichs* 2017, 204-215.

Thiessen, Jan, *Der Ausschluss aus der GmbH als „praktische Durchführung einer verbrecherischen Irrlehre' – eine Rechtsfortbildungsgeschichte*, Mohr Siebeck 2022.

Vollprecht, Hans, 'Das Reichsverwaltungsgericht und die Aufsichtsführung in Kriegsschädensachen', *Deutsche Verwaltung* (19) 1943, 426-428.

Wadle, Elmar, 'Das Reichsgericht im Widerschein denkwürdiger Tage', in: Wadle, Elmar (Ed), *Verfassung und Recht, Wegmarken ihrer Geschichte*, Böhlau 2008, 277-290.

Zarusky, Jürgen, 'Recht und Justiz in der NS-Diktatur. Neue Literatur', *Zeitschrift für Neuere Rechtsgeschichte* (28) 2006, 409-432.

About the Author

Martin Löhnig was Chair for Civil Law, Legal History and Canon Law at the University of Konstanz (2005-2008) and is now Chair for Civil Law, Legal History and Canon Law at the University of Regensburg. His research concerns Family Law, Succession Law, Comparative/European Legal History, and Legal Culture.

4 The Danish Supreme Court During the German Occupation

Ditlev Tamm

Abstract

This chapter discusses the role of the Danish supreme court during the German occupation in World War II. It explains how the Danish court system was left untouched by the minimal German occupation regime, and how the supreme court continued its traditional role, which it interpreted as a loyal branch of the civil service. Several significant cases are treated relating to assistance to the allied forces, which put some strain on the relations with the occupier. The introduction, by German demand, of anti-communist legislation caused a controversy within the court when its president advised on it and wrote about it without consulting his colleagues. The chapter is rounded off with a treatment of the post-war criticisms of the court's behaviour and an assessment of its role.

Keywords: Denmark in WWII; Danish Supreme Court; Anti-communist legislation; Troels G. Jørgensen; Post-war purge

1 Introduction

The position of the Danish Supreme Court during the Second World War was determined by the general agreement concluded between the Danish Government and the German authorities on 9 April 1940.[1] Germany had

1 For the Danish Supreme Court and its functioning during WWII, see Tamm 1984, p. 42-62. The following to a high degree is based on this work, in which further references can be found. Immediately after the end of the occupation, several books were published on wartime conditions. On legislation and the judiciary, see especially Petersen & Herfeldt 1948; on the specific question of how to keep Danish jurisdiction, Nissen 1973 passim and esp. p. 88f. A documentation of statutes, legal acts and courts' decisions is found in Alkil 1945. A so-called parliamentary

Venema, D. (ed.), *Supreme Courts Under Nazi Occupation*. Taylor & Francis Group 2022
DOI: 10.5117/9789463720496_CH04

invaded Denmark that same morning without warning. After a few hours of armed resistance, Denmark had capitulated and accepted the terms laid down in a so-called 'memorandum', which provided the basis for the German occupation over the following years. Germany, in this document, declared that it would neither act contrary to Denmark's territorial integrity nor its political independence. The following day, in another declaration, it further stated that it did not intend to interfere with the full functionality of the Danish police force. This meant that political life continued with a functioning parliament, with elections even as late as the spring of 1943; a public administration, which in practice was handled during the occupation without any interference from the German authorities; and a judiciary, which continued to conduct business as usual, according to legislation and other rules issued by Parliament and other Danish authorities.

This rather unique legal situation for an occupied country only had a parallel in Vichy France – with the marked difference, however, that even if political collaboration was necessary, it never amounted to sympathy, or any kind of voluntary siding, with the German cause. A German wartime administration was never introduced in Denmark. Relations continued on the level of foreign ministries, which, from the German side, were carried out by the German ambassador, who was substituted by a so-called *Reichsbevollmächtigter* in 1942. The occupation was a fact to be accepted, but no Danish government during the occupation had any members representing Nazi interests, or members who considered Denmark to be on that side or looked upon the German occupation with any sympathy.

The role of the Danish Courts was not changed and no specific Danish juridical bodies were set up to cope with special cases arising from, and relating to, the presence of the occupying forces in Denmark. To understand the Danish situation, it is important to keep in mind this specific legal situation and the existence of what Danish historians have called an 'official policy of collaboration or negotiation'.[2] The consequence of this policy was that, as long as there existed a Danish government, official policies aimed both at keeping jurisdiction over Danish citizens in Danish hands, and having all necessary wartime legislation prepared and issued by the Danish

commission consisting of members of Parliament after the war investigated the question as to whether former ministers could be held responsible for political acts committed during the occupation, the result of which was published as *Den Parlamentariske Kommissions Betænkning* 1945-1958. On the judiciary, see Vol VII: *Justitsministeriet* 1950.

2 The Danish minister of foreign affairs during the occupation (and in 1943 also prime minister) Erik Scavenius after the war published a book on this politics which he called the "policy of negotiation" (*forhandlingspolitiken*), see Scavenius 1948.

parliament. The role of the Supreme Court especially will be considered from this angle. The Court did not take a stand of its own, but saw itself as a player in the policy of protecting Danish jurisdiction. It therefore complied with what was seen as the necessary, and rather high, level of punishment, and even with the extraordinary legislation issued to fulfil German demands. A specific feature of the way in which the occupation of Denmark took place was that practically no German demands were made to the effect that specific persons with sympathies for Germany or members of a Nazi party be given any official posts. The Danish administration and the courts therefore functioned as before the occupation without changes in personnel or attitudes, besides those that occurred in their natural course. This ended in August 1943 when the Danish government chose to resign, instead of accepting new German demands – including accepting the death penalty for actions of resistance against the German occupation. After that time, no cases concerning extraordinary legislation were brought before the Supreme Court, which, nevertheless, continued its ordinary functions.

2 Cases before the Danish Supreme Court

The Danish Supreme Court at that time was – and to a certain degree still is – a traditional third instance supreme court, which received appeals from the two Danish High Courts. The Court heard civil, criminal, administrative, and constitutional cases. The Danish court system is constructed as a pyramid with generally competent municipal courts at the bottom and a supreme court at the top, consisting (at that time) of 15 justices. The German occupation, in principle, did not lead to any change in the function of the Court. Approximately the same caseload as previously was managed. There was no change as to the character of cases brought before the Court, except for a small number of cases to a rather limited, but nevertheless still somewhat important, degree, which dealt with such penal cases relating to certain legislation issued by the Parliament during the occupation. Most cases were dealt with in the first and second instance, and only a very limited number of cases were brought before the Supreme Court. An example is the case concerning a statute of 1 May 1940, which doubled the penalty for crimes committed during times of blackout or air raid alarm. Another statute, and the first to be denominated as a temporary one, was a statute issued on 18 January 1941. This statute was a more spectacular case of raised penalties, according to which sentences of prison for life could be meted out to those who entered into allied military service, committed acts of sabotage against German military installations, or "did similar acts which could seriously damage Danish interests with relation to foreign countries". By this statute, other normal principles of procedure were also set aside. No participation of lay judges (as in normal penal cases) was allowed; appeals could only occur with specific permit by the Ministry of Justice, which, after 1942, could also decide that appeals should be heard directly by the Supreme Court without previously having been heard by the High Court. The background for this statute is illustrative as to the way in which parliamentary statutes and the courts worked together as roles in a stage play, which aimed at keeping Danish jurisdiction over Danish citizens, even if German interests were at stake.

A tense situation, which led to extraordinary legal measures, arose when a Danish military officer, Lieutenant Colonel Ørum, was arrested in Berlin and charged with recruiting Danish citizens to enter the war on the allied side. It was feared that, before a German war court, he might receive a death sentence. Therefore, after negotiation between Danish and German government representatives, the necessary legislation was issued on 18 January 1941, which enabled Danish courts to give a sentence of life imprisonment as demanded by the German authorities. Accordingly, a week later, on 25 January 1941, Ørum was given a life sentence by the Copenhagen Municipal Court. Such decisions and legislation come close to legislation normally found as part of military or war penal law, with harsh penalties and vague descriptions of the criminal act.[3] The Ørum judgement was not brought before the Supreme Court and neither were a series of other judgements made according to the extraordinary penal legislation. The total number of such cases were 447 in 1940, 851 in 1941, and 1112 in 1942-3. Only six cases of this kind were brought before the Supreme Court in the years 1941-43.

The first case, decided in November 1941,[4] concerned an eighteen-year-old youth, under youth care, who, in July 1941, had made an attempt in vain to cross over to Sweden in a stolen fisherman's boat. This was a forbidden attempt to leave the country and he was charged accordingly under Art. 3 of the aforementioned statute from January 1941 for having committed one of '... similar acts which could seriously damage Danish interests with relation to foreign countries'. The municipal court had meted out a sentence of two years' imprisonment, whereas the High Court had acquitted him based on the reflection that he neither had in his mind, nor capacity to understand,

3 Tamm 1984, 45.

4 *UfR* (*Ugeskrift for retsvæsen*) 1942, 42.

the notion that his act could actually damage Danish interests. The Supreme Court voted differently. A sentence of one-and-a-half years of prison was given. It expressly stated that the sentence took into consideration the fact that, under the given circumstances, particular importance was laid upon the closure of Danish borders. From the Court's internal deliberations, we can see that mitigating circumstances in the minds of the judges had to give way to the pursuance of the main purpose of the law, which was to enforce claims from the occupying power. Danish points of view could not automatically prevail; the situation had to be considered from the German side, it was said. Therefore, it was important to give a strict sentence and signal that the High Court was wrong. Some judges referred to the High Court's decision as being based on a way of thinking that was not of this world. However, in this first case to be judged according to the extraordinary legislation, the justices were also aware of its lack of precision, which caused trouble for the courts in meting out correct sentences.

Two cases, which were particularly widely discussed, had to do with speeches given by academics. Vilhelm la Cour was a well-known historian – and well-known as someone who was not afraid of speaking up against the German occupation. In September 1941 and in January 1942, he had given speeches under the titles "Our Neutrality" and "The History of a Crusade". These had a critical content that was considered to be a transgression of the abovementioned Art. 3 in the statute of 18 January 1941. In his speeches, he had used expressions such as "the murderer's little canary bird", thinking of Denmark, and expressed the view "that any child could see how Germany would not be able to win the war". In the special municipal Court in charge of such extraordinary cases, he was sentenced to four months of light prison, a sentence that was elevated by the Supreme Court to imprisonment for seven months.[5] The Court quoted an opinion given by the Ministry of Foreign Affairs, which said that what la Cour had said complicated relations with the German authorities and also mentioned the intended anti-German tendency of these speeches. From the German side, the question had been raised of having la Cour sentenced by a German court and, consequently, there was in this case a specific Danish interest in giving a sentence that could satisfy German demands. The judges of the Supreme Court all agreed that la Cour had been too outspoken, considering the extraordinary situation, even if his motives were respectable. Sentences from five or six months to one-and-a-half years were considered. On the stricter end, we find judges who were bothered by the fact that la Cour might threaten the agreement

5 *UfR* 1942, 772.

between the Danish government and the occupying power, and even provoke fear and insecurity.

Another case concerning lecturing arose from a speech with the title "The Freedom of Denmark", given by the Danish journalist Peter de Hemmer Gudme before a closed audience in the Students' Association in Copenhagen. What was said in this speech was also considered damaging to Danish relations with foreign countries. The Supreme Court discussed in this case whether or not the lecture was to be qualified as a public lecture or as being given at a private assembly. A minority of the Court would acquit the accused on the ground that Gudme had not spoken in public. The majority, however, found that this question was less relevant and that the intention of the lecture should prevail. Therefore, on 26 November 1942, the Court sentenced him to four months of light prison.[6]

A much stricter decision was made by the Supreme Court in a case decided on 17 July 1942.[7] The accused were a ship owner and his assistant, who, on 1 May, had assisted a Danish politician, Wilhelm Christmas Møller, who wanted to escape from Denmark and join the so-called free Danish, who operated from London and from there called for resistance against the German occupation. Christmas Møller had sailed to neutral Sweden and from there travelled to London, where he made himself famous as a strong Danish voice with uncompromising speeches broadcast to Denmark. The case was tried in the municipal court: the sentence for the ship owner who had conducted the voyage was three years of prison, and one year for his assistant. The Supreme Court came to another result. The sentences were raised to six years of prison for the ship owner and three years for his assistant. In the Court, voices mentioned the possibility of passing down life sentences, which in the statute of 18 January 1941 was the 'normal' penalty. It was mentioned during the Court's deliberations, that helping by transporting an enemy of the occupying forces to England was a serious crime and normal Danish standards therefore could not be used. Again, we see in this case how the Court saw it as its role to support official Danish policies by meting out strict penalties where political interests were at stake, which would be especially sensitive for the Germans.

On 15 January 1943,[8] a penalty of forty days of prison for housing a German deserter during a few months in the beginning of the occupation period was elevated to three months of prison. On the other hand, later

6 *UfR* 1943, 56.

7 *UfR* 1942, 1030.

8 *UfR* 1943, 227.

the same year, the Supreme Court reduced the penalty in a case of people involved in anti-German propaganda by distributing a so-called "illegal" pamphlet, *De frie danske* ("The Free Danes").[9] Penalties of eight years were reduced to penalties of six years of prison, even though the prosecution had demanded harsh penalties considering "the dangerousness and the seriousness of the crime".

It is remarkable that the Supreme Court did not consider these extraordinary cases as something to be treated more as a show meant to satisfy the Germans than serious judicial business. The deliberations of the Court show clearly that at least a majority of the Court looked upon this matter and made a decision as they would in "normal" cases, based on the law and the intent of the statute, even if the statute from January 1941 was obviously provoked by the Germans. The Court considered itself a player in the fight for Danish jurisdiction and did not look benignly at those who actively or in their speeches endangered this official policy. However, as we have seen, the Court was also conscious of the fact that it was important that the Germans did not get the impression that Danish courts would not mete out strict sentences and therefore would have the accused put before a German court. It was an act of balance to find the "right" sentence but – at the same time – it is difficult to find any judge in the Court denouncing the extraordinary statutes as being contrary to Danish norms. The Supreme Court officially spoke in the same voice as the Danish government, which at that time did not want any conflict with a strong Germany and therefore adjusted its politics and its justice to such German demands to maintain the agreement made on the first day of the occupation. Danish judges at that time, as they still do, saw themselves as loyal civil servants – not as activists who should challenge the regime laid down by the Danish politicians, even if with regard to an occupying force. The policy was to maintain law and order, and not to be part of the resistance against the occupiers; the Supreme Court saw itself as an actor in maintaining this scheme. The extraordinary legislation was issued by a parliament established by ordinary elections before the occupation. With no tradition of a strong judicial review, the courts took the stand that this legislation should not be questioned. It was the task of the courts to fill in and interpret the rather general standard laid down, especially in the abovementioned statute of 18 January 1941, which even talked of German military forces as such "which according to agreement with the Danish government are present in this country". The Supreme Court made strict decisions according to such statutes following

9 *UfR* 1943, 819.

the intentions of the law. Clearly, there was a tendency in the Court not to look with specific sympathy at those who followed their own conscience and not the official rules of conduct laid down by the government.

3 The Anti-Communist Statute

A particularly controversial feature of legal life during the German occupation was the internment of Danish communists and the following legislation against communist activities issued by Parliament in the summer of 1941, after the German invasion of the Soviet Union on 22 June 1941. That same morning, leading Danish civil servants were summoned to a meeting at the German Embassy, informed of the German military action, and given certain demands, among which was the demand that leading Danish communists be taken into custody by the Danish police. This demand was accepted by the Danish Prime Minister and the Minister of Foreign Affairs. A card index with 72 names collected by German informants was handed over to the police by the German authorities. The Danish police, on its own initiative (as part of investigating communist activities feared to be unparliamentary), had collected more names and made its own card index, which they used, together with the German card index, to arrest a total of 147 persons in Copenhagen in the following days. Arrests were also made outside Copenhagen by local police authorities and, as a result, a total of 192 persons were taken into custody of which a majority was later released. By 22 August, 71 persons were kept in custody on the charge of being leading communists. The arrests were made without ordinary control by the courts. After the war, these arrests were openly derided as a blow to basic Danish values, which even under the given circumstances should not have been accepted. Criticism naturally came especially from organized communists or their sympathizers. On the other hand, it was argued that the communists were better off being arrested by the Danish police and that the action should be seen as a protection against such arrests by German authorities. Also, communists were seen as collaborators due to the pact between Germany and the Soviet Union, as at that time they had not actively taken part in the resistance movement, as was the case later.

The arrests were only a first step. It was now also demanded from the German side that communist activities should be expressly forbidden. This demanded, according to the Danish constitution, that in order for the government to dissolve such an association, a specific statute would have to be issued which qualified communist activity as an illegal purpose of an association. During the preparatory work for such a statute, the question was raised as to whether a clause should be inserted legalizing the arrests of the leading communists. The initiative to include such a clause stemmed from the President of the Danish Supreme Court, Troels G. Jørgensen, who had mentioned this possibility during a visit to the Minister of Justice without any express authority form the rest of the Court. He had expressed as his opinion that the general reference to the emergency, which had legitimized certain restrictions, and had also legitimized the arrests of the communists, could not include a continued detention without any legal basis. The President himself made a first draft, which after consideration in the Ministry was presented to the government. After the war, the President was subjected to heavy criticism for this intervention without informing his colleagues, using Court stationery, and referring generally to "a judicial point of view" as the reason for such a clause on detention. In the event, such a clause was inserted in the statute, which prohibited communist activities and allowed detention after a judicial scrutiny. This statute was approved unanimously by Parliament and enacted on 21 August 1941.

After the enactment of this statute, the Supreme Court President even published an article in a leading Danish law review,[10] in which he discussed arguments for and against the constitutionality of the statute and came to the conclusion that the statute was outside the scope of the constitution. According to both Parliament and the Minister of Justice, such a statute was necessary for the continuation of the detention of the communists. Both the article in the law review and the intervention in the preliminary procedure leading to the statute were seen by many as compromising the Supreme Court and its President. After that, he was isolated in his court and, after his retirement in 1944 upon reaching official retirement age, he was not invited to participate in any official acts of the court.

The legality of the detention was examined by the courts only two days after the enactment of the abovementioned statute. A series of communists challenged their detention, which was declared legal by the municipal court, in reference to the statute. In a case in which the question of the constitutionality of the statute was raised, the municipal court upheld the statute referring to the extraordinary situation and the unwritten principles of the law of emergency. The protection of liberty in the constitution, it was said, could not be upheld when the legislator, due to emergency and with regard to the security of the state and its relation to foreign powers, gives specific rules relating to a deprivation of liberty of a kind not foreseen

10 Jørgensen 1941, 497-504.

by the constitution. This decision was brought before the Supreme Court directly. The statute provided for such a direct appeal, with the exclusion of the High Court. In such cases, only three judges would make the decision. The Supreme Court, on 8 September, in a very short decision,[11] came to the conclusion that the question of unconstitutionality was raised without sufficient grounds and thus, in one sentence, the Supreme Court had legitimized the legal set-up around the internment of the Danish leading communists, as it was foreseen in the statute on communist activities.

After the war, the Supreme Court and the Danish Courts in general were scorned for what was seen as an uncritical attitude towards the extraordinary legislation and for having too easily accommodated official politics. The role of the Supreme Court in maintaining the anti-communist legislation was especially discussed. As to the question of setting aside a statute as unconstitutional, it must be stressed that, at that time, there was no strong Danish tradition of judicial review and till then no statute had been judged unconstitutional. As has already been mentioned, the Supreme Court considered itself a player in the performance of official Danish politics, which aimed at accepting German demands as long as this included the protection of Danish citizens against German jurisdiction. What, however, could be seen as a somewhat unusual step was the interference by the President of the Supreme Court in the preparation of the anti-communist statute and his article in a law review on the constitutionality of the statute, which was seen as an attempt to pressure his colleagues and led to his isolation. At the time, nobody raised their voice. However, after the end of the occupation, Danish lawyers were eager to manifest their criticism of the attitude of the President. However, there does not seem to be any reason to blame the President for what at the time was seen as lack of "national" motives. He was guided by a rather narrow way of legal thinking, which in the given situation had led him to the conclusion that a legal foundation was necessary to legitimate the extraordinary restraint on personal liberty. That might be true seen from a normal legal point of view. However, under the specific circumstances during the occupation, it might have been better not to compromise the courts and the integrity of the court system by interfering in the legislator's work. Yet, it is quite clear from the decisions made by the Supreme Court during the occupation, that there was no general opposition in the Court to the upholding of extraordinary measures. The criticism was aimed only at the public performance of the President, who made it clear to a general audience that the Supreme Court was to be found on the side

11 *UfR* 1943, 1030.

of the official politics and not on the side of the resistance movement. As we have seen, the Court did not even look positively at those first and early attempts of resistance that were brought before it.

4 Final Remarks

After the end of the German occupation, the question was raised by representatives of the Danish resistance movement: could the Danish courts legitimately take part in the purge foreseen against those who were considered to have been on the 'wrong side' and thus be sentenced according to new legislation, made immediately after the occupation, with retroactive effect? From the communist side, even the possibility of prosecuting the former President of the Supreme Court (who had retired upon reaching retirement age in 1944) was mentioned. In the end, the ordinary courts carried out the legal proceedings against those who were seen as collaborators. As a compromise, representatives of the Danish resistance movement were presented a list of judges and were authorized to delete those considered unfit. As it happened, only a few judges were deleted from the list and the legal proceedings as part of the transitional justice after the war were carried out with the same Supreme Court at the top, which had pronounced sentence during the first years of the German occupation against members of the resistance movement.

If there is a lesson to be learned from the story of the Danish Supreme Court during the occupation, it is a lesson of how easily judges of such a court, which in principle is independent, adapt to the existing political situation and behave more like loyal civil servants than as protectors of basic legal principles. During the occupation, official politics were taken as guidelines and, after the occupation, the Court did not hesitate to participate in legal proceedings and take attitudes, which could not completely be seen as compatible with what had happened during the war. The role of judges was compromised by the unanimous support of official politics, but Danish judges did not themselves reflect on their commitment when, after the occupation, they took upon themselves the cases brought before the Court. The Danish situation is often contrasted with the situation of the Norwegian Supreme Court, which had resigned in reaction to demands to uphold what was seen as both illegal and unjust legislation. The situation of the Danish Supreme Court was different, as was the wartime regime in Denmark. The Court chose to accept the official policies and to cover itself by referring to its official role. It is difficult to blame the Court for not openly joining the resistance, but one might have expected some more reflection from the judges as to the role they personally came to play, and the dilemmas presented both before and after the occupation. The mechanistic way in which the Court chose just to follow the rules on the other side does not portray the Court as a model of integrity in a situation that called for a firm attitude in protecting the rule of law.

References

Alkil, Niels (Ed), *Besættelsestidens Fakta* Vol I-II, Copenhagen: J.H. Schulz 1945.

Jørgensen, Troels G., 'En dansk lov mod kommunismen', *Juristen* 1941, 497-504.

Justitsministeriet og retshåndhævelsen under besættelsen: beretning (afgivet paa grundlag afforeliggende danske dokumenter) (Den Parlamentariske Kommissions Betænkning: Beretning til Folketinget afgivet af den af Tinget under 15. Juni 1945, 19. December 1945, 8. Januar 1948 og 25. Oktober 1950 nedsatte Kommission i Henhold til Grundlovens Paragraf 45: Bilag 12, Vol VII), 1950.

Nissen, Henrik S., *1940 Studier i forhandlingspolitikken og samarbejdspolitikken*, Copenhagen: Gyldendal 1973.

Petersen, Harald & Jens Herfeldt, *Retsvæsen og Politi under Besættelsen* (*Danmark under Verdenskrig og Besættelse* Vol III), Copenhagen 1948.

Scavenius, Erik, *Forhandlingspolitiken under besættelsen*, Copenhagen: Hasselbalch 1948.

Tamm, Ditlev, *Retsopgøret under besættelsen*, Copenhagen: Gyldendal 1984.

About the Author

Ditlev Tamm is a professor emeritus at the Faculty of Law, University of Copenhagen. As a lawyer and historian he has published books on Danish and European legal history, political history, and cultural history including literature and ballet. In 1984 he published a book on the role of Danish Courts during WWII and post-war transitionary justice.

5 The French *Cour de Cassation* During the Vichy Period

Clément Millon

'Il était des Nôtres.'[1]

Abstract

This chapter treats the position and attitude of the French Cour de Cassation during the German occupation and the Vichy regime. It introduces the position of the court in the French government system and explains how it continued to function while the country was split in two territories: German occupied territory and Vichy. Resistance and collaboration of judges is examined, such as in relation to anti-Semitic policies. Finally, the chapter describes the post-war fate of the court and its role in the assessment of its own war-time record.

Keywords: French Cour de Cassation; German occupation; Vichy France; Judicial personnel policy; State antisemitism

1 Introduction

In 1961, Léo Fénié honoured the memory of *conseiller* (judge) Gustave Abraham Laroque with this memorable phrase.[2] Laroque had been forced to accept early retirement on 13 November 1940 and had been excluded from the judiciary for 4 years until 20 December 1944. He specified that there should be no traditional eulogy presented by one of his former colleagues

1 'He was one of us.'

2 Léo Fenié, avocat général à la *Cour de Cassation*. Opening speech at the French *Cour de cassation*, 2 October 1961. This and other quoted speeches at the *Cour de Cassation* can be found at https://www.courdecassation.fr/agenda-evenementiel/.

Venema, D. (ed.), *Supreme Courts Under Nazi Occupation*. Taylor & Francis Group 2022
DOI: 10.5117/9789463720496_CH05

from the *Palais de Justice* upon his death. This illustrates the rupture within the French judiciary and the *Cour de Cassation*, as well as the desire to maintain continuity within one of the oldest French institutions. The *Cour de Cassation* has existed since the beginning of the French Revolution and is the highest judicial authority in the land.[3]

In 1940, France was divided by two elements: the occupation of a considerable amount of its territory and a new government that wished to create a new regime. The government was to remain in place, at Vichy, until 1944. It is particularly interesting to compare the situation of France with the other occupied countries, because France had a government that established itself in collaboration with the victorious Nazi Germany. The comparison is therefore of crucial importance: what real difference did the existence of a collaborating government make in overall government policy? Did the occupying forces have undue influence? Were French judges guilty of excessive complicity? What happened to them at the end of the war?

The French case is striking because it involves the two highest levels of the judiciary: the *Cour de Cassation* for civil and criminal cases, and the *Conseil d'Etat* for administrative cases. The latter's war history is ably summarized by Marc-Olivier Baruch in this volume.[4] The fundamental role of the *Cour de Cassation* is to harmonize case law by ensuring that all judicial texts are interpreted alike throughout the country. As it does not review the merits of the facts, the *Cour de Cassation* is not a court of third instance. *Prima facie*, it may appear that some countries had similar institutions, such as the Belgian *Cour de Cassation* and the Italian Council of State. However, these similarities are misleading given the unique historical and legal situation of the Vichy government, including the enemy occupation of all or a part of the national territory and collaboration with the occupying forces.

Between 1940 and 1944, the French judicial system continued to evolve. It remained influenced by members of the *corps judiciaire* who were in office during the German occupation, such as Marcel Rousselet[5] and Guy Raïssac.[6] After the Second World War, they documented the history of the judiciary in France.[7] Independent researchers, including Jean-Pierre Royer[8]

3 See the decree of 27 November and 1 December 1790.

4 Cf. Weil 2010, 75.

5 *Conseiller* at the French Court of appeal in Paris after the 4th october 1940.

6 General secretary of the *Cour de Cassation* between 1941 and 1944.

7 Rousselet 1957; Raïssac 1972.

8 Royer 1996.

and Alain Bancaud,[9] have written more about the nature of the judiciary and the careers of its members.

The study presented in this chapter is predominantly based on published decisions: the laws that appeared in the *Journal officiel*,[10] published court verdicts, the archives of the French Ministry of Justice, and German archives. However, it also considers the speeches given at the beginning of the year and published by the *Cour de Cassation*,[11] as well as biographical records provided by the Centre Chevrier de Lyon.[12]

On the surface, the old *Cour de Cassation* underwent little upheaval and the introduction of new special courts under the Vichy government suggested that its use was in decline.[13] In fact, it did suffer significant consequences from the beginning of the occupation and the establishment of the Vichy regime; it experienced several explicit pressures, some covert pressures, and a purge at the end of the war. An examination of these negative influences yields a balanced portrait of the *Cour de Cassation* from 1940 to 1944.

We will first examine the characteristics of France's specific situation: the territorial division due to the occupation, the organization of the French judicial system, and the role of the French *Cour de Cassation*. We will then study the consequences of the type of occupation, the policy of the occupier in France, the place of the French *Cour de Cassation* in the Vichy-regime, and the organization of the court during this period. We will finally examine the end of the occupation, including the purge, the new organization and the fate of the Vichy judges.

2 France's Specific Situation During the War

Between 1940 and 1944 the German occupation influenced the French areas where the judicial system continued to operate. We will consider three areas: Northern France, otherwise known as the *zone rattachée*, which was administered by the occupying forces based in Brussels; the Northern zone between 1940 and 1944; and the Southern zone from November 1942 to August 1944, when the *Cour de Cassation* had an overall jurisdiction over the territory.

9 Bancaud 2002.

10 https://www.legifrance.gouv.fr/.

11 First day of the judicial year; see https://www.courdecassation.fr/agenda-evenementiel/.

12 See https://annuaire-magistrature.fr/.

13 After the first years of the third republic in France, Vichy established a number of special courts. The kind of justice is not a feature specific of Vichy. See Codaccioni 2015.

A particular complexity is that there is only one single *Cour de Cassation* for the whole Republic, which has resulted in several difficulties for this Supreme Court: On numerous occasions, the authority of the *Cour de Cassation* was contested. For example, on 14 February 1941, the members of the French delegation at the *Commission allemande d'armistice* in Wiesbaden[14] were informed that the Head of the Nazi civil administration in Lorraine decreed that he would hear all cases intended for the *Cour de Cassation* concerning his territorial authority from 18 June 1940. On 18 August 1941, the German military commander responsible for supervising French institutions estimated that the occupied territories of Alsace and Lorraine still had 170 civil cases and 5 criminal cases pending before the *Cour de Cassation*.[15]

The existence of different areas of occupation was a stumbling block for the magistrates of the Court.[16] They presented their complaints to the French representatives of the German Armistice Commission, stating that their claims were justified by the competence of the *Cour de Cassation* in all jurisdictions throughout France.[17] At first sight, it seems that the occupying authorities had little to do with the *Cour de Cassation*. Most cases were of lesser importance for the winning army and thus their judges were unlikely to play any significant role during the occupation or for the new regime. Hence, despite receiving much credit and praise for his career, Luc Marigny, a *conseiller* (judge) at the *Cour de Cassation* who was responsible for interpreting legislation regarding rent, described his area of expertise as a 'rather thankless specialization.'[18]

In 1940, there was no important reform of the *Cour de Cassation*. The new situation did not change its fundamental role or structure. A new chamber, dedicated to social issues, had been created in 1938, and the next important reform would take place in 1947. During the war, a proposal to reform the *Cour de Cassation* was submitted to the Ministry of Justice. This was, of course, not a parliamentary proposition, given the adjournment of the Parliament, and hence it was dropped.[19] For the first time during

14 It was the German supervisory committee in the context of the agreement of 22 June 1940.

15 Correspondence of the German chief of civil administration in Lorraine, 28 April 1941, R3001/3006 Bundesarchiv, Berlin-Lichterfelde.

16 See the Decision of the *Cour de Cassation*, 21 October 1943, *Recueil Dalloz critique*, 1944, Jurisprudence p. 11.

17 From the French delegation at the Commission allemande d'armistice in Wiesbaden on behalf of the French Ministry of Justice Archives nationales, Paris, BB30 1712.

18 Côme (Maurice). Speech at the solemn session at the Fench *Cour de Cassation* on 16 October, 1947. See footnote 10 above.

19 Archives of the French secretary general of the ministry of Justice in Paris. Archives nationales, Paris, BB30/1708.

the Second World War, measures were taken that would prepare the *Cour de Cassation* to confront the conflict. On 16 June 1940, Marshal Pétain formed a new government and nominated *Cour de Cassation* president Charles Frémicourt for the post of Minister of Justice. During his short tenure as Minister of Justice and in an effort to ensure the effective smooth functioning of the Court, Frémicourt signed three decrees pertaining to the functioning of the *Cour de Cassation*, the regional boundaries of the repressive jurisdiction, and automobile theft, respectively.[20] The purpose of this government was to retain certain elements of the '*union sacrée*',[21] whilst leaving room for specialised civil servants. In precisely this manner, the most senior magistrate in the French judicial system, to his great surprise, took up this ministerial post, to which he had been appointed 'much against his will and even without his knowledge'.[22] This appointment could appear to be a vindication of the new institutions and the specialised civil servants against the remaining elements of the Third Republic, already deemed responsible for the defeat. However, this vindication seemingly did not last long. According to René Tunc's account at the solemn session at the Cour de Cassation in 1968, 'Mr. Frémicourt [...] was ill, when on 17 June he learned of this unexpected appointment by broadcasting. Joyless, but disciplined, devoted to France and the Republic, too much 'man of the North' to hesitate in the face of duty, he accepted this new post. He did not take part in the two councils of ministers which deliberated on the armistice. On July 10, he submitted his resignation. On July 12, a new minister of Justice was appointed and Mr. Frémicourt could rejoin – and he did so with all his heart – his Court of Cassation. On 13 August he presided at the resumption of his function in this very room and from the next day – the case law reports preserve the trace – he sat at the hearing of the civil chamber.[23]

Although, at first, the judiciary appeared to be stable, this was soon disproved by facts and laws – the very same laws that the *conseillers* were obliged to apply uniformly throughout the territory. But this stability did not hide the important exclusionary measures taken by the Vichy government. They did not provoke major protests from the high-ranking magistrates.

20 Tunc (René). Speech at the solemn session at the French *Cour de Cassation* on 2 October, 1968. See fn. 10.

21 The 'sacred union' meant the politically undivided front against Germany in 1914.

22 Ancel 1967, 966.

23 Tunc (René). Speech at the solemn session at the French *Cour de Cassation* on 2 October, 1968. See fn. 10.

3 The Consequences of the Type of Occupation

We will now examine the consequences of the occupation and its influence on the imposition of the Vichy regime, the *Cour de Cassation*, and the magistrates themselves. France was the only country in Europe where military defeat caused political change. The new legal government chose to collaborate[24] with Nazi Germany, both as a political choice and in an attempt to defend French sovereignty. The situation regarding the *Cour de Cassation* clearly demonstrates this. This attempt, however, was in vain: it was no significant softening of the regime of occupation. But we should address a broad overview of German policy. The law was interpreted by the Nazi authorities to their own advantage. For instance, the Germans established an armistice-style occupation over France, instead of a full-fledged military one. Some commentators consider the occupation of Southern France from November 1942 to be an 'occupatio pacifica', akin to the occupation of Denmark. This was only for justification of the new order in Europe.

As I have explained in my thesis,[25] the Third Reich considered that the occupation of France from 1940 to 1944 automatically conferred upon them the rights of an occupying power. They regarded themselves as fully justified by their military victory. The Germans gave the French limited autonomy on their territory and certain elements of the organization of their occupation. It is within this context of concessions granted from their solid power base that the German occupying forces attempted to take control over the French judicial system.

At first, the occupying forces assumed a right of information, and then a right of general surveillance, which they maintained until after 1942 in an increasingly oppressive form, whilst attempting to force the French judicial system into a compliant relationship. At the end of the occupation period, the Agreement of 22 June 1940 was used in an attempt to establish administrative control, but without any success.

After France signed the Armistice, Nazi Germany gradually used the Agreement to seek further control, with only a few employees. It is therefore difficult to evaluate the lives of the *Cour de Cassation conseillers* under the occupation, and thus, evaluating the effects of German manipulation over the policy of the Supreme Court is also difficult. Although there was only one *Cour de Cassation* for the entire Republic, it was obliged to accept all the geographical restrictions of the occupying forces. There has been a

24 This word is written in the French-German armistice of 22 June 1940.

25 Millon 2011.

great deal of discussion about the French *Cour de Cassation* and its system of jurisprudence. There were many debates in French doctrine[26] about legal methods to counteract German influence – for example, the principles of *nulla poena, nullum crimen sine lege* or *non bis in idem*, or article 43 of the Hague Regulations[27] – whilst the occupying forces took no real interest in these questions.

From time to time, incidents occurred which illustrated German pressure. A funeral speech contained the following example: Marcel Rey (*avocat général du service central à Paris*) was with Raoul Cavarroc (Attorney-General, appointed as *conseiller* in November 1943), when 'gentlemen, dressed in German army uniforms, presented themselves to demand case files which, of course, had escaped their investigation, despite hostage-takings lasting several days and threats against the person of the chief and his deputies'.[28] Nonetheless, it does not necessarily follow that French institutions were *completely* controlled, because the occupying forces could spare relatively few men for the task of surveillance. The French judicial system experienced occasional and irritating interventions which also concerned the *Cour de Cassation*.

Regarding its composition, the *Cour de Cassation* underwent a significant change (see table 1). This gave rise to doubts concerning the legitimacy of the institution due to the massive size of the reshuffle of *conseillers* (judges). From 17 June 1940 until 9 September 1944 (the period between Frémicourt's nomination to the Ministry of Justice and his departure), a total of 94 *conseillers* were active in the court. 54 magistrates were serving at the beginning of the period, of which 35 left their posts for various reasons: purged by the Vichy government, victims of illness, or simple resignation, for example, citing family and personal reasons. As a result, more than half of the senior magistrature was renewed in only four years. In September 1944, the majority of serving senior magistrates had been appointed by the Vichy government, and there were only 19 who had been in place prior to 17 June 1940.

Out of the 54 *Cour de Cassation conseillers* on which this study is based, 6 of them (11% of the members) were immediately forced into retirement due to the anti-Jewish (and anti-foreigner) legislation. This is no small number but an alarming statistic. Certain magistrates, affected by the anti-Jewish

26 See academic journal as *Gazette du Palais, Recueil Dalloz-Sirey, Recueil Dalloz Jurisprudence*.

27 See the introduction to this volume for the international law of military occupation.

28 Albaut (Daniel), avocat général at the *Cour de Cassation*. Speech at the solemn session at the French *Cour de Cassation*, October 2, 1970. See fn. 10.

measures, were as bitterly disillusioned by Republican France as by their colleagues. In light of this, we can best understand what was said about Pierre Lemant, forced into retirement in December 1941, in accordance with the law of 3 October 1940. 'He became terribly embittered. For four years he shunned this outside world, which for him was nothing more than a distorted universe.'[29] The action of the aforementioned Gustave Laroque eminently illustrates this sense of betrayal. The same can be said of Robert Dreyfus, dismissed in December 1941, who died alone and sick in 1943.[30] Some of the other reasons for dismissal are difficult to decipher. Paul Rolland was dismissed on 4 October 1940, and investigated, probably due to the fact that his son had left for England.[31]

Few judges protested against the anti-Jewish and anti-freemason laws, despite the shock they caused.[32] P. Birnbaum wrote that Alexandre Lyon-Caen had successfully pleaded his case in a letter to Marshal Pétain and obtained the lifting of his banishment.[33] More likely, however, is that this was an exception because he was permitted to retire. It contrasts with the case of Robert Dreyfus, a former member of the *Cour de Cassation*, who was dismissed during the Vichy regime as a Jew and sent to the detention camp at Compiègne.[34]

We will now examine some of the consequences of policies imposed by the Vichy regime. The Vichy government insisted on appointing a certain number of *conseillers* to the *Cour de Cassation*, as it wished to appear to be a law-abiding and responsible governing entity. However, they were largely unsuccessful in this endeavour.[35] The most important reshuffle concerned the top of the *Cour de Cassation*: the presidents and prosecutors. 10 *présidents de chambre* had been nominated by the Vichy-government. There were only 4 who had been in place before 17 June 1940 and only 2 of these remained in place until 1944. In fact, regular justice was regarded as too slow and too unlikely to profit the Vichy system, which presented itself as being more efficient. On 23 August 1941, a law was passed, banning communist

29 Ithier (André). Speech at the solemn session at the French *Cour de Cassation* on 3 October, 1955. See fn. 10.

30 He absolutely forbade any kind of speech after his death, because those speeches usually consist of glowing comments. Fretté-Damicourt (Paul), Speech at the solemn session at the French *Cour de Cassation* on 16 October, 1944. See fn. 10.

31 Reliquet (Jean). Speech at the solemn session at the French *Cour de Cassation* on 2 October, 1959. See fn. 10.

32 Charle 1994, 62.

33 Birnbaum 1992, 447.

34 Bernard 1944, 93.

35 Bancaud 2002.

and anarchist activity, and instituting a '*juridiction extraordinaire*', which was retroactively applied starting 14 August 1941. This law proclaimed that it was not possible to appeal to the *Cour de Cassation* from the special courts.[36] Appeal was assigned to the new political court of justice, the '*Tribunal d'état*' (law n° 3883 of 7 September 1941).[37] The same applies to law n° 4606, of 31 October 1941, banning communist or anarchist activity in all territories under the jurisdiction of the *secrétariat d'état aux colonies*.[38] A *section special* was instituted by law n° 318 on 5 June 1943, banning all communist, anarchist, terrorist or subversive activities.[39] On 14 May 1944, it was proclaimed that no appeal was possible against decisions of any of the special courts.[40]

It is conceded that a study of the decisions of the *Cour de Cassation* between 1940 and 1944 is not entirely meaningful. It was commonplace for court proceedings to take a very long time; a three-year wait was not uncommon for a judgment. After the initial judgment, there was the possibility of an appeal, which could be granted or quashed by the *Cour de Cassation*. During the occupation, legal procedures took so long that many cases could not be judged before 1944. This resulted in an insufficient number of significant cases passing through the highest levels of the judicial system. *The majority of decisions delivered by the Cour de Cassation between 1940 and 1944 concerned matters which dated from before the war, which were still being dealt with in 1942. From the end of the war, cases were decided concerning appeals submitted against decisions made after June 1940.* This makes it difficult to fully evaluate the influences of the Nazi occupation.

The original mission of the French *Cour de Cassation* was to regulate civil justice in accordance with the law. This demonstrates why the laws passed by the Vichy regime are so important. Due to the occupation, eight laws concerning the organization of the *Cour de Cassation* were published, including: the law of the 17th July 1940 concerning judicial vacations;[41] the law of the 9th December 1941 regulating prisoners;[42] and the law of the 12th August 1942 about the questions concerning La Réunion and French Antilles.[43]

36 *Journal officiel* of 23 August 1941, p. 3350.
37 *Journal officiel* of 10 September 1941, p. 3851.
38 *Journal officiel* of 4 November 1941, p. 4774.
39 *Journal officiel* of 24 June 1943, p.1714.
40 *Journal officiel* of 25 May 1944, p. 1366.
41 *Journal officiel* of 17 July 1940, p. 4533.
42 *Journal officiel* of 15 January 1942, p. 214.
43 *Journal officiel* of 19 August 1942, p. 2834.

Between 1940 and 1944, the *Cour de Cassation* was still comprised of the civil, criminal and social divisions, in addition to the *Chambre des Requêtes* (which determines whether appeals are to be examined by the Civil Division). Laws passed under Vichy illustrated the desire to defend the sovereignty of the *Cour de Cassation*. For example, a decree was passed on 7 August 1942[44] concerning the institution of a temporary *Chambre de Cassation* in Indo-China. Following a breakdown of communication between the French *Cour de cassation* in Paris and Indo-China during the Japanese occupation, France wanted to exercise its sovereignty over its territory. The Vichy government also wanted to simplify the procedural rules of the Cour de Cassation. A good illustration of this is the law passed on 19 June 1940, which concerned the number of *Conseillers* required for delivering judgments on behalf of the *Cour de Cassation*.[45]

Time has shown that there were two major pressures: the submission of the *conseillers*, and the coercion of the occupying forces. The Head of the government, Pierre Laval, believed that he had as much authority over the *conseillers* as over the police. On 12 November 1943, in an address to the magistrates, he attempted to seize control of the French judicial system by a '*Lit de Justice*', in the same manner that the King prior to the French Revolution used to issue royal edicts.[46] Indeed, the French *Cour de Cassation* was not genuinely independent: all the *conseillers* of the *Cour de Cassation* were obliged to swear an oath of allegiance upon their appointment. They had to renew this oath, pledging allegiance to the Vichy government,[47] which was effectively a vow of allegiance to Marshal Philippe Pétain. None of the *conseillers* at the *Cour de Cassation* refused to take the oath. It does not follow that they were all pro-Nazi, but this does indicate the subjugation of the judiciary to the Vichy government, which recommended 'collaboration' with the Third Reich. This is a good example of the '*illusoire séparation des pouvoirs en France*'.[48]

Another tool employed by the Vichy government, which had been in use since the 19th century, was the publication of judgments in the *Journal Officiel*, showing its political direction. These were accompanied by comments from jurists, and in the case of important decisions, by additional opinions

44 Decree of 7 August 1942, *Journal officiel*, 12 August 1942, p. 2762.

45 The law of 19 June 1940, *Journal officiel* of 20 June 1940, p. 4453.

46 Le Cocq & Poiroux 2015, 346.

47 Jugnot 2011, 118.

48 Garnot 2009, 544.

and reports. These decisions largely concerned hunting, the black market, inflation, the possession of firearms, and traffic accidents, all of which could be related to the interests of the forces of occupation. However, these matters were regarded as relatively trivial by the Third Reich: 'Peace and Order' was the watchword of the occupying forces. Compared to other occupied countries in Eastern Europe, like Poland, and, after 22 June 1941, the former territories of the Soviet Union, France was a relatively tranquil country, and Berlin did not wish to endanger this tranquillity. Concerning the fight against communism, the Vichy regime obtained better results than it had hoped for. This applied to some '*cours d'exception*' established by the Vichy government, and not to the *Cour de Cassation* itself. The political courts of law, namely the *Section Spéciale*, the *Cour Martiale*, and the *Haute Cour de Justice*, illustrate this fact. The occupying forces were never indifferent to the French judicial system, especially the *Cour de Cassation*, but they did not trust the institution to fight their enemies. It was considered a remnant of the French Revolution and hence not to be trusted. However, France witnessed the birth of an authoritarian regime – *l'Etat Français* – which established several new Tribunals (*Cour de Riom, Section Spéciale, Cour Martiale*). The Germans did not attempt to impose changes upon a judicial system which they distrusted.

The Vichy period is characterized by the establishment of special courts as an effective means in delivering political justice. The aim of these courts was to judge the opposition.[49] This reinforced Vichy's desire to limit the *Cour de Cassation* to a peripheral role. The special court judges were subservient administrators of the regime; they effectively contributed to the creation of a new system where political justice became possible. Robert Charvin wrote that there were two types of political justice in France: the first repressive and the second pedagogical. The Vichy regime, with its special courts, was by definition non-pedagogical (and hence repressive[50]), and used to legitimize the new regime.[51] For Alain Bancaud, the special courts are one of the '*exceptions ordinaires*' engaged during the Third Republic: a traditional process in France. Conversely, Jean-Claude Farcy considers that they originate from the current state: this process is directly linked to the war and the new regime of Vichy.[52] Regardless, the special courts were

49 Farcy 2001, 348.

50 Farcy 2001, 414.

51 See for the important role of the first degree of jurisdiction, the *tribunal correctionnel*: Sansico 1995.

52 '*Conjoncturel*', Farcy 2001, 347.

used to criminalise the opposition and to fight communism.[53] At the top of the judicial system stood firm the *Cour de Cassation*. The *conseillers* of the *Cour de Cassation* legitimised the new order by the old.

4 The End of the Occupation

Finally, we must examine the role of the *Cour de Cassation* during the last days of the war, when the Supreme Court preferred to emphasize its heroism. After the liberation of Paris on 16 October 1944, the President of the *Cour de Cassation* published a list of judges arrested by the Germans and the Vichy regime.[54] The most important factor for him was the continuity of the judicial system, as is illustrated by Maurice Rolland (a member of the French resistance, the first honorary President of the *Cour de Cassation*, and the '*inspecteur general de la magistrature*' in 1945) when he wrote that one should remember that the courts were by definition removed from the public and political realm.[55]

There were a few resistance fighters. One *conseiller*, Félix Mazeaud, was commended for an act of bravery: 'in May 1944, when his son had just fallen into German hands, he refused, at gunpoint, to salute a militia flag.'[56] Robert Mazoyer, who was nominated a magistrate in 1940, was complimented by President Picard during his inauguration into the court with these words: '[He] became, for the Resistance, the technical adviser for the Ministry of Justice of the underground authorities who would soon assume official control of the administration.'[57]

From the perspective of Vichy, the *Cour de Cassation* was meant to represent the stability of the judicial system in spite of the occupation and the new government. Georges Le Grix's career symbolised this wish. He had been a *conseiller* since 1932, became senate president on 4 October 1940, and was twice reappointed, despite having exceeded the normal age limit for this post. It was Jean Picard who delivered his funeral oration, stating that he believed that Georges Le Grix had acted '*to preserve the continuity*

53 Farcy 2001, 414.

54 Cointet 2008, 232.

55 Cointet 2008, 234.

56 Ithier (André), Speech at the solemn session at the French *Cour de Cassation* on 3 October 1955. See fn. 10.

57 Ithier (André), Speech at the solemn session at the French *Cour de Cassation* on 3 October 1955. See fn. 10.

of the adjudication of the civil chamber he presided.[58] This opinion had been expressed earlier by some members of the Cour de Cassation during the Vichy regime and the occupation. The Cour de Cassation wrote its own history. Thus, the Cour de Cassation did not have an important role to play, and it sometimes minimized the repressive force of the law that they had applied, by imposing a lower sentence.[59] Towards the end of the occupation, it appeared that the Cour de Cassation was showing more clemency towards small-scale black marketeers. However, this was revealed to be mere public relations.[60]

Ultimately, the Cour de Cassation lost control of the situation. In 1899, the monumental manual Droit Civil by Marcel Planiol appeared for the first time. Its successors, during the Second World War, stated that the Cour de Cassation did not control the law. It was not an arbiter of civil liberties (which was a pity in the prevailing circumstances), nor could it create laws. The author emphasizes the role of the cours d'appel, the second instance of the French jurisdiction. In the 1943 edition, George Ripert and Jean Boulanger insist the role of the cours d'appel has become 'more and more important' for two reasons. On the one hand, not all the questions had been submitted to the Cour de Cassation. On the other hand, the appeal courts avoided handing down decisions to avoid having their judgement annulled.[61] These motives were more relevant between 1940-1944. This suggests that the appeal courts played a major role in the interpretation of the law. Due to the short time period, much of the new legislation passed by Vichy was not put into effect, and few decisions were handed down based on the new principles. Furthermore, only a small part of this legislation was abandoned after Liberation, such as, for example, the anti-Jewish laws of 4 October 1940 and 17 June 1941.

The magistrates left the Cour de Cassation in two separate waves: in August 1942 and in March-April 1944. The Cour de Cassation would give the impression of being a safe haven. Raoul Cavarroc was nominated to the Court on 13 November 1943. This allowed him to leave his post in the

58 The avocat général à la *Cour de Cassation* said: *'Jamais il ne prit son parti de la capitulation, ni ne se rallia au gouvernement de Vichy dont il répudiait les théories et la politique'*. Blanchet (Marcel), Speech at the solemn session at the French *Cour de Cassation* on 16 October 1950. See fn. 10.

59 *Affair Verdier, Journal officiel of 4 January 1944, p. 69.*

60 *See affair 'Dussoreau, femme Prevost, prison pour vol', Journal officiel of 25 March 1944, p. 899.*

61 Planiol 1943, 55. In this book, the doctrine of Georges Ripert and Jean Boulanger is present.

Section Spéciale,[62] which was tasked with repressing 'terrorists' – a new responsibility that the Vichy regime had assumed retroactively.[63] However, membership of the Cour de Cassation is also known as a 'bâton de maréchal', an honour which is conferred upon magistrates of exceptionally long service and good reputation. At the same time (1943-1944), certain nominations permitted certain magistrates and associates of the Vichy leadership (the cabinet director, for example) to re-establish their careers (including Cavarroc, Crovisy and Dallant), whilst other nominees were elderly and experienced magistrates. This was rendered possible by new regulations adopted specifically for this occasion. Thus, the will to re-establish careers is clearly shown by changes in requirements for nominations to the Cour de Cassation.[64]

Many magistrates who were nominated at the end of the occupation, however, did not receive the traditional funeral oration upon their death (Deis, Stefanini, Chéron, Denoits). This does not indicate that they were collaborators, but it was the policy not to honour magistrates appointed during such a difficult period of French history, and who had remained in place until the early 1950s. However, there is one notable exception in the case of conseiller Victor Dupuich, who had discreetly edited the 'Palais Libre', a newspaper dedicated to the judicial arm of the resistance.[65]

The fates of the magistrates are very varied, and rarely lend themselves to a simplistic evaluation. The nominations after the Liberation were made with the continuity of the institution in mind. 16 conseillers appointed before the war and purged by Vichy or by others were recalled to their functions. The purge that occurred during the Liberation appeared very cautious. According to our research, out of the 94 conseillers having served during this period, only 4 were sanctioned by permanent dismissal, and only two of them did not receive their pension for collaboration. Another 3 who had been dismissed would be reinstated in the early 1950s. It is astonishing that many of these magistrates had been appointed before Vichy, whilst

62 Fénié, *avocat général* at the *Cour de Cassation*. Speech at the solemn session at the French *Cour de Cassation* on 2 October, 1961. See fn. 10.

63 The law 3515 of 14 August had retroactive effect (article 10). See *Legislation de l'occupation*, 1941, p. 421.

64 Loi nr. 64 du 14 février 1944. *Journal officiel* of 14 Febuary 1944, p. 486. Also, the loi n° 221 of 19 May 1944, *Journal officiel* of 21 May 1944, p. 1334.

65 The avocat général said: 'Si son action avait été soupçonnée par l'ennemi, il l'aurait sans doute payée de sa vie' (If his action had been suspected by the enemy, he would undoubtedly have paid for it with his life). Gégout (Henri). Speech at the solemn session at the French *Cour de Cassation* on 2 October, 1958. See fn. 10.

a collective sanction would have affected all the conseillers appointed by Vichy. This would have been a direct criticism of one of the measures taken by the regime.

It is certain that the measures taken against conseillers of the Cour de Cassation were not efficient. As I noted in my thesis, there was no moral obligation of 'heroism'.[66] Daniel Soulez Lariviere wrote that 10% collaborated, 10% resisted, and 80% were indifferent. He estimated that 51 of the 150 senior judicial staff members were guilty of collaboration.[67] The individual cases of the conseillers from the Cour de Cassation were examined by the Commission Nationale d'épuration in 1945. In 1947, an Avocat Général at the Cour de Cassation appeared before the disciplinary commission of the Cour de Cassation, but no penalties were imposed. Alain Bancaud wrote that only three members of the Cour de Cassation were found guilty of collaboration.[68] During the trials at the Haute Cour de Justice from 1944[69] (against Pétain, Laval, and other Vichy ministers), there was a manifest conflict of interest as some of the conseillers had previously served in the Cour de Cassation during the Vichy regime. The first President of this High Court, Paul de Mongibeaux, had been promoted to the Cour de Cassation during the Vichy regime.[70] André Mornet, a famous public prosecutor, was also honorary President of the *Cour de Cassation* in 1940. Despite wishing to put his past behind him, he had to explain his actions in 1945.[71]

It can be said that the historical record of the *Cour de Cassation* during the occupation is mirrored in the career of Charles Frémicourt: the organisation of the judiciary permitted this institution to continue its existence, but did not grasp the gravity of the situation. Confident in their positions, most judges maintained they did not need to be put on trial. They maintained they had done nothing to deserve any sort of investigation after the Liberation. In this way, Charles Frémicourt stayed in place, and upheld the zeal, the pride and the sovereignty of the court, as it had been at the end of the Ancient Regime. After Liberation, he was relieved of his functions,[72] briefly arrested in association with his role as a former minister, and then retired from office. However, following the decision of the *Conseil*

66 Millon 2011, 379.

67 Soulez-Larivière 1987, 17.

68 Bancaud & Badinter 1997, 232.

69 Created by ordinance of 18 November 1944. See the appointments, Archives Nationales, section 3W 1 to 27.

70 Bancaud & Badinter 1997, 233.

71 Mornet 1949.

72 Ancel 1967, 966.

Table 1 **94 *conseillers* in the *Cour de Cassation* between 17 June 1940 and 9 September 1944 (occupation and Vichy-regime)**

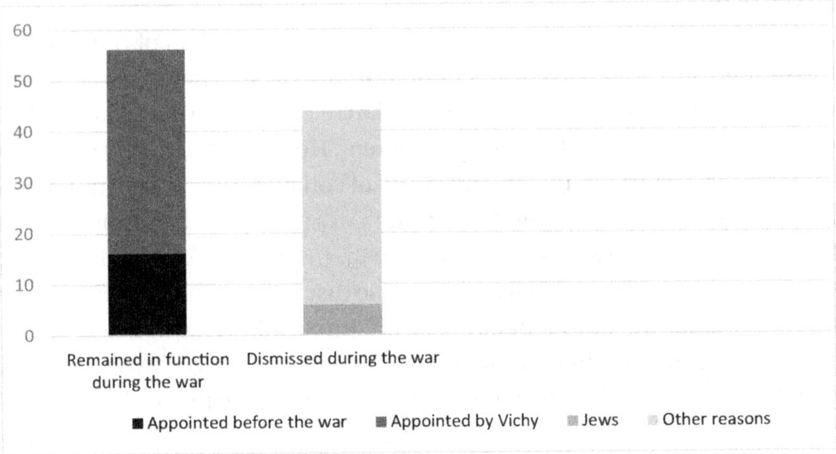

d'Etat of 4 June 1947, these decisions were annulled by the *Haute Cour de Justice,* which cancelled his forced retirement. Still, it was too late for Charles Frémicourt, now 70 years old, to re-join the *Cour de Cassation*. Frémicourt was appointed first honorary President of the *Cour de Cassation* by decree of 9 June, 1954. Effectively, through these decisions, the entire institution exonerated itself from all suspicion.

At the end of the war, the government, in association with the allies, formed a provisional *Chambre de Cassation.*[73] This caused the *Cour de Cassation* and the traditional French legal system to reclaim their rights. For this, the magistrates had to unite, even though it was painful. Today, there is still only one *Cour de Cassation,* which is established on the *Ile de la Cité de Paris.* The *Cour de Cassation* has thenceforth chosen to present itself as united, which is symbolised by Fénié's words: *'il était des Notres'.*

References

Alibert, J., *Treize années noires (1933-1946), Souvernirs et réflexions*, Paris: L'Harmattan 2001.

Ancel, Marc, 'Le Premier Président Charles Frémicourt', *Revue internationale de droit comparé* (19) 1967-4, 965-966.

73 See the Archives nationales, in Paris, under BB30/1716.

Aubusson de Cavarlay, B., Marie-Sylvie Huré & Marie-Lys Pottier, *La justice pénale en France. Résultats statistiques (1934-1954)* (Les cahiers de l'Institut d'histoire du temps present, Série Justice 23) 1993.

Bancaud, A. & R. Badinter, *Les ministres devant la justice,* Paris: Actes sud 1997.

Bancaud, A., *Une exception ordinaire, La magistrature en France, 1930-1950*, Paris: Gallimard 2002.

Barthélémy, J., *Mémoires*, Paris: Editions Pygmalion 1989.

Bernard, J. J., *Le camp de la mort lente, Compiègne 1941-42*, Paris: Albin Michel 1944.

Birnbaum, P., *Les fous de la République, Histoire politique des juifs d'état de Gambetta à Vichy*, Paris: Fayard 1992.

Charle, C., 'Les spécificités de la magistrature française en Europe (XIXe-XXe siècles)', *Crises* (4) 1994 (Les juges contre la République?), 61-68.

Charpentier, J., *Au service de la liberté*, Paris: Fayard 1949.

Charvin, R., *Justice et politique et évolution de leurs rapports*, Paris: Librairie générale de droit et de jurisprudence 1968.

Chomienne, C., 'Juger sous Vichy', *Le Genre humain*, (28) 1994, I, 117-131.

Codaccioni, Vanessa, *Justice d'exception. L'État face aux crimes politiques et terroristes*, Paris: CNRS Éditions 2015.

Cointet, J. P., *Expier Vichy, L'épuration en France, 1943-1958*, Paris: Perrin 2008.

Cotillon, J., *Raphaël Alibert, Juriste engagé et homme d'influence à Vichy*, Paris: Economica 2009.

Farcy, J.-C., *L'histoire de la justice française de la Révolution à nos jours*, Paris: Presses Universitaires de France 2001.

Gabolde, M., 'Le problème judiciaire pendant l'occupation', in: *La vie de la France sous l'occupation*, Fondation Hoover, Paris: Plon 1957, II, 619-642.

Garnot, B., *Histoire de la justice, France, XVIe-XXIe siècle*, Paris: Folio histoire, Gallimard 2009.

Israel, L., *Robes noires, années sombres*, Paris: Fayard 2005.

Jäckel, E., *La France dans l'Europe de Hitler*, Paris: Fayard 1968.

Jugnot, G., *Histoire de la justice française de l'époque franque à nos jours*, Paris: Ellipses 2011.

Le Cocq, V. & A. S. Poiroux, *Les notaires sous l'occupation (1940-1945), acteurs de la spoliation des Juifs*, Paris: Nouveau monde éditions 2015.

Lochack, D., 'La doctrine sous Vichy ou les mésaventures du positivisme', in *Les usages sociaux du droit*, Paris: PUF, 1989, 252-285.

Millon, C., Les *droits de la puissance occupante sur la justice judiciaire française, 1940-1944*, Paris, Dalloz Nouvelle bibliothèque de Thèses 2011.

Mornet, A., *Quatre ans à rayer de notre histoire*, Paris: Self 1949.

Paxton, R. O., *La France de Vichy, 1940-1944*, Paris: Le Seuil 1973.

Planiol, Marcel, George Ripert & Jean Boulanger, *Traité élémentaire de Droit Civil*, Paris 1943.
Raïssac, G., *De la Marine à la justice. L'orage d'une fin d'été. Un magistrat témoigne*, Paris: Albin Michel 1972.
Remy, D., *Les lois de Vichy, Actes dits « lois » de l'autorité de fait se prétendant « gouvernement de l'Etat français*, Paris: Romillat 1992.
Rousselet, M., *Histoire de la magistrature française: des origines à nos jours*, Paris: Plon 1957.
Royer, J. P., *Histoire de la Justice en France*, Paris: Presses Universitaires de France 1996.
Sansico, V., *La justice déshonorée*, Paris: Tallandier 1995.
Soulez-Larivière, D., *Les juges dans la balance*, Paris: Ramsay 1987.
Vergez-Chaignon, B., *Histoire de l'épuration*, Paris: Bibliothèque historique Larousse 2010.
Weil, P. & D. Pouyaud, *Le droit administratif*, Paris: Presses Universitaires de France 2010.
Weisberg, R., *Vichy, la justice et les Juifs*, Paris: Editions des archives contemporaines 1998.

https://www.courdecassation.fr/agenda-evenementiel/.

About the Author

Clément Millon is a historian and jurist, and holds a PhD in law from the University of Lille and Frankfurt-am-Main. He is affiliated to the Catholic University of the Vendée (ICES).

6 The *Conseil d'État* in Vichy France

Marc Olivier Baruch

'The worst servitude is to deny recognizing oneself as being a serf ...'
From a letter of the historian Lucien Febvre, 1942

Abstract
This chapter treats the position and attitude of the French *Conseil d'État* as the highest administrative court during the German occupation and the Vichy regime. It introduces the position of the court in the French government system and explains how it continued to function and cooperated with the Vichy government. Resistance and collaboration of judges is examined, such as in relation to anti-Semitic policies. Finally, the chapter describes the post-war fate of the court and how it secured its own survival.

Keywords: French Conseil d'État; German occupation; Vichy France; Judicial personnel policy; State antisemitism

1 Introduction

The case of France has a special status in this book, since no fewer than two papers are needed to analyze the impact of German occupation during WWII on French Supreme Courts. Any French (chauvinistic) law professor would find this situation normal, since no other country included in our project had, as is the case in France for at least two centuries, two systems of jurisdiction, namely judicial justice and administrative justice, headed respectively by the *Cour de cassation* and the *Conseil d'État.* The official website of the *Conseil d'État* goes back far into French history to legitimate the situation:

> In both the United Kingdom and the USA, the unicity of jurisdiction is the result of the principle of equality before the law, whereas in France

Venema, D. (ed.), *Supreme Courts Under Nazi Occupation*. Taylor & Francis Group 2022
DOI: 10.5117/9789463720496_CH06

> the distinction between judiciary and administrative law goes back to the *Révolution française* and even earlier. In 1641 a royal decree signed in Saint-Germain (*édit de Saint-Germain*) forbade courts to decide on administrative issues. When Napoleon seized the reins of power as *Premier Consul*, he founded the *Conseil d'État* as a specialized court empowered to decide on administrative issues since he well appreciated the specificities, idiosyncrasies and complexities of administrative issues. [...]. As Jean Foyer [a law professor who served for many years during the 1960s as General de Gaulle's Minister for Justice], rightly stated, "the *Conseil d'État* is not so much the judge of the administration as it is the administration judging itself" ("*le Conseil d'État n'est pas le juge de l'administration, il est l'administration qui se juge*").[1]

Some (even more chauvinistic) professors could claim a third system, with the *Cour des comptes* overseeing financial jurisdictions, and even a fourth one since 1958, when a Supreme Constitutional Court, the *Conseil constitutionnel*, was created, which now has – though only since 2008, as we will explain later – a monopoly on judicial review.

2 German Constraints on the *Conseil d'État*

If we go back to the so-called 'dark years' of 1940-44, this special treatment of the French case does correspond to the core of what was then France as an institution. The very concept of duality has also a strong historical meaning when applied to a country cut in half by a demarcation line, to a country with two governments (one headed by Marshal Pétain in Vichy and the other by General de Gaulle, in London until May 1943 and in Algiers after that), to a country that turned its back on its liberal and democratic institutions without formally adopting an autocratic constitution – or only with the provisional *Actes constitutionnels*.

Clément Millon's contribution has summarized the complex apparatus of occupation in divided France, the northern part German-ruled from Brussels. He has also dealt with Franco-German negotiations over the issue of penal repression of crime, thus emphasizing the ever-increasing grip exercised by the Nazis over the French police and judicial bodies – by retaliation and by the decision of shooting dozens of hostages for each German soldier that would be killed by the French Resistance ('river of blood' policies).

1 Foyer, 'Les juridictions' (my translation).

It is a completely different atmosphere that pervades the history of the French *Conseil d'État* between 17 June 1940 and 25 August 1944. There was no blood there, no direct threat from either the enemy or the French Resistance – not even a real *Diktat* from the occupier to have their policy schemes implemented. To wholly understand the situation, the role of both the *Conseil d'État* in the French State and the political situation faced by the Pétain regime in 1940 have to be taken into account.

Dramatic debates took place within the French government after the fall of Paris on 14 June between those who wanted the government to find refuge in Algiers, capital of French-owned Algeria, in order to continue the war, and those who reckoned that halting the hostilities was a necessary step both in granting them power and reconstructing France according to their strongly anti-democratic plans. The former were headed by Premier Reynaud, Minister of the Interior Mandel, and Undersecretary for War, de Gaulle; the latter by Marshal Pétain, then Vice-Premier, General Weygand, supreme commander, and Finance Minister Bouthillier. The latter won and a Franco-German armistice agreement was signed on 22 June in Compiègne, at the very place, and in the same railway carriage, where the Germans had signed the 1918 armistice.

Although the agreement stated that the Wehrmacht would occupy three-fifths of France, north of a line starting at the Swiss border by Geneva and running through Moulins and Tours down to the Spanish border, officially France remained an independent state, with her own government endowed – on paper – with full sovereignty over the entire territory of France and her colonial Empire. The deal advantaged both parties: Hitler realized that the defeated French would not easily stand up against an indigenous autochthonous government led by the very prestigious figure of Philippe Pétain, *"le vainqueur de Verdun"*, so that any problem arising from the occupation might successfully be dealt with by the French authorities, without requiring excessive German intervention.

On the new *État français*' side, political and juridical conditions were met that allowed the total reshaping of French society, by means of the sweeping anti-democratic, illiberal, and counter-revolutionary programme known as the *Révolution nationale*.

During the first two years of the regime – under the *de facto* leadership of former premier Pierre Laval until December 1940, when he was abruptly ousted by Pétain and replaced by the staunchly Anglophobic Admiral François Darlan – an impressively comprehensive series of decisions were made that were intended to wholly reorganize the State's political and administrative machinery: autocracy was to be preferred to democracy, decisions of the executive branch to parliamentary debate, decrees to laws.

Because of the well-known Aristotelian *horror vacui* principle, the space vacated by the dissolution of the Republican Parliament was to be filled, at least partly, by the *Conseil d'État*.

This institution had played a prestigious but uneven role in French juridical and administrative history. Historically, the *Conseil d'État* had found much to reproach in the parliamentary republic that had governed France from 1877 to 1940. As law professor Marie-Joelle Redor stated some thirty years ago in her PhD dissertation: in the Third Republic *l'État légal* (the legalist state) totally dominated *l'État de droit* (the rule of law).[2] So strong was the Rousseauian conception that nothing could overrule the power of the law, which expressed the general will of the Nation, that almost no one would advocate anything comparable to judicial review. The notion was discussed briefly in Parliament in 1901, in the troubled times of the Dreyfus case and state anti-clericalism, that some values – such as those stated by the Declaration of Human Rights proclaimed in 1789 – should be given pre-eminence over statutory law, but the proposition was rejected.[3]

It was a very long road indeed that led to the vote in 2008, under right-wing President Sarkozy, of the *Question prioritaire de constitutionnalité* (QPC) procedure, which introduced judicial review into French law. This stemmed ultimately, via a step-by-step progression, from an innovation introduced by de Gaulle in the Constitution adopted by the French people in 1958. In order to reduce Parliament's powers, the *Conseil constitutionnel*, a nine-member body (appointed by political authorities and not necessarily comprised of judges) was endowed with the power of nullifying, before its promulgation, any bill that the executive would consider contrary to the Constitution.

During WWII, no such body existed, and the rule was still the one firmly established by the *Conseil d'État* in November 1936: "The fact that a bill may not be in accordance with the Constitution has no effect in French public law as it is now."[4] Yet it should be noted that what Pétain's regime called 'law' had the formal appearance of a decree, since any text adopted in Cabinet meeting (*Conseil des ministres*) could be called a law. Julien Laferrière, a professor in the Paris Law faculty, therefore suggested, in a textbook published in 1942, that nothing would theoretically prevent the *Conseil d'État* considering that a law adopted in such conditions was, substantially

2 Redor 1992.

3 Rudelle 2002.

4 'En l'état actuel du droit public français, [le fait qu'une] loi serait contraire aux lois constitutionnelles n'est pas de nature à être discuté devant le Conseil d'État statuant au contentieux', *Conseil d'Etat*, Section, 6 November 1936, Arrighi, recueil p. 966, *Revue générale du droit* on line, 1936, numéro 5618. (www.revuegeneraledudroit.eu/?p=5618).

speaking, nothing more than a decree. As could be foreseen, this suggestion was met with total indifference. There was good reason for the *Conseil d'État* not to be too concerned with legal formalities at that moment of its history. It considered the new regime as a blessing; it would, at last, return to the institution the distinction and lustre it previously enjoyed under the two Bonaparte emperors, Napoléon I (1800-14) and Napoléon III (1852-70).

Most of the story that follows deals with the part played in occupied France by the *Conseil d'État*, both as the regime's top advisory body and as its supreme court for administrative law. As far as administrative law is concerned, neither the Vichy government nor the Germans created or demanded any specific institutional device, except for a few *ad hoc* committees – which makes a big difference with criminal courts. Should we therefore stop here? Of course not, because of the complex equation that linked the *Conseil d'État*, governmental projects, and the occupier's apparatus – an equation that makes the French case decidedly different from those of other European countries occupied by the Third Reich.

In order to understand this particular situation, one has to bear in mind the aims of the two partners involved. For Pétain and his followers, the objective was the so-called *Révolution nationale*, i.e. the installation of an authoritarian, non-democratic, and counter-revolutionary political system in France. Pétainists firmly believed Hitler had won the war – all the more so during summer and fall of 1940, the 'Britain alone' period when neither the US nor the USSR were at war with Germany; collaboration with the Nazi occupier seemed the only serious course of action. France's political renewal implied sovereignty (or the illusion of it), an aim that could not be implemented without the occupier's approval.

The Nazi perspective was different. Pétain's conservative government could implement whatever political renovations they wished, or nearly so, as long as France was kept a safe place for the German troops that occupied a large part of it. French politicians also had to comply with Hitler's dual strategy: first winning the war (which meant plundering the French economy, in order to bring Germany the wealth and resources that would help stabilize her home front) and, from 1942 onwards, annihilating the Jewish population of Europe. The deal can be summarized as follows:

> Vichy: Sovereignty for political renewal, collaboration for sovereignty – or the illusion of it.
> Nazis: Collaboration for pacification and plundering of France and for the promise of a strategic help to fulfil Hitler's priorities: winning the war and killing the Jews.

During a 1999 conference on the political implication of technical elites in occupied France, Swiss historian Philippe Burrin offered a thorough analysis of the evolution of the French civil service in their relationship to the Nazi occupier:

> The Germans, who never stopped evaluating French administrative cooperation throughout the four years of the occupation, highly praised the perfect cooperation they first obtained from the French civil service. In a report they drew up in 1944, as defeat was looming, the services of the *Militärsbefehlshaber* recalled with some kind of nostalgia the first years they worked with the French in obtaining from them "a cooperation widely exceeding the one to be normally expected from the administration of an occupied country".[5] In the years 1940 and 1941, the level of cooperation was high both because it was legitimized by Vichy's choice of state collaboration as a governmental priority and because it could be seen as a balanced deal. But from 1943 onwards, the Germans realized that high-ranking French civil servants were still ready to cooperate – an attitude that separated them from other parts of the French population – but in a noncommittal and hesitant way. [...] For instance, the prefects would still implement German decisions, but only after getting from the occupier a written order, so that the public would know where the decision came from.[6]

In a way, France was treated by Germany as a protectorate. Formally, France was a sovereign state, with Pétain at its head and its whole governmental and administrative machinery still functioning. In this framework, the *Conseil d'État* played its full part. Since Parliament was suspended, and later dissolved, the task of law-making devolved officially upon the Council, beginning in December 1940 with a new law aimed at restoring to the Council its former dignity and prominence. With France's administration expanding in many directions – some of them radically new, such as State antisemitism with the *Commissariat général aux questions juives* or State-control of industrial production with the *Comités d'organisation* – many members of the prestigious *Conseil d'État*

5 Tätigkeitsbericht der Gruppe allgemeine und innere Verwaltung, French National Archives, AJ40 536.

6 Burrin 2000, 93. For a general survey of the politics of collaboration, see Jäckel 1966; Burrin 1997.

Figures 1 and 2 Vichy regime posters showing Maréchal Pétain: "Do you understand the problems of the present better than him?" and "Are you more French than him?"

found unexpected opportunities in the highest spheres of Vichy's civil service.[7]

"Your only duty is to obey" (*Vous n'avez qu'un seul devoir, obéir*) was one of Pétain's favourite mottos to the French people – a motto that was even more directly applicable to civil servants, who were all theoretically considered as embodying a piece, however minor it may be, of the State's authority. More than ever in the twentieth century did the incestuous relationship between the administrative apparatus, and the *Conseil d'État* as its judge,[8] produce very dangerous consequences. At least until the beginning of 1943, the civil service would not object to the political priorities of the regime.[9]

7 Some members paid a high price after the war – although none of them were executed (in spite of some death sentences *in absentia*). For instance, the secretary-general of the Ministry of Justice, Georges Dayras, and the head of the Ministry of Interior in the occupied zone, Jean-Pierre Ingrand, both spent decades in exile after 1945, the former in Spain and the latter in Argentina.

8 Remember Jean Foyer's "*le Conseil d'État n'est pas le juge de l'administration, il est l'administration qui se juge*".

9 Baruch 1997.

3 The *Conseil d'État*'s Compliance with the Vichy Regime

Our investigation should therefore migrate from the study of Nazi constraint of the French administrative supreme court to the issue of the compliance of one of France's foremost public institutions with the undemocratic collaborationist regime that ruled the country from July 1940 to August 1944. It should moreover be kept in mind that important parts of the *Révolution nationale* programme often corresponded – although with a different ideological background – to the main items of the Nazi programme. Along with anti-communism and the persecution of freemasons, the implementation of state antisemitism was one of the most striking of these. The Nazis did not have to ask for a *judenrein Conseil d'État*, because the French government did the job itself.

As early as 3 October 1940 – three weeks before the solemn meeting between Pétain and Hitler that launched and symbolized collaboration between Vichy France and the Third Reich – the French promulgated their own Nürnberg laws, expelling Jews from the civil service, the media, the administration of justice, and all levels of the teaching professions. This was only the beginning of a whole range of laws and decrees that prevented Jews from earning their living, holding financial assets, or studying at university – all before, from the spring of 1942 onwards, the same Vichy regime let the French police force arrest and detain Jews, whom the Nazis intended to send to their deaths.

Not only did the *Conseil d'État* not object – because of the absence of judicial review in French public law, as we have seen – to the dozens of laws[10] that relegated people of Jewish origin to ghettos within French society, it often also, when asked to interpret texts, offered the harshest interpretation possible. For instance, as early as 12 December 1940 – a few days before the *statut des juifs* was supposed to be implemented in the French civil service – the government asked their higher administrative judges and advisers how the terms of the law were to be understood. The answer was unequivocal. For the *Conseil*, the aim of the law was crystal-clear: Jews were to be banned from all public jobs that could give them any influence or authority whatsoever within the State (*"interdire aux juifs l'accès et l'exercice de toutes les fonctions de nature à conférer une influence ou une autorité quelconque"*).[11]

10 Klarsfeld 1993.

11 Baruch 1997, 138.

Two months later, proof was given of the Kafkaesque logic of this 'narrowly legal' reasoning. It was a rule, in Republican France, that all civil servants of the same rank were deemed equal when a promotion was expected (*principe d'égalité des fonctionnaires*). The *Conseil d'État* used this principle to restrict even further the very narrow space left for Jews in the State. Not only should they be barred from all positions *de nature à conférer une influence ou une autorité quelconque*, as was decreed in December 1940, but the *Conseil* now decided that they should also be barred from all those positions from which they could be promoted to such a position, on the grounds that nothing could theoretically – very theoretically indeed! – prevent the minister from selecting a Jew for promotion.[12]

State antisemitism was strong enough in Vichy's high-ranking civil service to supersede the traditional corporatist inclination of bureaucratic institutions to protect their own. The results of the many purges led by the regime in its first year were impressive. Out of the 120 members of the *Conseil d'État*, no fewer than fifteen were ousted before the end of 1940: 9 of them because they corresponded to the definition of Jews given by the French *statut des juifs*, one due to a non-French father, and four by virtue of the application of an earlier law (17 July 1940) that allowed the government to expel from office any civil servant with no need for justification or show of cause. The last, Pierre Tissier, lost his position after having been stripped of French citizenship, a consequence of his decision to rejoin General de Gaulle in London, under whom he served as chief of staff.

There is little doubt that, for quite a long time, the *Conseil d'État* shared the ideological assumptions of the Pétain regime. This should not be surprising, since the same can be said of most of the more senior civil service, from the Ministry of Agriculture to the newly founded Sports section of the Department of Education. But the prestige and the influence of the *Conseil* played an important role in legitimizing the policies promulgated by the regime, as undemocratic as they were.

Historical scholarship on this period has recently become quite voluminous with regard to the French civil service and French courts, judicial as well as administrative. Many actors of the regime later published memoirs, such as Joseph Barthélemy, one of France's leading public law professors, who served as Minister for Justice between January 1941 and March 1943.[13] Less

12 Memorandum from the Secrétariat général de la vice-présidence du Conseil, Feb. 16th 1941.

13 Barthélemy 1989.

often quoted is the *Témoignage* written in 1977 by a then retiring *conseiller d'État*, Georges Maleville,[14] whose high court career began in 1941.

Born in 1914 and, at first, a mid-ranking clerk in the Paris City Hall, Maleville successfully passed the *Conseil d'État* exam at the end of 1940. He narrates in vivid terms his first years in office as an *auditeur au Conseil d'État*, the first step in his *Conseil* career. We follow his depiction of the institution through troubled times, first in Royat, a luxurious suburb of Clermont-Ferrand, the provincial capital of the region of Auvergne where Vichy lies:[15]

> We immediately started to work. The informal sessions during which we examined the issues took place in a small hotel room, in which a screen hardly hid the bathroom. Public hearings were held in the smoking-room of the Hotel Thermal, in Royat.[16]

More interesting is Maleville's analysis of the political attitude of his colleagues:

> The only viewpoint that could be uttered was that of colleagues who wished to see the *Conseil* [*d'État*] wholly aligned with the political choices of the Vichy government. They expressed the idea that we should take full advantage of the annihilation of the Republic and try to obtain some kind of leadership in the new regime, especially in helping them organize their political programme known as the *Révolution nationale* […]. In spite of a bill promulgated on Dec. 18, 1940 that stipulated that the *Conseil d'État* was to be involved with the writing of all laws, very little use was made of this prerogative. For another group of colleagues, this situation was seen as a blessing. They thought the *Conseil d'État* should stand apart from the strongly politicized Pétain regime and even, as much as was possible, take advantage of its influence to limit or even oppose the effects of its most objectionable decisions. Some of them, later, became active members of the *Résistance*. Yet, for the vast majority of us, the wisest attitude was to wait and see (*attentisme*), as did most of the French people then. Since

14 Maleville 1977.

15 It is to be remarked that the *Conseil d'État* did not travel back to Paris before the summer of 1942, whereas the *Cour de Cassation* was authorized to do the same as soon as December 1940. This should be seen as an indication of the lesser importance of administrative matters, as compared with judiciary ones, for the German occupier.

16 Maleville 1977, 24.

> no one, in the first half of 1941, had the slightest idea of the way WWII would end, caution was the best choice.[17]

Maleville also describes the way Pétain's government strove to politicize the institution. It has always been, and remains, the case that one nomination of *conseiller d'État* out of three is discretionary, a blessing for long-lasting governments that intend to have close friends in the *Conseil*. Here, according to Maleville, is the way this power was implemented in the strange times of France's occupation:

> The Vichy government strove to impose upon us men who they thought would influence us according to their will. In 1941 a vice-admiral joined us, who kept seeming both puzzled and bored by our activity. So did a former general secretary in charge of the police. Then followed a senior official of the Jewish Office[18] and a lawyer who had spent some time in the administration of the *Légion française des combattants*.[19] But the influence of these men was minimal, and they were expelled from the *Conseil d'État* after France's liberation in the summer of 1944.[20]

1941 was a turning point in the regime's attitude towards the civil service. Realizing that they were not being fully obeyed, the higher circles in charge of the civil service, grouped in the *secrétariat général de la vice-présidence du Conseil*, tried the carrot-or-stick policy. At the same time, they prepared the long-awaited statute for civil servants (*statut des fonctionnaires*) in which the government announced a series of very repressive measures against all types of dissidence: freemasons were ousted from all public offices, the police's legal powers and budget rose sharply. The government also decided to appoint political commissioners (*commissaires du pouvoir*), a small group of top officials with full powers to intervene in any branch of government to make sure that

17 *Ibid.*, p. 25-26. (My translation.)

18 I use this translation for the *Commissariat général aux questions juives*, a French institution settled, on German demand, at the end of March 1941. All three men who were put at the top of the *Commissariat général* (Xavier Vallat, Louis Darquier de Pellepoix, Charles du Paty de Clam) were staunch antisemites – the latter being the son of the major who falsely accused Captain Dreyfus of high treason in 1894.

19 This organization grouped all former veterans' associations, which had been dissolved by decree, in a state-ruled movement headed by Pétain. The Germans forbade the *Légion* in the occupied part of France.

20 Maleville 1977, 29 (my translation). Maleville slightly embellishes what happened after the end of the regime, since some political appointees from the Vichy period continued their career in the *Conseil d'État*.

the spirit of the *Révolution nationale* would permeate the whole of the French civil service.[21] The Nazi newspaper *Völkischer Beobachter* loudly applauded these measures, which embodied "the readiness of the French to build a wholly renovated state, apt to collaborate in construction of the new Europe".[22]

A symbolic measure was added to that already heavy lot: high-ranking civil servants were summoned to take an oath to the Chief of State. The *Conseil d'État* was considered so important a part of the new state that Pétain came in person to Royat, on 19 August, to receive the oath of "his" *Conseil d'État* ("*mon Conseil d'État*") – an expression that sounded shocking to the ears of republican Georges Maleville. Equally shocking were the words uttered, on this occasion, by both the Minister for Justice, former law professor Joseph Barthélemy: "The salvation of the state may require the sacrifice of legal forms." and by Pétain, whose tone was threatening: "The times of ambiguity are over. One is either on my side or against me, this being particularly true for those pillars of the state that you, gentlemen, have become."[23]

The remaining pages of Maleville's testimony deal with day-to-day life, first in the Auvergne exile, and then, from the summer of 1942 onwards, when the government returned – with German authorization – to Paris. Some interesting remarks are also to be found on the concept of resistance. It was out of the question, Maleville writes, to talk of it to anyone within the institution, although rumours credited a few younger members of the *Conseil* (such as future ministers of post-1944 France Alexandre Parodi or Michel Debré) with being important figures in the Résistance.

More cautious people distanced themselves by slightly, sometimes even imperceptibly, dissenting. From 1942 onwards, the *Conseil d'État*, acting as a supreme administrative court, overruled a few – less than ten out of hundreds – of the ministerial decisions that ousted civil servants for racial or political motives.[24]

4 The *Conseil d'État*'s Post-war Reputation

The last part of this study deals with the impact of the compliant attitude of the institution on its fate after the war. Although portions of the Résistance

21 The speech by which Pétain announced this severe programme is known in the historiography as *discours du vent mauvais*, since it started with these words: "I feel a bad wind is rising in many regions of France."

22 Quoted by Maleville 1977, 33.

23 Maleville 1977, 36-37.

24 Fabre 2001, 127-138.

asked that the whole administrative infrastructure, which had adhered for such a long time to Vichy's core programme of collaboration and the *Révolution nationale* anti-democratic policy, be abolished, de Gaulle (who then headed the French provisional government) understood history enough to realize that France, as a nation-state, could not do without her administrative elites – however compromised they were.[25] He dismissed the Vichy-appointed Vice-President Porché and replaced him with René Cassin, a law professor of Jewish origin who had joined the *France libre* (de Gaulle's movement) at the start and served as its top legal advisor throughout the war. Cassin was disappointed, since he thought he should have become Minister for Justice and the *Conseil* felt snubbed because Cassin was an outsider – a Jewish one, moreover.

Yet the institution survived, although some people had hoped to take this occasion to suppress it. Not only did it survive, but it would soon enough rewrite its own story in two ways. As the highest judge of the legal purges that occurred immediately after August 1944, it had the opportunity to draw a line between 'correct' and 'unpatriotic' attitudes adopted by the civil service during the Vichy years. As time went by, it became increasingly lenient, especially where some of its own members were concerned. The most striking case may be the less well-known one of Alfred Potier, a judge who served in Pierre Laval's office, where he dealt with the issue of forced labour and Jewish affairs. As one of the closest advisors to this very collaborationist chief of government, Potier was ousted at the end of 1944, with no right to pension, from the *Conseil d'État* in which Laval's favour had won him a seat in 1943. Potier brought this ministerial decision to the *tribunal administratif de Paris*, a first instance administrative court, where he won his case in 1950 on technical grounds. French society and its centre-right government longed for forgetfulness, and, consequently, the State did not make an appeal. The result was that a man associated, at a very high level, with some of the worst policies of the Vichy regime – Laval was sentenced to death and shot for having implemented them – quietly ended his career in one of the Republic's most prestigious positions.

The collective memory of the institution trod a similar path. As early as 1947, the respected *conseiller d'État* Tony Bouffandeau published in the institution's review a study long used as a powerful tool for institutional whitewashing.[26] One would have to wait more than six decades to hear Vice-President Jean-Marc Sauvé, a man eager to have the *Conseil d'État* come

25 See Baruch 2014a.

26 Bouffandeau 1947, 23-27.

to terms with its past, denounce this myth by declaring, at the beginning of the 2010s, that "the 'doctrine Bouffandeau' did not hesitate to depict the role of the *Conseil d'État* in Vichy France as a wall against the infringements on public freedoms from the regime (*un rempart contre les atteintes aux libertés portées par l'État français*)".[27]

Previously, modest steps had progressively prepared this shift in the opinion generally held from within the institution. Jean Massot, one of the Conseil's *présidents de section*[28] turned historian, published several papers in the 1990s that may today be read as too lenient but were, at the time, sharply criticized by older colleagues who still clung to the more comfortable Bouffandeau doctrine.[29]

By the end of the same decade, the master's thesis of a young and talented scholar, Philippe Fabre, on the part played by the *Conseil d'État* in the implementation of the antisemitic legislation adopted by the French state between 1940 and 1944, had been published as a book by the main law faculty of Paris.[30] This was the first thorough – and inevitably harsh – analysis of this shameful page in the history of the institution, and it was received as such. I used, at that time, to write reviews of history books in *Le Monde* and drew public attention to the book, which otherwise had little chance of reaching so large an audience, being published as it was by a specialized publishing house. I was quite surprised, shortly thereafter, to receive a letter from Philippe Fabre thanking me for "too laudatory a review", for which he was all the more grateful as "not a single law review had, for more than a year, published a single word on the book".[31] France has tended to be too strongly deferential to her public institutions, which have taken a very long time before being able to face their past.

The work is not finished: in the main hall of the Palais-Royal, the very hieratic building that hosts the *Conseil d'État*, a commemorative plaque lists all the members of the *Conseil morts pour la France* during the two world wars. Most of the names related to WWII are those of deported Jews, among them Jacques Helbronner, a former *conseiller d'État* who held high positions on Clemenceau's staff during WWI; he was gassed in Auschwitz,

27 Sauvé 2016. Mr Sauvé also uttered very strong words on the past of the institution over which he presided in his opening speech to a conference held in February 2013 in Paris, cf. Baruch 2014b, 17-18.

28 The hierarchy in the *Conseil d'État* is as follows (in 2016): auditeurs (15), maîtres des requêtes (64), conseillers d'État (108), présidents de section (10), vice-président (1).

29 Massot 1998.

30 Fabre 2001.

31 Private letter from Ph. Fabre, Sept. 23 2002.

aged 70. I was astonished, the first time I read the list, to find as well the name of Maurice Seydoux, who had served between 1941 and 1943 as a *commissaire du pouvoir*, the fanatically Petainist institution that aimed (and failed) to politicize the French civil service. I doubted Seydoux had joined the Résistance after this unequivocal Vichyist commitment, since I remembered from the archives that, although young, he was a sick man. The answer came quietly from the *conseiller d'État* who accompanied me: Seydoux died from illness in March 1944, and the institution had found it fair to consider that dying *in* France at that period was not, after all, so different for a member of the *Conseil d'État* from dying *for* France.

References

Barthélemy, Joseph, *Ministre de la justice, Vichy 1941-1943. Mémoires*, Paris: Pygmalion 1989.

Baruch, Marc Olivier, *Servir l'État français. L'administration en France de 1940 à 1944*, Paris: Fayard 1997.

Baruch, Marc Olivier, 'Changing Things so Everything Stays the Same: The Impossible "épuration" of French Society, 1945–2000', in: Nico Wouters (Ed), *Transitional Justice and Memory in Europe (1945-2013)*, Cambridge, Intersentia, Series on Transitional Justice, Vol 17, 2014(a), 63-94.

Baruch, Marc Olivier (Ed), *Faire des choix? Les fonctionnaires dans l'Europe des dictatures*, La documentation française, 2014(b).

Bouffandeau, Tony, 'La continuité et la sauvegarde des principes du droit public français entre le 16 juin 1940 et l'entrée en vigueur de la nouvelle Constitution', *Études et documents du Conseil d'État*, 1947, 23-27.

Burrin, Philippe, *France under the Germans. Collaboration and Compromise*, New York: The New Press 1997 (French edition: *La France à l'heure allemande*, Paris: Seuil 1995).

Burrin, Philippe, 'Les élites dans l'Europe nazie', in: Marc Olivier Baruch & Vincent Guigueno (Eds), *Le choix des X; l'École polytechnique et les polytechniciens 1939-1945*, Paris: Fayard 2000, 79-95.

Fabre, Philippe, *Le Conseil d'État et Vichy: le contentieux de l'antisémitisme*, Paris: Éditions de la Sorbonne 2001.

Foyer, Jean 'Les juridictions administratives, une spécificité française', http://www.vie-publique.fr/decouverte-institutions/institutions/approfondissements/juridictions-administratives-specificite-francaise.html

Jäckel, Eberhard, *Frankreich in Hitlers Europa; Die deutsche Frankreichpolitik im Zweiten Weltkrieg*, Stuttgart: Deutsche Verlag-Anstalg GmbH 1966.

Klarsfeld, Serge, *Le calendrier de la persécution des Juifs de France 1940-1944*, Les Fils et Filles des Déportés Juifs de France & The Beate Klarsfeld Foundation, 1993.

Maleville, Georges, *Conseiller d'État, Témoignage*, Paris: Litec 1977.

Massot, Jean, 'Le Conseil d'État et le régime de Vichy', *Vingtième siècle, revue d'histoire* (58) 1998-2, 83-99.

Redor, Marie-Joëlle, *De l'État légal à l'État de droit; l'évolution des conceptions de la doctrine publiciste française, 1879-1914*, Paris: Économica/Presses universitaires d'Aix-Marseille, 1992.

Rudelle, Odile, 'Constitutionnaliser la Déclaration des droits de l'Homme?', in: Marc-Olivier Baruch & Vincent Duclert (Eds), *Justice, politique et République de l'affaire Dreyfus à la guerre d'Algérie*, Bruxelles: Complexe, 2002, 125-143.

Sauvé, Jean-Marc, 'Le Conseil d'État et la protection des droits fondamentaux', lecture at Nagoya University, 27 October 2016.

https://www.conseil-etat.fr/actualites/discours-et-interventions/le-conseil-d-etat-et-la-protection-des-droits-fondamentaux.

About the Author

Marc Olivier Baruch was formerly a civil servant in the French Ministries of Education and Culture and in the Prime Minister's office; since 2003 he has been directeur d'études at the École des hautes études en sciences sociales. He researches the political history of the civil service in contemporary France.

7 Sacrificing the Pig in the Temple – The Supreme Court in Occupied Norway

Hans Petter Graver

Abstract

This chapter treats the Norwegian supreme court, the *Høyesterett*, under the German occupation in World War II. It explains how the court got into conflict with the occupier over the judicial review of occupation legislation and resigned in December 1940. After that, a new collaborating supreme court was installed, whose judges and judgments are described, as well as its relation to the government and the reactions of the judiciary, description of the return of the legitimate *Høyesterett* judges and the prosecution of the members of the collaborating court. The chapter is concluded with a discussion of legal continuity and discontinuity and an assessment of the court's legacy.

Keywords: Norwegian supreme court (Høyesterett); German occupation of Norway in World War II; legal continuity and discontinuity; judicial resistance; judicial collaborationism

1 Institutional Legacy

The working of the judiciary in countries occupied by Germany during the Second World War is perhaps not the most spectacular or important aspect of the history of the war.[1] Nevertheless, when we decide to investigate this part of history, Norway forms a very special case. It is one of the few examples of judges, in the face of an authoritarian turn, collectively resigning their positions, as the justices of the Supreme Court did over a controversy with the German

1 The work on this article led me to write a book in Norwegian, Graver 2019a. See also for a more general account of the courts in Norway under the German occupation Graver 2019b.

Venema, D. (ed.), *Supreme Courts Under Nazi Occupation*. Taylor & Francis Group 2022
DOI: 10.5117/9789463720496_CH07

Reichskommissar. This was over the question as to whether orders given by the German occupiers could be subjected to judicial review in the Norwegian courts. Following their resignation, the Norwegian collaborator government appointed new judges to fill the position of justices of the Supreme Court. The Supreme Court of the National Socialists was thus a new court and yet it was still the Supreme Court of Norway. It was housed in the same building and took over the workload left behind by its predecessors. This is the story of this court.

On the one hand, there was discontinuity. The legitimate government had been deposed by force and usurpers had taken their place, supported by German arms. This was not merely an occupation government set to maintain law and order under foreign occupation. Both the German occupiers and their Norwegian collaborators, the National Socialist Party, *Nasjonal Samling*, were set on transforming Norway into a National Socialist state, based on Nazi racial ideas of the primacy of the Germanic race. The judges of the Supreme Court were all appointed by the National Socialists and all but one were members of the party. Most of them had no experience on the bench and most of them were relatively young.

On the other hand, when we study the Court more closely, the picture that emerges is one of continuity. The Supreme Court operated as it always had: there were more or less the same types of cases and the same advocates who argued the cases. It adhered to precedents from the pre-war Supreme Court and did not try to transform the law into a National Socialist law.

After the war, the judges were removed and their four years were erased from the history of the Supreme Court. The eradication was so total that, when a historian proposed to include the period in a history of the Court, the representative of the Supreme Court withdrew from the project and proposed that the funding should be cut. The legacy of these years on the post-war legal order is scant. Nevertheless, the four years still tell us something about the Norwegian legal tradition. They demonstrate that removing the actual judges and replacing them with new ones does not necessarily break a tradition. The institution is more than the people occupying the positions. If we want a fuller understanding of the institution of the Supreme Court in Norway, we need to include the years when the places of the judges were filled by judges appointed by the National Socialist regime.

2 The Occupation of Norway

On 9 April 1940, German forces invaded Denmark and Norway. In Denmark, the national authorities capitulated without resistance to the invaders on the same day and the national authorities continued in their functions under German control. In Norway, Norwegian and allied forces put up resistance to the invasion for two months with heavy fighting. The King and the Cabinet evaded German capture by leaving the capital. The main cities of Oslo, Bergen, and Trondheim quickly came under German occupation, but in parts of the country fighting continued until the final capitulation of the Norwegian forces on 8 June. The cabinet and the King left the country, and established an exile government in England.

With the German occupation, Norway underwent an instantaneous transformation from a democracy based on the rule of law into an authoritarian state. Judges and courts were important, both to the German and national rulers, in upholding law and order in general, but also in combatting all forms of resistance. The German occupiers enacted a legal programme to transform Norwegian society into a National Socialist state, with the aid of the *Nasjonal Samling*.

By the *Decree of the Führer concerning the Exercise of Government Authority in Norway* (24 April 1940), Norway was set under German civil administration, under the leadership of a *Reichskommissar*.[2] Hitler himself gave the *Reichskommissar* 'supreme governmental authority', including the power to issue laws in the form of orders. The laws and statutes of Norway were to remain in force 'in so far as is compatible with the fact of occupation'. These events led to a five-year term of German occupation and Nazi rule in Norway, under a German civil administration.

The occupiers did not limit themselves to purely military aims for their occupation, but sought to remould Norwegian society into a Nazi state. In this, they had the support of Norwegian collaborators, led by Vidkun Quisling, the leader of the *Nasjonal Samling*. Quisling had founded *Nasjonal Samling* in 1933 with a national socialist platform. The party had competed in parliamentary elections in 1933 and 1936 without getting enough votes to have any representatives elected. On the day of the German attack on Norway (9 April 1940), he staged a coup and encouraged the Norwegian forces to lay down their arms. This was unsuccessful and after some weeks he had to step down. He had support from Berlin, however, and so no reprisals were enacted against him for his failed coup. On the contrary, after some months, the Germans decided to make him their puppet in the ruling of Norway. Party membership soared and at one point it had more than 40,000 members. Norway thus entered the group of states in Europe that were under Nazi or fascist rule, with rulers committed to a

2 This and other decrees in English translations are reproduced in Lemkin 2008, 498-505.

fascist ideology and to transforming society into a totalitarian National Socialist state.

3 The Establishment of a Norwegian Civil Administration

As German forces occupied the southern part of Norway, the government retreated north, leaving the occupied parts of Norway without a national government. Quisling unsuccessfully tried to fill this vacuum, as described above. The obvious need for a responsible authority to coordinate the efforts of the Norwegian civil administration led the chief justice of the Supreme Court, Paal Berg, to take the initiative to appoint a chief administrative council, which was to take on the functions of government in occupied Norway.

After the occupation of the whole of the country, the Germans wanted to establish a Norwegian government. Their preference was for this government to have a formal mandate from the Norwegian parliament and for parliament to dismiss the government in exile. Paal Berg was central in the negotiations over this during the summer of 1940. After the fall of France to the German forces, the Norwegian negotiators seemed willing to go along with such terms. The negotiations nevertheless broke down. This was partly because the King refused to accept any settlement with the Germans, and partly because Quisling, having travelled to Berlin, managed to convince the *Reichskanzlei* (the Reich chancellery) to support him and the *Nasjonal Samling* concerning the solutions proposed under the negotiations in Oslo. Paal Berg and the Supreme Court thus played a political role in the initial phases of the occupation.[3]

After initial negotiations with the remaining Norwegian authorities, the Germans decided to establish a Norwegian civil administration based on the *Nasjonal Samling*. At the same time, the *Reichskommissar* issued the *Order Prohibiting Political Parties in Norway*, on 25 September 1940. The Order did not apply to the *Nasjonal Samling* and its subsidiary organisation. On 7 October, the *Reichskommissar* issued orders concerning the *Prohibition of Activities on Behalf of the Royal House of Norway*, and concerning the *Dismissal and Transfer of Officials*. This, in effect, made all political opposition to the occupation and to the *Nasjonal Samling* illegal.

3 The main sources for the role of Paal Berg and the Supreme Court are the recollections by the Supreme Court Judge Ferdinand Schjelderup, Schjelderup 1945, and the biography of Paal Berg by Per E. Hem, Hem 2012.

The *Reichskommissar* appointed commissioners with the title of ministers to function as heads of each Norwegian ministry. This was done in consultation with Quisling, and most of the ministers were members of the *Nasjonal Samling*. The *Nasjonal Samling* was a small party without representation in parliament, but was placed in control of the civil administration, albeit backed by the force of the German occupier, and under German guidance and supervision. The party had an anti-democratic, revolutionary programme, which it now sought to impose on the country. Popular support for the party was negligible and, in the summer of 1940, its membership was less than 4,000. In the national elections in 1933 and 1936, it had obtained approximately 27,000 votes (2.25 per cent of the total). Its membership rose rapidly after the German occupation and approximately 60,000 persons, with a peak of 43,000 at one time, were members of the party during these five years.[4]

Most of the population generally regarded the party and its members as collaborators and traitors, and therefore met them with resistance and opposition in various forms. Much of the resistance during the occupation was in fact directed against the *Nasjonal Samling* and its measures of nazification, and not against the German occupying forces. This resistance was illegal and an important part of the work of the police consisted in protecting party members from harassment and attacks, many of which were symbolic in form, like the wearing of paper clips in coat lapels and the wearing of red woollen hats during winter.

The ministers exercised authority delegated from the *Reichskommissar* and under his supervision. They did not formally take decisions as a council, but they met regularly as a cabinet. Legally, there is no doubt that they were exercising power under German authority under international law. In occupied countries, state institutions are under direct foreign rule. The authority of the occupier rests directly on military supremacy and force. Yet, even under these conditions, there are aspects of legality, drawn up under the international law of war. International law declares that the occupier should respect the laws and the institutions of the occupied country insofar as possible, and maintain law and order in the occupied territories.[5] However, after a short while, the Germans claimed that the

4 See Andenæs, Skodvin and Riste 1966, 71.

5 *Convention Respecting the Laws and Customs of War on Land and its annex, Regulations Concerning the Laws and Customs of War on Land*, The Hague, 18 October 1907 (The Hague Rules) Art. 43: 'The authority of the legitimate power having in fact passed into the hands of the occupant, the latter shall take all the measures in his power to restore, and ensure, as far

war in Norway was over, and, therefore, that The Hague rules of the 1907 *Convention respecting the Laws and Customs of War on Land* did not apply. They therefore claimed that these rules did not limit their jurisdiction and right to change the laws of Norway.

4 The Occupation Regime's Policy toward the Judiciary and Legal System and the Resignation of the Supreme Court Judges

One of the first measures of the newly established *Nasjonal Samling* Minister of Justice, Sverre Riisnæs, was an attempt to control the composition of the courts. To this purpose, several decrees were enacted. The term for the appointment of lay members of the courts and jury members was due to expire by the end of 1940. The Minister issued a decree on 14 November, whereby he gave himself the power to extend the terms on an individual basis and to appoint new persons to the list of members. Soon thereafter, on 6 December, he issued a decree lowering the retirement age for civil servants, including judges, from seventy to sixty-five. The decree also empowered the Minister to extend the age of retirement of civil servants, including judges, beyond sixty-five on an individual basis. These rules gave the Minister the possibility of influencing the composition of the courts and of securing judges who were loyal to the regime. The creation of such measures to the Supreme Court was influenced by US president Roosevelt's court-packing scheme of 1937.[6]

The Supreme Court reacted strongly to these measures.[7] The Supreme Court justices held discussions over these developments and agreed that the measures were unacceptable attacks on the independence of the judiciary. They wrote a letter to the *Reichskommissar* stating that such legislation was *ultra vires* for an occupying authority under the international law of war and occupation, and that it fell to the Supreme Court to exercise judicial review over the measures enacted by ministers.

as possible, public order and safety, while respecting, unless absolutely prevented, the laws in force in the country.'

6 See the report written by Arne Vislie on the examination of Sverre Parelius Riisnæs 1. november 1945, found in the criminal case against Jacob Andreas Mohr, National Archives reference Oslo politikammer: dom 1821 – Jacob Andreas Mohr.

7 For an overview in English over the conflict that led to the resignation of the Supreme Court judges see Venema 2012.

The Supreme Court also wrote a letter to the Ministry protesting against the measure on lay judges and argued that it was contrary to the general principles of justice of the Norwegian constitution, as well as that it exceeded the powers of occupying forces under public international law. The judges got two reactions to these letters. The first was the regulation lowering the retirement age for public officials from seventy to sixty-five, combined with a right for the responsible minister to prolong the tenure indefinitely. The second was a letter from the *Reichskommissar* stating that the Norwegian courts did not have the power to review the legality of laws and regulations enacted by, or on behalf of, the occupation authorities.

With the new retirement arrangement, the conditions under which the justices of the Supreme Court were expected to function became unacceptable to them. Those deemed 'unreliable' would be dismissed at sixty-five and replaced with persons loyal to the regime. The letter from the *Reichskommissar* made it clear that the Germans would not accept judicial review of the legality of occupation measures against public international law. The *Reichskommissar* claimed to be the supreme source of law in Norway. On 9 December, all the judges signed a letter where they asked Minister Riisnæs to revoke the retirement regulation. Three days later, they sent a new letter to the minister where they all resigned, because "we cannot adhere to the view expressed by the *Reichskommissar* on judicial review without acting in contradiction with our duties as members of the Norwegian Supreme Court." The Minister replied by dismissing the judges who were sixty-five years or older, and by summoning the remaining ones to individual conferences at the ministry. When these conferences failed to provide submission by any of the judges, the ministry was forced to accept the resignation of the judges as a *fait accompli*.

The judges who left the Court on this day were, together with the President of the Court, Paal Berg: Jakob Andreas Rivertz, Thorvald Boye, Ulrik Anton Motzfeldt, Erling Broch, Jacob Aars, Thomas Bonnevie, Henrik Ludvig Larssen, Einar Hanssen, Edvin Alten, Emil Stang, Axel Theodor Næss, Ferdinand Schjelderup, Svend Josef Einar Evensen, Helge Klæstad, Sverre Grette, Sigurd Fougner, and Erik Solem. Berg, Rivertz, Boye, Hanssen, Larssen, Motzfeldt, Broch, and Næss were older than sixty-five, and were dismissed by Riisnæs. The other ten resigned in opposition to the order by Riisnæs to stay in their positions. None of them were subject to sanctions for their resignation, but only those over sixty-five were entitled to a pension from the state.

One should probably view the stance on judicial review by the Norwegian court against the background of the resistance against Quisling and his project, and the illegality under Norwegian law of an establishment of a government in substitution for the King and government in exile. The Supreme Court had been quite clear on this position in the negotiations and had made it publicly known in a statement of 15 June 1940.[8] The same position was taken by the King after a request forwarded by the presidents of Parliament asking him to resign. The position to review the legality of the measures of the administration established by the *Reichskommissar* was therefore directed as much against the Quisling administrators as against the Germans. When some months later it came to an open confrontation, this was also the case, as the topic of the conflict was a measure on the constitution of the courts issued by the commissarial minister of justice. The basic constitutional issue on the legality of the Quisling administration was therefore decided as an issue of the application of international law by national Norwegian courts. The resignation of the Norwegian Supreme Court judges at the beginning of the German occupation contributed to the general perception of illegitimacy of the Quisling regime during the occupation in Norway and was hailed after the war as an action deserving the gratitude of the Norwegian people.[9]

However, this did not stop the *Nasjonal Samling* from making attempts to nazify the judiciary. Judges of all courts were, mostly unsuccessfully, encouraged to join the party, with only eight actually doing so. The party also attempted to take control over the judges' association. This was part of a general measure to bring the trade unions and trade associations under *Nasjonal Samling* control. The attempt resulted in the disbanding of many of these organizations and the arrest of a large number of the Norwegian elite, but did not succeed in establishing working *Nasjonal Samling* organizations. As a result of this struggle, the Chairman of the judges' association was removed from his position as a district judge.

All in all, the Nazi administration removed fourteen judges from their positions because they were politically unreliable. The party had the opportunity to appoint 65 judges, most of whom were party members. Probably as many as 50 judges and assistant judges (referandaries) were members of

8 Schjelderup 1945, 117-118.

9 Report by the investigative Commission, published by the Norwegian Parliament: *Innstilling* 1946, 338.

the party during the occupation, or about 20 per cent. This was significantly lower than within the police and prosecution authorities, where membership among the lawyers was as high as 60 per cent.

5 The Establishment of a New Court

Minister Riisnæs had already started his work of finding new judges for the Supreme Court late in November. This shows that he wanted to take control of the Court even before the escalation of the conflict that led to the collective resignation of the judges. The work intensified after the letter from the Supreme Court judges announcing their resignation, but Riisnæs still had hopes that the judges under sixty-five years of age would continue in their positions.[10] By the end of December, he had eight persons that were ready to start work as new judges when the court started its new session in the beginning of January 1941. The eight judges were:

Table 2 Judges appointed in the new Norwegian Supreme Court

Name	Age
Jacob Andreas Mohr, President of the Court	58
Leif Ragnvald Konstad	51
Arthur Middelthon Dahl	41
Arnvid Birger Liljedal Vasbotten	37
Gustav Christian Selmer	36
Ottar Huuse	60
Edvard Aslaksen	43
Later the court was joined by	
Peter Nicolai Helseth	43
Wilhelm Christie Hofgaard	44
Birger Motzfeldt	37
Egil Reichborn-Kjennerud	38
Olav Bjarne Aalvik Pedersen	38
Christen Nicolai Endresen Apenes	42
Vilhelm Frimann Christie Bøgh	61
Per Schie	32

10 Schelderup 1945, 230.

It was not an easy task to find eight persons who were at least practically qualified and willing to take up such a position, particularly after the conflict with the existing judges had become known. Probably more than eighteen additional persons were asked, but they all refused. Some of them joined the Court later. In total, fifteen persons served as justices in the wartime Supreme Court. All but one were members of the *Nasjonal Samling* or joined the Party soon after they became members of the Court.[11]

The eight judges started their work on 4 January 1941. None of the former judges continued in their positions, so that in its composition it was a totally new court. The discontinuity was stressed both by the opposition at the time and in later works on the Court. In his chapter on the wartime Court, in his history of the Supreme Court in the twentieth century, the historian Erling Sandmo underlines that even though the Court continued in the tradition of its predecessor, the composition of the cases changed, making it more a criminal court than the general court that the former Supreme Court had been. The lack of civil cases was due to the lack of confidence and trust that the population and the lawyers had in the new judges.[12] Sandmo builds his description on the description given by the courts in the later collaborator trials against the judges after the war. A closer look at the historical sources reveals that this picture was distorted.

The Court was a smaller court than before: the number of justices in 1940 was eighteen, whereas they were now only eight. The number increased during the occupation, and at one time they were eleven. Both the judges themselves and the Ministry emphasised the continuity of the institution. They were still officially known as the Supreme Court, they operated in the same building, and had the same administrative staff. The same lawyers appeared as counsel and new lawyers continued to take the exam that gave permission to appear before the Supreme Court.

Seen in terms of the flow of cases, the Court fitted nicely into the steps of its predecessor. Contrary to the prevailing belief, there were but slight changes in the number of cases brought before the Court, or in the distribution between civil cases and criminal cases. The number of new cases is shown in the following table:

11 An overview of the members of the Court and their treatment in the collaboration trials after the war is given by the ministry of justice in its report to Parliament in St. meld. Nr. 17 (1962-63) Om landssvikoppgjøret, 125-127.

12 Sandmo 2005, 315-316.

Table 3 New Cases in the Supreme Court, 1937-44[13]

	1937	1938	1939	1940	1941	1942	1943	1944
Civil Cases	164	168	190	152	137	185	169	140
Criminal Cases	186	219	158	131	139	119	155	141

Initially, there were tendencies to boycott the new court by parties and counsel, and the Bar Association encouraged their members not to appear before the new illegitimate justices. Within a few months, however, the court functioned normally with parties and lawyers appearing. Cases that had been pending before the old court were dealt with by the new judges – seamlessly, as if there had been no change. In one of its first cases, two of the justices wanted to depart from the case law of the old court, but the majority ruled that the court should sustain the law that had been upheld by the Supreme Court in an extensive line of cases.[14] Adhering to the precedents of the old Supreme Court became the norm of the new court.

6 Reactions

The apparent continuity of the work of the Court does not mean that the resignation of the judges, and the appointment of new ones, was not met without a reaction. The Judges' Association wrote a letter on 7 January to the Ministry in which they voiced their concern over the fact that it had become necessary for the judges of the Supreme Court to resign. The Bar Association wrote a similar letter. Both letters were distributed to the members of the two organizations. In February, after the appointment of new judges loyal to the regime, the Bar Association stated in a new letter that the new judges did not have the support or confidence of the judiciary or of the Norwegian people.[15]

There seems, however, to have been little opposition from the Norwegian judiciary to the measures enacted by the *Nasjonal Samling* or to the new Supreme Court. As in the other countries that they occupied, the German

13 Figures from the document «Saker behandler ved HR 1940-1945» (cases by the Supreme Court 1940-1945), and from the document «notat fra Høyesteretts kontor av 17. november 1945 til høyesterettsadvokat Arne Vislie», (PM from the administration of the Supreme Court to supreme court attorney Arne Vislie), both documents in the criminal case against Helseth, National Archives file Oslo politikammer: dom 2175 – Petter Nicolai Helseth.

14 *NRT* (*Norsk Retstidende*, Norwegian Court Reports) 1941 p. 20.

15 Nissen 1983, 173.

authorities established military courts to deal with instances of civil resistance against its rule.[16] Contrary to the situation in Denmark, where the national authorities strove to keep jurisdiction in the national courts in cases where their citizens were involved, there were no such efforts from the Norwegian authorities.[17] When the Germans ruled that their military courts, and later an SS court, should deal with offences against their regulations, these courts consequently dealt with all cases against civilians accused of political offences and acts of resistance against the German occupiers. The *Reichskommissar* also ruled that a special court should be established to deal with political offences. This led to the establishment by *Nasjonal Samling* of a People's Court, staffed by party members. Except for a very small number of cases from 1940, before the establishment of the *Nasjonal Samling* judicial system, cases of political resistance were therefore not brought before ordinary Norwegian judges.

When the justices resigned, the President of the Supreme Court issued a statement that the other judges should stay in their positions and 'take such measures as called for by the situation'.[18] With a few notable exceptions, the lower courts functioned without questioning the legality or legitimacy of the occupation authorities or the new Supreme Court. A set of cases that seem to have formed an exception to this are cases on forced labour. The *Nasjonal Samling* enacted rules that empowered the labour authorities to conscript able men and women to work in agriculture and forestry, and other activities of "national importance". This included conscripting workers to construction work for the German occupiers. These measures were unpopular and the resistance encouraged people to refuse or evade conscription. Many crossed the border to Sweden; others moved to join relatives in rural areas, so that they could argue that they were already engaged in farming activities.

In the first cases brought to the Supreme Court against persons evading conscription, the court emphasised the need to react sharply. In two cases in December 1941, the Court raised the penalty from fines to an unconditional thirty-day prison sentence.[19] The Court continued to receive such cases from the lower courts where fines had been imposed. This shows that at

16 The history of this important part of the German judiciary is presented by Bohn 2000 pp. 91-114.

17 See Graver 2015a pp. 56-57. The Belgian courts, on the other hand, refused to apply the regulations of the German military administration, and violations of these were therefore tried by German courts, see Michielsen 2004 p. 36.

18 Nissen 1983, 174.

19 *NRT* 1941, 867 and 870.

least some lower court judges refused to accept the authority of the Supreme Court in such cases. This, however, was an exception to the general rule of subservience.

Opposition against the court continued through more political means. When asked about their opinion on the court, leading members of the profession stated that it was not a neutral court, but a political instrument in the hands of the *Nasjonal Samling*. The underground bar association in 1943 characterised the court as a "band of traitors".[20] They also reinforced the appeal to avoid dealings with the Court and warned that permissions for lawyers to appear before the Court that the judges issued would not be respected after the liberation of the country. The number of young lawyers submitting to the test fell sharply and, in the last two years of the occupation, only two National Socialist lawyers submitted to the test. But, as we have seen above, parties and their lawyers continued to appear before the Court as an ordinary supreme court during the years of its functioning. Even though it was opposed politically, in practice it was accepted as the Supreme Court.

7 The Legal Approach of the Court

The cases decided by the Court do not distinguish themselves in relation to the cases decided by the pre-war Court. The proportion between civil cases and criminal cases was roughly the same. The civil cases were typical cases involving contract, property, landlord and tenant, tort, family matters and paternity cases, taxation, and so on. The results were mostly in conformance with the law as it was regarded both before and after the occupation. After the occupation, a few parties sought to have the result in their cases overturned by the ordinary Supreme Court, according to a statute of restitution of judgements taken by National Socialist judges, but mostly without success. The number of crimes increased slightly during the occupation, mostly because of a rise in thefts and crimes against property. Crimes of violence decreased. These changes are also reflected in the composition of criminal cases before the Supreme Court, with many rather petty thefts of food, clothes, and rationed goods, together with wartime crimes such as violation of rationing regulations and blackout orders.

In some instances, the Court had to decide on more political issues. The first of such cases concerned the legality of a new procedural measure

20 Poulsson 1958, 159.

allowing for a court to be set without lay members in price control cases.[21] The appellant argued that the district court had been illegally established, because enacting such procedural measures was outside the scope of the occupant's authority under *The Hague Regulations respecting the Laws and Customs of War on Land*, Art. 43.

This was the same question that led to the resignation of the former judges, albeit on a different legal measure by the occupant authority. The regulation that triggered their resignation was one extending the function of elected lay judges, thereby giving the political authority the possibility of manipulating the constitution of the courts. This regulation was clearly an attack on judicial independence. Contrary to this, it could be argued that enacting measures to ensure an effective enforcement of price control measures was a legitimate task for the authorities during an occupation. The judges were asked, however, by a letter written by the Minister of Justice, to decide the case on a general basis and to establish a principle of non-interference by the courts against any regulation enacted by the occupation authority. And the Court complied. In a long ruling, it decided that the courts could not review the discretion exercised by the occupant authority when determining the necessity of measures "to restore, and ensure, as far as possible, public order and safety".[22]

An even more political statement was called for when Quisling prepared his *coup d'état* in 1942 and established a national government. Before announcing his government, he sought an opinion from the judges on the constitutionality of this course of action. In a statement dated 30 January 1942, the justices wrote that "[u]nder the present constitutional and political circumstances, the court sees no decisive constitutional case against the leader of *Nasjonal Samling*, Vidkun Quisling, forming a Norwegian national government".[23] In this, they laid the legal foundations for a National Socialist government backed by the strength of the Nazi occupying forces.

These two instances, however, do not mean that the Court in politically sensitive issues merely functioned as a puppet for the Germans and the Norwegian National Socialists. The issue on judicial review was open to argument both ways, and it was by no means obvious under international law or under Norwegian law that the courts could exercise review based on an application of rules under public international law. When the occupation

21 Reported in *NRT* 1941, 63.

22 *NRT* 1941, 63.

23 *Norsk Lovtidend* (Norwegian laws) 1942, 82.

ended, a new case regarding this question was pending before the Court. The case had been argued before a normal chamber of five judges, but had been referred to a hearing in a plenary session, because a majority of the judges wanted to invalidate the statute that had been enacted by Quisling's government.[24] In 1941, the Court was also asked to give a legal opinion on the status of the Norwegian Parliament. Elections would have been held in 1940 but for the occupation, so by the beginning of 1941 the term of office ended. Quisling wanted the backing of the Court to be able to regard the Parliament as defunct, since no new election had been held. The judges debated the issue over two days and concluded that the Parliament, under the circumstances, must be entitled to prolong its functioning until it became possible to hold elections. When the Minister of Justice was informed of this, the request for an opinion by the court was withdrawn.[25]

In a case concerning a Jewish defendant, the Court openly defied the approach of German law to the Jews.[26] On trial was a shopkeeper from the northern city of Tromsø. He was accused of selling articles of clothing to German soldiers without demanding coupons from their rationing cards. It has been claimed that this was a conscious provocation by the Germans to criminalise the Jewish trader.[27] The local court gave him a mild sentence, arguing that he, a Jew, had been in a precarious position with little possibility of refusing the demands of German soldiers to buy goods. The Supreme Court upheld this sentence and refused to follow the appeal of the prosecutor for a harsher sentence.

When the Germans heard about the lenient treatment, they arrested the merchant and shut down his shop. Nevertheless, the situation repeated itself. A few months later, two new defendants, also Jewish, had their appeals heard on the same grounds.[28] They were also treated leniently, both by the local court and the Supreme Court. The courts were not intimidated into treating Jews more harshly because of their Jewish origin and the justices appointed by *Nasjonal Samling* did not differ from other Norwegian judges in this respect.

24 Rapport 14. september 1945 from examination of Wilhelm Christie Hofgaard, dokument i sak mot Hofgaard.

25 This instance was described both by Hofgaard and Konstad after the war, see Rapport 4. september 1945 from examination of Leif Ragnvald Konstad, dokument i sak mot Konstad and forklaring avgitt av fange nr. 774 på Ila fengsel Wilhelm Hofgaard 19. juni 1945, dokument i sak mot Hofgaard.

26 *NRT* 1941, 18.

27 Bruland 2017, 103.

28 *NRT* 1941, 238 and 239.

A case where the National Socialist sympathies of the judges were obviously in play was a conflict between a divorced couple over the custody of their son. The husband was an ideologically convinced National Socialist, whereas the wife shared the resentment of most of the population against *Nasjonal Samling*. The boy lived with his mother, together with his two sisters. The custody question had already been decided by the courts in 1938, but, in 1941, the father decided to make a new appeal. The local court upheld the judgement from 1938, but the father appealed to the Supreme Court. He argued that it was best for a child to be raised in the spirit of the "new times", and that this was also in accordance with the political programme of the *Nasjonal Samling*. He had excellent testimonies from the school and local authorities, all by persons who were members of the Party. The Supreme Court decided to award custody to the father, overturning all previous court decisions. The judges were careful not to use an explicit political motivation for the decision, but it is difficult to understand it outside of its political context.

In general, the Court maintained the traditional respect of Norwegian courts for legality and the rule of law, and adherence to precedents. In some cases, the Court deviated from this, but such examples can also be found in the cases of the Supreme Court from both before and after the occupation.

8 The Capitulation and the Aftermath

The German forces capitulated on 8 May 1945 and the leading authorities of the National Socialist regime were arrested in the following days. This included the Supreme Court judges. Justices of the Court at this time were: Jacob Andreas Mohr, Leif Ragnvald Konstad, Arthur Middelthon Dahl, Edvard Aslaksen, Peter Nicolai Helseth, Wilhelm Christie Hofgaard, Olav Bjarne Aalvik Pedersen, Christen Nicolai Endresen Apenes and Per Schie. Of the eight appointed in December 1940, only four – Mohr, Konstad, Dahl, and Aslaksen – were left. Two, Helseth and Hofgaard, had been serving since March 1941. Of the judges no longer serving, Selmer had fallen fighting on the Eastern Front in Caucasia in July 1942. One judge, Vasbotten, had left the Court to take the position of Minister for the Interior in November 1944. Justice Reichborn-Kjennerud, who joined the court in 1942, had also been a soldier on the eastern front. Towards the end of the war, he was trained in Germany to form part of a stay-behind group to undertake guerrilla warfare after the capitulation of the regular troops. He was, therefore, no longer a member of the court when the capitulation was made. Two judges were allowed by the Ministry to leave and took up positions in lower courts. In total, fifteen judges served on the bench of the Supreme Court during the occupation. Before the war, and after, the number of Supreme Court judges was eighteen. This shows the difficulties that the *Nasjonal Samling* faced in recruiting judges to the Supreme Court.

All judges were prosecuted and given severe sentences for treason and collaboration with the enemy. After the war, the trials against the main collaborators were heard directly by the Court of Appeals. Under Norwegian criminal procedure, the Court of Appeals was the court of first and last instance regarding the facts in serious criminal cases. Normally, cases were tried by a jury, but in the collaborator cases, the jury was substituted by a panel of three professional and four lay judges.

Questions of law could be appealed to the Supreme Court. Shortly after the liberation, the judges who had resigned resumed their function as the Supreme Court. As five died during the war, five new judges were appointed. These were the ones to hear the cases against the judges of the Supreme Court during the occupation.

Mohr, who functioned as the Court's President, was sentenced to life imprisonment. He died in prison in 1951. The others were given sentences from six to fifteen years in prison. They were mostly pardoned and released by 1951-1952. Some of them took up practice as lawyers, two quite successfully. Some were employed as lower-level civil servants: one in the Ministry of Finance and one in the national social security agency. Others just disappeared from public life, leaving little trace to be found.

The first case against the judges was the case against President Mohr.[29] Mohr was a justice at the City Court of Oslo when he was approached in December 1940 by the Minister of Justice and asked to take office as President of the Supreme Court. He accepted this appointment and was assigned immediately. A unanimous Supreme Court found Mohr guilty both of collaboration and of treason. By accepting appointment to this court, Mohr had contributed to substituting the legal judges, who had resigned their offices for reasons grounded in international law and the constitution, with a set of justices who were willing tools in the hands of Quisling and the Germans.

The justices were not held accountable for their individual judgments. Participation in the ruling on judicial review of rules given by the occupying authorities was part of the indictment against the judges of the Supreme Court. However, in the verdict against Mohr and the others, the Supreme Court did not see this as a separate criminal offence, and

29 *NRT* 1946, 1139.

the courts after the war therefore saw no need to go into the legal issue of the relationship between an occupier and the courts in an occupied county under international rules of war. This may be seen as according the members of the illegal Supreme Court some immunity for judgments issued according to their exercising of normal judicial functions.[30] It may also be interpreted, however, in the light of the obvious dilemma that it was the opinion of the Quisling Court, and not the opinion of the Supreme Court, that best accorded with accepted opinion in international law. In this way, the Norwegian courts after the war circumvented this thorny issue.

They were, on the other hand, held accountable for their support for Quisling's formation of a government in 1942. By legitimizing this *coup d'état*, they had made themselves accomplices to the crime of treason.

9 Disruption and Continuity

The staffing of the Supreme Court was in one way a clear break with the past. The existing Supreme Court judges all resigned, in a manner that clearly stated their view on the illegality of the new regime. The new judges were all hand-picked by Minister Riisnæs and they were mostly loyal party members. The National Socialist authorities, however, did not intend to create a new type of court. Riisnæs, the Minister of Justice, wanted a majority of judges who accepted the new regime as a legitimate authority of state, at least for the duration of the occupation. Like Roosevelt, he wanted judges who understood the demands of the time and who did not cling to an obsolete past. Yet, he wanted an independent court that operated according to the basic tenet of the rule of law. The People's Court, established to deal with political cases, was to be a spearhead in the transformation of Norwegian society into a National Socialist state.[31] Riisnæs never expressed a similar ambition on behalf of the Supreme Court.

In the political resistance against the regime, the Court was perceived as a political tribunal and the judges regarded as criminals, guilty of treason and collaboration with the enemy. This was also the way that they were treated by the authorities after the occupation. During the occupation, however, the Court functioned as an ordinary court of last instance. This was certainly

30 To the question of holding judges under authoritarian regimes accountable for their rulings, under criminal law, see Graver 2016.

31 Graver 2015b, 92.

the way that the judges perceived themselves. They argued in their defence that they had done the country a favour by accepting unpopular posts as judges in the Supreme Court. The country needed this institution for the normal functioning of the judicial system and they feared that German judges or bureaucrats would review the cases from the Norwegian lower courts and exert their power over them, should a Norwegian Supreme Court cease to exist.

They based their judgments on the existing law and did not attempt to reinterpret it in a National Socialist direction. They adhered loyally to the precedents of their predecessors and emphasized continuity in the law. In some instances, they refused to accommodate the interests of the regime, although it can by no means be characterized as a court in opposition to the regime. Basically, it followed the tenet that it had established in 1941: it was not for the courts to review the legality of measures enacted by the regime.

In practice, if not in words, they were regarded as an ordinary court also by the legal complex. Parties continued to bring cases to the Court, in around the same amount as previously, and the cases were argued by the same advocates. Young lawyers continued to submit to the test to gain recognition as advocates of the Supreme Court, at least until the resistance warned them from doing this in 1943. In general, their rulings were followed by the lower courts and seen as a basis for determining the law. The National Socialist authorities respected the independence of the judges and there is no evidence that they tried to influence their rulings in individual cases. The Court was in other words a court, as we know courts within the western legal tradition.

In its operation, it did not function very differently from the functioning of the Supreme Courts of other western European countries under German occupation, such as, for instance, the Supreme Court of Denmark and the Higher Court of the Netherlands. To the extent that this is true, we may say that the resignation of the judges of the Supreme Court, and the appointment of new judges by the National Socialist authorities, did not change the institution of the Norwegian Supreme Court. It is, of course, merely speculation, but one may hypothesize that, had the incumbent judges not resigned, they would have been forced to surrender on the question of judicial review and would have functioned much in the same way as their successors on the bench.

This case then, is an example of the force of institutions on persons, whether they operate as individuals or collectively within organizations. Institutions are not first and foremost rules of the game, but self-enforcing systems of rules, beliefs, norms, and organizations.[32] Institutions enforce themselves through strong mechanisms of path dependence, which operate both on formal rule-changes and changes of personnel. Germany itself presents examples of this: even the SS courts and the Special Courts that were established to deal with political enemies of the regime operated as independent courts according to basic tenets of the rule of law.

In the Norwegian setting, many factors contribute to this path dependence. The self-images of the judges, as judges according to Norwegian law and the Norwegian tradition, kept them on the path of law. They perceived themselves as appointed to serve on a Supreme Court and not on a people's court established to be a vanguard of National Socialism.[33] The same mindset seems to have also influenced the Minister of Justice, Sverre Riisnæs. He did not see it as illegitimate to attempt to copy the court-packing plan of US President Roosevelt. This attempt was, we should remember, not universally seen as illegitimate at the time. Roosevelt had broad support for his proposal in the US until the court changed and submitted to the New Deal.[34] In the presentation of the scheme to the Norwegian legal community, the comments were generally sympathetic or neutral to the proposal. Riisnæs was, on the other hand, careful to assure his candidates that they would be expected to function as independent judges, and not be under his or anyone else's instruction.

Riisnæs did not show the same respect for judicial independence when it came to using special courts as a mere appearance of legality in trials against members of the Norwegian Resistance. The *Nasjonal Samling* government was one of the few governments in Western Europe that used special courts for show trials to legitimize decisions taken in advance by the party concerning the guilt and punishment of the would-be accused.[35] Together with Vidkun Quisling, he also sought to instruct the judges of the Peoples' Court. This only serves to underline his reverence for the institution of the Supreme Court within the legal order. The beliefs and informal norms of judicial independence also operated in the minds of the National Socialists.

Lawyers and others critical of the regime may have seen the judges as political appointees, and regarded them as traitors to the cause for legality and judicial independence that was fought by the resigning judges.

32 See Graver 2018.

33 Even the judges of the People's Court saw themselves as independent judges and refused to take instructions from the political authorities in individual cases, see Graver 2015b, 148-149.

34 Leuchtenburg 1995, 135.

35 See Graver 2015b, 149.

Nevertheless, habits, personal interest, and the rules of the game made them play along as before. The actions of the parties and their lawyers also demonstrate that they had faith in the value of legal argument, even in the courtroom of the National Socialist judges.

10 The Legacy of the Court

After the removal and conviction of the judges, the collaborating court and its members sank into oblivion. The years of 1941-44 were removed from the history of the Supreme Court and its cases not included in the indexes of case law. When an electronic database of legal sources was established, the cases of the wartime court were not included. The judges do not appear in the record of Supreme Court judges of Norway and their cases are never referred to in the rulings of the Supreme Court. There are, however, some references to its cases in rulings by lower courts after the occupation and in scholarly legal works, despite the fact that the official view is that they have no force whatsoever as legal sources. When the historian commissioned to write the history of the Supreme Court in 2000 proposed to include a chapter on the wartime court, the judge in the steering committee of the project demanded that the project should be terminated immediately and suggested to the Ministry that it should withdraw its funding.[36] No study of this court going to the sources has to date been undertaken – either by lawyers, legal historians, or historians. The prevailing view is the one that was established in the collaborator trials against the judges. Otto Kirchheimer warns us, in his book on political trials, of the limited usefulness of political trials in establishing meaningful interpretations of the past.[37]

The harsh sentences, and total erasure of the court and its judges from legal memory, demand an explanation. According to the standards established by the retribution trials in Norway after the occupation, the judges were collaborators as members of the *Nasjonal Samling*. As prominent members, they faced prison terms. But the sentences were unusually harsh, even within the contemporary context. The judges had, after all, not been active in developing the policies or strategies of the regime; they had not taken orders from, or performed tasks for, the Germans. They had, by accepting office, contributed to bestowing a shroud of legality on the regime, but so did the other judges who stayed in office in the lower courts.

36 Sandmo 2007, 119.
37 Kirchheimer 1961, 47.

Their acceptance of office could be seen as an act to undermine, or at least counter, the strong statement that the resigning judges gave by their resignation, but the actual course of history proved that it did not have this effect. The Norwegian people got the message and were not confused by the establishment of a new Supreme Court. Why then the severe sentences? They were desecrators; they violated the sanctity of the holiness of the institution. They had dared to enter the temple of justice and dress themselves in the robes of the consecrated. The National Socialists had sacrificed a pig in the temple and the judges were the executors of this act. For this, there could be no leniency.

Their acts were, however, not totally devoid of implications for the law after the occupation. In the eyes of the people, the legitimacy of the Supreme Court was greater than ever after the war. The "Nazi judges" could be held up as a counterpoint to the "untainted" judges. The shortcomings of the judiciary in general during the occupation were dealt with by the trials against the usurpers. In this way, the judiciary as a whole emerged as cleansed of the grime acquired from five years of dealing as judges of the regime with cases bordering on, and sometimes crossing the line to, illegitimacy.

The story of the judges of the Supreme Court during the occupation also shows that institutions are greater than men. Although the creations of men, institutions consist of informal norms that are changed with more difficulty than formal rules. They shape the knowledge and values of society, and also its fundamental values. Neither the Minister of Justice nor the judges themselves wanted to change the Supreme Court. The question is why they did not want to do so, when they wanted to change so much else.

References

Andenæs, Johs, Magne Skodvin and Olav Riste, *Norway and the Second World War*, Oslo: Aschehoug 1966.

Bohn, Robert, *Reichskommissariat Norwegen: "Nationalsozialistische Neuordnung" und Kriegswirtschaft*, München: Oldenburg Wissenschaftsverlag 2000.

Bruland, Bjarte, *Holocaust i Norge. Registrering, deportasjon, tilintetgjørelse*, Oslo: Dreyers forlag 2017.

Graver, Hans Petter, *Judges Against Justice. On Judges When the Rule of Law is Under Attack*, Heidelberg: Springer 2015a.

Graver, Hans Petter, *Dommernes krig. Den tyske okkupasjonen 1940–1945 og den norske rettsstaten*, Oslo: Pax forlag 2015b.

Graver, 'Judging without Impunity: On the Criminal Responsibility of Authoritarian Judges', *Bergen Journal of Criminal Law and Criminal Justice* (4) 2016-1, 125-149.

Graver, Hans Petter, 'Judicial Independence Under Authoritarian Rule: An Institutional Approach to the Legal Tradition of the West', *Hague Journal on the Rule of Law*, 2018, https://doi.org/10.1007/s40803-018-0071-8

Graver, Hans Petter, *Okkupasjonstidens Høyesterett*, Oslo 2019a.

Graver, Hans Petter, *Der Krieg der Richter Die deutsche Besatzung 1940-1945 und der norwegische Rechtsstaat*, Baden-Baden: Nomos 2019b.

Hem, Per E., *Megleren Paal Berg 1873-1968*, Oslo: Aschehoug 2012.

Innstilling fra undersøkelseskommisjonen av 1945, Oslo: Aschehoug 1946.

Kirchheimer, Otto, *Political Justice: The Use of Legal Procedure for Political Ends*, Princeton: Princeton University Press 1961.

Lemkin, Raphael, *Axis Rule in Occupied Europe Law of Occupation, Analysis of Government, Proposals for Redress*, second edition, Clark: The Lawbook Exchange 2008 (Orig. 1944).

Leuchtenburg, William E., *The Supreme Court Reborn The Constitutional Revolution in the Age of Roosevelt*, Oxford: Oxford University Press, 1995.

Michielsen, J.N.M.E., *The 'Nazification' and 'Denazification' of the Courts in Belgium, Luxembourg and the Netherlands*, Maastricht: University of Maastricht Press 2004.

Nissen, Gunnar, 'Krigstid og Landssvikoppgjør i etterkrigstid', in: Gunder Egge, Gunnar Nissen & Johannes Dannevig, *Den dømmende makt. Domstolenes organisasjon og virksomhet*, Oslo: Universitetsforlaget 1983.

Poulsson, Erik T., 'Den Norske Sakførerforening juli 1941-mai 1945', in: Christophersen, Rolf (Ed), *Den Norske Sakførerforening 1933–1958*, Oslo: Den Norske Sakførerforening 1958, 91-121.

Sandmo, Erling, *Siste ord. Høyesterett i norsk historie 1905–1965*, Oslo: Cappelen 2005.

Sandmo, Erling, "Just Past: on Historical and Legal History", in Kenneth Johansson and Marie Lindstedt Cronberg (red.), *Vänskap över gränser. En festskrift til Eva Österberg*, Lund: Studentlitteratur AB 2007, 113-128.

Schjelderup, Ferdinand, *Fra Norges kamp for retten. 1940 i Høyesterett*, Oslo: Grøndahl & Søn Forlag 1945.

Venema, Derk, 'The Judge, the Occupier, His Laws, and Their Validity. Judicial review by the Supreme Courts of occupied Belgium, Norway, and the Netherlands 1940-1945 in the context of their professional conduct and the consequences for their public image', in: Koster, M. de; Heirbaut, D. (Eds), *Justice in Wartime and Revolutions, Europe, 1795-1950*, Brussels: State Archives 2012, 203-223.

About the Author

Hans Petter Graver is a professor of private law affiliated with University of Oslo; his research concerns public law and legal theory. He is the author of *Judges against Justice. On Judges when the Rule of Law is under Attack* (2015) and *Der Krieg der Richter. Die deutsche Besatzung 1940-1945 und der norwegische Rechtsstaat* (2019).

8 The Belgian Court of Cassation in the Turmoil of the Second Occupation

Françoise Muller and Kirsten Peters

'Die Vormachtstellung der Justiz ist gebrochen'
('The Predominance of Justice is Broken')[1]

Abstract
This chapter looks back at the policy of the lesser evil adopted by the Belgian authorities during the Second World War, namely the fact that they remained in place under the supervision of the Occupier. This policy allowed the national institutions, including justice, to be safeguarded. But this preservation had a price: the institutions were required, in accordance with international law, to compromise with the occupier and adopt a loyal attitude towards him. The Court of Cassation thus continued its role as guardian of the law. But the German ordinance of 14 May 1942, which prohibited the judges from examining the legality of the orders of the secretaries general, placed the Belgian high court before the most difficult decision in its history.

Keywords: Policy of the lesser evil; Secretaries-General; Control of legality; Delegation of powers; Senior magistracy; Judicial crisis

1 Introduction

Drawing lessons from the First World War, the Belgian authorities examined, during the inter-war period, measures to ensure that the national institutions would continue to function in the event of another occupation. What

1 *Gruppe Justiz an das Oberkommando des Heeres, Generalquartier*, 6 July 1942, Freiburg: Bundesarchiv-Militärarchiv (BA-MA), RW 36/400, p. 22.

Venema, D. (ed.), *Supreme Courts Under Nazi Occupation*. Taylor & Francis Group 2022
DOI: 10.5117/9789463720496_CH08

emerged from this process of reflection was the idea that the interference of an occupying power could be restricted by combining two principles. The first was the obligation for civil servants to remain in office and to continue to work in accordance with international law. The second was the principle of delegation, whereby officials, who for reasons of war were prevented from performing their duties, would be automatically replaced by their subordinates for urgent matters. In this way, the national institutions would continue to function, making interference by the invader superfluous.

In May 1940, these principles were applied right up to the top of the state. The powers of the ministers – who had been forced to flee the country in order to continue the struggle on the side of the Allies – were exercised by the highest official of each ministry: the secretary-general. The story of the Belgian judiciary (corresponding to the French 'magistrature' as used in Belgium, including both judges and prosecutors) during the war is intrinsically linked to that of the secretaries-general ('secrétaires-généraux'). Firstly, this is because the Secretary-General of Justice was the intermediary between the Belgian judiciary and the German military administration. Jean Hubrecht (16 May 1940–1 August 1940), Antoine Ernst de Bunswyck (2 August 1940–31 January 1941), and Gaston Schuind (4 April 1941–17 September 1943) are three of the five persons who carried out this function.[2] These are omnipresent players in this study on the relationship between the judiciary and the occupier. Secondly, and more fundamentally, this is because the secretaries-general were responsible for administering the country by means of decrees ('arrêtés'). The Belgian legislators, who wanted the secretaries-general to be able to confront all eventualities, had remained intentionally imprecise as to the extent of the powers conferred on them; a gap that would be for case law to fill.

This study examines, in its first part, the lead advisory role played, in this period of great legal uncertainty, by the senior judiciary in the adoption of the 'Protocol' of June 1940, i.e. the agreement between the occupying power and the secretaries-general, defining the scope of their respective powers. This Protocol formed the basis of the modus vivendi between occupier and occupied. It enacted the power of the secretaries-general to issue, within certain conditions (including a right of veto of the occupier) decrees having force of law. However, there is one crucial question that the Protocol did not regulate: Were such acts the expression of executive or legislative authority? If the former, then, under Article 107 (former) of the Constitution, they were

2 The two others are E. Wauters (3/2/1941-31/3/1941) and Robert De Foy (1/10/1943 until the end of the occupation).

subject to the control of the courts and tribunals, which, in cases of illegality, must refuse to apply them. If the latter, then they escaped this control of legality. It is therefore understandable that, from the beginning of the war, the Germans were concerned about this essential prerogative of the Belgian judiciary and sought a means of conferring the force of law on the acts of the secretaries-general. This vagueness as to the nature of the latter contained the seeds of potential conflict between the judiciary and the occupying authority, should the former consider itself justified in exercising a right of control of the legality of the secretaries-generals' acts. In 1942, the risk took concrete form, leading to a crisis of rare intensity with the occupying authorities. This crisis, and the difficult choice that the Belgian Court of Cassation ('Cour de Cassation' – Supreme Court) had to make between the strict respect of the law and the interests of the population, is the subject of the second part of this study.

2 From Delegation of Powers to Protocol: The Shadow Action of the Senior Judiciary in the Early Days of the War

2.1 Uncertain Times

In an increasingly tense international context, Belgium adopted, from 1936 onwards, what has been described as a 'hands-free' foreign policy. Faced with Germany's violation of its international commitments (Locarno Agreement, 1925) and the helplessness of the League of Nations, Belgium considered itself released from its obligations and took its international policy back into its own hands. In so doing, it opted for de facto neutrality, while investing heavily in its defence systems so as to dissuade its neighbours from using its territory for fighting their wars.

The fact of strongly playing the neutrality card did not prevent the authorities from preparing simultaneously – though secretly – for war. This possibility, and the measures to be taken as a result, were discussed in both the military and political spheres.[3] Jean Servais,[4] an eminent magistrate

3 "Several times a week, under the chairmanship of the Minister of Justice, and usually in the presence of the Minister of National Defence, the three general prosecutors (*'procureurs généraux'*) at the Courts of Appeal met with the auditor general to examine the measures concerning the organization of justice and the exercise of public action, to be taken in case of invasion of the territory" (Ganshof van der Meersch 1971, 13).

4 Jean Servais (° 25 Sept. 1856 – † 30 Nov. 1946). After a few years at the bar, he joined the judiciary in 1880 as deputy public prosecutor at the Brussels Court of First Instance. Eleven

(member of the judiciary)[5] and minister of state, played a leading role in this process. From 1933, Servais developed the idea that, if a subordinate authority depending on a public institution is cut off from its hierarchical leaders as a result of war, this does not necessarily result in a lack of executive power, to be replaced by the occupying power. On the contrary, the subordinate authority may, during this period of uncertainty, replace the higher authority in cases of emergency. Servais – whose reputation was such that he was described as “the law incarnate”[6] – based his reflections on the experiences of the First World War. On the first day of the invasion, 4 August 1914, a law concerning delegations in time of war had been passed in haste. Its scope was limited to the provinces and municipalities;[7] for Servais, a frame too small to be effective.[8] Accordingly, he drafted a bill to fill these gaps.[9]

years later, he was appointed deputy public prosecutor at the Brussels Court of Appeal. He was promoted to public prosecutor at the court of appeal (‘*avocat-général*’) three years later. Appointed counsellor to the Court of Cassation in 1908, he was charged by the government in 1918 with reorganizing the Brussels public prosecutor’s office (‘*parquet général*’) after the First World War, a function he maintained until his retirement 1928.

5 Belgian *magistrates* have often held the positions of both judge and prosecutor in their career, which is why this general term is used. To distinguish it from the Anglo-Saxon term ‘magistrate’, it is put in italics, except in quotations.

6 ‘Jean Servais’, 343.

7 This law was repealed by the occupier on 3 December 1914, when the powers exercised by the provincial governors, under the delegation law, were transferred to the German military governors. The powers exercised by the King were transferred to the Governor General, von Bissing (‘*Decree repealing the law of 4 August 1914 on the delegation of powers in case of invasion of the territory, and regulating the exercise of powers which belong to the provincial governors and to the King of the Belgians by virtue of the laws on the administration of the provinces and municipalities*’, in *Bulletin officiel des lois et arrêtés pour le Territoire belge occupé*, 7 December 1914).

8 “Under the pretext of ensuring public order in the occupied country, the occupier profited from this [legislative] deficiency to interfere in our public life in a way that always injured the patriotic feelings of our population and which was at times indecent” (Preliminary draft of the Honorary Prosecutor General Servais, annexed to a letter from Lieutenant General Cattoir, Head of the National Mobilization Department, to the members of the Permanent National Mobilization Commission, 8 January 1936, in *Archives Raoul Hayoit de Termicourt concernant le travail des institutions belges pendant l’occupation* 1933-1973, CEGESOMA, AA mic 48).

9 This senior magistrate also left his mark on the *Livret de mobilisation civil* (*civil mobilization booklet*). This text sought to ensure the continuity of national institutions in the event of enemy occupation. If civil servants, *magistrates*, and other public servants remained in place or were replaced by their subordinates – according to the principle of delegation – the continuity obtained in this way would prevent the occupier gaining control of the national administration.

2.2 The Invasion and the Exile of the Government

It was only on the day of the German invasion (10 May 1940) that the draft bill on the delegation of powers in time of war, largely inspired by Servais' thinking, was submitted to Parliament.[10]

> Secretly buried, as early as 1936, in a cupboard of the General Secretariat of Justice, they [the "Servais documents"] were exhumed only on 10 May 1940, to be placed preciously in the ministerial briefcase, in view of the debates in the legislative assemblies. And on using shortly afterwards, in the House, the right of initiative, Mr. Janson [Minister of Justice] took from the morocco briefcase solely the draft bill, the only document in the dossier of which Parliament was ever apprised.[11]

The text was adopted the same day, in a hurry, by a majority (143 out of 146 votes). The central provision of this law lies in Article 5, which sets out the framework for the delegation of powers:

> When, as a result of military operations, a magistrate or civil servant, a corps of magistrates or civil servants [...] is deprived of all communication with the higher authority on which he or it depends, or if this authority has ceased to function, he or it exercises all the powers of this authority in the course of his/its professional activity and for urgent cases.

The law of 10 May thus established a new institutional reference framework within which the judiciary and the occupier interacted through the secretary-general of the Ministry of Justice. The secretaries-general were responsible for the most important administrative tasks within their respective ministries; overseeing the organization of all the departments reporting to them.[12] Even before the war, the secretaries-general would meet at times on global matters concerning several ministries; these meetings having then only an informal character.[13] This character, as we will see,

10 Loi du 10 mai 1940 relative aux délégations de pouvoirs en temps de guerre, *Pasinomie*, 6e série, Brussels: Bruylant, 1940, 198-199.

11 Leclercq 1946, 5.

12 Van den Wijngaert 1975, 1.

13 Van den Wijngaert 1975, 1.

was transformed in the context of the occupation, and especially after the first judicial crisis in 1942.

The scope of powers conferred on the secretaries-general in the framework of the delegation of power was deliberately vague. As Jean Servais had already noted in October 1935:

> The text needs to be very general and even a little vague, in order to lend itself to all the interpretations that patriotism and practical necessities could provoke if Belgium were to relive the 1914-1918 period.[14]

The military campaign on Belgian soil was very short. The fort of Eben-Emael, one of the most powerful in Europe and considered 'impregnable', fell in just over a day. In the days that followed, German troops advanced rapidly. Faced with the situation, the Belgian government, which believed that Belgium must continue to participate in the war alongside the Allies, prepared its departure to France. The King was asked to follow suit. However, Leopold III refused, judging that his role as commander-in-chief of the army compelled him to share the fate of the soldiers to the end, even at the risk of being taken prisoner.

With the departure of the Belgian government,[15] 16 and 17 May marked the concrete beginning of the administration of the country by the secretaries-general. Prudence and uncertainty characterized the attitude of these senior officials, who initially pointed to the unofficial nature of the committee and the narrowness of their newly acquired prerogatives.[16]

14 Letter from Honorary Public Prosecutor Servais to Secretary-General of the Ministry of Justice, Ernst de Bunswyck, 3 October, 1935, in *Archives Raoul Hayoit de Termicourt concernant le travail des institutions belges pendant l'occupation*, 1933-1973, CEGESOMA, AA mic 48.

15 The government moved to Paris, then Poitiers, Bordeaux, and Vichy. There was great hesitation as to which decisions to take, but, as early as 18 July, the return to Belgium of the members of the government-in-exile was formally prohibited by a German ordinance ('Ordonnance du 18 juillet 1940 relative à l'exercice d'une activité publique en Belgique', in *Verordnungsblatt*, 25 July 1940, No. 1, page 132). At the beginning of August, Prime Minister Hubert Pierlot was finally convinced that the government-in-exile should establish itself in London. Nevertheless, the ministers were far from complete in the British capital. Only Pierlot, Albert de Vleeschauwer (Minister of the Colonies), Paul-Henri Spaak (Minister of Foreign Affairs), and Camille Gutt (Minister of Finance), installed their government-in-exile in October 1940, dividing ministerial responsibilities among them ('Gouvernement de Londres' 2008, 212). They would now address the Belgian people via BBC airwaves. Most other ministers resigned on 27 August and remained in France.

16 Van den Wijngaert 1975, 13.

2.3 Role and Positioning of the Judiciary during the Events of May 1940

During this period of great uncertainty, the senior magistrates, like other notables remaining in the country, were called upon to discuss urgent issues.[17] As members of the establishment with their legal knowledge, the senior magistrates were authoritative figures. The gravity of the events compelled them to move beyond their traditional reserve and conferred on their legal opinions a real political influence.

Among these judicial figures that marked this period, one should mention the Attorney General ('avocat général') at the Court of Cassation, Raoul Hayoit de Termicourt – "a veritable incarnation of the judiciary".[18] On 24 May 1940, he gave an opinion to the King which greatly influenced the history of the country.[19] The King wanted to replace the ministers in exile in order to have a new government at his side to negotiate with the occupier. Not knowing whether the Constitution authorized him to do so, Léopold III turned to Hayoit de Termicourt, in whom he had particular trust, as testified by his proposing to him in March 1939 the post of Prime Minister.[20] In a consultation he sent to the King on 24 May, Hayoit de Termicourt opined that "the appointment of new ministers is not currently essential to the administration of the country," stating that a countersignature (i.e. the signature of at least one minister of the current government) would need to be obtained before any ministerial appointment.[21] Consequently, Leopold III turned, on 26 May, to the government which was then in Paris.[22] Faced with the negative answer received from it, the King considered himself in an impossible position. The government-in-exile, which supported the continuation of the war, remained legitimate. Hayoit de Termicourt's opinion would be the subject of criticism after the war. Part of the legal doctrine considers, in fact, the King to enjoy complete freedom of choice regarding his ministers; this avoids the risk of an institutional blockage if the ministers

17 For example Gérard-Libois and Gotovich 1971, 167-199.

18 Bayot 1971, 12.

19 'Note remise par Hayoit au Roi, à sa demande', in *Documents en relation avec la campagne des 18 jours, la capitulation et le problème de la restructuration politique*, in *Archives de Hendrik De Man*, 1940, CEGESOMA, AA 624/120; *idem* dans: *Archives Raoul Hayoit de Termicourt concernant le travail des institutions belges pendant l'occupation, 1933-1973, Documents concernant la Campagne des Dix-huit jours, 1940-1943*, CEGESOMA, AA mic 48, 24/5/1940.

20 He declined the offer (Stengers 1992, 46-47).

21 Cf. item I in 'Note remise par Hayoit au Roi, à sa demande, 24/5/1940', in *Archives Raoul Hayoit de Termicourt concernant le travail des institutions belges pendant l'occupation, 1933-1973, Documents concernant la Campagne des Dix-huit jours, 1940-1943*, CEGESOMA, AA mic 48.

22 Stengers 1992, 44.

of the outgoing government refuse to countersign the appointment of their successors.[23]

On 28 May, the Belgian population learned of the unconditional surrender of Belgium and of the King's status as a prisoner of war.[24] The King's attitude to the events was strongly condemned by Belgian Prime Minister, Hubert Pierlot, who, in a radio speech the same day, called for the continuation of the fight alongside the Allies. This break between the King and his ministers worried the establishment that had remained in the country and, in particular, the bar and the Brussels judiciary.[25] The senior figures, fearing – and the future would prove them right – a division of the Belgian population around the position of the King, sought to avoid this rupture. A meeting was held on 29 May, chaired by former Finance Minister Albert-Edouard Janssen. At least six senior magistrates were apparently present,[26] along with representatives of the bar, politicians, and bankers. They agreed to try to obtain and publish a declaration by the King giving the Belgian people an opportunity to understand their sovereign's political and military choices. Cardinal Van Roey, solicited for this mission, met the King on 31 May, after Hitler had authorized the interview.[27] The Cardinal's pastoral letter,[28] the outcome of the interview with Leopold III, containing a series of declarations defending the King and justifying his actions, was read in churches during mass on 2 and 9 June 1940.[29]

After meeting with the King, Van Roey organized, together with the President of the Bar Council ('bâtonnier de l'Ordre des avocats') of the Court of Cassation, Paul Veldekens, a "meeting of some personalities whom the

23 According to historian Jean Stengers, Hayoit de Termicourt probably did not act out of political calculation – which one might be tempted to suspect – he simply made a mistake owing to lacking the necessary documentation (Stengers 1992, 44-45).

24 Until June 1944, this captivity was comparable to house arrest at the Laeken Palace.

25 Etienne Verhoeyen comes to the conclusion that the initial initiative in this process indeed came from these two groups of the *'judicial family'* (Cf. Verhoeyen 1978, 221-242).

26 Jamar and Gesché, respectively First President and Prosecutor-General at the Court of Cassation; de Lichtervelde, Collard, and Van Durme, respectively First President, General Prosecutor, and General Advocate at the Brussels Court of Appeal; as well as the President of the Brussels Court of First Instance, Gilson de Rouvreux (Verhoeyen 1978, 228).

27 On this occasion, the Cardinal handed a legal opinion to Leopold III, stressing the legality of the act of the capitulation of the King as commander-in-chief of the army. A countersignature was not required for this act, contrary to what was erroneously advanced by Pierlot in his broadcast speech. This opinion had been prepared by a trio of eminent jurists: advocate-general Raoul Hayoit de Termicourt, and former ministers Joseph Pholien and Albert Devèze.

28 The pastoral letter of 31 May 1940 is published, *inter alia*, in Verhoeyen 1978, 241-242 and Dantoing 1991, 58.

29 Boudens1996, 13.

Cardinal could apprise of the situation".[30] Among the eight people selected for this meeting were the two highest magistrates in the country: the first President of the Court of Cassation, Jean Jamar,[31] and its Prosecutor General, Adolphe Gesché.[32] All expressed their desire to support the King. At this meeting, dated 1 June, Jamar declared that the members of the Court of Cassation opted for continuity of the executory formula 'in the name of the King'[33], whereas the government-in-exile had ordered, by its decree-law of 28 May 1940 that, 'establishing that the King is unfit to reign'[34] the decrees and sentences of the Belgian courts and tribunals were now to be pronounced 'in the name of the Belgian people'.[35]

2.4 The Consolidation of the Powers of the Secretaries-General after the Capitulation

Germany established a military administration, under the direction of Infantry General von Falkenhausen.[36] The introduction of a military administration excluded, in the short term, the annexation of the occupied

30 Verhoeyen 1978, 231.

31 On Jamar's role during the war, consult Hansen 2008.

32 Conférence du samedi 1er juin 1940, à 11 heures, à la Fondation universitaire à Bruxelles. Cf. Verhoeyen 1978, 232.

33 Executory formula prescribed by the Royal Decree of 23 February 1934.

34 'Arrêté-loi du 28 mai 1940 réglant la formule exécutoire des arrêts et jugements des cours et tribunaux, des ordonnances, mandants de justice et de tous actes emportant exécution parée', in *Bulletin usuel des lois et arrêtés, Législation promulguée par le gouvernement belge en exil, mai 1940-31 décembre 1943*, Brussels: Bruylant, s.d., p. 1.

35 In his *Mémoires de guerre*, Joseph Jamar justifies the decision taken with respect to the executory formula with the following reflections: "The insertion of the executory formula on the first authentic copy of the judgments is not the work of the judicial authority, but the work of the clerk of court, a mandated agent of the executive power; the judiciary cannot in this respect give orders to the clerk. The Germans did not indicate any desire to have the name of their governor-general included in the formula. On the other hand, the Belgian administration continued to exist under the direction of the secretaries-general. No authority would have thought of removing from the formula the name of Leopold III, King of the Belgians, the legitimate sovereign" (Joseph JAMAR, *Mémoires de guerre 1940-1944*, CEGESOMA, AB 778, pp. 14-15). See also: Van den Wijngaert 1975, 33 and Verhoeyen 1978, 234.

36 This military administration extended to Belgium, with the exception of its eastern parts annexed to the Reich (Eupen, Malmedy and Saint-Vith) as well as to the French departments of Nord and Pas-de-Calais. These two French departments had been cut off from the rest of France by the rapid advance of the German troops in the region between Laon and the coast. In the absence of a military administration in the rest of France, the two departments were attached to the territory governed by von Falkenhausen (Kossmann 1963, 309). Among the historians who have analyzed this choice, we refer in particular to Albert de Jonghe: De Jonghe 1972 and De Jonghe 1974-1984. In July 1944, Hitler would order the introduction of a civil administration.

territories. On the contrary, it involved the "superposition on the same territory of two sovereignties and in any case of two administrations".[37] In preparing for the occupation administration in the West, the principles of the continuation of indigenous services and respect for the 1907 Hague Convention were emphasized.

Article 43 of this international convention makes it a duty for the occupying power to ensure the maintenance of order and public life in the occupied country. In the exercise of this administrative mission, the occupying power is required to respect, "unless absolutely prevented, the laws in force in the country". However, the Hague Convention is extremely imprecise, allowing the Germans to define what constituted being 'absolutely prevented'.

As early as 10 May, the Germans announced their intention to keep the Belgian institutions in place and to assume only a supervisory role. The proclamation, issued by the Commander-in-Chief of the German Army, Walther von Brauchitsch, stated that: "the local authorities may continue their activities providing they observe a loyal attitude towards the German Army."[38] In his 'Notice to the Entire Press in the Occupied Western Territories' of the same day, Von Brauchitsch furthermore stated that the orders of the German military leaders would have force of law during the occupation and would prevail over domestic law.[39] In this way, Belgian and German legislation coexisted in Belgium during the occupation. The ordinances issued by the occupier did not become part of national legislation; they were only provisional, limited to the duration of the occupation.[40]

From the outset, the Germans aimed at a modus vivendi with local institutions. For them, this situation had the double advantage of (a) facilitating a return to calm and (b) tying up only a small number of German troops to administer the country. Very quickly, and at this stage informally, German military officials took the pulse of the Belgian civil authorities remaining in the country,[41] especially the secretaries-general. On the whole, the attitude of the secretaries-general regarding their powers was marked, at the very

The ephemeral nature of the latter did not fundamentally alter the relationship between the judiciary and the occupier.

37 Burrin 2004, 94.

38 'Proclamation à la population de la Belgique', in *Heeresgruppen-Verordnungsblatt für die besetzten Gebiete*, No 1, 10 May 1940, p. 2.

39 'Notice destinée à toute la presse dans les territoires occupés de l'ouest', in *Heeresgruppen-Verordnungsblatt für die besetzten Gebiete*, No. 1, 10 May 1940, p. 16.

40 'Note sur la nature des décrets de l'occupant', in *Archives Hayoit de Termicourt*, CEGESOMA, AA 48/14.

41 Gérard-Libois and Gotovich, p.186; Van den Wijngaert 1975, 13.

beginning of the occupation, by a certain degree of wait-and-see. To learn more about the will of the government, an exchange of letters took place, as late as 15 May, between the Committee of Secretaries-General, represented at this time by Alexandre Delmer, Secretary-General of the Ministry of Public Works, and Prime Minister Pierlot. The secretaries-general were seeking clarification on the interpretation of the law of 10 May, but the Prime Minister remained relatively vague in stating that it was impossible for him to foresee the cases of application of the law that could arise during the occupation.[42]

At first, the secretaries-general, uncertain as to the type of occupation that was going to be established,[43] took their inspiration from a final draft ministerial decree of Pierlot's cabinet of 16 May, which, as a result of the hasty departure to France that same day, had not been enacted.[44] According to this decree, the power of a secretary-general cannot go beyond the scope of the delegation conferred on him by his minister:

> In the event of the absence or incapacity of the Minister and without prejudice to the delegations that may be granted to the heads of administration, the secretary-general shall be responsible for dispatching all administrative matters pertaining to the Department and signing, for the Minister, in conformity with existing laws and regulations, all items except those requiring ministerial countersignature.[45]

Once the military administration was finally installed and functioning, the question of the limits of the delegated powers – and, in particular, that of the legislative power of the secretaries-general – rapidly required clear answers. On 1 June, upon his arrival in Brussels, Wilhelm van Randenborgh, director of the department for the monitoring of the Belgian legal system and a specialist in legal matters, met with the newly appointed Secretary-General

42 'Pierlot, Premier Ministre, à Delmer, Secrétaire-général du Ministère des Travaux publics', 15 May 1940, in *Archives Hayoit de Termicourt*, CEGESOMA, mic 48/15.

43 Thus, the acting secretary-general of the Ministry of Justice, Jean Hubrecht, explained in 1944, the conception he had in 1940 of the scope of the powers of the secretaries-general: "This was a question I did not ask myself at that moment. My impression, strengthened again by my conversation with the minister, was that we would not stay long in office. We were under the impression of news published about Poland, where the officials had apparently immediately been driven out by the occupier" ('Procès-verbal d'audition de M. Hubrecht, en qualité de témoin', of 13 December 1944, in Rapports de réunions et rapports dans la commission d'enquête des secrétaires généraux CEGESOMA, AA 43/39, p.2).

44 Van den Wijngaert 1975, 11.

45 Charles and Dasnoy 1974, 38.

of Justice, Jean Hubrecht, and then with the Secretary-General of Public Health and Food Supply, Raymond Delhaye. The two senior officials were of the opinion that secretaries-general did not have the right to legislate.[46] Following these interviews, the Militärverwaltung (military administration) addressed specific questions, to which the secretaries-general were asked to reply within ten days:

1. Do the secretaries-general in office in Brussels represent the government?
2. If so, which government, that of the King or the one presided over by Mr. Pierlot?
3. Do they possess legislative power?
4. If not, could the occupying power confer it on them?[47]

In this way, the secretaries-general were forced to abandon their wait-and-see attitude.[48] In a meeting of 3 June 1940, Secretary-General Jean Vossen "recalled that there can be no question of derogating from the existing laws and that, in the current state of the powers of the Secretaries-General, legislating is not possible". Nevertheless, in the face of pressure from the Germans and in order to limit their interference, it seemed almost inevitable to envisage a broader interpretation of the legislative power of the secretaries-general. Vossen continues in this direction: "In any case, we need to be duly authorized and covered for this purpose and it would be advisable to continue the conversations with the competent judicial authorities".[49]

Jean Hubrecht, charged with obtaining the opinion of the judiciary, visited the Attorney-General at the Brussels Court of Appeal, Norbert Van Durme on 3 June.[50] Other eminent magistrates were also present during this discussion, such as: the Acting President of the Court of Appeal, François Convent; the President of the Court of First Instance, Joseph Gilson de Rouvreux; and the Appeal Court Counsellor (and future Secretary-General of Justice), Gaston Schuind.[51] The interpretation given by the magistrates as to the powers of the secretaries-general was more extensive than the latter had judged until then. The magistrates took a pragmatic approach:

46 'Procès-verbal d'audition de M. Hubrecht, en qualité de témoin…', p. 3; Leclercq 1946, 2.
47 Gérard-Libois and Gotovich 1971, 188.
48 Leclercq 1946, 3.
49 Charles and Dasnoy 1974, 41.
50 Charles and Dasnoy 1974, 40.
51 Van den Wijngaert 1975, 4; Gérard-Libois and Gotovich 1971, 188.

maximizing the legislative power vested in the secretaries-general might serve in order to minimise and limit, insofar as possible, German interference.[52] Strangely, the possibility of the direct intervention of the occupier in the composition of the Committee of Secretaries-General – an essential question with regard to the attitude of the committee vis-à-vis the occupier – does not appear to have been taken into account by the jurists. The experience of the occupation would show, however, that the danger of the replacement of the persons meant by the law of 10 May was very real and that one of the major weaknesses of the system established by this law lay in the fact of not having made provision for it.[53] At the meetings in early June 1940, this question seems to have been neglected; the notables mentioned above seem to have been preoccupied with presenting, via the delegation, a strong Belgian power in the face of the occupier. The haste with which political decisions had to be taken at that moment probably did not allow the time needed for deep reflection and consideration of all the related issues.

On 5 June, the first official meeting took place between the secretaries-general and the occupying power in the person of the head of the military administration, Eggert Reeder. At this meeting, Reeder promised to "allow the Belgian administration to work with the widest autonomy, in the hope that it will justify the trust he was placing in its loyalty".[54] The autonomy promised by Reeder would, in fact, be very limited, with any decree having to be submitted to the occupier for approval prior to promulgation. Additionally, Eggert Reeder announced that the interpretation of the Hague Convention was reserved for the Militärverwaltung.[55]

52 Van den Wijngaert 1975, 4.

53 Thus, upon Liberation, Deputy Military Prosecutor Roger Ockrent, asking himself about the extent of the powers of the secretaries-general, noted that before looking at the limits of this power, it was essential to set the framework of persons covered by the law of 10 May 1940. He observes that: "This law, as its title indicates, is a delegation law. Its principle resides in the confidence of the legislator towards the officials in question. It goes without saying that Parliament, in passing this law, the King sanctioning it and enacting it, could place their trust only in the secretaries-general who remained in the country and who were in office by virtue of the laws, regulations and acts of appointment, taken by the bodies of the sovereign and independent Nation, authors of the law of 10 May 1940. They alone are 'functionaries' within the meaning of Article 5 of that law. Excluded from the benefit of the delegation would therefore appear to be those persons appointed, appointed, designated or charged with secretary-general functions under the enemy occupation [...]". Ockrent 1944, 43.

54 Charles and Dasnoy 1974, 42.

55 Van den Wijngaert 1975, 29.

On the question of the legislative activity of the secretaries-general, his position was clear:

> Exceptional periods, such as the one we are going through, call for exceptional measures. Legal provisions and decrees are designed for normal times. It is obvious that these can only partially respond to the current situation. It is for this reason that legislative measures must be taken to meet the needs and to ensure somewhat regular conditions.[56]

The German administration hoped to get the unpopular measures accepted more readily by having them issued by the Belgian authorities.[57]

The secretaries-general did not, at the outset, present any common front in terms of their analysis of the situation or attitude to be taken. In addition, they took no decisions without first consulting leading jurists, whether senior magistrates or politicians. Nevertheless, as time passed, they increasingly accepted the idea that "the abandonment of the regime of secretaries-general would entail such serious harm for the country that, in order to avoid this, great sacrifices must be made."[58]

The consultations continued in the days that followed. Jean Hubrecht met the highest authorities of the Court of Cassation – First President Jamar and Attorney-General Gesché – and informed them of the three possibilities envisaged at that moment by the military administration:

> the secretaries-general recognize themselves as having legislative powers, by resorting to a broad interpretation of the law of 10 May 1940; or
> the Germans delegate to the secretaries-general the right to issue decree-laws; or
> the secretaries-general confine themselves to executing the German ordinances, without legislating themselves.[59]

56 Charles and Dasnoy 1974, 42.

57 Certain people were not fooled by the German plans, like the Prince de Merode, who wrote in June 1940 that "the German authorities have preferred to leave to the Belgian authorities, whose precariousness they are aware of, the apparent and hateful responsibility for the measures of every kind and sanctions they had decided to apply […]". Quoted in Gérard-Libois and Gotovich 1971, 196-197.

58 'Notes personnelles sur plusieurs Secrétaires-généraux', s.d., in *Archives Raoul Hayoit de Termicourt concernant le travail des institutions belges pendant l'occupation, 1933-1973, Documents concernant la Campagne des Dix-huit jours, 1940-1943*, CEGESOMA AA mic 48.

59 'Procès-verbal d'audition de M. Hubrecht, en qualité de témoin', du 13 décembre 1944, in *Rapports de réunions et rapports dans la commission d'enquête des secrétaires généraux*, CEGESOMA, AA 43/39, p. 3.

Gesché and Jamar apparently advised opting for the first solution.[60]

On 9 June, Raymond Delhaye invited six senior figures from the worlds of politics, banking, and the judiciary to discuss the same issue.[61] At this first meeting, which was no longer restricted to jurists, the topic was discussed "in 'political' terms, that is to say in terms where the answer was motivated by considerations of strategy and tactics relating to the existence of the Belgian state and society in an occupation situation".[62] The possibility of a delegation of legislative power by the occupying power was definitively rejected in favour of a broad interpretation of the powers of the secretaries-general. At this meeting, magistrate Hayoit de Termicourt advocated the solution involving 'the lesser evil' ('politique du moindre mal'), in so doing formulating for the first time an expression which would go down in history as characterizing the political choices made under the occupation. Hayoit de Termicourt purportedly intervened in the 9 June discussions with the following words:

> It is quite obvious that the independence of our secretaries-general will not be complete, we are perfectly aware of it. But, between two evils, we must choose the lesser and I ask you: is not the continuation of public life by means of indigenous bodies, even under enemy control, a less harmful solution than the personal administration of the occupier and its constant interference in the management of the country?[63]

Then, referring to the experiences of the judiciary under the first German occupation, Hayoit de Termicourt explained that, for public prosecutors, administration by the occupier would represent a "subordination to this power in the normal measure of their dependence on the executive power", while for judges it would involve the "choice between resigning and direct collaboration with the occupier" (with, for the litigant, the risk of being delivered to German judges).[64]

60 'Procès-verbal d'audition de M. Hubrecht, en qualité de témoin…', p. 3.

61 Secretaries-general Raymond Delhaye and Jean Hubrecht, the lawyer and former Minister Joseph Pholien, the acting Chairman of the Board of Directors of the Banque de Bruxelles and former Minister of Finance Max-Léo Gérard, the governor of the Province of Brabant Baron Houtart, former Defence Minister Albert Devèze and Advocate General Raoul Hayoit de Termicourt.

62 Gérard-Libois and Gotovich 1971, 190.

63 Leclercq 1946, 3.

64 Leclercq 1946, 1-2.

The seven senior figures present at the meeting of 9 June 1940 were finally unanimous on the need to refuse delegation by the occupier and, consequently, to present the secretaries-general as the legitimate Belgian power. Prudence had given way to pragmatism: Article 5 of the Law of 10 May 1940 being intended to ensure the safeguarding of indigenous institutions, as well as administrative and economic recovery, by granting wide-ranging powers to the secretaries-general.[65] A Protocol of Understanding ('protocole d'accord') between the secretaries-general and the military administration was drawn up on 12 June. By this Protocol, the secretaries-general recognized "that ordinances made under the Hague Convention [...] are executed in the same way as the Belgian laws".[66]

As to Article 5 of the Law of 10 May 1940, they declared that it:

> authorizes each secretary-general, within the scope of his jurisdiction and in urgent cases, to issue decrees having the force of law. When several ministries are involved, the secretaries-general of these ministries will issue a joint decree. Each matter can therefore be settled with force of law by the secretaries-general, provided that it is not political in nature.[67]

The Belgian drafters involved in the formulation felt at this stage relatively reassured by the fact that the Protocol was anchored in the framework of the Hague Convention.[68] The right of veto of the head of the military administration with respect to the decrees of the secretaries-general was also set out in this text of 12 June.[69] The scope of the secretaries-general's powers was broad but limited to urgent cases and excluded political matters.

For the Germans, however, there remained a shadow in the picture. From the beginning of the occupation, one provision of the Belgian Constitution worried them particularly. Article 107 of the Constitution enjoins the courts not to apply, in a dispute submitted to them, an unlawful act of the executive power.[70] This is a fundamental feature of the Belgian judicial power,

65 Gérard-Libois and Gotovich 1971, 191-192.

66 'Protocole du 12 juin 1940', in Charles and Dasnoy 1974, 48-49.

67 'Protocole du 12 juin 1940', in Charles and Dasnoy 1974, 48-49.

68 'Procès-verbal d'audition de M. Hubrecht, en qualité de témoin...', p. 4.

69 Delhaye had tried in vain to get this clause removed from the protocol. Cf. Van den Wijngaert 1975, 29.

70 "Courts and tribunals shall enforce general, provincial, and local decrees only as long as they comply with the law."

inscribed in the Constitution in response to the abuses of the executive committed under the Dutch regime.[71]

The presence and repetition of the terms 'force de loi' (force of law) in the Protocol with regard to Article 5 of the Law of 10 May 1940, are therefore far from being innocent: the occupier was hoping to remove the control of legality by the courts and sought confirmation of this from Hubrecht:

> The occupying power essentially wanted to obtain assurance that any decrees that we might issue would be equated with royal decrees and that, consequently, the courts would not refuse to apply them. I pointed out to the representatives of the Military Commander that in Belgium the judiciary enjoyed a great deal of independence and that we were unable to give them the guarantees they seemed to expect from us.[72]

The final version of the Protocol, approved by the First President of the Court of Cassation, Jamar, was signed by all the secretaries-general on 17 June.[73]

Additional opinions, supporting the powers of the secretaries-general, as defined in the Protocol, were added during the autumn of 1940. For example, the one rendered on 20 September 1940 by the five members, all of whom were senior magistrates,[74] of the Advisory Committee on Administrative Litigation and General Administration ('Comité consultatif de contentieux administratif et d'administration générale');[75] and that submitted on 16 October 1940 by the Standing Committee of the Legislative Council ('Comité permanent du Conseil de Législation'),[76] composed mainly of magistrates from the Court of Cassation.[77]

71 Thonissen 1876, 326 et seq.

72 'Procès-verbal d'audition de M. Hubrecht, en qualité de témoin...', p. 4.

73 Van den Wijngaert 1975, 31.

74 Baron Paul Verhaegen, Honorary President of the Court of Cassation, the three counsellors to the Court of Cassation Hodüm, Fauquel, and Bail, and the First Advocate General at the Court of Cassation, Léon Cornil. Cf. Hanquet 1946, 37-38.

75 Hanquet 1946, 37.

76 In its consultation of 16 October 1940, the Legislative Council is appreciably more cautious with respect to the interpretation of the scope of the secretaries-general's powers by insisting on the prohibition of legislating in the political sphere and on the state of urgency as a prerequisite for any legislative measure ('Avis du Comité permanent du Conseil de Législation au Secrétaire-général du Ministère de la Justice, concernant la nomination éventuelle de bourgmestres-fonctionnaires, 16/10/1940', CEGESOMA, AA mic 48 / 16).

77 Composition: lawyer Resteau; First Advocate General at the Court of Cassation, Léon Cornil; Advocate General at the Court of Cassation, Raoul Hayoit de Termicourt; law professor at the Free University of Brussels and former magistrate, Henri de Page; Secretary-General of Justice, Ernst de Bunswyck: the Honorary Attorney General and Minister of State, Jean Servais; and the Counsellor at the Court of Cassation, Soenens. Cf. Hanquet 1946, 38.

3 The Judicial Crisis of the Summer of 1942

'It Is for the Life of a People that We Shall Have to Give Account One Day'[78]

During the first half of the occupation, the archives mention only one incident relating to a judicial review of the orders of the secretaries-general.[79] In September 1941, the Vice-President of the Court of First Instance in Ghent, Charles Reychler, handed down a judgment declaring illegal a decree involving a question of food supplies. The occupier suspended him in retaliation. Faced with this attack on the independence of the judiciary, the Court of Cassation threatened to go on strike if Reychler was not reinstated. The suspension was lifted a few weeks later and the matter went no further.

The situation became tense in 1942 when the Court of Cassation was in turn called upon to rule on the application of Article 107 of the Constitution to the acts of the secretaries-general.

3.1 The Origins of the Crisis

At the origin of the conflict between the judiciary and the military administration were the decrees creating the National Agriculture and Food Corporation ('Corporation nationale de l'agriculture et de l'alimentation' (CNAA)) and the introduction of administrative jurisdictions. On 27 August 1940, the Secretary-General at the Ministry of Agriculture and Food, De Winter, promulgated a decree establishing the CNAA,[80] a corporate body tasked with controlling production and food supply during the occupation. To speed up legal proceedings against fraud relating to food supplies, rationing, and price fixing, De Winter introduced an exceptional jurisdiction. By the decree of 15 February 1941, he established the Higher Administrative Jurisdiction ('Juridiction Administrative Supérieure') in order to circumvent the procedural slowness of the regular courts.[81] This procedure allowed

78 '*Secrétaire général de la Justice, Schuind, au Premier président de la Cour de cassation, Jamar, 31 mai 1942* (p. 13)', CEGESOMA, *Fonds Jamar*, No 106.

79 Memorandum entitled 'Suspension du Vice-Président Reichler, de Gand', CEGESOMA, *Fonds Jamar*, n° 70. See also the same archival fund, Nos 144 and 305.

80 'Création d'une corporation nationale de l'agriculture et de l'alimentation', in *Moniteur belge des arrêtés ministériels et autres arrêtés des Secrétaires généraux*, No 85, 30 August 1940, pp. 580-583.

81 'Arrêté instituant une procédure administrative en matière de répression des infractions concernant le ravitaillement, le rationnement et la fixation des prix', in *Moniteur belge*, n°52, 21 February 1941, p. 1175.

the administrative tribunals – i.e. the mayors and district commissioners ('commissaires d'arrondissement') in the first instance, and provincial governors and secretaries-general on appeal – to sanction infringements of the various decrees of the secretaries-general concerning food supplies. The judicial route was not totally absent from this procedure. The courts of appeal constituted a third instance. The administrative jurisdictions could also decide to report a case to the public prosecutor's office. This new administrative jurisdiction, which upset Belgian legal traditions, violated the principle of the separation of powers, because the mayors, governors, and secretaries-general do not fall under the judicial power, but rather the executive power, as underlined by the Brussels Bar Association in a motion of 14 March 1941.[82]

In March 1941, a Food Supply Control Service ('Service de Contrôle du Ravitaillement') was established, the agents of which could, inter alia, seize goods and control vehicles or buildings suspected of being used to hide food. During these 'visits', "the presence of the justice of the peace of the legal canton was not required, nor even the written authorization of this magistrate".[83]

During the following summer, affiliation to the CNAA (and hence financial contribution) become obligatory, accentuating the disfavour enjoyed by the institution among the population.[84] Faced with a large number of farmers refusing to pay their dues, CNAA leaders applied harsh measures to break the resistance. But these stringent measures only strengthened the climate of insurrection. With the measures taken by the Secretary-General of the Ministry of Agriculture and Food Supply no longer sufficient in the eyes of the Germans to guarantee 'Ruhe und Ordnung' ('peace and order') in the occupied territory, the military administration intervened by promulgating an ordinance dated 2 August 1941.[85] This Ordinance on Administrative Criminal Law in Belgium ('Ordonnance concernant le droit pénal administratif en Belgique') amended the De Winter Decree of 15 February and excluded appeals to the ordinary courts against decisions

82 'Lettre de l'Ordre des Avocats à la Cour d'Appel de Bruxelles, Cabinet du Bâtonnier, adressée au Secrétaire Général du Département de la Justice' in *Archives de guerre Jean Vossen, secrétaire-général des Affaires Intérieures*, CEGESOMA, mic 73.

83 Colignon 1993, 67.

84 Louveaux 1981, 65-66.

85 'Deuxième ordonnance du 2 août 1941 concernant le droit pénal administratif en Belgique', in *Verordnungsblatt des Militärbefehlshabers in Belgien und Nordfrankreich für die besetzten Gebiete Belgiens und Nordfrankreichs, herausgegeben vom Militärbefehlshaber (Militärverwaltungschef)*, No 51, 13 August 1941, p. 1.

of the administrative courts in order to speed up proceedings against the fraudsters.[86] The German intervention discredited the CNAA even further, which looked increasingly like an institution subservient to German interests.

Despite the obvious unconstitutionality surrounding the CNAA legislation, the judiciary was not as quick to protest as were the lawyers.[87] It was only in the spring of 1942 that the question of the legitimacy of the secretaries-general's decrees became a subject of open opposition between many Belgian magistrates and the occupier.

Summonses-constraining orders were sent by the CNAA to a large number of farmers in the Liège region to collect unpaid contributions. Liège lawyer Paul Tschoffen, a former Minister of Justice, and lawyer Jean Discry pleaded in front of the Louveigné Justice of the Peace, Guillaume Hanson, on behalf of 121 farmers who had refused to comply. Hanson handed down his judgment on 20 March 1942, a judgment that would cost him his freedom and his life.[88] Referring to Article 107 of the Constitution, he refused "to apply these orders because of their illegality, the law of 10 May 1940 permitting only the taking of urgent and necessary measures," which was not the case here.[89] Thereby, he declared illegal the decree setting up the CNAA and, in so doing, the Louveigné judgment called into question the modus vivendi on which relations between occupier and the occupied were based, and triggered the judicial crisis. Notwithstanding the German ban on its dissemination, the Louveigné verdict very quickly became known in Wallonia and Brussels.[90] During the months of March and April 1942, this decision was followed by other justices of the peace.[91]

86 *'No appeal against administrative sanctions decisions is admissible in the ordinary courts* [...] *Instead of being brought before the ordinary courts, the appeal may be brought before the administrative authority* [...]', *idem*, p. 2.

87 Gotovitch 1972, 6.

88 *Jugements de la justice de paix de Louveignée, Liège et Schaerbeek dans l'affaire paysans contre le C.N.A.A.*, 1942, CEGESOMA, AA 270; *Jugement rendu par Monsieur le Juge Hanson dans une affaire concernant la Corporation Agricole*, CEGESOMA, AA 271/12.
Hanson was arrested on 29 April 1942 and died on 26March 1944 in a German prison.

89 Louveaux 1981, 624.

90 *Meldungen aus* extract *Belgien und Nordfrankreich, Nr. 7 / 42,* 1 August 1942, BA-MA, RW 36/400, pp. 424-425.

91 'Juge de Paix de Walcourt: Mr Clément, En cause Neirinck contre Groupement Général Cheptel, Viande et sous-produits, contre Etat Belge Ministère de l'agriculture et du Ravitaillement', undated, in *Documents ZERO*, CEGESOMA, AA 1078/850; 'Jugement rendu par Monsieur le Juge de Paix de Schaerbeek – 1er canton, le 15 avril 1942', in *Documents Zéro*, CEGESOMA, AA 1078/1034/55.

In the eyes of the occupier and the collaborationist movements, this series of lawsuits around the legality of the secretaries-general's decrees had been premeditated by a handful of 'politicized' lawyers who had encouraged the farmers' complaints in order to undermine the authority of the secretaries-general. Lawyers like Tschoffen and Discry were indeed hostile to innovations inspired by the New Order, and it is "reasonable to doubt that their recourse to justice was devoid of ulterior motives".[92] Joeri Michielsen went even further:

> Tschoffen challenged the constitutionality of the decree establishing an administrative criminal proceeding, probably intending to go before the Court of Cassation in order to get an explicit ruling on the status of the decrees of the secretaries-general.[93]

While the Secretary-General of Agriculture and Food Supplies tendered his resignation to the Chairman of the Committee of Secretaries-General, the Director of the CNAA immediately appealed against the Louveigné judgment before the Liège Court of First Instance. The proceedings, announced for 20 March, were adjourned to 3 April 1942, pending proceedings before the Court of Cassation to decide whether the courts could examine the legality of decrees of secretaries-general (in this case the decree of 15 February 1941, establishing the Higher Administrative Jurisdiction). The military administration was expecting the Court of Cassation to declare itself incompetent on this question; this would solve the problem in favour of the occupier, but without its having to intervene.[94]

3.2 The Position of the Court of Cassation and the German Response

The judgment of the Court of Cassation[95] confirmed the right of the secretaries-general to take measures which, in times of peace, fall within the legislative power. It should be noted that this judgment was handed down under the chairmanship of Hodum and that the rapporteur was Fauquel – two of the five magistrates on the Advisory Committee on Administrative Disputes and General Administration who had 'endorsed' the Protocol

92 Colignon 1993, 74.

93 Michielsen 2004, 55.

94 *Die belgische Justiz und Gesetzgebung*, BA-MA, RW 36/397, p. 70.

95 'Copie d'un arrêt rendu le 30 mars 1942 par la 2e chambre de la Cour de Cassation', in *Documents ZERO*, CEGESOMA, AA 1078/1034/89.

in 1940. At the same time, however, the Court examined the limits of the power of the secretaries-general. Thus, Article 5 of the Law of 10 May 1940 "excludes any political measure and any other measure that would breach either the Constitution or the essential principles of national legislation, and in particular those relating to various jurisdictions". Moreover, each secretary-general cannot issue decrees that concern any area of administration other than his own. But, above all, the Court of Cassation reiterated that the legality of the orders of the secretaries-general can and must be reviewed by the courts and tribunals.[96] It was this item of the judgment of the Court of Cassation that especially posed a problem to the military administration:

> Das Kernproblem lag darin, dass die Generalsekretäre zwar auf Grund des Vollmachtgesetzes vom 10.5.1940 auf allen Gebieten Verordnungen erlassen konnten, dass aber die Rechtsgültigkeit dieser Verordnungen jederzeit der rechtlichen Nachprüfung unterlag, und dass es selbst auf lebenswichtigsten Gebieten keine Möglichkeit gab, ein Gesetz zu erlassen, das von vornherein allen Angriffen entzogen gewesen wäre. Diese Schwäche wurde in dem Augenblick zu einer ernsten Gefahr, [...] zu einer Lähmung der gesamten Verwaltung zu führen drohte.[97] (The key problem was that, while the secretaries-general could, based on the Delegation Law of 10.5.1940, issue decrees in all areas, the legal validity of these decrees was subject at all times to judicial control, and that even in vital areas there was no possibility of issuing a law which was from the outset safe from attack. This weakness became at this time a serious danger [...], threatening to paralyse the entire administration.)

The military administration, very dissatisfied with the decision of the Court of Cassation, reacted promptly. On 1 April, it sent a draft ordinance to the Secretary-General of Justice. This text prohibited the courts and tribunals from examining the legality of the decrees of the secretaries-general. The military administration gave the Secretary-General of Justice a fortnight to find a 'Belgian solution' to the 'problem', failing which the ordinance would be published. This draft ordinance was discussed during several meetings of the Committee of Secretaries-General. Most of them were well aware of

96 *Die belgische Justiz und Gesetzgebung*, BA-MA, RW 36/397, p. 71.

97 *Gruppe Justiz an das Oberkommando des Heeres, Generalquartier*, 6 July 1942, BA-MA, RW 36/400, pp. 21-22.

the blockage that the publication of the ordinance risked causing.[98] The Committee of Secretaries-General, therefore, made numerous proposals to the occupier. All were rejected. Several extensions of deadlines were requested.[99] Deadlocked, the Committee of Secretaries-General turned again to the Legislative Council, but this shared the position of the Court of Cassation.[100] Finally, the military administration issued its ordinance on 14 May 1942:

> Review of the legality of the general decrees of the secretaries-general taken or to be taken in future with express reference to the law of 10 May 1940 on the delegation of powers in time of war is forbidden.[101]

The German Ordinance of 14 May 1942 sent a shockwave through the Belgian judicial world. A shockwave made worse, two days later, by the arrest, during a full hearing, of the lawyers at the origin of the Louveigné judgment. Paul Albert Stasse, Paul Tschoffen, and Smolders were imprisoned. On 17 May 1942, The Prosecutor-General and the First President of the Court of Cassation attempted, unsuccessfully, to intervene with General von Falkenhausen to obtain their release, stressing that the lawyers had "used a right [to bring an appeal under Article 107] that is denied to them only by an order of the occupying authority issued subsequent to the acts which motivated their arrest".[102] The two senior magistrates also protested against the conditions of these arrests (during an in camera hearing and without prior warning to the President of the Court), thereby undermining the dignity of the judiciary.

The Court of Cassation, meeting on 19 and 20 May, opined that, as a result of this ordinance "the courts will no longer be able to accept or instigate legal proceedings based on the illegality of one of these decrees [based on the Law of 10 May 1940],"[103] because the question of legality is, in essence,

98 Charles and Dasnoy 1974, 131-153.

99 Van den Wijngaert 1975, 254-255.

100 *Die belgische Justiz und Gesetzgebung*, RW 36/397, p. 73.

101 'Ordonnance du 14 mai 1942, relative à l'application de certains arrêtés des Secrétaires généraux', in *Verordnungsblatt des Militärbefehlshabers in Belgique und Nordfrankreich für die besetzten Gebiete Belgiens und Nordfrankreichs, herausgegeben vom Militärbefehlshaber (Militärverwaltungschef)*, No 76, 15 May 1942, p. 915.

102 'Protestation du procureur général près la Cour de cassation, Hayoit de Termicourt, et du premier président de la Cour de cassation, Jamar; 17 mai 1942', CEGESOMA, Fonds Jamar, No 105.

103 'Cour de cassation, Assemblée générale du 20 mai 1942', in *Archives du réseau ZERO*, CEGESOMA, 1S1 – ZERO – AA 1078/1034/149, p. 2.

indivisible from the rest of the dispute. Therefore, if the courts cannot rule on the dispute, their operation is impossible.

The minutes of the general meeting of the Court of Cassation, acting as 'supreme guardian of the law', was rapidly disseminated through the courts. A large part of the Belgian courts suspended all criminal proceedings related to the orders of the secretaries-general.

On 29 May 1942, the military administration requested that the Secretary-General of Justice make known to the judiciary the firm position of the occupying authority with regard to the application of the Order of 14 May 1942, and demanded that the distribution of the minutes of the general meeting of the Court of Cassation be ceased. It made known that such distribution would henceforward be considered as an 'incitement to strike action' and hinted that severe measures would be taken against any magistrates who did not comply with this prohibition.[104] Contrary to the expectations of the occupier, the Secretary-General, a former senior magistrate, affirmed his solidarity with the judiciary:

> 1) Personally, I do not see the possibility to make known to the judiciary the sanctions which you envisage with regard to it;
> 2) Personally, I do not recognize myself as having the right to apply such sanctions;
> 3) If the envisaged sanctions were to be taken against members of the judiciary, I should conclude that my functioning at the Ministry of Justice is unsuccessful, making it impossible for me to pursue it.
>
> Accordingly, I would ask you to apply against me the sanctions you might think fit to take against the members of the judiciary.[105]

The Committee of Secretaries-General at once set to work to find a 'Belgian solution' to put an end to the judicial crisis, which concerned many Belgians who still remembered the tragic consequences of the strike of the judiciary in 1918. The military administration waited for proposals while announcing the non-payment of salaries and the imprisonment of magistrates taking part in the strike. It tried, by every means, to eradicate this first strike movement, well aware that the country could be administered only by relying

104 *Reeder à Schuind*, 29 May 1942, in *Documents ZERO*, CEGESOMA, AA 1078/1034/156, or a copy of the same letter in German in: BA-MA, RW 36/400, p. 300.

105 *Gaston Schuind, General Secretary, Ministry of Justice to Egmond Reeder, President of the Military Administration*, 30 May 1942, BA-MA, RW 36/400, p. 293. This statement would only amplify the demands from collaborationist circles who regularly called for Schuind's replacement (See BA-MA, RW 36/400, pp. 297-299 and 319-328).

on the Belgian institutions.[106] From both the material and psychological standpoints, it would have been difficult, if not impossible, to replace Belgian officials with German staff.[107]

3.3 The Pact

In the days that followed, intense oral and written exchanges took place between Secretary-General Schuind and First President of the Court of Cassation Jamar. The two men were under pressure, the former by the occupying authority, which wanted to end the control of the legality of the decrees of the secretaries-general, and the latter by the Cassation Bar Association and the Brussels Bar Council ('conseil de l'ordre'), which were ready to support the judiciary in the event of a repetition of the 1918 strike. The tension grew by the day, with the legal uncertainty engendered by the crisis having repercussions on the ground. The population and the control bodies were questioning the legality of provisions relating to food supplies, a crucial issue at a time when famine loomed. The situation on the ground was, to say the least, confusing and the authority of the secretaries-general severely undermined. The occupier demanded that a way be quickly found out of this impasse.

Secretary-General of Justice Schuind found, in the law of 7 September 1939 conferring extraordinary powers on the King, the legal face-saver, which made it possible to satisfy the German interests. Under this law, the King, confronted with urgency and necessity, may, in time of war, make "provisions having force of law by decree deliberated in the Council of Ministers". These extraordinary powers covered many areas and were aimed at maintaining public tranquillity and health, food supplies, the state's financial income, and the regular functioning of judicial and administrative institutions. The idea was to transfer these exceptional legislative powers from the person of the King to the Committee of Secretaries-General. In this way, the decree-laws of the secretaries-general would have the force of law and their legality could no longer be reviewed by the courts and tribunals. At first, the Court of Cassation took a particularly legalistic stance, distinguishing between the role of the executive, tasked with looking after the material interests of

106 *Die belgische Justiz und Gesetzgebung*, BA-MA, RW 36/397, p. 75.

107 This is a recurring theme in the reports of the military administration and especially in the *Group Justice* (see *Gruppe Justiz an das Oberkommando des Heeres, Generalquartier*, 6 July 1942, BA-MA, RW 36/400, 21).

the population, and the judiciary in charge of maintaining the country's legal traditions:

> [The members of the Court] are fully aware that the public authorities, and first and foremost the secretaries-general, have the mission of safeguarding, to the best of their abilities and within the framework of our institutions, the life of the Belgian people. Yet we cannot forget that the safeguarding of the soul of a people and its fundamental traditions is as important as that of its material subsistence.[108]

The Court also displayed a certain touchiness:

> Thus, the collaboration of the judiciary is today considered essential to the respect for the regulations concerning the food supply of the country, whereas yesterday this collaboration was pushed aside or progressively restricted. Moreover, you seem to be saying that it is the Judiciary that will be held responsible for the fact that, tomorrow perhaps, the Belgian population will be subject to the military law of the occupying authority in terms of food supplies.[109]

The German administration regarded Schuind's proposal as "eine brauchbare Grundlage für eine Staatsverwaltung" (a viable basis for a state administration).[110] The Court of Cassation, "taking into account the exceptionally tragic situation in which the country finds itself",[111] ended up siding with this proposal, but specified that the restrictions of the Law of 10 May 1940 would continue to apply. In other words, the courts could still examine whether the decree-laws were political in nature or whether they changed the political structure of the country, in which case they would be illegal.[112] The military administration refused these conditions: the decree-laws to be promulgated on the basis of the Law of 7 September 1939 were to have the character of law and their legality was in no event to be examined. The crisis then reached a climax, with the Secretary-General going so far as to request being replaced.

108 '*Premier président de la Cour de cassation, Jamar, au secrétaire général de la Justice, Schuind, 4 juin 1942*', CEGESOMA, *Fonds Jamar*, No 106.

109 *Ibidem*.

110 *Gruppe Justiz an Herrn MVVchef von Craushaar*, 5 June 1942, BA-MA, RW 36/400, p. 215.

111 '*Premier président de la Cour de cassation, Jamar, au secrétaire général de la Justice, Schuind, 4 juin 1942*', CEGESOMA, *Fonds Jamar*, No 106.

112 *Die belgische Justiz und Gesetzgebung*, RW 36/397, p. 76.

At the same time, the Sicherheitsdienst (security service) discovered, following a denunciation, a strike fund in Liège, intended for preparing passive resistance by senior Belgian officials.[113] Part of this fund was intended to support magistrates in the event of a strike. The funds were immediately confiscated by the occupier, while Cassation Counsellor Nestor Louveaux and First Attorney-General Léon Cornil, who had purportedly participated in setting up the fund, were arrested.[114] Winded by this case, the Court of Cassation eventually yielded to the occupier's demands.[115] On 25 June 1942, President of the Court of Cassation Jamar wrote to the Secretary-General of Justice.[116] On behalf of the Court, he stated that the courts and tribunals could not examine the political character of the decree-laws of the secretaries-general issued on the basis of the Law of 7 September 1939. The Court of Cassation, however, posed a condition: that these decree-laws based on the 1939 Act be adopted by the Committee of Secretaries-General and not by a single secretary-general. The legality of the decrees based on the Law of 10 May could, for its part, always be examined by the courts.

The military administration had achieved its goal: a "Belgian" solution whereby the acts of the secretaries-general had real force of law. This end to the crisis was felt to be a victory by the military administration, as evidenced by the letter of the Gruppe Justiz to headquarters in Berlin: "Die Vormachtstellung der Justiz, die sie bisher mit der Entscheidung über die Rechtsgültigkeit der VOen der GSe innehatte, ist gebrochen".[117] (The dominant position that the judiciary had until now, with the right to determine the legality of the decrees of the secretaries-general, has been broken.)

The minutes of the general meeting of the Court of Cassation having been made public, the occupier asked in return that the letter of the First President of the Court, written on behalf of the Court and blessing the 'Pact', also be made public. The Court of Cassation, in its weakened position, even accepted two of the modifications to its original text required by the

113 *Geheimer Bericht des Beauftragten des Chefs der Sicherheitspolizei und des SD für den Bereich des Militärbefehlshabers in Belgien und Nordfrankreich. Protokollierte Aussage des Vertrauensmannes der hiesigen Dienststelle,* 15 June 1942, BA-MA, RW 36/399, p. 100. See also: Archives générales du Royaume, *Ministère de la Justice, Secrétariat général, Série III,* n°2886.

114 They would be imprisoned for two months (*Vermerk einer Unterredung mit Generalsekretär Schuind,* 19 June 1942, BA-MA, RW 36/399, page 103 and Archives of the Court of Cassation, personal file of Nestor Louveaux).

115 *Die belgische Justiz und Gesetzgebung,* BA-MA, RW 36/397, p. 77.

116 *Cour de cassation, Cabinet du Premier Président. Lettre adressée à Monsieur le Secrétaire Général du ministère de la Justice,* 25 juin 1942, BA-MA, RW 36/399, p. 124.

117 *Gruppe Justiz an das Oberkommando des Heeres, Generalquartier* (Gruppe Justiz to the Oberkommando, General Headquarters), 6 July 1942, BA-MA, RW 36/400, p. 22.

occupier.[118] The military authority was of the opinion that the text as it then stood could "incite certain people to ill-considered and spectacular attitudes".[119] The amended letter, dated 30 June 1942, was intended to be sent to all magistrates.[120]

The military administration, having achieved its goal, suspended its order of 14 May 1942, and the lawyers Tschoffen, Stasse, and Smolders were released.[121] The decrees of the Committee of secretaries-general concerning the CNAA and the administrative procedure were rapidly re-promulgated as decree-laws based on the Law of 7 September 1939 and their legality was no longer examined by the courts.[122]

The fact that the legality of the secretaries-general's decree-laws could no longer be examined by the courts represented a significant diminution of the power of the Belgian institutions as it existed before the occupation, while the powers of a new institution, the Committee of Secretaries-General, was considerably strengthened, aided by the 'assistance' of the German military administration. This fact was condemned not only by the underground press, but also by the government-in-exile. The latter expressed, via radio broadcasts from London, its anger at the increasingly visible change in the Belgian institutions under the influence of the occupier.[123]

A second judicial crisis occurred in late 1942 in the context of the creation of 'large agglomerations'. As this does not involve the central question of the legality of the secretaries-general's decrees and given its lesser intensity, we will not address it in these pages. It should be noted only that, if the intensity of the crisis were less, it was because the judiciary, in this case the Court of Cassation and the Brussels Appeal Court, which had suspended their hearings, yielded relatively quickly to the ultimatum of the occupier to resume – within three days and without conditions – their duties. Reeder, through Secretary-General Schuind, threatened the magistrates with harsh measures and drew their attention to an order in preparation – to be promulgated four

118 About these final negotiations between the Court of Cassation and the military administration, see: BA-MA, RW 36/399, pp. 137, 139, 143 and 147.

119 'Schuind (relayant les directives du Chef de l'Administration militaire) à Jamar, 30 juin 1942', CEGESOMA, Fonds Jamar, No 106.

120 *Die belgische Justiz und Gesetzgebung*, BA-MA, RW 36/397, p. 78.

121 *Edmond Reeder à Gaston Schuind*, 18 juillet 1942, BA-MA, RW 36/400, p. 18.

122 *Die belgische Justiz und Gesetzgebung*, BA-MA, RW 36/397, p. 79.

123 These broadcasts are partly conserved in the archives of the German intelligence service, for example: *Funkabhörbericht, Sender London* [Discours du premier-ministre Pierlot, lu par le secrétaire d'État de l'Enseignement, Julius Hoste], *5. 6. 42*, BA-MA, RW 36/400, pp. 211-213; *Funkabhörbericht, Sender London, 6.6.42*, RW 36/400, p. 210; *Funkabhörbericht, Sender London, 9 Juni 1942, 21 Uhr*, BA-MA, RW 36/400, p. 194.

days later – punishing harshly, and, in serious cases, by the death penalty, "whoever prejudices the interests of the German occupation by ceasing work without regular termination of his labour or employment contract [...], and whoever incites others to cease work".[124]

4 Epilogue and Conclusions

"Our own honour is saved".[125] This was the view taken retrospectively by First President of the Court of Cassation Jamar on these five years of war, which deeply marked him. This senior magistrate, who appeared only rarely in public after his retirement in 1945, was decorated with the Civic Cross First Class, illustrating that his attitude – like that of the Supreme Court – was deemed patriotic by the Belgian authorities. Despite this high distinction, Jamar spent his last years justifying the attitude of the Court of Cassation during the war.[126] This latter did indeed come under criticism.[127]

The policy of 'the lesser evil' could not fail to arouse this. This policy, devised during the interbellum and introduced by the Belgian authorities on the day of the invasion, made it possible to safeguard the national institutions, including the institutions of justice. However, this maintenance had a price: the institutions were required, in accordance with international law, to compromise with the occupier and adopt a loyal attitude towards it. The notion of civil resistance was out of place.[128] In addition, the policy of the

124 'Ordonnance du 10 décembre 1942 relative à la protection de la paix du travail', in *Bulletin législatif belge*, 1942.

125 'Agenda sommaire de Joseph Jamar, date du 26 févier 1951', CEGESOMA, Fonds Jamar, No 6. Underlined in the text.

126 See his 'Memoires de guerre' (unpublished), kept at CEGESOMA.

127 Certain *magistrates* were also personally targeted in the same way as Advocate General Hayoit de Termicourt, whose support for the policy of the *lesser evil* at the beginning of the occupation still raises criticism among circles of former resistance fighters in the judicial world: "Everyone knows the eminent role played, as early as May 1940, by Mr. Hayoit de Termicourt, first advocate general at the Court of Cassation. His remarkable faculty as a jurist, his penetrating intelligence, and the moral credit he rightly enjoyed led the secretaries-general to solicit his advice, from the first days of the occupation, on all questions relating to the political orientation of Belgium. Sometimes personally, sometimes in the Standing Committee of the Legislative Council where he held a prominent place, Mr. Hayoit de Termicourt gave advice that, we have no doubt, was probably followed only partially. But it remains that, convinced as he was of the policy of the lesser evil, his opinion was, in many cases, decisive." ('Toujours debout', 6).

128 Van Goethem 2006, 122.

The Court of Cassation illustrated this well in the support it showed to *magistrates* who had been the victims of harsh measures. This support – protests to the occupier, letters to the

lesser evil required occupied and occupier to negotiate a modus vivendi. These negotiations were done in the shadows. Even during the conflict, voices were raised – especially through the clandestine press organ Justice libre – criticizing the secrecy surrounding the relations between the Court of Cassation and the occupier, whether on the occasion of the 1940 Protocol or the 1942 Pact.[129]

Because of this state of affairs, the judiciary and, in particular, the body at its top – the Court of Cassation – did not emerge haloed in glory, as it had in 1918. One should, however, avoid such hasty comparisons. Occupation regime, food supply situation, and the existence in 1940-45 of a precedent are all examples of differences at the origin of very distinct contexts of occupation.[130] In many ways, the second occupation was more brutal than the first. We will mention just two examples that particularly involved the Court of Cassation.[131] The first is the German hostage policy, the most notable of which was the execution of hostages as a retaliation of violence against German soldiers. Authorized by German law, in violation of the Hague Convention, this practice by which persons were executed without trial, for acts which they had not necessarily committed, could not but deeply offend the senior magistrates as representatives of justice. The Court of Cassation made representations on this subject to the Secretary-General of Justice in 1941 and officially protested from 1942 onwards. The Court managed to prevent the execution of fifteen hostages in Liège and obtained some success in favour of another category of hostages, those used as human shields to protect German troop transports.

The Court of Cassation also expressed its indignation at the system of compulsory labour started in 1942 (in March, the work was to be carried out in Belgium, and, from October, in Germany). While failing to obtain

families – was shown to *magistrates* targeted in the course of their duties; in other words, when the independence of the judiciary was undermined. *Magistrates* who in their personal capacity undertook acts of resistance, rarely received the support of their superiors (See Bost and Peters 2016, 259).

129 "For two and a half years the Belgian "authorities", up to and including the first president of the Court of Cassation, have surrounded with the most absolute secrecy the facts that the country has the greatest interest in knowing, and which the country, of which gentlemen seem to forget that they are the mandated agents, has the right to know. Why do we still know nothing about the conditions in which "the highest judicial authorities" considered it necessary to deal last June with the occupying power, through the secretaries-general? Why, if not because these conditions are shameful for these authorities?" ('Un point d'Histoire', 13).

130 See Bost and Peters 2016, 233-260, and on the First World War, Bost 2013.

131 See the Fund Jamar at the CEGESOMA examined by Nicolas Hansen. The Jamar archives contain only a few items on the lot of the Jews (see Hansen 2008, pp. 52-62).

results, the protest of the Court of 20 March 1943, disseminated among the population to the great discontent of the occupier, somewhat revived the honour of the Court in public opinion.

These fundamental attacks on life and individual liberty helped to strengthen the ranks of the Resistance and radicalize a certain fringe; this led to an escalation of violence on both sides.

The occupation of 1940-44 was also more brutal towards the judiciary itself, which took more blows than in 1914-18.[132] From 1940, an ordinance allowed the Germans to prohibit the exercise of judicial functions by the chief magistrates of the different courts. In November 1942, in the context of the aforementioned political radicalization, the scope of this ordinance was extended to all persons exercising public office, thereby including all magistrates. In December 1942, the occupier issued its ordinance on the protection of labour peace, which could have served as a legal basis for sanctioning a possible strike by the judiciary. Between 1940 and 1944, twenty to thirty magistrates were prevented from performing their duties.[133] In addition, about fifty were arrested as political prisoners and twenty to thirty were arrested as hostages (with some used as human shields). At least twelve magistrates died as a result of the war, executed by the enemy or dying in captivity.[134] Finally, let us mention, to cite only one, the attempted assassination by collaborators of the country's leading judge, Jamar, one night in February 1944.

Despite this difficult context – in which, to refer to the terminology used in the aftermath of the First World War, 'Law, rebuffed, has to bow to Force'[135] – and, following the line traced by the law of 10 May 1940, the Court of Cassation – like most of the judiciary – remained in place[136] and continued its traditional missions.

In so doing, it sought to be faithful to its role of reflecting the unity of the country. It did so by ensuring the unity of interpretation of the law and with a composition reflecting the unity of the country; by choosing to range itself, at

132 See Bost and Peters 2016, 233-260.

133 Bost and Peters 2016, 254-255.

134 Archives générales du Royaume, *Ministère de la Justice, Secrétariat général, Série II*, n°4566.

135 The collective memory associates the First World War with the 'triumph of the Law over Force'.

136 On the question of desertions, see: Peters 2011, 163-186. The Court of Cassation had only one 'desertion', that of Chamber President Henri Rolin. The quotation marks are necessary, the Rolin case being particularly complex (Jewish wife, mental disorders, etc.). He was finally considered to have resigned in a regular fashion by the Court and allowed to receive his pension with retroactive effect from 10 May 1940 (see the personal file of Henri Rolin in the archives of the Court of Cassation).

the very beginning of the war, behind the King, the "supreme personification of the Fatherland in danger".[137] In so doing, the representatives of the Court of Cassation supported the idea that the King must justify himself publicly in order to maintain the confidence of the people. Similarly, the Court of Cassation refused to comply with the demand of the government-in-exile to no longer render judgments in the name of the sovereign.

The Court of Cassation is also traditionally the supreme guardian of the law, a mission undermined in 1942, when the German ordinance of 14 May prohibited courts and tribunals from examining the legality of the orders of secretaries-general. This ordinance placed before the Court of Cassation the most difficult decision in its history, forcing it to recognize its inability to judge on a number of disputes. The result was a blocked situation, with the course of justice suspended and the risk of seeing, as in 1918, the establishment of German courts. The exchanges with the Secretary-General of Justice testify to the fact that, initially, the Court of Cassation considered its sole duty to be to act in the interest of the law. For the Court of Cassation, it was for the executive to look after the interests of the people, in this case to solve the vital issue of food. This was perfectly consistent with the doctrine and jurisprudence that, since its establishment in 1832, had considered the Court of Cassation to be an agent of the legislative power vis-à-vis the courts and tribunals.[138] The Secretary-General of Justice, himself a former senior judge, used some poignant words to try to make the supreme court realize that it is useless to preserve at all costs the law and the rule of law if there is no longer a population to live them: The Court of Cassation resorted to pragmatism,[139] the same pragmatism that had already reigned in the establishment of the Protocol in June 1940.

The choice it was forced to make in 1942 modified, in our opinion, the way the Court of Cassation perceives its mission. During the war, a shift took place in its conception of its role. Until the interbellum, the Court of Cassation saw itself as established only in the interest of the law, tasked with ruling on the lawfulness of judicial decisions.[140] Conversely, the courts and tribunals, which constitute the judicial power, were responsible for the interests of the parties. After the Second World War, the Cassation magistrates

137 Verhoeyen 1978, 235.

138 Leclercq 1946, 1137-1153; Faider 1886, 10-11.
Cass., 18 mai 1933, *Pas.*, 1933, I, pp. 234-245. For more information on this question, see: Muller 2011, 11-28.

139 Deltour 1995, 153-161.

140 Cornil 1948, 453-461; Cornil 1950, 489-498. The only person to have ventured to formulate this idea before the Second World War was Cassation Counsellor Henri Rolin: Rolin 1938, 229-344.

defended a new conception of their institution: it is placed at the head of the judicial power, the Court of Cassation and the basic jurisdictions being established both in the interest of the law and in the interests of parties. The interest of the law and the interest of parties are no longer considered as opposing but complementary concepts. This evolution is understandable when one analyses the choice that the Court of Cassation had to make between either (a) maintaining its legalistic position by defending a strict application of the law that would have delivered Belgian litigants to the German war councils, or (b) sacrificing some of the sacredness of the law and concluding a 'pact' with the enemy in the interest of the population. In doing so, it reminds us that the population is an essential component of the state in the same way as the sovereignty exercised through the constituted powers.

In this way, the Court of Cassation took important 'political' decisions in these troubled times. This period and the choices made then constitute the darkest page in the history of the Belgian judiciary, the evocation of which was to remain taboo within the profession for nearly half a century.

References

Bayot, J., 'Eloge funèbre de M. le procureur général vicomte Hayoit de Termicourt', *Journal des tribunaux* 4729, 1971, 79-81.

Bost, Mélanie and Kirsten Peters, 'Belgian Magistrates and German Occupiers, A Diachronic Comparison (1914-1918/1940-1944)', in: Annie Hondeghem, Xavier Rousseaux and Frédéric Schoenaers (Eds), *Modernization of the Criminal Justice System and the Judicial System. New insights on trust, cooperation and human capital*, Springer 2016, 233-260.

Bost, Mélanie, *Traverser l'occupation 1914–1918. Du modus vivendi à la grève, la magistrature belge face aux occupants allemands*, unpublished PhD thesis, Louvain: Université catholique de Louvain, 2013.

Boudens, Robrecht, *Kardinaal Van Roey en de Tweede Wereldoorlog*, Averbode: Altiora 1996.

Burrin, Philippe, 'Faire l'histoire des occupations militaires', in: *La France sous Vichy. Autour de Robert O. Paxton*, Paris: Complexe 2004, 91-104.

Charles, Jean-Léon and Philippe Dasnoy, *Les secrétaires généraux face à l'occupant – Procès-verbaux des réunions du comité des secrétaires généraux (1940-1944)*, Brussels: Arts & Travel, 1974.

Colignon, Alain, 'C.N.A.A., L'agriculture en rangs d'oignon', *Jours de Guerre* (9) 1993, 49-93.

Cornil, Léon, 'La Cour de cassation. Considérations sur sa mission. Discours prononcé par M. le Procureur général Cornil à l'audience solennelle de rentrée de la Cour de cassation le 15 septembre 1950', *Journal des Tribunaux* 3863, 1950, 489-498.

Cornil, Léon, 'La Cour de cassation. Mercuriale prononcée par M. Léon Cornil, procureur général, à l'audience solennelle de rentrée de la Cour de cassation le 15 septembre 1948', *Journal des Tribunaux* 3778, 1948, 453-461.

Dantoing, Antoine, 'Le cardinal Van Roey de la neutralité à la présence', *Jours de Guerre* (5) 1991, 55-67.

De Jonghe, Albert, *Hitler en het politieke lot van België (1940-1944): de vestiging van een Zivilverwaltung in België en Noord-Frankrijk*, Antwerpen: Nederlandsche Boekhandel 1972.

De Jonghe, Albert, 'La lutte Himmler-Reeder pour la nomination d'un HSSPF à Bruxelles (1942-1944)' (Part I-IV), *Cahiers d'Histoire de la Seconde Guerre Mondiale* (3-8) 1974-1984.

Deltour, Pol, 'Het weinig heroïsch pragmatisme van de Belgische oorlogsmagistratuur (1940-1944)', *Panopticon* 1995, 153-161.

Faider, Charles, 'La Cour de cassation. Discours prononcé par M. Ch. Faider, procureur général, à l'audience solennelle d'installation de M. le Conseiller Lelièvre le 7 décembre 1885 et dont la Cour a ordonné l'impression', *Bulletin des arrêts de la Cour de cassation de Belgique* 1886, 1569-1575.

Ganshof van der Meersch, Walter, 'Eloge funèbre de M. le procureur général vicomte Hayoit de Termicourt. Discours de M. W. Ganshof van der Meersch', *Journal des Tribunaux* (4729) 1971, 81-84.

Gérard-Libois, Jules and José Gotovitch, *L'an 40, La Belgique occupée*, Brussels: CRISP 1971.

Gotovitch, José, *Note relative à la magistrature sous l'occupation*, Brussels: C.R.E.H.S.G.M. 1972.

'Gouvernement de Londres,' in: Paul Aron and José Gotovitch (Eds), *Dictionnaire de la Seconde Guerre mondiale en Belgique*, Brussels: Versailles 2008.

Hanquet, René, *Les pouvoirs des secrétaires généraux pendant l'occupation*, Brussels: Goemaere 1946.

Hansen, Nicolas, *Un haut magistrat belge face à l'occupation. Joseph Jamar, Premier président de la Cour de cassation de 1940-1944* (unpublished history M.A. dissertation), Louvain-la-Neuve 2008).

'Jean Servais', *Annales du notariat et de l'enregistrement*, December 1946.

Kossmann, Richard, 'Das Arbeitsgebiet der Gruppe Qu 2', in: Elisabeth Wagner (Ed), *Der Generalquartiermeister. Briefe und Tagebuchaufzeichnungen des Generalquartiermeisters des Heeres General der Artillerie Eduard Wagner*, Munich: Olzog 1963, 302-312.

Leclercq, Paul, 'Du pouvoir judiciaire. Discours prononcé par M. Paul Leclercq avocat général à l'audience solennelle de rentrée de la Cour d'appel de Bruxelles le 2 octobre 1911', *Belgique Judiciaire* (72) 1911, 1137-1153.

Leclercq, Pierre, 'L'interprétation de la loi du 10 mai 1940', *Journal des Tribunaux* (3671) 1946, 65-70.

Louveaux, Charles, 'La magistrature dans la tourmente des années 1940-1944', *Revue de Droit pénal et de Criminologie* (7) 1981, 620-665.

Michielsen, Joeri, *The 'Nazification' and 'Denazification' of the Courts in Belgium, Luxembourg and The Netherlands. The Belgian, Luxembourg and Netherlands courts and their reactions to occupation measures and measures from their governments returning from exile*, Maastricht: Universiteit Maastricht 2004.

Muller, Françoise, *La Cour de cassation belge à l'aune des rapports entre pouvoirs: de sa naissance dans le modèle classique de la séparation des pouvoirs à l'aube d'une extension de la fonction juridictionnelle (1832-1914/1936)*, Bruges: La Charte 2011.

Ockrent, Roger, *Les crises constitutionnelles du pouvoir législatif en Belgique. Les pouvoirs des Secrétaires généraux sous l'occupation ennemie, suivie de: Délégation du Pouvoir législatif au Roi, Avant-projet de réforme constitutionnelle*, Brussels: Office de Publicité 1944.

Peters, Kirsten, 'Les abandons de poste dans la magistrature lors de la Seconde Guerre mondiale', *Cahiers d'histoire du temps présent* (24) 2011, 163-186.

Rolin, Henri, 'Procédure en cassation', in: *Réforme de la procédure*, Vol III, Brussels: Centre d'études pour la réforme de l'État 1938, 229-344.

Stengers, Jean, *L'action du Roi en Belgique depuis 1831, Pouvoir et influence*, Paris: Duculot 1992.

Thonissen, Jean-Joseph, *La Constitution belge annotée offrant sous chaque article l'état de la doctrine, de la jurisprudence et de la législation*, 2nd ed., Brussels: Bruylant 1876.

'Toujours debout', *Justice libre, affilié au Front de l'Indépendance* (3) May 1945.

'Un point d'Histoire', *Justice Libre* [clandestine], November 1942.

Van den Wijngaert, Mark, *Het beleid van het comité van de Secretarissen-generaal in België tijdens de duitse bezetting 1940-1944*, Brussels: Paleis der Academiën 1975.

Van Goethem, Herman, 'La convention de La Haye, la collaboration administrative en Belgique et la persécution des Juifs à Anvers', *Cahiers d'Histoire du Temps Présent* (17) 2006, 117-197.

Verhoeyen, Etienne, 'La lettre pastorale du Cardinal van Roey sur la capitulation du 28 mai 1940 – Le rôle du barreau et de la magistrature', *Cahiers d'Histoire de la Seconde guerre mondiale* (5) 1978, 221-242.

Zurné, Jan Julia, *Tussen twee vuren. Gerecht en verzet tijdens de Tweede Wereldoorlog*, Tielt: Lannoo 2017.

About the Authors

Françoise Muller holds a PhD in contemporary history. She wrote her doctoral thesis on the history of the Belgian Court of Cassation, from the perspective of the relations between the different constitutional powers. She is postdoctoral researcher at Université Catholique de Louvain. She is also Bachelor of Law and Bachelor of Political Science.

Kirsten Peters studied history at the Université Libre de Bruxelles and Tourism at the Institut Roger Lambion. As a research assistant at the Université Saint Louis, she researched Belgian judges and lawyers under German occupation (1940-1944). She now works with the Permanent Representation of Germany to the EU.

9 The *Hoge Raad* during the German Occupation of the Netherlands

Derk Venema

Abstract

This chapter discusses the role of the Dutch Supreme Court (*Hoge Raad*) during the German occupation. After explaining the position of the court in the context of the occupation regime, international law and domestic law and politics, it turns to the effects of several occupation regime measures like the introduction of new courts and personnel policy on work of the court. As a pivotal case representing the court's occupation strategy, the review case from 1942 is treated in detail. The post-war period and the court's legitimacy crisis are considered before evaluating the performance of the court in light of their constitutional and societal task.

Keywords: German occupation of the Netherlands; Hoge Raad; legal ethics; Dutch review case; judicial legitimacy

1 Introduction[1]

On Friday 28 and Saturday 29 June 1940, less than two months after the German attack on the Netherlands, the first meeting of the Dutch Lawyers Association (NJV) under Nazi-German occupation took place at the *Hoge Raad* in The Hague. The second day fell on the birthday of Prince Bernhard, Crown Princess Juliana's husband and adjutant to Queen Wilhelmina.[2]

1 This chapter is primarily based on Jansen & Venema 2011, Venema 2007, and also on Mazel 1984. Details on the archival materials and other sources can be found in Venema 2007 and Jansen & Venema 2011. The author is also indebted to Jan Barendsen, Joseph Fleuren, Marcel Verburg and Frank de Vries for many fruitful conversations on this topic.

2 Although as a student German-born Prince Bernhard von Lippe-Biesterfeld (1911-2004) had briefly been a member of NSDAP, SA and SS, any association with the Nazis had ceased before

Venema, D. (ed.), *Supreme Courts Under Nazi Occupation*. Taylor & Francis Group 2022
DOI: 10.5117/9789463720496_CH09

Only a few days earlier, he had held a radio speech for the BBC Overseas Service expressing his confidence in a British victory over the 'German tyrant' Hitler.[3] To express alliance with the royal family and aversion to the German occupier, a member of the *Hoge Raad* handed out white flowers to the participants of the meeting, referring to the white carnation Bernhard used to wear in his buttonhole.[4] Bernhard's habit was adopted throughout the country and the day came to be known as 'carnation day.' A couple of Nazis amongst the lawyers protested, but the meeting was not disturbed. When it had ended, the president of the *Hoge Raad*, Lodewijk Ernst Visser, stood at the door and shook everyone's hand as they stepped outside.[5] They all understood the new political situation would bring difficulties for this eminent jurist, because of his Jewish ancestry. Indeed, infuriated by the display of anti-German sentiment, the occupier immediately took the first, seemingly unimportant, of a long series of measures increasingly marginalising the Jewish population of the Netherlands.[6]

This chapter will explain how the *Hoge Raad* navigated between on the one hand pacifying the occupier and staying out of harm's way, and on the other hand defending the Dutch democratic nation and helping its population. The predicament the judges found themselves in has become known in the Netherlands as the 'mayor in wartime problem'.[7] It constitutes a multi-facetted dilemma. The one option that was open to mayors, judges, and other public servants who were not Nazis, was pacifying the enemy by remaining in office and cooperating with the occupation authorities. The advantages of this tactic were: keeping the civil service in non-Nazi hands, which could moderate the occupier's policies, and retaining an income and staying out of trouble personally. The downside was that by working with the enemy, one 'got their hands dirty', which are not always easy to wash clean. And of course, less symbolically, one could be forced to execute very harmful policies. The other option was leaving office: actively, as an act of protest, or by being fired as a sanction for other acts of protest or resistance activities. The benefits were that it might encourage the suppressed population and

meeting his future wife in 1936. As the symbolic 'commander of the Dutch armed resistance' (from September 1944), he acquired the image of a war hero. On Bernhard, see for example: Fasseur 2009 and Aalders 2014.

3 De Jong 1972, 132.

4 Interview with C.W. Dubbink, 7 December 2005, on file with the author. Dubbink (1914-2014) attended the meeting as a young solicitor, and later became president of the *Hoge Raad* (1976-1981).

5 On the meeting, see also Jansen & Venema 2011, 90-91; Lokin & Jansen 1995, 19-20.

6 De Jong 1972, 301. Jews were banned from the air-raid defence.

7 See, for example: Romijn 2000, 178-179.

yield clean hands, an unblemished personal reputation. On the negative side, the risk loomed large of being replaced by a more loyal collaborator or even a true Nazi, which might make things worse for some people.

After a brief overview of the occupation administration and the *Hoge Raad*'s position at the start of the Second World War, I will describe the new courts that were created during the occupation, and explain how the occupation regime used a very important instrument of control on the judiciary: personnel policy. An overview of the regime's new laws and other measures and the way the *Hoge Raad* reacted to them, together with some important *Hoge Raad* cases, will complete the picture of this supreme court's war history.

2 The Civil Occupation Regime

In his 'magnanimity' towards the 'blood-related' Dutch people,[8] Hitler had decided to install a civilian occupation regime instead of a military one, or so the Austrian lawyer Arthur Seyss-Inquart assured his audience in his official proclamation upon assuming office as *Reichskommissar* of the occupied Netherlands.[9] Although Hitler never said so, it has been supposed that the primary reason for choosing a civilian regime was that it would serve a policy of nazification better than a military one.[10] Other reasons could have been the flight of the Queen and her government, planned acquisition of the Dutch colonies, and utilization of the Netherlands for the war economy.[11] Queen Wilhelmina and her cabinet ministers had fled to London, which made the secretaries-general the highest civil servants in the government departments.[12] Their new supervisors were four German *Generalkommissare*, two of whom were relevant for the judiciary: Friedrich Wimmer, *Generalkommissar für Verwaltung und Justiz*, was responsible

8 Arthur Seyss-Inquart, 'Aus Anlass der Übernahme der Regierungsgewalt', Den Haag, May 29th 1940, in: Reichsminister Seyss-Inquart, *Vier Jahre in den Niederlanden. Gesammelte Reden*, Amsterdam: Volk und Reich Verlag 1944, p. 7-12, published in an abridged version as Verordnung (ordinance) 2/1940 'Aufruf des Reichskommissars für die besezten [sic] niederländischen Gebiete', *Verordnungsblatt für die besetzten niederländischen Gebiete*, where the vast majority of the ordinances can be found, and which will be referenced as Vo [number]/[year].

9 Neuman 1967, 136-141, See on Seyss-Inquart also Koll 2015.

10 De Pater 1972, Cohen 1972. It is suggested, for example, by Kurt Rabl (head of the section Legislation and Constitutional Law of Wimmer's *Kommissariat-General für Verwaltung und Justiz*) in Rabl 1941, 84.

11 Romijn 2017, 47.

12 Verburg 2016, 29-32.

for the justice department, and Hanns A. Rauter, who was also *Höhere SS- und Polizeiführer*, led the *Generalkommissatiat für das Sicherheitswesen* (security). While the exiled lawful government was preparing its return to a liberated Netherlands, the country was administered by Dutch and German agencies working together. This was perceived, by both sides, as a necessary evil.

The justice department[13] was led, first, by acting secretary-general Jan C. Tenkink, who was appointed after secretary-general Johannes R.M. van Angeren had been ordered at the last minute to join the cabinet in their departure for London. Tenkink was a legalist who executed the law, whether it was from Dutch or German origin, and abhorred acts of sabotage by the resistance, because they would only lead to reprisals. But as a principled man of the law, he viewed the fundamental changes in Dutch society the Germans were preparing by legal means as contrary to international law. Ten months after his appointment, he was therefore forced by his conscience, and allowed by the Germans, to resign. For three months in 1941, the much more idiosyncratic Johannes P. Hooijkaas took over as acting secretary-general, before the Germans replaced him on the first of July with Jaap J. Schrieke.[14] Schrieke was, contrary to his predecessors, a loyal National Socialist and member of the Dutch Nazi party NSB (Nationaal-Socialistische Beweging). After a career in the Dutch East Indies civil service, culminating in the position of director of the Justice department, but failing to achieve the customary promotion to the Dutch East Indies Council, in 1934 Schrieke accepted a professorship at Leiden University in Dutch East Indies constitutional law. As the leader of the justice department, he was loyal to the occupier, but careful not to antagonize the overwhelming non-Nazi majority of his staff.

It has become customary in historiography to divide the occupation of the Netherlands, more specifically the relation between occupier and occupied, into several phases.[15] The first phase was one of a careful mutually cooperative spirit. Several German functionaries have emphasized that the Hague Regulations for Land Warfare were regarded and respected as the legal foundation for the occupation regime's power.[16] This claim was

13 See mainly Verburg 2016.

14 On Schrieke, see: Vogel & Schulten 1996.

15 Here I use the periodisation of Romijn 2017, 58-73.

16 Ernst Althaus, head of personnel management of Verwaltung und Justiz, in his book *Personalangelegenheiten* 1943, p. 42; Lecture by Kurt Rabl (Rabl 1941), probably second half of 1941, NIOD Institute for War, Holocaust and Genocide Studies, Archive 020 (Verwaltung und Justiz), 2353.

apparent from the wording of the first organic ordinances,[17] and was even explicitly announced in the *Frankfurter Zeitung*.[18] In the summer of 1941, when the German army had optimistically begun marching into Russia, the first phase of the occupation in the Netherlands ended in deception for both sides. It had become clear to the Germans that the Dutch were not as receptive to National Socialism as they had hoped, and as a consequence the Nazification of Dutch society would acquire a more coercive nature. In this context, local democracy in the Netherlands was abolished, and the Nazi party NSB acquired some official powers. Furthermore, in 1942 the deportations of Dutch Jews to the extermination camps commenced, and in 1942 and the beginning of 1943, after the German defeat at Stalingrad, more than 300,000 men were drafted into forced labour in Germany. This antagonized the Dutch people even further, and the renewed captivity of all previous Dutch military provoked spontaneous strikes, in April and May 1943, which marked the beginning of the phase of hard confrontations. The fourth and final phase, of chaos, violence, and humanitarian emergency, started in September 1944 when the south of the country was liberated, and rumours of total liberation caused many NSB members to flee to Germany. A railway strike led to Seyss-Inquart's decision to stop deliveries of coal and foodstuffs to the Western part of Holland, causing the 'hunger winter' of 1944/1945. We shall see that policy regarding the judiciary reflects these phases.

Of crucial importance for the understanding of the conduct of judges and civil servants were the 1937 Instructions (Aanwijzingen) from the government for the attitude to be taken by all members of the civil service and the judiciary in case of an enemy attack.[19] In the 1930s, hoping that a possible second outburst of German aggression would pass the country by as it did in 1914, the Netherlands had observed a politics of strict neutrality. Nevertheless, legal and other preparations were made for the eventuality of war. The 1937 Instructions, an improved version of similar instructions

17 Vo 1/1940, 2/1940, 3/1940 and 23/1940. All legislative powers of German and Dutch members of the administration were based on the Führer's decree (Vo 1/1940), and thus on international occupation law, not on the Dutch constitution.

18 Signed 'X.': X. 1940.

19 Cabinet decision of 1 May 1937, Aanwijzingen betreffende de houding, aan te nemen door de bestuursorganen van het Rijk, de Provinciën, Gemeenten, Waterschappen, Veenschappen en Veenpolders, alsmede door het daarbij in dienst zijnde personeel en door het personeel in dienst bij spoor en tramwegen in geval van een vijandelijke inval. On these Instructions: Sikkes 1985, Verburg 2001, 442-448, Romijn 2006, 50-57, Jansen & Venema 2011, 84-89; Venema 2007, 143-153.

from 1914, ordered all addressees, in case of an enemy occupation, *to remain in office as long as possible, until their functioning would benefit the occupier more than the civilian population*. The following year, a month after Austria's *Anschluss* to the Reich, minister of justice Goseling sent a letter to all courts and Public Prosecutor offices to inform their personnel of the decision that they should in any event remain at their posts.[20] Both the Instructions and the letter were highly classified, lest the Germans should feel insulted by the suggestion that the Netherlands was anticipating an attack. When the attack did come, on 10 May 1940, the Instructions were either not yet distributed to all local authorities, or were stored so safely by them that many civil servants, including some mayors and other high ranking officials, did not learn of their existence until later in the war, or even after liberation.[21] The *Hoge Raad*, however, studied the Instructions at their first meeting during the occupation, on 20 May 1940,[22] and took them out of the safe (together with the Hague Regulations of Land Warfare) every time they faced difficult decisions related to the occupation.[23] It will become clear that the members of the *Hoge Raad*, like most judges, paid heed to the clear message of the government's Instructions to the proverbial mayor in wartime: remain in office to serve the people. This would not, however, serve their reputation.

3 The *Hoge Raad* in 1940

Created in 1838, the *Hoge Raad* was modelled after the French *Cour de Cassation*, which means that it considers only matters of law, not matters of fact. In 1940, it consisted of divisions for civil law, criminal law, and tax law,[24] whose task it was to quash verdicts of lower courts in case of 'incorrect application or violation of written law'.[25] Although at the beginning of the twentieth century Dutch lawyers were not convinced of its necessity, in the

20 'Minister van Justitie aan Autoriteiten, Colleges en Ambtenaren, ressorteerende onder het Departement van Justitie, 25 April 1938. Afdeling A.S. No 2350. Zeer Geheim.' Reproduced in Barendsen & Venema 2004, appendix 2. The text is also printed in Verburg 2001, 445-446.

21 Sikkes 1985, 21-23.

22 *Hoge Raad* Archive, Minute Book 1921-1958, plenary meeting of 30 May 1940.

23 As M.J.Ch. Reyers (deputy registrar at the *Hoge Raad* 1942-1958, registrar 1958-1978) has told Eveline Hartogs (registrar at the *Hoge Raad* 2002-2011). Information from Mrs. Hartogs. Jansen & Venema 2011, 86-87.

24 The Central Appeal Council dealt in the highest instance with some other categories of administrative law cases, mainly involving civil servants.

25 Article 172 of the Dutch Constitution and article 99 of the Law on the Judicial Organisation (Wet op de Rechterlijke Organisatie), Fruin 1940.

following decades several ground-breaking decisions secured the positive image of the *Hoge Raad* from the 1930s onwards. The introduction in 1932 of the obligatory retirement age of 70 may also have helped.[26] There were seventeen judges in total, presided over by Lodewijk E. Visser, whose Jewish ancestry would lead to his dismissal in 1941. According to custom, five positions in the *Hoge Raad* were reserved for Roman Catholics, the only group who enjoyed this guarantee. When there is a vacancy, the *Hoge Raad* sends a list of six recommended persons to the house of representatives, which virtually always nominates the top three to the King (or Queen), who appoints the number one. In case of a catholic vacancy, Catholics are placed at the top of the list.[27] The procurator-general and his deputies the advocates-general have as their main task to advise the *Hoge Raad* in all cases. These advisory opinions are usually published along with the judgements selected for publication.[28]

Although the age of legalistic formalism had passed, and extensive interpretation of statutory law had its prominent advocates, the *Hoge Raad* was very cautious not to overstep its competency boundaries: it considered itself a non-political body, for which political neutrality was especially important in times of political upheaval. The making of laws was the province of the chosen legislator, their application was the courts' job. Among jurists, some leeway for more extensive judicial legal interpretation was granted in civil law, but generally denied in criminal law, where the principle of *nulla poena sine lege* (no punishment without written law) was paramount.[29] This attitude contrasted with the National Socialist ideal of a judge who is the representative of the people's sense of justice and is guided more by lofty ideals of an ethnocentric common good than by the letter of the – 'utterly out-dated' – liberal democratic law.[30]

What the Nazis thought about law, the state, Jews, and international politics was not unknown in the Netherlands. Of course people were familiar with the political ideas of the Nazi party NSB. But legal journals had also written about new German laws such as the Nuremberg race laws.[31] So the judiciary knew who they were dealing with in May 1940. Still, in the first phase of the occupation, many civil servants and members of the judiciary

26 See for the *Hoge Raad* during the interbellum: Jansen & Venema 2011, 21-38.

27 Donner 1962, 3-7.

28 The main source for published court decisions is *Nederlandsche Jurisprudentie* (1913-present). Some important older decisions are being published on https://uitspraken.rechtspraak.nl/.

29 Jansen & Venema, 2011, 39-50; Venema 2007, 74-86.

30 Venema 2007, 105, and generally 86-128.

31 Jansen & Venema, 2011, 53-60.

allowed themselves, some as optimists, others perhaps as fatalists, to become part of the occupation administration which from the very start bore the risk of entrapment. As time went by, it became increasingly difficult to judge for whom one's functioning was more beneficial: the Dutch people or the German occupier. And even more problematic was the question of what to do when one suspected that the Germans profited most from one's remaining in office. Yet those were exactly the questions all government personnel were left with by the government's Instructions from 1937. I will return to this predicament in the discussion of two court cases that play a central role in the literature on the Dutch judiciary under the occupation: the *Hoge Raad*'s judicial review case and the Leeuwarden Appeals Court judgement concerning detention camp Ommen.

4 New Courts

Directly following their invasion, the Germans set up military courts in the Netherlands.[32] This is a normal and logical measure, because an army must be able to adjudicate unruly behaviour of its members. But also acts of Dutch citizens against the German army, SS, or police services came within the jurisdiction of these courts-martial and *Sondergerichte* (special courts),[33] which constituted a novelty in international law.[34] The Netherlands were the only country besides the Protectorate of Bohemia and Moravia where also German *non-military* criminal courts were introduced.[35] This *Landgericht* (district court) and *Obergericht* (appeal court as well as first instance for graver crimes) could try Dutch citizens who had acted contrary to the interests of Germans or Germany or against the common interest, especially the food distribution system.[36] Hearings took place in Dutch courtrooms. The *Obergericht* often used the main courtroom of the *Hoge*

32 See on German courts in the Netherlands Von Frijtag Drabbe Künzel 1999.

33 Verordnung des Oberbefehlshabers der Heeresgruppe B 10 Mai 1940 über die Einführung des Deutschen Strafrechts in den von Deutschen Truppen besetzten der Niederlande und Belgiens, *Heeresgruppen-Verordnungsblatt für die besetzten Gebiete* 1, 4/1940, § 1: 'Soweit eine Handlung, die nach deutschem Recht strafbar ist, zur Aburteilung durch Wehrmachtgerichte oder Sondergerichte gebracht wird, wird das deutsche Strafrecht angewandt.' (When an action which is punishable under German law is brought before a court martial or a special court, German law will be applied.) Nestler 1990, 93-94 (also available at: https://opac.cegesoma.be/en/archview/list).

34 Moritz 1955, 26.

35 Best 1941, 65.

36 Verordnung [decree] (Vo) 52/1940 (20 July).

Raad, which meant that the *Hoge Raad* judges had to resort to their other, smaller courtroom.[37] As there were also several different police organizations meting out punishments, and even the German *Volksgerichtshof* could deal with acts of high treason in the Netherlands, competition resulted between the different instances with overlapping competencies.[38]

Because the occupier was determined to prevent Dutch judges from deciding on any politically sensitive matters, especially the persecution of the Jews, civil law cases with a political aspect, or against Germans, could be decided by the *Reichskommissar* himself or persons appointed by him.[39] Finally, some specific matters of civil law could be decided by German instances: in 1943, custody cases were entrusted to the *Landgericht*, possibly as a result of an earlier custody case between two German parties in which the *Hoge Raad* had decided that Dutch law was applicable.[40]

What started as normal measures of one belligerent on the occupied territory of another, gradually expanded into ever further reaching infringements on the jurisdiction of the national courts. Nevertheless, some measures would probably also have been taken by the Dutch government in comparable circumstances. The creation of an economic criminal court system is such a measure, taken in the period of mutual cooperation. As the black market was growing fast, and theft and food coupon fraud were on the rise, the ordinary criminal courts were flooded with cases. Therefore, in April 1941, at all nineteen district courts, a specialized criminal court for 'economic crime' was created.[41] Economic divisions at the appeal courts were instated, and the *Hoge Raad* formed an economic division presided over by its *deutschfreundliche* president Johannes van Loon (to whom I will return later), who had special powers to speed up the procedure (introduced by *Verordnung* (decree, Vo) 92/1942). Nevertheless, before and after this Verordnung, the *Hoge Raad* rendered rather formalistic decisions that did not support the political aims of severe, deterrent sentences.

Soon, *Generalkommissar* Wimmer and two public prosecutors, both prominent Dutch Nazis, complained to secretary-general Hooykaas about the sentences meted out by economic judges, which they thought were much too lenient. Later, Nazi secretary-general Schrieke approached not only the Public Prosecutor but also the economic judges with this concern. Although

37 *Hoge Raad* archive: Minute Book 1921-1958: plenary meeting of 1 September 1941.

38 Von Frijtag Drabbe Künzel 1999, 128-132.

39 Vo 230/1940 (19 December).

40 Vo 97/1943; *Hoge Raad* 15 January 1942, *Nederlandsche Jurisprudentie* 1942, 286.

41 Vo 71/1941. Venema 2007, 246-251.

he confessed that he realized that it lay beyond his authority to instruct judges, he still wished to emphasize how devastating the consequences of black market trade could be for the food supply, which called for more serious sentences. To this end, the economic divisions at the appeal courts were replaced by an Economic Appeals Court (Vo 38/1943). Notwithstanding its objective necessity (it was not abolished after the liberation), the economic criminal court system was still tainted because it was set up under enemy administration.

A new court that by no means had an ambivalent status, was the 'peace court'. In August 1941, the beginning of the period of coerced nazification, four months after the introduction of the economic criminal courts, five district courts received a second novel division for criminal cases, staffed by a 'judge of the peace' (vrederechter), who was competent in all criminal cases with a 'political aspect' (Vo 156/1941).[42] Only in case of a prison sentence or a fine of more than 200 guilders, could an appeal be filed with the Peace Appeals Court (*Vredegerechtshof*) which was also the highest instance, precluding recourse to the *Hoge Raad*, and as such, a special supreme court. The immediate cause for the creation of these courts were complaints by members of Nazi party NSB that persons calling them 'traitors' were punished too lightly. The judges of the peace met their demands by pronouncing sentences of two weeks' imprisonment instead of the usual two guilders fine in such cases. The *Vredegerechtshof* was presided over by Johan H. Carp, an internationally renowned Spinoza expert turned Nazi and advisor to NSB leader Anton A. Mussert. Although he was not as rabid and vindictive as Roland Freisler, the fearsome president of the *Volksgerichtshof* in Berlin, Carp did apply some wild interpretations of the criminal law in order to acquit fellow Nazis.[43]

Apart from being highly politicized and staffed exclusively by NSB members and other loyal collaborationists, the judges of the peace were competent to try anew cases in which a final judgement had already been rendered by a regular criminal court. A letter of protest against this violation of the principles of *ne bis in idem* and non-retroactivity was signed by almost all members of the judiciary, and the *Hoge Raad*'s criminal law section also filed a protest. Several courts discussed the possibility of collective resignation, but found no majority. Three individual judges did leave office in reaction to

42 On the Peace Courts, see Venema 2007, 253-275, 338-346; Jansen & Venema 2011, 115-120.

43 Carp wrote a book about his court, in which he proudly presents his clever inventions: Carp 1942. More judgements are recorded in: NIOD Archive 249 (Doc II), 876: Vredegerechtshof en vrederechtspraak.

the peace court system. Interestingly, Carp together with another member of the *Vredegerechtshof* also expressed his worries about the violation of *ne bis in idem* to his fellow party member secretary-general Schrieke, who explained that the Germans had insisted upon the contested provision. One of the grievances against the *Hoge Raad* was that its collaborationist president had sworn in the judges of the peace without protest from any of the other members against the institution itself (except for the violation of *ne bis in idem*).[44]

5 Personnel Policy

In his decree from 20 August 1940 (vo 108/1940), Reichskommissar Seyss-Inquart reserved for himself the power to appoint members of the *Hoge Raad* and the presidents and chief public prosecutors of the appeal courts (art. 1, section 3 & 4), leaving the appointment of other judges to the secretary-general (art. 3), but reserving the right to appoint them himself if so desired (art. 4).

Most of the appointments in the judiciary were made by secretary-general of Justice Schrieke. Although he was an NSB member, he was careful not to antagonise the courts by appointing Nazi fanatics. Another reason for appointing cooperative non-Nazis was that there weren't many Nazi jurists who were qualified for the job. Especially after staffing the economic criminal courts and the peace courts, there were very few eligible *deutschfreundliche* jurists left. Among non-Nazi jurists, the vast majority, accepting a position in the judiciary from enemy hands was not generally approved of, it became increasingly difficult to find willing and able judges. This was an aspect of the 'mayor in wartime' problem: some argued that good patriots should above all be willing to serve their country, to avoid further Nazification of the government, while others strongly advocated observing strict moral hygiene which meant not accepting any favours or appointments from the Germans or the NSB.[45]

As instructed, Schrieke always consulted with the Germans and the NSB before appointing a new judge. Although he had the authority to appoint judges in most positions, he always needed German approval, which he

44 See the apologia of the *Hoge Raad*, published under the name of judge Nicolaas C.M.A. van den Dries, Van den Dries 1945, 46.

45 Venema 2007, 311.

secured for non-NSB members by including the phrase 'very good political orientation', regardless of the candidate's political opinions.[46]

The occupation regime used a three-way strategy to create vacancies in the judiciary that could be filled with politically reliable and racially acceptable jurists.[47] The first method was dismissal on special grounds: Jewishness and unreliability. Although obviously all German measures against the Jews in occupied Europe were illegal according to international law, and specifically in violation of Hague Regulations article 43 because those measures were not 'absolutely necessary' to uphold public order, two *Hoge Raad* judges and a professor of international law have pointed, during and after the war, to the highly authoritative opinion in Hersch Lauterpacht's 1935 edition of Lassa Oppenheim's treatise on the international law of war, which they thought justified the dismissal of Dutch Jewish judges by the Germans.[48] Indeed, this authoritative treatise on the international law of war stated that '[t]here is no doubt that an occupant may suspend the judges as well as other officials.' And in a footnote, it is stated: 'As to the removal of Jewish judges by the Russians during their occupation of Lemberg in the World War, see Cybichowski [...].'[49] As it turns out, one of the Dutch judges referring to this passage apparently did not consult Cybichowski's article, and the other, who did read the relevant passage, interpreted it very creatively, because Cybichowski does not approve of the removal at all: 'In June, the highest commander ordered the removal of all persons of Jewish descent from the justice system [...]. Austrian law recognizes the principle of equal treatment of religions; there was no ground for the violation of this norm.'[50] This seemingly insignificant example illustrates how Dutch legal experts, in the phase

46 Venema 2007, 313-314.

47 The sources for the appointments and dismissals/resignations are Register rechterlijke macht 1934-, Register economische kamers en vrederechters 1941-, a chronological index of appointments and dismissals in the judiciary 1934-1951 and the registration cards of members of the judiciary (all in the archive of the Ministery of Justice, The Hague); *Staatscourant* 1940-1945, *Gids voor de rechterlijke macht* 1940-1943, *Bestuursalmanak voor het bezette Nederlandsche gebied*, 1942-1943 en 1943-1944, *Naamlijst van de leden der (van de) rechterlijke macht* 1936 and 1951 and Koppen & Ten Kate 2003. New counts and calculations have been made to correct some of the numbers mentioned in Venema 2007.

48 See the report by *Hoge Raad* judge Kosters, published in Venema et al. 2008, 63; Van den Dries 1945, 41-42. Cf. François 1933, 445; Published post-war parliamentary hearings: *Enquêtecommissie* 1955, 598 and 600-601: hearing of Hooykaas.

49 Oppenheim/Lauterpacht 1935, § 172, 357.

50 Cybichowski 1916, 452 (translation DV). Lemberg, now Ukrainian L'viv, was Austrian at the time.

of mutual benevolence, went out of their way to legally justify even highly questionable measures by the occupier.

To bring this first measure into effect, the Germans first needed to know which judges (and other civil servants) were Jews. As there was no religious registration by the state, a form was sent to all government personnel requiring them to state whether they or their spouse had any Jewish parents or grandparents, on the penalty of discharge. Virtually everyone filled out this 'Aryan Declaration' truthfully and sent it back.[51] Only *Hoge Raad* member Donner wrote on his form: 'Providing this information should not in the least be regarded as cooperation with the measures for the purpose of which the information was requested.'[52] Before that, *Generalkommissar* Wimmer had already compiled a list of Jewish judges and advocates, against which he could check the statements.[53] A delicate matter for the *Hoge Raad*, and for the judiciary as a whole, was the fact that among the Jewish judges was, as previously mentioned, *Hoge Raad* president L. E. Visser. Notwithstanding several letters of protest, the *Hoge Raad* judges decided in a meeting to sign and submit the statements. Visser did not take part in the deliberations because he did not want to defend his personal interest in the matter. On 23 November 1940, nine judges and eighteen part-time judges were suspended on the grounds of being Jewish. They were formally dismissed on 1 March 1941. President Visser was glad that attempts by others to keep him in office until his retirement age (1 September 1941) had failed, because: 'it would have hindered me if I had not been able to stand in the lines of those who have been treated so unjustly'.[54] Of all 317 full-time judges in all courts, nine were dismissed because of their Jewish ancestry. Four of them survived the war, four died in extermination camps, and Visser, who had been left alone by the Germans, suffered a fatal heart attack in February 1942. One Jewish judge had already committed suicide on 15 May 1940, not awaiting any possible measures. Nineteen part-time judges, amongst whom were two prominent law professors, were also dismissed.[55]

At least nine, at most twelve judges were dismissed on grounds of political unreliability. Most of them were involved in resistance activities, one had a Jewish wife, and two were members of the court that had decided the detention camp Ommen case, which will be dealt with later.

51 See Jansen & Venema 2011, 90-96; Michielsen 2004, 125-131.

52 Jansen & Venema 2011, 77 and photo section [xi].

53 De Jong 1972, 748.

54 Cited in *Nederlandsch Juristenblad* 1946, p. 363 (obituary L.E. Visser).

55 See Venema 2007, 298-302, 387.

Lowering the obligatory retirement age was the second strategy. Introduced only in 1932 and set at 70 years of age,[56] it was changed to 65, taking effect on 1 September 1941 (VO 130/1941). The transitional arrangement for judges who at the time were between 65 and 70 years old provided a gradual dismissal, and replacement, of this group until 1 March 1943, but this was applicable only to the lower and appeals courts, not to the *Hoge Raad*. On the basis of this decree, as much as 33 judges were retired one month to five years before their 70th birthday. Naturally, many of them were high ranking judges, and four were members of the *Hoge Raad* (see table 1). Exceptions could be made when 'the interests of the justice system' demanded them.

The third instrument of nazification was the creation of new courts. Although the economic courts were not intended as instruments of nazification, they were still a creation of the occupation authorities, which made it problematic to accept an appointment to the somewhat tainted position of economic judge. As a result, a disproportionate number of 'deutschfreundliche' judges staffed the economic courts. The peace courts were, as explained, fully staffed with convinced Nazis.

These three instruments created a total of close to eighty vacancies. A further 21 vacancies were created by voluntary resignations. This means that almost one hundred positions of a total of 322[57] had to be filled. In the peace courts, there were eleven positions to be filled, which were all staffed by Nazis and convinced collaborationists.[58] In the economic criminal courts, twelve of twenty judges were members of either the Nazi party NSB or the *Rechtsfront*, the Nazi organisation for the police and the legal professions. Thus the new courts together accounted for 23 *deutschfreundliche* judges or almost a quarter of the vacancies. The resignations and the dismissals left 63 vacancies, of which 21 were filled by collaborationists. This yields a total of 44 out of almost a hundred. Consequently, the other vacancies were filled with non-Nazi jurists, or weren't filled at all.[59]

56 Then article 84 of the Judiciary Act (Wet op de Rechterlijke Organisatie), *Staatsblad* 1932, 576.

57 Excluding: part-time judges (mostly solicitors occasionally hearing cases together with full-time judges), lay judges (the military members of military senates and of the Peace Appeals Court, and members of land lease senates). Source: *Gids voor de rechterlijke macht* 1943.

58 Sources for membership of Nazi organisations are: Rechtsfront archive, NSB archive (both at NIOD), Justice purge archive (Archief Zuivering Justitie), Centraal Archief Bijzondere Rechtspleging (CABR) (both at National Archives), and Vliegenthart archive (at Brabant Historisch Informatie Centrum); *Nationaal-socialistisch jaarboek* 1942, *Nationaal-socialistische almanak* 1943-1944.

59 See Venema 2007, 318-320, 391-392.

On top of this, twelve pre-war appointees were members of Nazi organisations. This amounts to a total of 56 judges who were Nazis or at least openly sympathized with the occupier. They did not serve all at the same time. In 1943, in the confrontational phase of the occupation, their number reached its highest point: of a total of 322 full-time judge positions, there were 51 collaborationists, which amounts to almost 16%.

6 Personnel Changes in the *Hoge Raad*

In the *Hoge Raad*, after president Visser was dismissed and another member died, a new president was appointed on 23 July 1941: Johannes van Loon.[60] This law professor, specialized in industrial and intellectual property law, had no experience in the judiciary, but had been friends with one of the most ruthless fanatics among Germany's Nazi lawyers: Hans Frank. Before the war, Van Loon, who was not a Nazi, saw Europe's future as an economic union under German leadership, and in 1935 became a corresponding member of the *Akademie für Deutsches Recht*, which was led by Hans Frank. In 1941, he had founded the 'Social-Economic Society The Netherlands and Europe'. Van Loon was introduced to Seyss-Inquart only weeks after the latter's installation as Reichskommisar, probably by Frank, and met with him regularly until late 1943. After discussing Van Loon's candidacy with Commissary-general Wimmer, Secretary-general Schrieke did not consult nor inform the *Hoge Raad* about their new president.

But why Van Loon? Why this inexperienced jurist as president of the highest court of the country? First, there were very few other candidates both (somewhat) qualified and willing, and secondly, no other candidate had such good standing with the Germans. The suspension of president Visser, and his replacement with the loyally collaborating Van Loon, 'beheaded' the *Hoge Raad* at an early stage, making it unable to play a more critical and heroic role as did for example the intact Norwegian Høyesterett.

As Van Loon had no experience with judicial work, he was 'more or less "managed"' by L.A. Nypels, who chose not to 'expose Van Loon in his incompetence', which would have been an option.[61] Van Loon's performance as president was ambiguous: on the one hand, he helped many Dutch citizens,

60 On Van Loon, see mainly Hermans 2008, Jansen & Venema 2011, 163-170.

61 J. Donner to R.P. Cleveringa, 25 January 1949, Jansen & Venema 2011, 166, 292. See on Donner and Cleveringa below.

including Jews, aided by his good relationship with Seyss-Inquart.[62] On the other hand, as we shall see, he often frustrated collective action by the *Hoge Raad* against the occupier's policies. In subsequent appointments in the *Hoge Raad*, formally made by Seyss-Inquart, Schrieke consulted with Van Loon, who did not let his colleagues participate in the process. When he thought a *Hoge Raad* judgement would be of interest to the German authorities, he sent it to them on his own initiative.[63]

The new retirement age threatened to create four vacancies at once, in addition to the one left by the death of one judge, and it was far from easy to find suitable replacements. Two *Hoge Raad* judges were retired because one, J. van Gelein Vitringa, was held responsible for a judgment from 1941 the Germans rejected,[64] and the other, vice-president J. Kosters, advocated a critical stance towards the occupier, and did not wish to be eligible for the exception.[65] The two others were left in function until they reached seventy: R. de Menthon Bake and B. Taverne, who must have been viewed as not unreliable. And two suitable candidates had been found, who both had enough experience and did not sympathise with the occupier: J.A. de Visser, who had been a public prosecutor for over twenty years, and, very briefly, minister of Justice; and P.H. Smits, who had had twelve years of experience on the bench. They were the last war-time appointees who would have qualified in normal circumstances as well. In fact, before the war Smits had already appeared on the list of nominees.

After De Visser and Smits, appointed in September 1941, no suitable candidates could be found anymore, which led to the appointment, one month later, of W.M.A. Weitjens. This colourful character had been a textile merchant and a judge in the Netherlands Antilles, which was how he knew Van Loon, whose wife was from Curaçao. Van Loon recommended him to Schrieke, who had to convince him to join the *Hoge Raad*, by explaining that he wanted to 'protect the judiciary from an invasion by extremists [i.e. Nazi fanatics]'.[66] Weitjens' merchant blood caused him, besides his judicial work, to keep trading in paintings and acting as an intermediary in lucrative transactions between Dutch and German citizens, for which he was convicted after the war.

62 See also Meihuizen 2010, 134.

63 Venema 2007, 230.

64 Mazel 1984, 52.

65 De Jong 1975, 657.

66 Weitjens 1946, 6-8.

The next two appointees had good connections via another Dutch colony, the Dutch East Indies, where they had become acquainted with Schrieke. H.A. Helb had been head of the legislative section of the Dutch East Indies department of Justice. In August 1941, he had been appointed to the Peace Appeals Court. His steep career landed him in the *Hoge Raad* in September 1942. H.W.B. Thien, appointed in June 1943, had had a long career as a judge in the Dutch East Indies. Neither was a Nazi, but they wilfully collaborated, and in most matters sided with president Van Loon. Meanwhile, three other judges had reached retirement age, one of them after having been exempt from the new age limit. This left the court one judge short.

In March 1944, vice-president Taverne died, and four days later judge J. Donner was dismissed at his request, one year after a two-year period of internment by the occupier as a hostage. Although well into the period of hard confrontations, Schrieke managed to find one last new member for the *Hoge Raad*: S.A. van Lunteren, the only NSB member ever in the *Hoge Raad*, was appointed on 13 March 1944. Van Lunteren was a convinced Nazi, who had been an NSB member since 1932 (with an interruption from 1939-1941) and authored one of the official NSB publications, a booklet on National-Socialist Philosophy of the State.[67] As a Hegelian philosopher, he belonged to a group of prominent Hegelians who drifted towards fascism and National Socialism. In 1936, after three years of teaching jurisprudence at Utrecht University, Van Lunteren became chief editor of *Volk en Vaderland*, the NSB weekly. With no experience in the judiciary, he was first appointed to the Hague Appeals Court in 1942. In the *Hoge Raad*, he did not have much opportunity to exert any influence, as Nijmegen, where the court resided at the time, was liberated six months later, in September 1944. By then, Van Lunteren had fled to Germany, leaving an infuriated Schrieke and only one published judgement bearing his name.[68]

Showing Schrieke's reluctance to accept current developments, he wrote a letter to *Hoge Raad* judge G. van der Flier to inform him of his retirement at age 65 effective 1 November 1944. The letter was dated 30 March 1945, well after the liberation of Nijmegen and the south of the Netherlands (September-October 1944), and a day before the start of the military campaign that liberated the rest of the country. The letter probably never reached Van der Flier.[69]

67 *Nationaal-socialistische (fascistische) staatsleer* (NSB brochure 3), 1933.

68 Hoge Raad 14 July 1944, *Nederlandsche Jurisprudentie* 1944/45, 477.

69 Jansen & Venema 2011, 99.

According to judge P.H. Smits, the *Hoge Raad* did not have much trouble with Van Loon, Weitjens, Helb, Thien, and Van Lunteren in the deliberations on cases: 'they initialled everything'. Deputy clerk M.J.Ch. Reyers reported that the other judges often met without the collaborators.[70]

Table 4 Personnel changes in the Dutch *Hoge Raad* under the German occupation

	out	in
23 November 1940	Jewish President L.E. Visser suspended	
1 March 1941	Visser officially dismissed	
23 June 1941	P. van Regteren Altena †	
23 July 1941		J. van Loon*
1 September 1941	*New retirement age: 65 instead of 70*	
1 September 1941	J. van Gelein Vitringa >65	J.A. de Visser
	J. Kosters >65	P.H. Smits
8 October 1941		W.M.A. Weitjens*
30 September 1942		H.A. Helb*
1 October 1942	G.A. Servatius 65	
1 April 1943	J.L.M. Meckmann 65	
1 May 1943	R.W.J.C. de Menthon Bake 70 (exception to new retirement age)	
8 June 1943		H.W.B. Thien*
9 March 1944	B. Taverne † at 69 (exception to new retirement age)	
13 March 1944	J. Donner dismissed at request	
13 March 1944		S.A. van Lunteren*

* Would normally not have been regarded as suitable candidates for the *Hoge Raad*.

7 Other Interventions in the Justice System

In one of his first decrees, VO 3/1940, Reichskommissar Seyss-Inquart announced that the administration of justice would remain independent (art. 6). He also declared existing law would remain in force, 'as far as it is compatible with the occupation' (art. 2), which was based on a rather

70 Conversation of the author with P.R. Smits, son of P.H. Smits; communication of former *Hoge Raad* clerk E. Hartogs to the author, from a conversation of Hartogs with Reyers. See also Van den Dries 1945, 5.

extensive interpretation of Hague Regulations art. 43, which allows legal changes only when the occupier is *absolutely prevented from upholding public order using existing law*.[71]

All government personnel, including judges, had to make a formal statement (not an oath), in which they promised to 'conscientiously follow the decrees and other provisions of the Reichskommissar and of the German instances under his command, and [...] refrain from any act directed against the German Reich or the German army.' (vo 3/1940, art. 7). In this first cooperative period of the occupation, even professor of international law B.M. Telders, one of the most ardent legal critics of the German occupation regime, in an optimistic vein wrote in a newspaper that 'no loyal public servant can have any objection to this statement [...]. The duty it contains forms the consideration which is indissolubly linked to the trust invested in him [...].'[72] His subsequent public criticisms, however, led to his arrest, and eventual death in concentration camp Bergen-Belsen.[73]

The same decree ordered in art. 6 that judgements were no longer to be given 'in the name of the Queen', but rather 'in the name of the Law' (*in de naam van het Recht*). Some criticized this as a denial of the Dutch nature of the justice system, although it did not violate international law.

Before we move to more substantial interventions in the work of the judiciary and especially the *Hoge Raad*, it is important to make clear how the marginalization and deportation of the Dutch Jews was kept out of reach of the courts. Some of the anti-Jewish measures were published as official decrees, many others were published only in the Jewish Weekly (*Joodsche Weekblad*) or not published at all. The first measure was taken already on 31 July 1940: a ban on the slaughter of animals without anaesthetic (vo 80/1940), which outlawed the slaughter method prescribed by Judaism. The Germans wanted to prevent any public discussion of anti-Jewish criminal laws, so they put their enforcement in the hands of the German criminal courts in the Netherlands. Litigation in relation to anti-Jewish decrees was not allowed, and when in a court case before a Dutch court, one of those measures threatened to become relevant and be discussed, the case was taken away from the Dutch court and decided by Seyss-Inquart (vo 230/1940).[74]

71 See the introduction to this book.

72 Telders 1947, 304 (from newspaper *NRC*, 8 June 1940).

73 For a short biography, see Telders 1972.

74 Venema 2007, 212-214, 287-289.

I will now discuss the measures of the occupation regime which were relevant for the *Hoge Raad*. A fundamental legal principle which the Nazi occupation regime tried to undermine, was the legality principle in criminal law: *nulla poena sine lege*. Brought into Dutch law by Napoleon, it was one of the hallmarks of 19th century formalism, and has retained the support of the vast majority of jurists until today. In the 1920s and 1930s, however, several prominent legal scholars and public servants advocated what they called 'analogous application of the criminal law', which meant that acts worthy of punishment, but not falling under the exact wording of any criminal offence, could still be punished, as long as they showed enough similarity with acts that did fall under one of the legally defined offences.[75] Two important advocates of this idea were J.P. Hooykaas, who in 1941 had briefly been acting secretary-general of Justice, and B.M. Taverne, vice-president of the *Hoge Raad*.

Paragraph 1 of article 1 of the Dutch criminal code contained, as it still does, the legality principle: 'No act is punishable except on the grounds of a prior statutory criminal law'. In June 1943, during the period of confrontations, VO 1943/62 added a second sentence:

> If an act does not fall under the wording of a statutory offence, the statute is still applicable, if the act falls under the underlying rationale of the statutory offence, and merits punishment according to a sound (gezond) sense of justice.

The text was inspired by the German equivalent from 1935, containing the infamous phrase 'gesundes Volksempfinden' (literally 'the people's healthy feeling', meaning something like 'sound public judgment').[76] The Dutch version changed this to 'gezond rechtsgevoel' (sound sense of justice). In the official explanation in the most read national law journal, Hooykaas mentioned as grounds: protection of state interests, protection of well-meaning citizens, the unforeseeability of the nature of all future misbehaviours, and the fast changes in society and public opinion. All of this demanded, according to Hooykaas, a more flexible criminal law.[77]

The procedure to create this amendment had started before the period of confrontations, in April 1942. Secretary-general Schrieke had requested the

75 Venema 2007, 112-117.

76 See especially the new articles 2a of the criminal code and 170a and 267a of the code of criminal procedure, *Reichsgesetzblatt* 1935, Vol. I, 839 & 844.

77 Hooykaas 1944, 13-14.

advice on the proposed amendment of the *Hoge Raad*, the Peace Appeals Court, the Rechtsfront, and the Institute for Legal Renewal (Instituut voor Rechtsvernieuwing).[78] The latter institutions' advice came in late and was not useful, according to Schrieke. President of the Peace Appeals Court Carp objected that most judges did 'not yet fully understand the demands of the coming times', and therefore would not be able to apply the new law in the desired manner. This objection was not met. Van Loon had formed a commission to prepare an advice, consisting of Taverne, known supporter of the idea, W.A.J.M. Fick, and G. van der Flier, who had no objections in principle to the analogous application of the criminal law, but did object to implementation during the occupation. The *Hoge Raad* had also received a lengthy essay on the subject by Peace Appeals Court judge Helb, who would join the *Hoge Raad* later that year.

The commission was of the opinion that the proposed addition to the criminal law would in most cases make little difference. It would merely be used in cases where the court would otherwise call its argument an (extensive) interpretation, such as in the case from 1892 where a defendant was convicted for damaging telegraph poles, whereas he had in fact damaged *telephone* poles, a relatively new phenomenon, which hadn't made it into the lawbooks yet. The *Hoge Raad* had argued, that in this context, the legal term 'telegraph' could also mean telephone.[79] The occupation was, in the eyes of the commission, however, not the right time to introduce the possibility of punishing *per analogiam*, because of the difficulty to assess the 'people's sense of justice'. As the *Hoge Raad* was divided over the whole question, it was decided to send Schrieke merely some editorial comments, and add the commission's report as an attachment. Schrieke accepted all editorial comments, including, not unimportantly, the change of the less binding 'the statute may be applied' to the stricter 'the statute is still applicable'.

All the trouble was eventually in vain: there is no evidence of the new article ever having been applied by a regular criminal court. In only one reported case did a district court *consider* its application, but decided against it, because it judged that the two reasons Hooykaas had mentioned in his official explanation were not relevant in the matter at hand.[80] Ironically, the one reported case where it *was* applied, was a case before the Peace Appeals Court, which had advised *against* its introduction.[81]

78 Venema 2007, 283-286.

79 Hoge Raad 21 November 1892, *Weekblad voor het Recht* 6282.

80 Rechtbank Rotterdam 21 March 1944, *Nederlandsche Jurisprudentie* 1944, 299.

81 Venema 2007, 356-357.

Another ideologically motivated plan also ended in failure: a proposal to change the legal grounds for divorce.[82] In the Netherlands, divorce by mutual consent was legally forbidden (civil code art. 263), but nevertheless possible when both spouses declared that (at least) one of them had committed adultery, which they often enough had not. The courts knowingly cooperated with what was in fact illegal, and commonly called 'the big lie'. The occupier wished to end this and to expand the list of grounds for divorce with, amongst other things, 'such discord as to damage the foundation of the marriage' (the German *Zerrüttung der Ehe*), 'refusal to procreate without sufficient grounds', and 'untimely infertility, without children having been born'. The anonymous government commentator explained that the new grounds were especially in the interest of the family, 'the most important cell of the community'.

In December 1942, still in the second phase of the occupation, of 'coerced nazification', Schrieke went through the trouble of requesting advice from the *Hoge Raad*, two appeals courts, two archbishops, three churches, and two national-socialist institutions: the Rechtsfront and the Institute for Legal Renewal. The *Hoge Raad* took its time, and sent in its advice a full year later, mentioning the forced removal to Nijmegen in May 1943 as an excuse. In the discussion of the internal commission's report, president Van Loon did not agree with the commission's opinion that changing the divorce grounds fell outside the scope of the occupier's powers according to Hague Regulations article 43, as not being necessary to guarantee public order and civic life. Also, the committee argued, the amendment did not reflect public opinion. In sum, the occupation was not the right time for such a fundamental change in the law. In Van Loon's view, only the occupier himself could assess whether a measure was necessary in the sense of art. 43 or not. *Hoge Raad* judge Donner, who was not a member of the committee, defended their standpoint by saying: 'The only thing we have vis à vis the occupier are the Hague Regulations. That is our foothold.' Van Loon lost, and the advice to Schrieke opened with the rejection based on international law.

Especially in the last two phases of the occupation, those of open confrontations (from April 1943) and chaos (from September 1944), several alterations were made in procedural law. The main objective was to speed up procedures. More cases could be heard by a single judge instead of a court of three (VO 13/1943), and appeal and cassation limits were raised in civil and criminal matters (VO 91/1942; VO 79/1943; VO 3/1945; VO 4/1945). The first time

82 Venema 2007, 278-281.

those limits were raised, still in the period of coerced nazification, the *Hoge Raad* had been able to give its advice, which resulted in a lesser increase than the regime had wished.[83] The second time, in the confrontations period, the *Hoge Raad* learned of the new cassation limits from the newspapers. Not even Van Loon was consulted.[84]

On 28 December 1943, Schrieke introduced the *Führerprinzip*, the leader's principle, to the judiciary.[85] This awarded more powers to the court presidents, including *Hoge Raad* president Van Loon, who did not sign the *Hoge Raad*'s letter of protest against this violation of the collegial nature of judicial decision making. Neither did the war-time appointees Weitjens, Helb and Thien. For Donner, who had recently returned from captivity, this law was the last straw, leading him to resign. Schrieke was glad to see Donner go, and called him 'blind for the demands of this time'.[86]

Two other types of intervention affected the work of the *Hoge Raad*: its removal from The Hague to Nijmegen, and the forced labour programme. Since mid-1942, the German authorities had considered seriously the possibility of allied troops landing on the North Sea coast.[87] This led to the construction of the *Atlantikwall*, which necessitated evacuations of people and institutions and the demolition of many buildings in the long coastal area. As The Hague lies near the coast, it was decided to relocate government departments and other institutions to different towns in the eastern part of the country.[88] This had two other advantages for the occupier: the Dutch civil service would be scattered and less able to resist occupation measures *en bloc*, and German officials would be nearer the German border in case of the need for retreat to the *Heimat*.

In May 1943 Schrieke published the decision to move the *Hoge Raad*'s seat to Nijmegen, the oldest city in the Netherlands, across the country from The Hague, close to the German border.[89] The judges' protest had not had any effect. The court used a private property as office space, and the nearby auditorium of the closed Catholic University of Nijmegen functioned as courtroom. Some judges moved to the Nijmegen area, others stayed in their homes in or near The Hague, and organized temporary

83 *Hoge Raad* archive, General Meetings Book of Minutes 1921-1958, meeting of 6 January 1942.

84 *Hoge Raad* archive, General Meetings Book of Minutes 1921-1958, meeting of 29 september 1943; J. Donner archive, Hooge Raad der Nederlanden to Secretary-General of Justice, November 1943.

85 *Nederlandsche Staatscourant* 1944, 3.

86 Jansen & Venema 2007, 107-109.

87 De Jong 1975, 60.

88 Verburg 2016, Ch. 26; De Jong 1975, 765-779.

89 *Nederlandsche Staatscourant* 1943, 89.

lodgings in Nijmegen. The office building was bombed by the American air force on 22 February 1944,[90] destroying part of the *Hoge Raad* archives. After Taverne died on 9 March 1944 and the Nazi Van Lunteren was subsequently appointed, the latter was quartered in Taverne's house in Nijmegen, to the horror of the latter's widow and children.[91] Luckily for them, Van Lunteren fled to Germany on 'mad Tuesday', 5 September 1944, when rumours of the imminent liberation of the whole country chased many an NSB member across the border. In fact, only the south was freed that month, and a large part of the Netherlands had to wait at least six more months.

While in Nijmegen, the *Hoge Raad* was confronted with the so-called 'arbeidsinzet', the forced labour programme. Begun in 1942, it was expanded in 1943 with the obligation for all men between 18 and 35 years of age to report to the local labour agency for work in Germany (VO 43/1943).[92] Initially, civil servants were exempted, but this was soon informally repealed. The *Hoge Raad* procurator-general, W.J. Berger, refused to provide the requested information on his staff, and was subsequently dismissed. The judges agreed with Berger that the forced labour programme violated the Hague Regulations, especially art. 52, allowing 'requisitions in kind and services' only 'for the needs of the army of occupation'. Van Loon, however, did not want to discuss the matter in the *Hoge Raad* meeting. Therefore, the other judges held a secret pre-meeting and decided to refuse the information as well, and they said so in the official meeting, ignoring Van Loon's ban on the subject. Van Loon cut the discussion short and reported to Schrieke the decision of his colleagues. To avoid conflict, Schrieke retracted his request, and the *Hoge Raad* did not protest publicly against the forced labour programme.[93]

With regard to post-war discussions on the *Hoge Raad*'s war-record, the symbolic culmination point of all these developments is a judgement from 12 January 1942, which has become known as the *Toetsingsarrest* (Judicial Review Case). As it is often contrasted with a judgement of the Leeuwarden Appeals Court from 1943, I will devote the next section to these judgements that came to symbolize surrender and protest respectively.

90 Destroying much of the old city, this was a badly executed bombing of the Nijmegen railway area, a secondary (or even tertiary) target of an American bombing squadron that hadn't been able to bomb its primary target, an airplane factory in Gotha, Germany. See Rosendaal 2009.

91 Conversation of the author with Taverne's daughter N. van Lookeren Campagne-Taverne.

92 See also Klemann 2002, 265-276.

93 Jansen & Venema 2011, 104-106; *Hoge Raad* archive, General Meetings Book of Minutes 1921-1958, meeting of 29 september 1943.

8 The Judicial Review Case

In the Dutch monistic system, international treaties automatically become an integral part of the Dutch legal order. At least from the beginning of the 20th century, all forms of national legislation, including acts of parliament, whether created before or after a treaty, were considered lower in rank. Nowadays, national legislation contradicting a treaty will be declared unlawful by the courts and consequently not applied, but before the war, the *Hoge Raad* had always avoided explicit judicial review by creatively interpreting national laws as conforming with the treaty they may in reality have conflicted with.[94] So actually reviewing legislation by the occupier against Hague Regulations art. 43 would have been, although not contrary to Dutch law, a novelty.

The problem of judicial review had concerned the *Hoge Raad* from the beginning of the occupation. Professor of international law B.M. Telders compiled over a hundred pages of documentation (excerpts from international handbooks, international case law, etc.) on the subject, which vice-president J. Kosters used in the autumn of 1940 to write a thorough report on judicial review of occupation ordinances.[95] In 1940 and 1941, there were more jurists who addressed the problem of the review of occupation ordinances in legal and illegal publications. Some argued that judicial review would violate Dutch law (which was not very convincing, or at most a minority view), others that it would be unwise given the circumstances, and still others argued both.[96]

The case before the *Hoge Raad*[97] involved a conviction for buying meat without valid food distribution coupons. The defendant was tried by an economic criminal court, created by the secretary-general of Justice under authority of the occupier. In his cassation appeal, the defendant pleaded the quashing of his conviction on the grounds of incompetence of the court, arguing that the ordinance establishing the economic court system did not live up to the criterion of Hague Regulations art. 43, which demanded the absolute impossibility of upholding public order and civic life without

94 Fleuren 2004, 10-18, 98-132.

95 De Ruiter 2003, 197.

96 The most important wartime and post-war commentaries on the legal background and on the verdict have been published and introduced, along with the verdict itself, in Venema et. al. 2008. See also De Ruiter 191-196.

97 *Hoge Raad* 12 January 1942, *Nederlandsche Jurisprudentie* 1942, 271, published on-line in 2021: https://uitspraken.rechtspraak.nl/inziendocument?id=ECLI:NL:HR:1942:244&showbutton=true.

creating new laws. In other words, according to the defence, the economic courts were not necessary to secure public order and civic life, and thus illegal and lacking competence.

Procurator-general Berger in his advice to the *Hoge Raad* offered a way to side-step the review problem altogether, suggesting that in peace time the Dutch government would have taken similar necessary measures and that the economic courts were not so foreign to the justice system so as to constitute a case of 'not respecting the laws in force in the occupied country.' In arguing towards this conclusion, however, an implicit review of the legislation was nevertheless made. The *Hoge Raad* did not follow this suggestion. The most important elements of the judgment are the following:

1. The occupier is competent to issue laws *within the restrictions of Hague Regulations art. 43: those laws must be aimed at ensuring public order and civic life*. The ordinance establishing the economic court system, issued under the occupier's authority, is *such a law*.
2. Therefore, under the 'present conditions' [i.e. that said ordinance was issued under the authorities of those who, according to Dutch treaty law, exercise factual sovereignty over the occupied territory[98]], that ordinance is to be considered Dutch law [i.e. law which is valid in the occupied Netherlands].
3. Dutch courts may, however, not review legislation against treaties.
4. There is nothing in the Hague Convention, nor in its history, nor in the Dutch parliamentary discussions that bears witness to the intention to award courts in occupied territory the power to review ordinances *aimed at ensuring public order and civic life* against the requirement of Hague Regulations art. 43 that this aim cannot be reached using only the existing laws of the land.
5. Therefore, the appeal is denied.

The surprising step is of course the third, as review would have been novel, but in accordance with the law, as explained at the start of this section. Nonetheless, as the first and fourth steps show, the court distinguishes between two requirements of Hague Regulations art. 43, and does assess whether the ordinance in question meets the first one: that the occupier's ordinances must be aimed at ensuring public order and civic life. Only after having concluded that this is the case regarding the ordinance in question, does the court decide that *this type of ordinance*, falling in the category of

98 As explained in a later deleted sentence in the draft version of the decision. National Archives, Archive 2.09.65: *Hoge Raad* der Nederlanden, (1939)1940 – 1979(1980), inventory number 780.

'Dutch laws' cannot be reviewed against the second requirement, which is that such ordinances may only be issued when public order and civic life cannot be guaranteed using only existing law. An important element is that the ban on review is applied only to ordinances 'aimed at ensuring public order and civic life'. This means that other ordinances, such as anti-Jewish or forced labour measures, have not been classified by the *Hoge Raad* as 'Dutch laws'[99] and consequently were not 'protected' by this judgment, as some have complained. From the occupation to the present day, less meticulous and more casual readings of the *Hoge Raad*'s decision have led to strong, yet somewhat misguided, moral criticisms. Usually, an oversimplified good-and-evil and heroes-and-villains perspective lies at the basis of those arguments.[100]

The court's arguments listed under 4 are legally irrelevant and thus superfluous, and it seems that they are given to deflect from the court's decision, which was unprecedented, and, according to Dutch law, not at all self-evident. This means that the choice to introduce into Dutch law a ban on judicial review was prompted by other considerations.

This decision has given rise to a longstanding, still ongoing debate in Dutch legal (academic) circles which touches upon various themes of legal and political theory. I will address these more extensively in the concluding chapter of this book. Here, I will focus briefly on opinions during the occupation and its immediate aftermath. Two *Hoge Raad* judges defended the decision in writing. They were not members of the senate that heard the case, as it is not customary for judges to comment on their own decisions. The first recorded defence appears in the 1943 correspondence between judge Losecaat Vermeer and professor Cleveringa, a highly principled, patriotic anti-German jurist noted for his famous protest speech as faculty dean on 26 November 1940 against the dismissal of Jewish professors from Leiden University.[101] In Cleveringa's opinion, a judge should always assess the legal validity of the laws he is asked to apply, and when he is prevented from doing so, he should resign, because he can no longer be a proper judge. But when a judge refuses to assess the law's validity and nevertheless remains in office, he is in the wrong, and when the highest court in the country does this, the court is guilty of 'undermining the law', which amounts to

99 Cf. Frank de Vries, unpublished manuscript on the review case, on file with the author. See also Van den Dries 1945, 38 fn 45.

100 See Venema et. al. 2008 for an overview, as well as the discussion in the final chapter of this book.

101 Venema et. al. 2008, 75-85. On Cleveringa: Schuyt 2018.

'the self-elimination of the judiciary', because all past and future measures of the occupier are thereby approved and rendered untouchable. Moreover, according to Cleveringa, the people were longing for a public cry from the heart to encourage them.[102]

Against Cleveringa's severe moral criticism, Losecaat Vermeer defends the *Hoge Raad*'s decision with pragmatic reasoning: it is more important to remain in office in order to be able to help the population than to antagonize the occupier and risk dismissal of the court and replacement by collaborationists or even the abolishment of all courts.[103] Judge N.C.M.A. van den Dries, under whose name the post-war apology of the *Hoge Raad* was published, stated this mayor in wartime dilemma clearly: when the *Hoge Raad* would resign or be dismissed, the majority of the courts would follow and legal chaos would result. Remaining in function, as the government had instructed, would enable the courts to mitigate the force of the occupier's measures.[104]

A case in point is a famous 1943 judgment of the Leeuwarden Appeals Court.[105] This court lowered the sentence of a thief because the temporary penal facility, Camp Ommen, where he would be sent was rather horrible: cruel guards made the badly fed inmates work so hard that they often ended up in hospital. Besides presenting these circumstances as grounds for leniency, the court also mentioned that it did so 'for conscience's sake'. This was immediately understood, by Dutch and Germans alike, as expressing disapproval of the occupation regime for allowing such inhumane circumstances in Camp Ommen. But it was also strongly felt as a general cry from the heart against the Nazi occupation as a whole. As such, it was hailed, by Cleveringa and others, as a necessary morally principled stand which should be an example to the *Hoge Raad*. Others, such as Losecaat Vermeer, called it a 'tactical error', because by infuriating the Germans, the Leeuwarden verdict endangered the careful and discreet lobby to achieve the closing of Camp Ommen. *Generalkommissar* Wimmer confirmed this in a post-war interview: 'They handled it completely the wrong way.'[106] One of the principal lobbyists was B.M. Taverne, the presiding judge in the judicial

102 Venema et. al. 2008, p. 80, 81, respectively.

103 See also Van den Dries 1945, 23-33.

104 Van den Dries 1945, 9-10.

105 Published after the war: Hof Leeuwarden 25 February 1943, *Nederlandsche Jurisprudentie* 1951, 501, and published on-line in 2021: https://uitspraken.rechtspraak.nl/inziendocument?id=ECLI:NL:GHLEE:1943:22.

A book was devoted to the history of this case and the judges who decided it: Hermans 2003.

106 Blom 2005, 367.

review case.[107] He managed to convince president Van Loon to protest to the German authorities. After Seyss-Inquart dismissed the Leeuwarden judges responsible, Taverne participated in the protest against this as well.[108]

The consequences of the ban on judicial review of occupation regime ordinances are difficult to determine, because we do not know for certain how the occupier would have reacted against a review, or what the judiciary would have done if the *Hoge Raad* had stepped down or been dismissed. In any case, neither the *Hoge Raad* nor any other Dutch court found themselves in the position where they would have to decide on the application of measures concerning the persecution of the Jews, or any other politically sensitive matters, as explained earlier.[109] That did not mean, however, that no questionable ordinances would ever be relevant in a court case. In late 1943, after the Ommen question had been resolved, the *Hoge Raad* applied an ordinance concerning the *Kultuurkamer* (Chamber of Culture). It decided, with a senate consisting of two collaborationists and three other members, against the lower courts, that the term 'art' applied to mass produced paintings that would normally not be considered 'art', thus ensuring a wide scope of the *Kultuurkamer* membership obligation.[110] The *Hoge Raad* tax division also handed down a decision in which a questionable measure (imposing a collective fine, termed a 'reconciliatory payment') was excluded from judicial scrutiny by not awarding it the status of a tax.[111]

While the Germans and the Dutch Nazis were content with the decision in the review case, many others were discouraged, especially lawyers.[112] Still, in early September 1944, a lawyer requested a temporary injunction at the Arnhem District court, on the grounds that the ordinance establishing the Pharmacists Chamber was illegal. The judge, F.M.O. van Nispen tot Sevenaer, granted the request, arguing, amongst other things, that there were solid grounds for the rejection of the ordinance in the light of Hague regulations article 43, and that the civil senate of the *Hoge Raad* might decide to review it, even though the criminal senate had decided against it.[113] This was not unimaginable, as the *Hoge Raad* had also referred to Hague regulations article 43 in its advisory opinion rejecting the proposed amendment of the divorce law. This Arnhem case renders the lawyers' argument that the

107 Jansen & Venema 2011, 137-139.

108 Hermans 2003, 128-142; Jansen & Venema 2011, 141-144; Jansen 2018.

109 See footnote 39 and accompanying text.

110 Venema 2007, 357-358.

111 See also Essers 2012, section 6.2.

112 See Meihuizen 2010, 85, 415-416.

113 Rechtbank Arnhem, 4 September 1944, *Nederlandsche Jurisprudentie* 1944/1945, 653.

review case dissuaded or even prevented them from requesting judicial review in court cases less convincing, especially since this case was the last in a series of similar cases with similar pleas.[114]

The Arnhem case did not go further due to the battle of Arnhem that started two weeks later as part of the allied Operation Market Garden, destroying the courthouse and other parts of the city, and probably preventing the judge's otherwise expected arrest.[115] In this period of chaos, the occupying authorities were mainly concerned with emergency measures.

9 Liberation and Aftermath

While the liberation of Arnhem failed, Operation Market Garden did successfully liberate nearby Nijmegen, which became part of the frontline for several months.[116] In this period of social chaos, the *Hoge Raad*, having its seat in Nijmegen at that time, stopped functioning. Van Lunteren, the only NSB-member in the *Hoge Raad*, had fled from Nijmegen to Germany a few weeks earlier, and many other judges were in The Hague and unable to travel to Nijmegen. Secretary-general Schrieke's attempt to convince the judges to resume their duties in The Hague failed, because president Van Loon refused to cooperate, on the grounds that since the liberation of Nijmegen, the occupier had lost authority over the *Hoge Raad*.[117] On 22 November, Schrieke formally abolished cassation for pending cases, effective from 17 September 1944.[118] But on 20 September, martial law had been declared in Nijmegen, and on the same date the returning government issued the order to suspend all *Hoge Raad* judges. Only two of them were in Nijmegen, so the others learned about their suspension from the radio. The exiled government as well as the resistance movement had been disconcerted by the *Hoge Raad*'s policy – as far as they were aware of it – for some years, and this measure surely did not improve its public image. A deadlock between the government and the judges resulted: the judges felt deeply aggrieved by the government's lack of tact, especially since, in their opinion, the government did not have an adequate picture of the situation in the Netherlands under the Nazi occupiers, 'wrathfully hurling its lightning bolts from the

114 Venema 2007, 351-354.

115 Barendsen & Venema 2004, 59-65

116 See for this section especially: Jansen & Venema 2011, Part 3.

117 Hermans 2008, 86-87.

118 Jansen & Venema, 110-111 and VO 49/1944.

unreachable heights of the London Olympus towards Dutch soil,"[119] as it was formulated in the *Hoge Raad*'s post-war pamphlet.[120]

To restore public confidence in the judiciary, the returned government wanted the remaining *Hoge Raad* judges to resign of their own accord,[121] as they enjoyed independence from the executive, who could not fire them – except the war-time appointees, whose terms ended automatically upon the restoration of sovereignty. But the judges held firmly to their most important guideline for their wartime conduct: the government's own pre-war instructions to remain in office as long as possible for the benefit of the population. To be able to do so, they could not have protested publicly against any of the occupier's measures: the dismissal of their Jewish president, the appointment of Van Loon and other *deutschfreundliche* judges, the installation of the peace court judges, the dismissal of the Leeuwarden judges, or any other decision. The judgment in the review case should also be seen in this light. The Germans had made it clear that they wanted absolutely no public signs of disapproval from any of the remaining Dutch government offices. Heated correspondence between the *Hoge Raad* and the government and critical pamphlets from other jurists were published.[122] Although the stalemate remained unresolved, the understaffed *Hoge Raad* was allowed to resume its duties on 10 October 1945.

The solution to the '*Hoge Raad* problem' was the appointment on 8 November 1946 of J. Donner as president instead of the judge whose seniority would have made him eligible: Van den Dries, the formal author of the apologetic pamphlet. Donner was the only judge who did not bear the stain of collaborating with the enemy, because he had been involved with the resistance and, also as the only *Hoge Raad* judge, been arrested twice and held hostage for two years, before resigning on 13 March 1944, when he no longer felt morally able to remain in office.[123] As a hostage, he was held in several Dutch camps and in camp Buchenwald. However, although in captivity, he was not isolated from the rest of the world: in the camps, he met many prominent politicians and corresponded with colleagues and family. The *Hoge Raad* tax law senate even managed to send him a cake while in captivity![124] What the public (and many members of government)

119 Van den Dries 1945, 73.

120 Jansen & Venema 2011, 227-236.

121 Minister of Justice Gerbrandy to all members of the *Hoge Raad*, excluding Donner and the wartime appointees, 21 June 1945. Jansen & Venema 2011, 253-257.

122 Collected in Venema et. al. 2008.

123 See on Donner: De Ruiter 2003, esp. Chs. 10-15.

124 De Ruiter 2003, 162.

did not know, was that he completely agreed with the way the *Hoge Raad* had handled the occupation, and with Van den Dries' pamphlet, to which he had also contributed. Indeed, in a letter to Van den Dries, he called the draft defence of the review case 'masterly'.[125] In public, Donner not once uttered a word about the *Hoge Raad*'s occupation history. Even at his installation as president, in November 1946, he did not commemorate his predecessor L.E. Visser, which was particularly painful as he was wearing Visser's robe, a present from Visser's surviving daughter.[126]

Together with Donner, finally new members could be appointed to the *Hoge Raad* vacancies. Donner promoted the appointment of jurists who were trusted by the former resistance, such as A.L.M. van Berckel (1948) and H. Haga (1951), who had stepped down as judges in protest against the Peace Courts in 1941, and had been vice-president and president of the Special Court of Cassation (see next section). Cleveringa, moralistic as ever, kept commenting publicly and otherwise on all the appointments in the court he liked and disliked. Even the regular promotions of Van den Dries, Fick, and also of Nypels, who had 'managed' Van Loon during the occupation, to vice-president led him to air his disgust in letters and a publication.[127]

10 Purges and Prosecutions

While Smits was reappointed in November 1946, and De Visser returned to the Public Prosecutor's office at the Arnhem Appeals Court, the other wartime appointees in the *Hoge Raad* would not return to the judiciary. Thien was the only one who was not prosecuted, merely purged. Although there were no grave objections against his conduct, and he was a competent and experienced jurist, according to the purge committee he should never have accepted an appointment while he knew that his acquaintance with secretary-general Schrieke was the only reason his name was put forward. He was banned from any future function in the judiciary, as was Weitjens, who had traded illegally with the Germans. To account for his shady dealings, Weitjens also had to appear before a tribunal of the 'Special Criminal Court System', created by the exiled government in 1943 and 1944 to try collaborators. This tribunal found that intellectuals had a special responsibility,

125 De Ruiter 2003, 217.

126 De Ruiter 2003, 234.

127 Jansen & Venema 2011, 291-292.

and therefore disenfranchised him from the right to vote and to stand for election.[128]

The Special Criminal Court System consisted of 'tribunals' for the less serious cases, 'courts of justice' for the more serious cases and a 'Special Court of Cassation' as an appeal court.[129] Helb, Van Lunteren and Van Loon were tried before the same court as Weitjens: the Hague Tribunal. This means that these judges were not viewed as major traitors, but that their conduct did merit a more serious than merely administrative reaction. Helb's acceptance of an appointment in the political criminal court *Vredegerechtshof* (Peace Appeals Court) was the major reason that he was prosecuted as a collaborator, unlike Thien, the other Dutch East Indies connection from Schrieke, who was only purged. Helb justified his actions by arguing that he had accepted the positions in the *Vredegerechtshof* and the *Hoge Raad* only with good intentions: to help uphold law and order, and because Schrieke preferred not to appoint an NSB member in the *Hoge Raad*. Prominent former government officials from the Dutch East Indies testified to Helb's good character. The tribunal's sentence was mild: internment for the period that he had already been interned (until 8 October 1946), and confiscation of shares. He did not lose his voting rights, because of his remorseful attitude.[130]

Van Lunteren had more to answer for: he had been a long time NSB member, been involved with the National Socialist 'Institute for Legal Renewal', and he had bought a house from the *Niederländische Grundstücksverwaltung*, the organization for the administration of stolen Jewish property. The sentence was: internment for the period that he had already been interned (until 24 October 1946), disenfranchisement from the right to vote and to stand for election, and the harshest punishment: confiscation of his large library, which was subsequently put at the disposal of the Council for Legal Reparations (an institute handling claims arising from theft or illegal transactions during the occupation).[131]

The exponent of collaborating jurists in the *Hoge Raad* was of course president Van Loon, who had accepted an appointment from the German occupier to the position left vacant by the dismissal of his Jewish predecessor Visser. Van Loon was the kind of person who 'liked his own way and [...] got his own way.'[132] His opponent before the tribunal was the equally stubborn

128 Jansen & Venema 2011, 279-282, 307-308.

129 See Venema 2019a and Romijn 2002.

130 Jansen & Venema 2011, 184-187, 302-304.

131 Jansen & Venema 2011, 304-306.

132 According to his eldest son, in Hermans 2008, 104.

and ambitious prosecutor J. Zaaijer, who had been frustrated by his failure to make the trial against NSB-leader Mussert, in 1945, into a trial against the NSB as a whole.[133] During the impasse between the returned government and the *Hoge Raad*, however, Zaaijer initially tried something similar with respect to Van Loon in May 1946: without consulting with his superiors, he sent Van Loon an indictment that in fact constituted a charge against the whole *Hoge Raad*.[134] Van Loon was to appear before a Special Court of Justice. Zaaijer's aim was to put pressure on the *Hoge Raad* in order to force a solution to the conflict, preferably the judges' voluntary resignation. It was probably Donner who convinced the minister of Justice Kolfschoten to order Zaaijer to repeal his indictment, which he did, five days after it had been issued.[135]

After a second draft was also rejected by the minister, and finally in March 1947, Van Loon was tried – not before a Special Court of Justice, but before a tribunal,[136] because after new interventions by the new *Hoge Raad* president Donner at the ministry, it was decided that Van Loon was one of the less serious cases. Because the government nor the *Hoge Raad* wished any more public discussion on the *Hoge Raad*, it was undesirable either to let Van Loon be acquitted or to discuss the *Hoge Raad* at length at the trial. Therefore, the indictment was short and easily proved: Van Loon was accused of accepting the position of president of the *Hoge Raad* from the hands of the occupier whose intention it was to appoint willing collaborators in key positions, expecting them to promote the interests of the occupying regime. This strange accusation was partly obvious, as no-one would deny that Van Loon had been *Hoge Raad* president, partly obscure: not *Van Loon's actions* as president but *the occupier's expectations* were part of the formal accusation.[137] The verdict does not clarify this, but simply declares this part of the indictment proven.[138] The presiding tribunal judge, A.W.J. van Vrijberghe de Coningh, has been depicted as a priggish little man who was harsh in his verdicts.[139] Van Loon complained to his

133 See on the Mussert trial: Venema 2019b, originally published in Dutch as Venema 2015; The relevant documents are published in: *Het proces Mussert* 1987.

134 Hermans 2008, 90-92.

135 Meihuizen 2003, 400-401n290.

136 See Hermans 2008, 89-102.

137 Less important parts of the indictment were: paying social visits to Reichskommissar Seyss-Inquart, attending national-socialist (legal) events, and having several subscriptions and memberships in the national-socialist spectrum.

138 Reproduced in Hermans 2008, 139-156.

139 Meihuizen 2003, 233, 706-707, 722-723.

lawyer that this judge had done the same thing that he was now judging him, Van Loon, for: indeed, Van Vrijberghe de Coningh, as a judge in the Hague district court, had accepted an appointment to the Hague Appeals Court from the occupation regime in 1942.

Van Loon was sentenced to internment until the day of the verdict, disenfranchisement from the right to vote and to stand for election, and confiscation of his farmhouse and his large legal library. Although there was no ordinary legal remedy, a High Authority had to authorize the execution of the tribunals' verdicts. The confiscation of Van Loon's farmhouse was repealed, but the library, which had nothing to do with aiding the enemy, and was not worth much in relation to Van Loon's property in total, remained confiscated, although this severely harmed him. The books ended up in several court libraries.[140]

11 Conclusion

As the only one of the three state powers whose organization remained virtually intact, the judiciary, and especially its supreme national organ, the *Hoge Raad*, was a focus of hope for the people. With government in London and parliament dissolved, the courts were the only remaining check on regulations and other measures taken by the occupation authorities. It was therefore only logical that people were looking to the *Hoge Raad* for some kind of critical evaluation of, or even protest against, the occupier's measures and policies. It did not come. Faced with the mayor-in-wartime predicament and German warnings against public criticism, the judges had decided against open confrontation and instead chosen the path of silent diplomacy and underground aid. They felt supported by the pre-war government Instructions and by their own conviction that the country would be much worse off with a collaborationist *Hoge Raad*, or even a general court strike. That their diplomatic interventions were not known to the public, and not valued by the cabinet in exile (as far as the ministers did know about them), led to a bitter impasse after the liberation.

Starting with the dismissal of their Jewish president Visser in 1940, which decapitated the *Hoge Raad* and the judiciary as a whole, a series of measures were accepted and partly implemented by the *Hoge Raad*, implicating the institution in the occupier's policy. Some of the most salient measures were: the Aryan declaration as basis for dismissing all Jews from

140 Hermans 2008, 102.

government service and their subsequent persecution, the lowering of the retirement age for judges, the introduction of the 'judge of the peace', and the appointments of *deutschfreundliche* judges in the *Hoge Raad* and other courts. Some other measures were largely symbolic, such as the introduction of the *Führerprinzip* in the judiciary and the analogous application of the criminal law.

Although in three appeal courts and five district courts, the post of president has been filled by a regime-friendly judge for a certain period,[141] and the five chief public prosecutors were Nazis for most of the occupation,[142] the judiciary was not 'nazified' in the way for example local government was.[143] There were simply not enough qualified jurists who were also *deutschfreundlich* to fill the vacancies.[144] Moreover, the national socialist secretary-general of justice Schrieke did not want to appoint fervent Nazis, as he knew that would cause problems for the cooperation in the courts.

The *Hoge Raad*'s remaining in office and not reviewing the occupier's ordinances may have added an appearance of legitimacy to the occupation regime, but it is hard to assess whether it weakened the resistance, as has been argued by some. On the contrary: on the district court level, some resistance organizations had very different experiences with judges, as they were helped by courts in economic crime cases where food for people in hiding was at stake.[145] Because there are many types of resistance, with many different consequences, it is very hard to draw general conclusions on this point. The same holds true for the more general criticism that a different tactic would have served public morale, and fed the spirit of resistance against the oppressor.

Should the *Hoge Raad* judges have aspired to become war heroes and to 'secure a place in post-war heaven', as judge Losecaat Vermeer formulated it in a letter to professor Cleveringa? To the judges, remaining at their posts felt as a selfless act of patriotism. To Cleveringa and some others, it seemed like the line of least resistance, choosing the lesser evil instead of the greater good. Protest or resignation might have resulted in praise, because of the moral support it would have lent to the people. The *Hoge Raad* judges doubtless acted in what they saw as the best interest of the country and its people.

141 Venema 2007, 391-392.

142 Verburg 2005, 47, 69-73.

143 On local government: Romijn 2006.

144 This makes the title of Michielsens study *The 'Nazification' and 'Denazification' of the Courts in Belgium, Luxembourg, and the Netherlands'* somewhat misleading, notwithstanding the parentheses.

145 Venema 2007, 250.

Nevertheless, the need for a public protest was more strongly felt than the unprovable practical necessity of remaining in office to prevent worse.

References

Aalders, Gerard, *Niets was wat het leek, Prins Bernhard*, Boom 2014.

Barendsen, Jan, & Derk Venema, *De rechtbank Arnhem en de Duitse bezetting*, Nijmegen: Wolf Legal Publishers 2004.

Best, Werner, *Die deutschen Aufsichtsverwaltungen in Frankreich, Belgien, den Niederlanden, Norwegen, Dänemark und im Protektorat Böhmen und Mähren, vergleichende Übersicht*, Typescript 1941, https://www.delpher.nl/nl/boeken/view?coll=boeken&identifier=MMKB18B:056057000.

Blom, J.C.H., et. al. (Eds), *A.E. Cohen als geschiedschrijver van zijn tijd*, Amsterdam: Boom 2005.

Carp, J.H., *Een halfjaar rechtspraak van het Vredegerechtshof*, Utrecht: Nenasu 1942.

Cohen, A.E., 'Opmerkingen over de notitie van dr. de Paterover het doel van het Duitse civiele bestuur in Nederland', in: A.H. Paape, *Studies over Nederland in oorlogstijd*, Den Haag: Nijhoff 1972, 48-58.

Cybichowski, Sigmund, 'Die Besetzung Lembergs im Kriege 1914/15' *Zeitschrift für Internationales Recht* (26) 1916, 427-478.

De Jong, L., *Het Koninkrijk der Nederlanden in de Tweede Wereldoorlog, deel 4, Mei '40 – Maart '41*, Den Haag: Martinus Nijhoff 1972.

De Jong, L., *Het Koninkrijk der Nederlanden in de Tweede Wereldoorlog, deel 6, Juli '42 – Mei '43*, Den Haag: Martinus Nijhoff 1975.

De Pater, J.C.H., 'Doel van het Duitse civiele bestuur in Nederland', in: A.H. Paape, *Studies over Nederland in oorlogstijd*, Den Haag: Nijhoff 1972, 39-47.

De Ruiter, J., *Jan Donner jurist*, Amsterdam: Boom 2003.

De Vries, Frank, [unpublished manuscript], 2015.

Donner, J., *Plaats en taak van de Hoge Raad der Nederlanden*, Calvinistische Juristen Vereniging 1962.

Enquêtecommissie Regeringsbeleid 1940 – 1945. Verslag houdende de uitkomsten van het onderzoek, Vol 7c Leiding en voorlichting aan ambtenaren en burgers in de bezette gebieden – het contact met en de politiek ten aanzien van de verzetsbeweging in Nederland (punten G en H van het enquêtebesluit) Verhoren, 's-Gravenhage: Staatsdrukkerij- en Uitgeverijbedrijf: 1955.

Essers, Peter, *Belast verleden. Het Nederlandse belastingrecht onder nationaalsocialistisch regime*, Kluwer 2012.

Fasseur, Cees, *Juliana & Bernhard. Verhaal van een huwelijk. De jaren 1936-1956*, Balans 2009.

Fleuren, J.W.A., *Een ieder verbindende bepalingen van verdragen* (PhD Diss), Boom Juridische uitgevers 2004.

François, J.P.A., *Handboek van het volkenrecht, Tweede deel*, Zwolle: W.E.J. Tjeenk Willink 1933.

Fruin, *De Nederlandsche wetboeken*, 's-Gravenhage: Martinus Nijhoff 1940.

Gids voor de rechterlijke macht 1943.

Hermans, H.L.C., *Om des gewetens wille. De geschiedenis van een arrest in oorlogstijd*, Leeuwarden 2003.

Hermans, H.L.C., *Een ambitieuze jurist in gevaarlijk vaarwater. Johannes van Loon, President van de Hoge Raad in oorlogstijd*, Den Haag 2008.

Het proces Mussert (NIOD Bronnenpublicaties, Vol. 4), Amsterdam: Sijthoff 2nd edition, 1987.

Hooykaas, J.P., 'Toepasselijkheid van wettelijke strafbepalingen', *Nederlands Juristenblad* (19) 1944-1, 13-14.

Jansen, Corjo, 'De opstelling van de Nederlandse rechters en raadsheren tijdens de bezetting', *Trema* 2018-3, https://trema.nvvr.org/editie/2018-03/de-opstelling-van-de-nederlandse-rechters-en-raadsheren-tijdens-de-bezetting.

Jansen, Corjo, in collaboration with Derk Venema, *De Hoge Raad en de Tweede Wereldoorlog. Recht en rechtsbeoefening in de jaren 1930-1950*, Amsterdam: Boom 2011.

Klemann, H.A.M., *Nederland 1938-1948, economie en samenleving in jaren van oorlog en bezetting*, Amsterdam: Boom 2002.

Koppen, J.P. van & J. ten Kate, *De Hoge Raad in persoon. Benoemingen in de Hoge Raad der Nederlanden 1838-2002*, Deventer: Kluwer 2003.

Lokin, J.H.A. & C.J.H. Jansen, *Tussen droom en daad. De Nederlandse Juristen-Vereniging 1870-1995*, Zwolle: W.E.J. Tjeenk Willink 1995.

Mazel, P.E., *In naam van het recht..., De Hoge Raad en de Tweede Wereldoorlog*, Arnhem: Gouda Quint 1984.

Meihuizen, J., *Noodzakelijk kwaad, De bestraffing van economische collaboratie in Nederland na de Tweede Wereldoorlog* (PhD Diss), Amsterdam: Boom 2003.

Meihuizen, Joggli, *Smalle marges. De Nederlandse advocatuur in de Tweede Wereldoorlog*, Amsterdam 2010.

Michielsen, J.N.M.E., *The 'Nazification' and 'Denazification' of the courts in Belgium, Luxembourg and the Netherlands, The Belgian, Luxembourg and Netherlands. Courts and their Reactions to Occupation Measures and Measures from their Governments Returning from Exile* (PhD Diss Maastricht), Maastricht: Universitaire Pers Maastricht 2004.

Moritz, G., *Gerichtsbarkeit in den von Deutschland besetzten Gebieten 1939-1945*, (*Studien des Instituts für Besatzungsfragen* Vol 7), Tübingen: Institut für Besatzungsfragen 1955.

Nationaal-socialistisch jaarboek 1942.

Nationaal-socialistische almanak 1943-1944.

Nationaal-socialistische (fascistische) staatsleer (NSB brochure 3), 1933.

Nestler, L., *Die faschistische Okkupationspolitik in Belgien, Luxemburg und den Niederlanden (1940-1945)*, (*Europa unterm Hakenkreuz*, Vol 4), Berlijn: Deutscher Verlag der Wissenschaften 1990.

Neuman, H.J., *Arthur Seyss-Inquart. Het leven van een Duits onderkoning in Nederland*, Utrecht: Veen 2nd edition 1989.

Oppenheim, L. & H. Lauterpacht, *International Law, A Treatise*, Vol. II: *Disputes, War and Neutrality*, London: Longmans, Green & Co. 5th Ed, 1935.

Rabl, Kurt, 'Das Reichskommissariat', in: Du Prel & Janke, *Die Niederlande im Umbruch der Zeiten* 1941, 83-90.

Romijn, Peter, '"Restoration of confidence": The Purge of Local Government in the Netherlands As a Problem of Postwar Reconstruction', in: *The Politics of Retribution in Europe* 2000, 173-193.

Romijn, Peter, *Snel, streng en rechtvaardig. De afrekening met 'foute' Nederlanders*, Olympus 2002.

Romijn, Peter, *Burgemeesters in oorlogstijd*, Amsterdam: Balans 2006.

Romijn, Peter, *Der lange Krieg der Niederlande. Besatzung, Gewalt und Neuorientierung in den vierziger Jahren*, Wallstein Verlag 2017.

Rosendaal, Joost, *Nijmegen '44. Verwoesting, verdriet en verwerking*, Nijmegen: Vantilt 2009.

Schuyt, Kees, *R.P. Cleveringa. Recht, onrecht en de vlam der gerechtigheid*, Amsterdam: Boom 2018.

Seyss-Inquart, Arthur, 'Aus Anlass der Übernahme der Regierungsgewalt', Den Haag, May 29th 1940, in: Reichsminister Seyss-Inquart, *Vier Jahre in den Niederlanden. Gesammelte Reden*, Amsterdam: Volk und Reich Verlag 1944, p. 7-12.

Sikkes, J.H., *... In geval van een vijandelijken inval. Ambtelijk gedrag in bezettingstijd en de daarvoor geldende aanwijzingen*, Deventer: Kluwer 1985.

Telders, B.M., *Verzamelde geschriften*, Vol IV, Den Haag: Martinus Nijhoff 1947.

Telders, C.S., 'Ben', in: C.S. Telders et al. (Eds), *Levensbeschrijving van prof. mr. B. M. Telders*, 's-Gravenhage: Martinus Nijhoff 1972, 11-54.

Van den Dries, N.C.M.A., *De Hooge Raad der Nederlanden tijdens de bezetting*, Leiden: Brill 1945 (partly published in Venema et al. 2008).

Venema, Derk, *Rechters in oorlogstijd, De confrontatie van de Nederlandse rechterlijke macht met nationaal-socialisme en bezetting* (PhD diss. RU Nijmegen), Den Haag: Boom Juridische uitgevers 2007.

Venema, Derk, 'Een levensgevaarlijke marionet. De terdoodveroordeling van Anton Mussert', in: R. Baas et al. (Eds.), *Rechtspleging en rechtsbescherming. Liber amicorum voor prof. dr. Leny E. de Groot-van Leeuwen*, Deventer: Kluwer 2015, p. 293-306 (=Venema 2019b), http://repository.ubn.ru.nl/handle/2066/37572.

Venema, Derk, 'The Netherlands', in: Lavinia Stan & Nadya Nedelsky (Eds), *The Encyclopedia of Transitional Justice. Vol. 2: Country Studies*, Cambridge: Cambridge University Press, 2nd Edition 2019a.

Venema, Derk, 'A Perilous Puppet. The Trial of Dutch Nazi Leader Anton Mussert', in: Andreas Raffeiner (Ed), *Auf der Klaviatur der Rechtsgeschichte. Festgabe für Kurt Ebert zum 75. Geburtstag* (Rechtsgeschichtliche Studien, Band 84), Hamburg: Verlag Dr. Kovač 2019b, 967-976. (=Venema 2015)

Venema, Derk, Leny de Groot-van Leeuwen & Thomas Mertens (Eds), *Onder de huidige omstandigheden, De Hoge Raad en het Toetsingsarrest 1942*, Den Haag: Boom Juridische uitgevers 2008.

Verburg, M.E., *Geschiedenis van het Ministerie van Justitie. Deel II: 1898-1940*, Den Haag: Sdu Uitgevers 2001.

Verburg, M.E., *De procureurs-generaal in vergadering bijeen, Grepen uit de notulen van 60 jaar*, Den Haag: Sdu Uitgevers 2005.

Verburg, Marcel, *Geschiedenis van het Ministerie van Justitie 1940-1945. Een departement in oorlogstijd*, Amsterdam: Boom 2016.

Vogel, J. & P. Schulten, 'Het dwaalspoor van een praktisch staatsrecht, Jaap Schrieke (1884-1976)', in: P.J. Knegtmans, P. Schulten & J. Vogel (Eds), *Collaborateurs van niveau, opkomst en val van de hoogleraren Schrieke, Snijder en Van Dam*, Amsterdam: Vossiuspers AUP 1996, 30-154.

Von Frijtag Drabbe Künzel, G., *Het recht van de sterkste, Duitse strafrechtspleging in bezet Nederland*, Amsterdam: Bert Bakker 1999.

Weitjens, W.M.A., *Hoor en wederhoor*, 1946.

X., 'Occupatio bellica', *Frankfurter Zeitung*, 4 August 1940, 3.

About the Author

Derk Venema is assistant professor at the Law Faculty of the Open University in the Netherlands. He has published on the Dutch judiciary in WWII and transitional justice theory, amongst other subjects. He teaches professional ethics at the Training Centre for the Judiciary SSR, and is an associated researcher at CegeSoma, Brussels.

10 The Supreme Courts in the Protectorate of Bohemia and Moravia

Jaromír Tauchen

Abstract

This chapter analyzes the activities of the three Supreme Courts in the period of Protectorate of Bohemia and Moravia (1939-1945): Constitutional Court, Supreme Court and Supreme Administrative Court. It also outlines the functions of the complicated Protectorate legal system and the fates of these courts in the post-war period. Personalities who have served on the supreme courts are also mentioned.

Keywords: Protectorate of Bohemia and Moravia; Supreme Administrative Court; Supreme Court; Constitutional Court; Emil Hácha

1 Introduction

The supreme courts during the Protectorate of Bohemia and Moravia (1939-45) have not been the object of thorough research in Czech legal historiography. Therefore, the current chapter may be considered the first comprehensive treatment of the organization and activities of the supreme courts in that period.[1] To better understand the functioning of the

1 The archive of the Supreme Court, Supreme Administrative Court, and the Constitutional Court is located in the National Archive in Prague. For the period until 1939, there is a sufficient number of records. For the period of the Second World War, the situation is the opposite. For this chapter, all the remaining records from the archives of the three courts were studied. Therefore, the information presented in this chapter could be considered as the maximum of what could be discovered about the functioning of these institutions and on personal questions. There is a sufficient quantity of archival material on the activity of the Supreme Administrative Court. However, in the case of the Supreme Court, a large part of the records is missing. This can be attributed to the bombing of Brno in 1944, when one of the buildings of the Supreme Court was damaged and part of the archived records was destroyed.

Venema, D. (ed.), *Supreme Courts Under Nazi Occupation*. Taylor & Francis Group 2022
DOI: 10.5117/9789463720496_CH10

Supreme Court, the Supreme Administrative Court, and the Constitutional Court during the Protectorate, it is first necessary to introduce the quite complicated legal system of the Protectorate and the changes that took place in the court system.

2 Outlines of the Functions of the Protectorate Legal System

According to the terms of the Munich Agreement – concluded by Germany, the United Kingdom, France, and Italy at the end of September 1938 – Czechoslovakia was forced to cede to the German Reich its vast border areas, known as the 'Sudetenland'. German representatives assured the world public that this was the solution for the "Czech problem" and that Germany would make no further territorial claims against Czechoslovakia. The truth was exactly opposite, as was proven in the spring of the following year.

On 15 March 1939, Czech territories were occupied by the German army and the so-called Slovakian State was proclaimed in the Slovak territory. One day later, the Führer, who was also the Reich Chancellor, issued the decree on the Protectorate of Bohemia and Moravia.[2] This decree, composed of a preamble and thirteen articles, was the legal basis for a new state.[3]

Article 12 stated that: "The legal order of Bohemia and Moravia remains in force insofar as it does not contradict the purpose of protection under the German Reich". Consequently, most of the legal order from the First and Second Czechoslovak Republics, which in turn stemmed from the former Austrian empire, could be adopted. This ensured the continuity of the Czechoslovakian legal order. Laws that remained in force after 15 March 1939 had to be interpreted according to the ideology and interests of the National Socialist Greater German Reich. The Protectorate period did not last long. Nevertheless, during the six years of its existence, both private law and public law were definitely and significantly influenced by Nazi ideology.

In addition to the so-called Czech autonomous law (Czechoslovakian law and new Protectorate laws), some of the Reich's laws were applied.[4] The

2 *Reichsgesetzblatt* 1939 I, p. 485.

3 On the development of the Protectorate law from contemporary literature, see detailed description by Tauchen 2013, 701-716; Maršálek 2002; Pasák 1998.

4 For characterization of Reich's law, see, for example Mandl 1939; Nýdl 1939, 18-19; Knapp 2002; from new literature, see Tauchen 2009.

application of Czech or Reich's law usually depended on the nationality of the addressees of the legal norms. German nationals who resided in the Protectorate fell under the scope of German courts and also enjoyed the rights of Protectorate nationals. The Reich's law, however, did not apply to Protectorate nationals or to German nationals as a whole; only a select number of laws applied to them. German nationals in the Protectorate were bound by some of the norms of the Reich's law (for example, criminal law and laws governing personal status), but also by some Czech laws, especially administrative law. Some of the norms of the Reich's law – for example, criminal law (such as treason) – also related to Czech nationals in the Protectorate.

During the Protectorate, the legislative powers belonged to the state president and government. The National Assembly (parliament) was dissolved by the President only a few days after the establishment of the Protectorate. The Empowering Law of 15 December 1938, No. 330/1938, awarded the President of the state the authority to issue decrees having the power of a constitutional act upon unanimous proposal by the government, if these decrees related to issues that would otherwise have to be regulated by a constitutional act. For the first two years of the new Empowering Law, the government had the authority to take all necessary measures by means of government decrees, although for such steps it would otherwise be necessary to pass a law.

The President, however, did not use his power to issue decrees having the power of a constitutional law. Therefore, the government became the exclusive autonomous lawgiver issuing governmental decrees. However, from the very beginning of the Protectorate's existence, the German authorities significantly influenced this "autonomous" law-making. The Reichsprotektor[5] could interfere with the law-making activity of the autonomous lawgiver. By Article 5, section 4 of Hitler's decree, the Reichsprotektor had the right to be informed of all of the measures of the Protectorate government and to grant his advice. He could also object to measures that could damage the Reich. In case of imminent danger (*Gefahr im Verzug*), the Reichsprotektor could issue his own ordinances to protect the common interest, and thus to intervene in the autonomous law. If he objected, the autonomous authorities could not promulgate the law in question, or enforce administrative or court decisions to which he objected. If required by the common interest,

5 The Reichsprotektor's Office was held by Konstantin von Neurath, Reinhard Heydrich, Kurt Daluege, and Wilhelm Frick.

the Reichsprotektor could even change the autonomous law. He also had the right to issue police decrees.

Courts and administrative bodies of the autonomous authority were not entitled to question the legal measures or the provisions of the Reichsprotektor. Protectorate authorities were subordinate to him and the Reichsprotektor could order the Protectorate authorities to issue reports for him on certain topics without further request.

From the foregoing, it is obvious that the autonomy of the Protectorate government was only an empty phrase; all the legal activities of the Protectorate government and Protectorate ministries were strictly directed, from the very beginning of the existence of Protectorate of Bohemia and Moravia, by the Reichsprotektor's Office.[6]

3 Order and Changes in the System of Courts

In the period of the Protectorate of Bohemia and Moravia, we must distinguish between the so-called autonomous (Czech) system of courts, which was based on the structure of courts in Czechoslovakia before the war, and the German court system, which was adopted from the Reich.[7]

As in the Reich, the following jurisdictions were established in the Protectorate:

a) twelve German local courts (*Amtsgerichte*);
b) two German district courts (*Landgerichte*) – in Prague for Bohemia and in Brno for Moravia, where they formed the second instance;
c) the German regional court in Prague (*Oberlandesgericht*); and
d) the Protectorate was included in the jurisdiction of the *Reichsgericht* in Leipzig and the *Volksgerichtshof* in Berlin.

The difference between the composition of German Office courts in the Protectorate and in the Reich was that there were no lay courts (*Schöffengerichte*) in the Protectorate. The Protectorate also had so-called special courts (*Sondergerichte*), located at the *Oberlandesgerichte* in Prague and Brno. These special courts were especially competent to prosecute crimes

6 For details on the characteristics of the autonomous and occupation administrations, see: Janečková 2013; Maršálek 2002, 2009 and 2012.

7 For more details on the legal system of the Protectorate, see Schelle and Tauchen 2009 and 2010, 62; Vlček 2006, 41; Moravčík 1993; Mířička 1939.

against the State. Each German court in the Protectorate had its own public prosecutor's office.[8]

After the establishment of the Protectorate of Bohemia and Moravia, the then existing system of courts remained. Even the procedural rules applied before the autonomous courts in the Protectorate were not changed significantly. When requested by the German prosecutor, the Public Prosecutor and the courts of the Protectorate had to stop any proceeding that they had begun and hand it over, if the German prosecutor found it to belong to the German jurisdiction. German courts in the Protectorate and protectorate courts had to provide legal and official assistance and legal information to each other. German courts, however, could refuse to send records to the Protectorate courts, if it was against the interests of the Reich.

In connection with the liquidation of the Czechoslovak Armed Forces, the Czechoslovakian military courts and Military Offices of Public Prosecution ceased to exist.[9] Protectorate nationals, who were previously under the jurisdiction of the military court system (military personnel as well as, for example, *gendarmerie*), were now under the jurisdiction of general criminal law or laws of the Reich, which were applicable to their proceedings. In November 1939, the Supreme Military Court was abolished as well. All pending cases were transferred to the Supreme Court.

4 The Constitutional Court[10]

The Constitutional Court was established in 1921;[11] its official seat was Prague. It consisted of seven members, three of which were appointed by the President of the Republic based on a joint proposal by the Chamber of Deputies and the Senate of the National Assembly. The Supreme Court and the Supreme Administrative Court each contributed two of their judges as members and two as substitutes. They were elected in plenary sessions of each of these courts. The term of office of the judges at the Constitutional Court was ten years.

8 More information on the German contemporary legal system can be found in contemporary literature, such as Hochberger 1939-1940, 121; Lorenz 1939, 177; Schmidt 1939; Krieser 1940, 1745; Nüßlein 1940, 2085; Veselá und Lepšík 1939.

9 Government decree of 7 September 1939 no. 255/1939 on Dissolution of the military judiciary.

10 For more on Constitutional Court in between the Wars, see: Osterkamp 2009.

11 Law from 9 March 1921 no. 162/1920 Coll. (= *Collection of laws of the Protectorate of Bohemia and Moravia*), on Constitutional Court.

The Constitutional Court did not decide on complaints of citizens concerning violation of rights that were guaranteed by the Constitution (this was the competence of the Supreme Administrative Court). The sole purpose of the Constitutional Court was to decide on the compliance of laws and provisional measures of the Permanent Committee of the National Assembly with the 1920 Constitution.[12] For this reason, the results of its decision-making were quite modest.

The Constitutional Court held hearings when it was needed. For a decision to be made, there had to be at least five votes. If the votes were tied, the president's vote was the deciding one. A petition against a particular law to the Constitutional Court could be sent within five years after its promulgation. It could be submitted only by the following institutions: either chamber of the Parliament, the (never realized) Assembly of the Carpathian Ruthenia, the Election court, the Supreme Court, and the Supreme Administrative Court. The Constitutional Court's decisions had no retroactive effect in a dispute involving a law that was ruled unconstitutional.[13]

The first term of office of the Constitutional Court judges expired in 1931. However, throughout the following six years, the political parties were unable to agree as to whom to assign the positions of judge within this Court. The Constitutional Court only resumed its activity and functionality in April 1938 with the appointment of Jaroslav Krejčí (1892-1956) as its President. Krejčí had been a secretary of the Constitutional Court for a long time, as well as an extraordinary professor of constitutional law in the law faculty of Masaryk University in Brno. From December 1938, he was also the Minister of Justice and, from January 1942 to January 1945, he was the Prime Minister.

Shortly after the occupation of the Czech territories, the situation of the Constitutional Court was unclear. The decree of the Führer on the Protectorate of Bohemia and Moravia from 16 March 1939 did not mention the institution of the Constitutional Court. Other laws, whether issued by the occupying or autonomous administration, did not ban the activity of the Constitutional Court either, even after the political changes. A public meeting of the Constitutional Court was scheduled for 21 March 1939. However, due to unclear conditions, it eventually did not take place. A few weeks later, the President of the Constitutional Court – and, concurrently, the Minister of Justice – Jaroslav Krejčí decided to call a plenary meeting of

12 The permanent committee was a 24-member body of the Chamber of Deputies and the Senate of the National Assembly, which issued laws if there was no Chamber of Deputies. Such laws were subject to review by the Constitutional Court.

13 Princ 2015, 116-118.

the Constitutional Court for 16 May 1939. In the meantime, the declaration on the Protectorate of Bohemia and Moravia also immediately impacted the staffing of the Constitutional Court. On 7 April, the Vice-President of the Court, Adolf Záturecký (1884-1958), was dismissed. Záturecký, a Slovakian national, went on to serve the Slovakian state, which had been declared one day earlier than the Protectorate. At the end of April, Maximilian Pokorny (who was initially a judge in the Supreme Court) left his office of substitute Constitutional Court judge. With the establishment of the Protectorate, he gained Reich nationality and left to join the Reich's judiciary. The same circumstances caused substitute judge, Josef Orglmeister, who had acted as the Head of the District Office in Děčín, to leave office. The secretary of the Constitutional Court, Gejza Zigo, left for Slovakia.

The plenary meeting took place on 16 May 1939. At this meeting, the Constitutional Court decided on two submissions concerning the unconstitutionality of two laws. This situation was extremely paradoxical and even absurd, since the Constitutional Court was evaluating the compliance of laws with the 1920 Constitution, which had not been officially abolished, but in practice was no longer valid. Both findings, not having found any contrariety with the 1920 Czechoslovak Constitution, were announced in summer of 1939 in the collection of laws.[14]

Minister of Justice and Constitutional Court president Jaroslav Krejčí tried to normatively adapt the Constitutional Court to the new conditions of the Protectorate with regard to the question of the appointment of the Court's members. There was a problem in that it was impossible to appoint new members, because suggestions for three candidates were supposed to be submitted by the Chamber of Deputies and the Senate. Those two bodies were dissolved by the President of the state, Emil Hácha, after the German occupation. Therefore, Krejčí initiated in the Protectorate government an amendment to the Constitutional Court Act, which was approved by the government on 6 June 1939. This, however, had never entered into force – probably due to opposition of the Reich's Protector's office.

Hence, in the summer of 1939, the representatives of occupying forces noticed that they had forgotten to abolish the Constitutional Court. Officially, this did not happen under any law. However, from that summer, the judges of that court did not convene. The judges did not lose their mandates officially. Even though the Constitutional Court had no further activity,

14 The Collection of laws was also published during the period of the Protectorate. Government regulations and ordinances of Ministries were published in the Collection of laws. The Collection was published both in German and in Czech.

its seat had to be moved from its permanent building into a rented six-room apartment in Lucerna Palace in Prague at the end of August 1939. In March 1940, all of the judges of the Constitutional Court had to swear an oath of allegiance to the leader of the Great German Reich, Adolf Hitler, as well as to the *Reichsprotektor* of the Protectorate of Bohemia and Moravia. The salary of Head of Office at the Constitutional Court was paid only until the end of March 1941, which signalled the definitive end of this institution.[15]

5 The Supreme Administrative Court

The Supreme Administrative Court (SAC) was established in Prague on 2 November 1918.[16] It was composed of a President, a Vice-President, four Senate Presidents, and twenty other judges. The jurisdiction and the proceedings before the SAC were subject to the then existing laws from the Habsburg era. The internal organization of the Court and the rules of procedure remained unchanged, but the scope of its jurisdiction had grown. One of its important competencies was deciding on complaints by citizens as to violations of their political rights. The SAC decided in cases where a person claimed that his or her rights were harmed by an illegal decision or decree of an administrative body. The Supreme Administrative Court had also decided on disputes over the powers of public administrative bodies.[17]

The SAC was clearly overloaded with cases; proceedings could last longer than three years. For this reason, in 1937, a significant change was made to the regulations, which should have eased the burden of the SAC.[18] However, it did not have any significant effect. The Supreme Administrative Court did not decide meritoriously, but on the legality of an administrative act.[19] The Supreme Administrative Court had proven to be very effective between the two World Wars. It had celebrated unique achievements during the establishment of the legal order of the new state. For example, in the twenties, it was responsible for the smooth course of the territorial reform, which had a positive influence on the social stability of Czechoslovakia in the

15 Langášek 2011, 166-169.

16 Law from 2 November 1918 no. 3/1918 Coll., on the Supreme Constitutional Court and solution of competence conflicts.

17 More on the Supreme Administrative court during the First Czechoslovak Republic can be found in, for example: Kliment 1937; Joachim 1937.

18 Law from the 16. June, 1937 no. 164/1937 Coll., on the Supreme Administrative court.

19 Ondruš 2001, 15.

post-revolution period. According to the president, T. G. Masaryk: "The Supreme Administrative Court is one of the foundation stones at the base of the international political credit of the First Czechoslovak Republic".[20] A major part of the work of the SAC involved the publishing of judicial precedents. This activity was independent and progressive. The SAC thus heavily influenced administrative practice in the First Republic. By this, the SAC was helping to create a feeling of legal stability and safety.[21]

The decisions of the Supreme Administrative Court were published in the collection of court decisions, which was organized by the Senate President of the SAC, Josef V. Bohuslav (1863-1952). The relevant volumes of the collection included clearly organized legal principles expressed in the findings of the Supreme Administrative Court in the area of administrative and financial issues. From 1918 until abolition of the SAC, several tens of thousands of findings were published in almost one hundred volumes. In the era of the Protectorate of Bohemia and Moravia, the findings were issued in two versions: Czech and German.

As a result of the forced cession of the *Sudetenland* in October 1938, and the establishment of an independent Slovakian state on 14 March 1939 (which meant a decrease in population and a transfer of part of the public administration to the Reich's institutions), the number of claims submitted to the SAC significantly decreased.[22] Because of changes in the constitutional order, the SAC had to reorganize the cases and the German courts were handed more than 4,500 cases in 1939. This transferral of cases was undertaken following a decision by the three-member Senates of the SAC.[23] In the first half of 1940, the Slovakian administration was given almost 2,800 cases.[24]

From the period of the First and Second Czechoslovak Republics, the SAC still had almost fourteen thousand cases, which had not yet been decided. Dealing with some of the complaints became irrelevant after the changes in the government and legal system, and it was decided to 'file' these claims. An example of such a case was a complaint about a disciplinary punishment that was imposed on administration workers of German nationality for their membership of a banned Nazi party.[25]

20 Introduction by Emil Hácha in Rádl 1933, 11-12.

21 Novotný 1999, 81.

22 NA (=National Archive in Prague), SAC fund (=fond NSS), carton 45, sign 5, official remark of SAC from 15 March 1939.

23 NA, SAC fund, carton 45, sign 5, SAC Activity Report for the year 1939.

24 NA, SAC fund, carton 45, sign 5, official remark of SAC from 2 June 1940.

25 NA, SAC fund, carton 47, sign 5, official remark of SAC from 20 November 1942.

New relationships after the German occupation led to many questions that had to be answered by the judges of the SAC. Firstly, it had to decide whether the Court could deal with complaints submitted by German nationals who lived in the territory of the Protectorate, and who were generally under the scope of German jurisdiction. The SAC stated that German nationals were under the scope of German jurisdiction only in criminal and civil cases, though, in administrative cases, they could apply to the SAC.[26] As for the language aspect of the cases, applications written in Czech had to be treated in Czech. If the application was submitted in German, the court was obliged to solve it in German.[27] If the complaint was submitted in Czech by the Protectorate office or a public law corporation, and one of the involved parties was a German national, then that office had to submit a German translation.[28] All forms that were used by the Court had to be bilingual.

Some laws of the Reich also applied to the territory of the Protectorate. Because of this fact, and based on the instructions of the SAC President, its judges were obliged to keep themselves informed of the laws published in the *Reichsgesetzblatt*, of which the SAC received a total of three copies.[29]

The occupation of Czechoslovakia by the German army and the establishment of the Protectorate of Bohemia and Moravia did not considerably affect the work of the SAC. Even though the Nazis were trying to unify the entire administrative law in the Reich and to refuse judicial protection of citizens' civil rights against the state, the SAC was active throughout the entire existence of the Protectorate. The former long-time president of the SAC – Emil Hácha – expressed, in an article in 1943, the need to keep the administrative legal system and the need to keep the SAC, which was in contradiction with Nazi ideas.[30] However, German lawyers, for their part, never reacted to Hácha's article.

It is typical for a democratic, rule-of-law state that its administrative authorities' decisions are reviewable by the administrative justice system. It was the same during the First Czechoslovak Republic, when the Supreme Administrative Court had had the reviewing function for the decisions of

26 NA, SAC fund, carton 45, sign 5, official remark of SAC from 24 May 1939 (the outcomes of the meetings with heads of Senates).

27 NA, SAC fund, carton 45, sign 5, a decision of the government of the Protectorate on usage of the languages in the Protectorate of 19 August 1939.

28 NA, SAC fund, carton 46, sign 5, a note from the Government of the Protectorate of 17 October 1941.

29 NA, SAC fund, carton 45, sign 5, official remark of SAC from 6 September 1939.

30 Hácha 1943, 165.

administrative authorities. However, during the Protectorate, the competence of the SAC to review several types of administrative decisions was completely excluded; they were non-reviewable (for example, decisions of the Employment Bureaux concerning forced labour). As a result, the Supreme Administrative Court had no opportunity to stand up against the occupying regime by reviewing its possibly illegal administrative decisions.

First of all, the Court had no possibility of reviewing the decisions of the German authorities in the Protectorate, mainly the Reichsprotektor and the *Oberlandräte*. An example of a class of decisions outside the scope of the SAC review, issued by the two occupation organs, is the confiscation of Jewish property as part of the Aryanization policy.[31] In 1940, the Reichsprotektor authorized himself to decide on complaints against decisions made by the Ministry of Agriculture (Territorial Authority) in matters of confiscation of property.[32]

It quite often happened that autonomous (Czech) offices of the Protectorate issued decisions on direct instruction by the Reichsprotektor or *Oberlandräte*. However, if a citizen submitted a complaint against this decision to the SAC, those complaints were discussed by a special Senate,[33] which usually declined them.

As time passed, more and more decisions by protectorate authorities were removed from the competency of the SAC. Most of the non-reviewable decisions concerned the functioning of a system of controlled war economy or the system of forced and controlled labour. The free market and the freedom to set prices were abolished shortly after the establishment of the Protectorate in May 1939, which significantly influenced everyday economic life in the Protectorate.[34] Prices for goods and services were no longer the result of a supply and demand ratio, but the product of state regulation. The pricing agenda, grown extremely large, was entrusted to a special price apparatus, headed by a special central authority: the Supreme Price Authority.[35] In order to ensure economically justifiable prices, that authority could take all necessary measures, in particular to set the lowest or highest, indicative or fixed prices for goods and services of all kinds. From 1 January 1940, complaints against decisions, measures, and findings of the Supreme Price Authority were excluded from the competence of the SAC.

31 Tauchen 2015, 110-124.

32 NA, SAC fund, carton 45, sign 5, A note from the Reichsprotektor of 28 August 1940.

33 NA, SAC fund, carton 46, sign 5, official remark from 18 October 1941.

34 Černý 1940, 374-384; for more on price management: Rentrop 1939, 235-242.

35 Government regulation from 10 May 1939 no. 121/1939 Coll., on establishment of Supreme Price Authority.

Similarly, it was not possible to submit a complaint to the SAC against decisions of the administrative authority: on alienation, leasing or acquisition of real estate;[36] on territorial planning;[37] on hunting;[38] on the imposition of preventive police custody or planned police surveillance;[39] by the Labour Office or the Ministry of Economy and Labour concerning certain measures in the labour law field;[40] or decisions on the suspension of business activities and the transfer of employees.[41]

From 1918, the seat of the SAC was the former cadet school building in Prague. After the separation of border areas in October 1938, the military administration had a shortage of office space and, therefore, in December 1938, requisitioned the SAC building. However, this did not take effect during the Second Czechoslovak Republic. The occupation authorities ordered the eviction of the SAC on 11 April, 1939. The SAC started to move out the same day. Moving took three days and, since no moving company could be found for such an urgent removal, even criminals were allowed to render their services. The building was subsequently handed over to SS units, which made it into military quarters.

From that time, the SAC held its meetings in the building of the former shelter for the poor in Vyšehradská Street. The move to this less important building was a symbolic manifestation of the noticeable decline in the glory of this institution.[42] The shelter's former chapel was used as a courtroom for public hearings. At the front, a large marble frame was preserved and the statue of the first Czechoslovak president, Tomáš G. Masaryk, was placed on it. This conflicted, on the one hand, with the established requirements for courtrooms, according to which the national emblem had to be at the front, and, on the other hand, with the new conditions, which forbade the depiction of former representatives of the extinct Czechoslovakia. This is why the heads of the SAC asked the government to give it prompt instructions

36 Government regulation from 18 December 1941 no. 443/1941 Coll., on expansion of real estate leases.

37 Government regulation from 23 June 1941 no. 299/1941 Coll., on preparation for territorial planning.

38 Government regulation from 31 March 1941 no. 127/1941 Coll., on hunting.

39 Government regulation from 9 March 1942 no. 89/1942 Coll., on preventive measures against crime.

40 Government regulation from 7 December 1942 no. 404/1942 Coll., on ensuring stability of salary and pay and labour morality.

41 Government regulation of 11 February 1943 no. 44/1943 Coll., on letting workforce for war related acts.

42 NA, SAC fund, carton 52, sign 6, a note by SAC for Ministry of Finance of 2 June 1939.

as to what to do with the statue.[43] In October 1939, the judges were asked to remove from their robes all the features and symbols reminiscent of the Czechoslovak Republic.[44] According to the new state symbol system, new bilingual versions of all stamps and seals were made. If the state signs of the former Czechoslovak Republic had adorned the offices of judges or courthouses, it was necessary to remove them. In July 1940, the bronze signs of the former Czechoslovak state were handed over to the ongoing collection of metals, organized by the authorities of the Protectorate. Paintings reminiscent of earlier constitutional regimes, as well as busts and stamps, had to be given by the SAC to the National Gallery. The new offices of the First and Second President of the SAC, and the courtroom, were newly decorated with a portrait of the Führer, the Reichsprotektor, and the President.[45] From 1941, the SAC building was marked with a large letter "V" (Victory) as a "symbol of victory of the Reich for a new Europe".[46]

The leadership of the SAC considered the placement of the Court in the shelter building to be temporary. Therefore, it requested to move the court into more appropriate accommodation.[47] This, however, did not happen until the end of the war. The SAC management also had to solve the issue of furniture and other inventories after the very fast and unexpected move, since they did not manage to take everything from the original seat and, after the move, the SS units had not allowed SAC staff to enter the building.[48] In the following years, the SAC received paintings for decoration that were borrowed without charge from the Bohemian-Moravian National Gallery.

Anti-Jewish measures and discrimination against the Jewish inhabitants of the Protectorate also affected the SAC. Under the government resolution from 27 January 1939, government employees of Jewish origin had to be dismissed from active service. Thus, in March 1939, one judge and two office workers of Jewish origin were retired.[49] In addition, two judges of SAC who had Jewish wives were affected: part of their salary payments had to be paid into an escrow bank account. Until the end of 1940, all the employees of the SAC had to provide evidence of their origin, to which they

43 NA, SAC fund, carton 52, sign 6, official remark of SAC for the government of 9 May 1939.

44 NA, SAC fund, carton 45, sign 5, a note by the Ministry of Justice of 14 October 1939.

45 NA, SAC fund, carton 46, sign 5, a note by the President of the SAC of 28 August 1941.

46 NA, SAC fund, carton 46, sign 5, a note by the government for the presidium of SAC of 18 June 1941.

47 NA, SAC fund, carton 52, sign 6, a note of the government for the presidium of SAC of 3 February 1940.

48 NA, SAC fund, carton 52, sign 6, official remark of SAC of 20 January 1942.

49 NA, SAC fund, carton 32, official SAC record of 21 March 1939.

had had to attach the baptismal letters of their parents and grandparents.[50] Only two of the SAC judges had a parent of Jewish origin. Furthermore, judges were required to report which of them was a member of the Lodge of Freemasons. In the SAC, there were three such judges and they were barred from promotion.[51] If Jews wanted to visit the SAC, they could do so only during certain hours – from 8 a.m. until 9 a.m.[52]

In 1943, the Ministry of Justice started to prepare a more radical amendment to the law on the SAC and its procedural rules. Its purpose was to speed up the handling of complaints, increase the effectiveness of the whole administrative justice system, and reduce the number of judges in the enlarged Senate (thus saving manpower).[53] This amendment was not accepted until the end of the war, because of extreme circumstances caused by the war; during the last months, the government of the Protectorate did not carry out any essential steps.

For different reasons, mentioned above, the numbers of complaints submitted to the SAC gradually decreased during the Protectorate period. In 1939, 43% of the SAC's findings were in favour of the complainants and 57% were in favour of the defendant authorities. When comparing this result with the result of 1938, when the ratio was 36% to 64%, it is possible to point out a change to the disadvantage of the defendant authorities.[54] In 1940, the SAC had received 2,316 complaints, which was 18% less than in the previous year. The reason for this decline were the extraordinary circumstances caused by the first year of war. The SAC also gradually managed to reduce the number of pending cases from previous years. The duration of procedures was also shortened from 2.5 to 4 years in the pre-war period to an average of 2.5 years. In 1940, the number of findings in favour of the defendant authorities increased from 40% to 60%.[55] The decrease in the number of complaints submitted to the NSS was also notable in the following years (there were 1,800 in 1941;[56] 1,512 in 1942;[57] 933 in 1943;[58] and 812 in 1944[59]).

50 NA, SAC fund, carton 32, an entry in the file of 26 August 1940.

51 NA, SAC fund, carton 33, official remark of SAC from 25 November 1941.

52 NA, SAC fund, carton 46, sign 5, letter of SAC for the government of 13 November 1941.

53 NA, Ministry of Justice fund (=Ministerstvo spravedlnosti-dodatky), carton 2009, a proposal for change of the act on SAC.

54 NA, SAC fund, carton 45, sign 5, SAC Activity Report for the year 1939.

55 NA, SAC fund, carton 46, sign 5, SAC Activity Report for the year 1940.

56 NA, SAC fund, carton 47, sign 5, SAC Activity Report for the year 1941.

57 NA, SAC fund, carton 47, sign 5, SAC Activity Report for the year 1942.

58 NA, SAC fund, carton 47, sign 5, SAC Activity Report for the year 1943.

59 NA, SAC fund, carton 48, sign 5, SAC Activity Report for the year 1944.

However, during the period of the Protectorate, the SAC management several times criticized the work-rate of a number of the judges, which showed a decrease as compared with the previous period. Decreases in performance were caused, amongst other things, by the fact that all decisions had to be bilingual. During the Protectorate period, the general legal system, including the SAC, was subject to criticism and strict control. However, the SAC could not name the restrictions from occupation authorities as the possible cause for this decrease. For this reason, the management of the Court compelled some judges to explain the causes of their decreased work-rate.[60] In order to prevent discussions about the SAC's possible abolition, the judges regularly contributed to the German Red Cross collections of metals or winter supplies for the army (such as blankets). The SAC also participated in a waste-paper collecting event by donating some old writings, as well as superfluous books and law journals from the library.[61] The SAC management also recommended that the judges make contributions from their salaries to the social assistance fund.[62] The purpose of the fund was to help orphans, mothers and children, etc.

In the thirties, the personality of its President, Dr. Emil Hácha (1872-1945), was indelibly linked to the activity of the Supreme Administrative Court. He was elected to the presidency of the Czechoslovak Republic in November 1938 and, in March of 1939, he became the President of the Protectorate of Bohemia and Moravia, while remaining in office as president of the CAS. The Vice-President of the SAC was Dr. Egon Zeis (1880-1955). The period of occupation, however, affected the organization and staffing of the court. Even when Emil Hácha became the President of the Protectorate of Bohemia and Moravia, political persecution did not spare the Supreme Administrative Court. One of his employees was executed and another, namely Dr. Jiří Havelka (1892-1964), was imprisoned for a long time.[63] He was an SAC judge from 1933. In 1939-41 he was Minister of Transportation in the Protectorate government and, after having been removed from this office in April 1941, he again started to work at the SAC, where he was, however, arrested in September 1941.

Based on the agreement between the Minister of Justice, Jaroslav Krejčí, and the Secretary of State, K. H. Frank, all general authorities of the Protectorate, including the Supreme Courts, were obliged to send their nominations

60 NA, SAC fund, carton 47, sign 5, SAC Activity Report of 21 April 1942.

61 NA, SAC fund, carton 47, sign 5, official SAC record of 1 June 1943.

62 NA, SAC fund, carton 47, sign 5, official SAC record of 21 September 1943.

63 Ondruš 2001, 98.

for the appointment of new officials or courts to the Reich Union of German Officials (*Reichsverband deutscher Beamten*) in Prague.[64] In 1940, all judges had to make a new pledge of allegiance, which was worded as follows:

> I promise to be loyal to the Leader of the Greater German Empire, Adolf Hitler, as the protector of the Protectorate of Bohemia and Moravia, and to protect the interests of the Greater German Empire and the Protectorate, and to uphold the laws and to perform my duties conscientiously.

In some cases, judges were promoted to the position of Senate President directly at the request of the Reichsprotektor, even though it contradicted the existing order of seniority and other judges were skipped over in the process.[65] Judges were gradually required to present their knowledge of the German language. If they came into official contact with a person of German nationality and did not have sufficient knowledge of German themselves, they were required to immediately invite a person with knowledge of the German language.[66]

In September 1940, the management of SAC organized courses in the German language for individual judges and strongly encouraged them to attend the courses. These voluntary and free courses were held twice weekly for two hours.[67] Moreover, the judges were required to pass a German language exam. *Oberlandräte* were responsible for the organization of such examinations, which were composed of both written and oral parts. It was possible to re-sit the examination once. Those who failed were at risk of retirement or dismissal.

In 1941, the SAC had 51 judges and 59 members of staff. During the last years of the war, some of the workers had to leave the SAC to take part in the German forced labour programme. Some judges had to assist in the harvest in summer 1944. In June 1942, the Vice-President of the SAC, Egon Zeis, was retired after reaching the age of 62 years, which was the retirement age. Although the SAC Presidium requested that Zeis be left in post due to his broad knowledge, the Reichsprotektor did not give his consent.[68] On 6 July 1942, according to the order of the Reichsprotektor, a German national, Dr. Walter Nobis (1883-?), was appointed as the SAC's Vice-President. He

64 NA, SAC fund, carton 45, sign 5, official remark of SAC of 14 December 1939.

65 NA, SAC fund, carton 32, official remark of SAC of 16 September 1940.

66 NA, SAC fund, carton 46, sign 5, letter of SAC Presidium of 6 October 1941.

67 NA, SAC fund, carton 45, sign 5, official remark of SAC of 23 September 1940.

68 NA, PMR fund, carton 4270, JUDr. Egon Zeis – retirement.

functioned as such until 1944. Since Nobis was a German national, and until his appointment had worked as a ministerial counsel at the Office of the Reichsprotektor, the SAC was viewed as having German leadership. Until the end of the war, four German nationals were judges at the SAC.

On 25 March 1944, Dr. Josef Kliment (1901-78) was appointed President of the SAC. Before that, he had acted as the secretary to the previous President, Emil Hácha. The appointment ceremony was attended by the protectorate government and leaders of the German occupation authority. After the appointment of Kliment to the head of SAC, Walter Nobis felt unappreciated. He felt that he should have been the one promoted.

When Josef Kliment acted as the head of the Court, it was considered as having Czech leadership. Later, after the war, Kliment was accused of not mitigating German administrative regulations.[69] Although he was not very successful, after his arrival at the SAC, Kliment arranged that Senate meetings would be held in Czech, unless the judges involved were of German nationality. In the last months of the Second World War, the German occupation authority was preparing to honour a number of SAC judges with St. Wenceslas Eagle badges. Kliment himself had to propose the names of specific judges. German awards given before the end of the war would have unambiguously discredited the judges after the liberation. Therefore, Kliment wrote to the State Ministry for Bohemia and Moravia that he had received the awards as the leader of the Court, and it was valid for the entire Court, so it was no longer necessary to award it to individual judges.[70]

Kliment's last day of service was 5 May 1945. A few days later, he was arrested and then sentenced to life. He was released under an amnesty only in 1960.

6 The Supreme Court

The Supreme Court was established immediately after the declaration of an independent Czechoslovak state in 1918.[71] Its headquarters were first in Prague, but they were transferred to Brno as soon as 1919. The Supreme Court was composed of a President, a Vice-President, four Senate Presidents and twenty-five judges. The number of Senate Presidents and advisors increased

69 NA, SAC fund, carton 48, sign 5, official SAC record of 12 June 1945.

70 National Museum archive, fund of Josef Kliment, 20 let v úřadovnách Emila Háchy, p. 71/2.

71 Law from 2 November 1918 no. 5/1918 Coll., on Supreme Court.

in the following years of the First Republic. The Supreme Court was the final instance in deciding on all disputes and other private law cases decided by a court of a second instance against which it was possible to appeal. As for criminal cases, the Supreme Court was empowered to cancel the challenged decisions. Furthermore, the Court also decided competence disputes among the particular courts. The Supreme Court was also competent to initiate requests for changes or passages of laws concerning the judiciary.

The President and Vice-President assigned cases to individual judges, appointed co-rapporteurs, assembled chambers, and were authorized to chair any court session. The Supreme Court Senates in criminal and civil matters had five members. Regarding criminal matters at the Supreme Court, there was a Prosecutor-General (the supreme state attorney), who fell under the authority of the Ministry of Justice.[72]

As with the SAC, after 15 March 1939, the Supreme Court had to transfer its records from the German Reich and Slovakia. Because of constitutional changes, some judges of German, Slovak, Hungarian, and Carpathian-Ruthenian nationalities had left. A decrease in the number of judges also happened as the result of lowering of the age limit for active duty of judges, which led to the retirement of many old and experienced experts. In the beginning of 1939, the SC had 77 judges. In April that year, SC President, Dr. Vladimír Fajnor (1875-1952), retired. In the following years, his position remained vacant and the court was led by the oldest Senate President, Dr. Theodor Nussbaum (1880-1965).

At the beginning of 1940, there were 43 judges. In this year, a significant change in staffing occurred, as several judges retired. In June 1940, Dr. Theodor Nussbaum was appointed as Vice-President and, in November 1944, he was appointed President of the Supreme Court. The decisions of the Supreme Court were published in the collection of decisions of the Supreme Court. From 1942, it was published bilingually. The collection of decisions in criminal matters was published in the Czech language throughout the war. Unlike the SAC, the Supreme Court did not have its authority limited by the Protectorate; it remained the highest instance for submission of appeals against the decisions of the Protectorate (Autonomous) courts. Its authority did not extend to the German justice system.

As in the Reich, the organization of the justice system was relaxed towards the end of the war. The aim of the change was mainly to achieve acceleration and economization of court proceedings, as well as savings of manpower in the judiciary system, which could be used differently in the war economy.

72 Princ 2015, 80-83.

This relaxation process did not leave the Supreme Court unaffected, where the number of Senate members for decisions in civil and criminal cases was reduced from five to three.[73]

During the war, the judges had to work under atypical conditions, which could be considered harsh. Due to the war economy and the need to decrease coal consumption, rooms of the courts could not be heated to more than 18°C. The heating season could begin only after the temperature remained under 12°C for three days in a row. Persons responsible for managing the heating of the courts had to undergo training in heating properly.[74] During the winter months, the judges often had to cover themselves with blankets during work.

The activities of the Supreme Court and Supreme Administrative Court were influenced by obligations arising from the anti-aircraft defence. After court working hours, some judges had to stay alert in their homes. If the anti-aircraft alarm sounded, they had to hurry to the court house to perform some prescribed duties. In some cases, judges were required to take part in fire patrols in the court building during nights or weekends.[75] Moreover, judges were required to undergo anti-aircraft defence training. In case of air-attack, some specific records and items had to be placed in specially prepared sacks and carried into the basement without delay, in order to prevent their being damaged.[76] In order to prevent damage, as many records as possible had to be kept in the cellar.[77]

The heavy bombing of the city of Brno on 20 November 1944 had an impact both on the activity and the personnel of the Supreme Court; several employees and judges were killed in the shelter of a detached office building during an air raid.

7 The Post-War Period

After the Second World War ended, the Constitutional Court did not regain its activity. The post-war period immediately showed some features of a

73 A Decree issued by the Minister of Justice on 2 September 1944, No 194/1944 Coll., on simplifying the organization of justice (the first decree on war measures in the area of organization of justice of the Protectorate).

74 NA, SAC fund, carton 52, sign 6, a note of the Reichsprotektor of 20 November 1942.

75 NA, SAC fund, carton 52, sign 6, a note of the head of anti-aircraft defence of 9 October 1943.

76 NA, SAC fund, carton 52, sign 6, a note of the SAC presidium for the employees of SAC of 20 April 1943.

77 NA, SAC fund, carton 52, sign 6, a note from Ministry of Interior Affairs of 7 May 1943.

non-democratic state, which was aiming for totalitarianism. It could not contain the institution of a Constitutional Court. The idea of constitutional justice was discredited, because of the last president of the Constitutional Court Jaroslav Krejčí, who had been Minister of Justice and Prime Minister during the Protectorate, and who was convicted for collaboration after the war. The communist members of parliament used the roles of the previous First Republic leaders for attacks against the existing judiciary system, which in their eyes should be replaced by a new justice system. They criticized the roles of Emil Hácha (President of the Supreme Administrative Court and, later, Protectorate President), Josef Klìment (judge and, later, the President of the Supreme Administrative Court, who served as a personal secretary to the State President, Hácha, during Protectorate), as well as Jaroslav Krejčí.[78]

The democratic political parties, when imagining the future state, made their calculations with the existence of the Constitutional Court in mind. They wanted to anchor this court in the newly-written constitution, which was to replace the original constitution of 1920. However, the new constitution was approved on 9 May 1948 under the Communist party rules. Thus, the days of the Constitutional Court were limited. Ideologically, it contained the idea of a single state power with closely cooperating branches, which was to replace the classical separation of powers approach. In this approach, the constitutional court had no role. During the so-called Prague Spring (1968), which brought some political freedom, discussions on renewal of constitutional justice began again. Although the constitutional court was restored in the legal order,[79] it was not really established during the time of the socialist reign. The court was established again only two years after the Velvet Revolution in 1991.[80]

The Election Court has never been renewed after the Second World War and was definitively cancelled in 1946.[81]

In 1945, the operation of the Supreme Administrative Court could not be fully restored to its pre-war extent. Among the reasons for that were long-lasting problems with court staffing and the activity of the competing Administrative Court in Bratislava, which was established during the Slovakian state period. The division of the competency between the courts remained unclear until 1949. It was definitively resolved by transferring the seat of the court to Bratislava. This was, however, a purpose-oriented

78 Langášek 2011, 205-208.

79 Constitutional laws no. 143/1968 Coll., on Czechoslovak Federation.

80 Schelle & Tauchen 2009, 30.

81 Constitutional law from 11 April 1946, no. 65/1946 Coll., on the Constituent National Assembly.

solution aimed at the extinction of the court – a decision that was politically determined soon after the Communist Party seized power in February 1948. Already at this point, it was clear that independent judicial supervision of public administration authorities and the protection of citizens' civil rights were incompatible with the new regime. After personnel purges of the justice system in February 1948, and after the forced retirement of "First Republic" judges in June 1948, the court in Prague became practically non-functional. Some of its Senates could not be assembled and there were no Senate Presidents. No new judges were appointed. After the seat of the court was moved to Bratislava in the fall of 1949, the Supreme Administrative Court operated until the end of 1952.[82]

After the liberation, the Supreme Court continued its work and was preserved, even during the Communist regime.

8 Summary

In the period of the Protectorate of Bohemia and Moravia, the Supreme Courts had had very limited possibilities to prevent measures taken by the occupying power. The reason for that lay, mostly, in the fact that legal norms were totally excluded by occupying administration from autonomous examination by (Czech) courts. Considering that the Constitutional Court was inactive, there was no possibility of pronouncing unconstitutional and repealing the regulations of the Protectorate or of Protectorate Ministries. The Supreme Administrative Court could, therefore, only cancel the decisions of some of the Protectorate authorities. If a decision was not issued in accordance with the law, the Supreme Administrative Court was not afraid to quash it, even when, for example, it was a police decree prohibiting the entry of Jews into certain enterprises. In this respect, the decision-making process of the supreme courts does not show any significant deviations from their pre-war judgments. Even if the courts were to make judgments that would be contrary to the interests of the occupying power, the Reichsprotektor would have been able to cancel them, which in some cases actually happened. This was a clearly visible subordination of the judiciary branch to the German occupation apparatus.

As regards the personnel changes made among the judges: in the case of the Supreme Administrative Court, there were no major interventions. The number of judges having to leave the SAC for political or racial reasons was

82 Ondruš 2001, 98-99.

not very high. However, from 1942 until 1944, the Supreme Administrative Court had German management. In the Supreme Court, despite greater changes of personnel, it was always led, throughout the war, by a Czech president, which was also reflected in the activities of this institution. Judges of the supreme courts (with some exceptions, e.g. Dr. Jiří Havelka), did not join the resistance; some of them held less important functions in the authorities or organizations of the Protectorate. An example of collaboration is the last chairman of the Constitutional Court, Jaroslav Krejčí, who was the Minister of Justice and later the Prime Minister of the Protectorate.

Neither the Supreme Administrative Court nor the Supreme Court played any essential important role in the period of the Protectorate. Neither had representatives who joined the resistance in an essential way, nor had these courts rendered any decisions which would have broken the law of the Protectorate.

References

Adamová, Karolina, Karel Schelle, Jaromír Tauchen and Antonín Lojek, *Velké dějiny zemí Koruny české. Tematická řada. Stát*, Praha: Paseka 2015.

Adamová, Karolina, Karel Schelle, Jaromír Tauchen and Antonín Lojek, *Velké dějiny zemí Koruny české. Tematická řada. Právo*, Praha: Paseka 2017.

Černý, Bohuslav, 'Tvorba ceny v našem řízeném hospodářství', *Obzor národohospodářský*, (45) 1940, 374-384.

Hácha, Emil, 'Gedanken eines ehemaligen Verwaltungsrichters', *Prager Archiv für Recht, Verwaltung und Wirtschaft* (25) 1943, 165-168.

Hochberger, Ernst, 'Die deutsche Gerichtsbarkeit im Protektorat Böhmen und Mähren', *Zeitschrift für osteuropäisches Recht*, (6) 1939-1940, 121ff.

Janečková, Eva, *Státoprávní uspořádání Protektorátu Čechy a Morava (1939-1945)*, Plzeň: Vydavatelství a nakladatelství Aleš Čeněk 2013.

Joachim, Václav, *Nový zákon o Nejvyšším správním soudě ze dne 16. června 1937 č. 164 Sb. z. a n.*, Praha: V. Joachim 1937.

Kliment, Josef, *Zákon o nejvyšším správním soudě a jeho jednací řád*, Praha: Čin 1937.

Knapp, Viktor, *Problém nacistické právní filosofie*, Dobrá Voda: Vydavatelství a nakladatelství Aleš Čeněk 2002.

Krieser, Helmut, 'Die deutsche Gerichtsbarkeit im Protektorat Böhmen und Mähren – Ausübung und Umfang', *Deutsches Recht* (10) 1940, 1745-1754.

Langášek, Tomáš, *Ústavní soud Československé republiky a jeho osudy v letech 1920-1948*, Plzeň: Vydavatelství a nakladatelství Aleš Čeněk 2011.

Lorenz, Max, 'Die Neuregelung der Strafgerichtsbarkeit im Protektorat Böhmen und Mähren', *Deutsche Justiz* 1939, 177ff.

Mandl, Vladimír, *Právní soustava Německé říše*, Praha: V. Linhart 1939.

Maršálek, Pavel, *Veřejná správa Protektorátu Čechy a Morava v letech 1939-1945*, Praha: Vodnář 1999.

Maršálek, Pavel, *Protektorát Čechy a Morava: státoprávní a politické aspekty nacistického okupačního režimu v českých zemích 1939-1945*, Praha: Karolinum 2002.

Maršálek, Pavel, *Pod ochranou hákového kříže: nacistický okupační režim v českých zemích 1939-1945*, Praha: Auditorium 2012.

Miřička, August and Vladimír Solnař, *Nová úprava trestního soudnictví v Protektorátu Čechy a Morava*, Praha: Melantrich 1939.

Moravčík, Ctibor, *Organizace soudnictví Protektorátu Čechy a Morava*, Brno: Masarykova univerzita, 1993.

Novotný, Josef, 'Nejvyšší správní soud: (historické poohlédnutí na naše správní soudnictví, jeho přítomnost a nutnost neodkladných změn.). I. část', *Správní právo* (32) 1999, 73-92.

Nüßlein, Franz, 'Die deutsche Gerichtsbarkeit im Protektorat Böhmen und Mähren – Strafrechtspflege', *Deutsches Recht* 1940, 2085-2091.

Nýdl, Bohumil, 'Základy nacionálně-socialistické nauky právní', *Právník*, (78) 1939, 1-20.

Ondruš, Radek, 'Nejvyšší správní soud 1918-1952 a jeho odkaz pro současnost', *Justiční praxe* (1) 2002, 91-99.

Ondruš, Radek, *Vybraná rozhodnutí Nejvyššího správního soudu ve věcech administrativních 1918-1948 a jejich využití v současné aplikační praxi*, Praha: Linde 2001.

Osterkamp, Jana, *Verfassungsgerichtsbarkeit in der Tschechoslowakei (1920-1939): Verfassungsidee, Demokratieverständnis, Nationalitätenproblem*, Frankfurt am Main: Klostermann 2009.

Pasák, Tomáš, *Pod ochranou říše*, Praha: Práh 1998.

Princ, Michal, *Soudnictví v českých zemích v letech 1848-1938: (soudy, soudní osoby, dobové problémy)*, Praha: Wolters Kluwer 2015.

Rádl, Zdeněk, *Nejvyšší správní soud*, Praha: Nákladem Československého Kompasu 1933.

Rentrop, Wilhelm, 'Preise im Protektorat', *Prager Archiv für Gesetzgebung und Rechtsprechung*, (21) 1939, 235-242.

Schelle, Karel and Jaromír Tauchen, *Recht und Verwaltung im Protektorat Böhmen und Mähren*, München: Dr. Hut 2009.

Schelle, Karel and Jaromír Tauchen et al., *Protektorát Čechy a Morava – jedna z nejtragičtějších kapitol českých novodobých dějin (vybrané problémy)*, Brno: The European Society for History of Law 2010.

Schelle, Karel and Jaromír Tauchen et al., *Demokratiserung der tschechischen Rechtsordnung (1989-2009)*, München: Dr. Hut 2009.

Schmidt, 'Deutsche Strafgerichtsbarkeit im Protektorat Böhmen und Mähren', in: *Prager Archiv für Gesetzgebung und Rechtsprechung*, 1939, 1099ff.

Tauchen, Jaromír, 'Prameny práva v nacistickém Německu', in: *Dny práva 2009 – Days of Law*, Brno: Masarykova univerzita 2009, 2757-2773.

Tauchen, Jaromír, 'Právní řád a publikace právních předpisů v Protektorátu Čechy a Morava', in: *Dny práva 2012 – Days of Law 2012*, Brno: Masarykova univerzita 2013, 701-716.

Tauchen, Jaromír, 'Legislation on the Disposal of Jewish Property in the Protectorate of Bohemia and Moravia', in Martina Fiamová (Ed), *Anti-Semitic Legislation in Slovakia and in Europe*, Bratislava: Ústav pamäti národa 2015, 110-124.

Tauchen, Jaromír, 'Das Protektorat Böhmen und Mähren und seine Rechtsordnung (1939–1945)', *Beiträge zur Rechtsgeschichte Österreichs* (10) 2020-2, 260-268.

Veselá, Jarmila and Jaroslav Lepšík, *Německé trestní řízení. Německé vojenské trestní řízení*, Praha: Českomoravský kompas, 1939.

Vlček, Eduard, *Dějiny trestního práva v českých zemích a v Československu*, Brno: Masarykova univerzita 2006.

Wnuck, Felix Tilman, 'Rechtspraxis im Protektorat Böhmen und Mähren. Eine Mikrogeschichte des Amtsgerichts in Brünn im Jahre 1942', *Journal on European History of Law* (9) 2018-2, 50-58.

About the Author

Jaromír Tauchen is associate professor at the Department of History of State and Law of the Faculty of Law, Masaryk University Brno. He researches German legal history, especially the Third Reich, and the history of Germans in the Czech lands. His publications include *Labour and its Legal Regulation in the Protectorate of Bohemia and Moravia (1939-1945)* (2016).

11 The *Cour Supérieure de Justice* and the Luxembourg State Collapse

Vincent Artuso

Abstract

This chapter outlines the fate of the *Cour Supérieure de Justice* in the context of the Collapse of the Luxembourg State. It describes the extensive measures concerning the incorporation of the Luxembourg courts (and administration) in the German state. The actions of the judges and their justifications are discussed and weighed in their context.

Keywords: Luxembourg Cour Supérieur de Justice; German occupation of Luxembourg in World War II; Judicial collaborationism; German Quasi-Annexation of Luxembourg; State collapse

1 Introduction

The occupation period holds a central position in Luxembourg's historiography. It is the equivalent of popular uprisings and liberation wars in other national narratives. According to the long-standing authoritative version of events, the government and the head of state (Grand Duchess Charlotte) left the country on the day of invasion to keep up the fight on the Allies' side, in accordance with a long-established plan. During their absence, the people maintained its unity by resisting the Germanization and nazification policies pursued by the occupying authorities that had destroyed and replaced domestic institutions. The readiness of Luxembourgers to shed their blood for their country irrefutably proved that they were a distinct nation.[1]

Recent publications have shown that this national myth masks certain facts. Luxembourgian society was actually deeply divided during the war.

1 Weber 1946; Majerus 1980; Dostert 1985; Haag & Krier 1987; Trausch 2003.

Venema, D. (ed.), *Supreme Courts Under Nazi Occupation*. Taylor & Francis Group 2022
DOI: 10.5117/9789463720496_CH11

A strong resistance movement had certainly existed, but there was also a substantial minority of Luxembourgers who were ready to assimilate into the National-Socialist *Volksgemeinschaft*.[2] The flight of the members of the executive branch had been ill-prepared and had left the state headless. The *de facto* government that formed in its absence chose to collaborate with Nazi Germany. As to the state apparatus, it did not simply vanish, but, instead, was taken over by the Gauleiter's administration. Senior positions might have been entrusted to Germans, but most Luxembourgian civil servants remained in office.[3] Many aspects of this process have to be studied further. This is certainly the case for the absorption of the *Cour supérieure de Justice* (Superior Court of Justice – CSJ), a long-ignored topic.

The fate of the judicial system, as a whole, was briefly addressed in Paul Dostert's reference work on occupied Luxembourg.[4] It was then more extensively described in Joeri Michielsen's comparative analysis on the impact of National-Socialist rule on the Belgian, Dutch, and Luxembourgian courts.[5] Michielsen was able to describe the process by which the latter were incorporated into the German judicial system, but ultimately he could not verify whether his central thesis applied to them.[6] The main reason he stated for this was that many sources had either been destroyed or remained inaccessible, notably the records on cases conducted before the tribunals during the war. However, the Luxembourg National Archive has since opened access to the records of the post-war purges, including those of the "administrative inquiry" (*Enquête administrative*).[7] During this large-scale undertaking, the attitude of some 20,000 persons – mainly civil servants, including the members of the CSJ – were scrutinized.[8]

2 Artuso 2013.

3 Artuso 2015.

4 Dostert 1985, 193-196.

5 Michielsen 2004.

6 Michielsen's thesis was based on the assumption that the court's positivist attitude towards legal measures, in those three pre-war democracies, condemned them to become executive tools for the policies of the occupant and the governments returning from exile. "Courts will be assumed to have extended the doctrine of supremacy of acts of parliament, which did not allow courts to review these measures, to measures resulting from the occupant or the government returning from exile. This would have put the courts in a position whereby the only choice was to apply the measures, regardless of their legal validity or morality", Michielsen 2004, 2.

7 Archives nationales de Luxembourg (ANLux), Fonds Epuration.

8 After this contribution was finalised, a doctoral thesis on this subject was defended: Wingerter 2021. In her introduction, the author states that she had to face obstacles similar to those encountered by Michielsen almost 20 years ago: "Throughout the writing process, the author has met a variety of people who viewed this endeavour with great scepticism, or even opposition. Some of this opposition was voiced at the very beginning of this task when the

Their individual files have provided a better understanding of the ways in which the Luxembourgian magistrates tried to cope with the new situation. Almost all of them, including the members of the CSJ, were ready to abide by the requirements of the new regime.

2 A Tendency to Violate the Principle of Universality

The modern Luxembourg State was shaped by the institutions and liberal values of the French Revolution.[9] The legal system of the Grand Duchy derives from the Napoleonic Code; its supreme court, the *Cour supérieure de Justice*, is the equivalent of the French and Belgian *Cours de cassation*. The CSJ, whose legal foundations are rooted in Articles 49 and 84 of the country's constitution, is the supreme appellate court for criminal, civil, and commercial cases, as well being the court of last resort; it is also empowered to try members of the government and take disciplinary measures against magistrates. The members of the CSJ are civil servants, appointed by the head of state. In 1940, the institution was composed of a President, two Vice-Presidents, ten counsellors, as well as one Chief and one Deputy Clerk.

The CSJ also hosted another crucial legal institution: the Public Prosecutor's Office (*Parquet général d'État*). It was headed by a Chief Public Prosecutor (*Procureur général d'État*), himself assisted by two Advocates-General. The public prosecutors answered directly to the Minister of Justice. Their missions were to conduct the activities of the criminal police, represent the public in court, and manage the extracts from police records.[10] They also supervised the activities of the immigration police (*police des étrangers*), a task that would lead them to get accustomed, and to some extent adopt, National-Socialist legal vocabulary and concepts right before the war.

author had nothing but a subject and a vague idea of what "purge" meant in the Luxembourg context. Frequent doubts about this project were voiced with statements such as "We already know everything about it" and "Paul Cerf already wrote a book on it, and that is enough." The author has also witnessed a conversation in which other researchers who worked on this subject in previous years were discredited by stating that their source references were not authentic and that some of their research was based on hearsay. These situations are vivid indicators that this research means a great deal to many and remains highly debated. It is sometimes difficult for "outsiders" to research Luxembourgish history of the 20th century." Wingerter 2021, p. 21.

9 The Duchy of Luxembourg, which had been part of the Austrian Netherlands, became a French department from 1795 to 1815.

10 Grand-Duché de Luxembourg, publications de l'Office de Statistiques, *Annuaire Officiel 1940*, Luxembourg, Imprimerie de la Cour Victor Buck 1940, 87-92.

Between 1933 and 1940, the Jewish population had doubled with the arrival of thousands of refugees fleeing the Third Reich. This influx exacerbated the anguish of *Überfremdung* (foreign overflow), which already existed in large portions of the majority Catholic population at a time of economic, political, and identity crisis. This led the authorities to take measures to restrict Jewish immigration. By the mid-1930s, some public servants, particularly those collaborating with the immigration police, grew accustomed to treating foreign Jews as a special category. Immigrants considered Jewish by racial standards were counted separately and were prohibited from engaging in certain professions. Moreover, expressions such as "Non-Aryan" started to appear – without brackets – in official documents.[11] This was a clear breach of the Luxembourg State's traditional refusal to differentiate individuals on religious or racial grounds.

This tendency to violate the principle of universality also appears in a debate that took place towards the end of 1935, when some of the most influential magistrates in the country argued about the necessity of enforcing the Third Nuremberg Law in the Grand Duchy whenever a planned marriage involved at least one German partner.[12] The question had arisen because Luxembourg had, as well as Germany, signed the Hague Convention of 12 June 1902, which had resolved legal conflicts regarding marriage. A state could, however, refuse to apply a foreign law if it considered it to be in contradiction with its own. Other signatories to the Convention, such as France and Belgium, had already decided not to apply the law. District Prosecutor of Luxembourg, Frédéric Gilissen, who would become President of the CSJ in 1940, advised renouncing the Hague Convention, since Luxembourg's legislation did not accept impediments to marriage based on religion or racial differences.[13] Public Prosecutor General Léon Schaack argued, for his part, that the application of this law could not be refused, especially as it was motivated by concerns shared by many Luxembourgers:

> Public opinion and political authorities are concerned about the excessive number of foreigners that are continually pouring into the Grand Duchy. Why, in these conditions, and after reasoning in direct opposition with this fact, should we incite foreigners to commit in our lands an act that their national law qualifies as crime subject to imprisonment and considered

11 See Artuso 2015.

12 This 'Law on the Protection of German Blood and German Honour' dated 15 September 1935 prohibited German citizens of 'German blood and related' from marrying 'Jews'.

13 ANLux, J 57 (30), pièce 0108, opinion from the district court of Luxembourg, 2 November 1935.

null and void unequivocally as to its civil effects, under the pretext of safeguarding a rather vague domestic law and order? Is it not also in our very country that we demand legal measures for the preservation of the race, without contradicting law and order? For example, I noted this wish expressed in a Luxembourg daily newspaper quite recently: 'In the interest of our national economy, social hygiene, and the future of our race, beings who are physically inferior should not be allowed to marry. For this, we should establish a required Health File, as the Medical College has suggested in the past'.[14]

3 The Absorption of the Judicial System

The Grand Duchy was invaded by Germany on 10 May 1940. The Wehrmacht's rapid advance compelled the grand ducal family and the government to flee hastily, without leaving any instructions to the administration left behind. The next day, to overcome the political vacuum, the Chamber of Deputies voted for a resolution creating a Governing Committee (*Commission de Gouvernement*), which was soon thereafter renamed the 'Administrative Commission' (*Commission administrative*).[15] The Deputies did not only give this *ad hoc* executive body the means to function effectively; they granted it the full powers that the emergency laws of 28 September 1938 and 29 August 1939 had conferred on the government.[16] The Chamber of Deputies thus endowed the new institution with a legitimacy rivalling that of the government-in-exile.

Which of the two could claim to be the legal holder of the State's authority? The members of the Administrative Commission addressed this question, among others, after the war in a document handed to the government on 15 January 1945[17]. According to them, the government had ceased to exist after it had left the country since Article 109 of the Constitution excludes any

14 'Im Interesse unserer Volkswirtschaft, der sozialen Hygiene und der Zukunft unserer Rasse, müssten alle physisch minderwertigen Ehekandidaten ausgeschlossen bleiben. In diesem Sinne wäre nach den früheren Anregungen des Medizinalkollegiums, ein Casier sanitaire als obligatorisch einzuführen'. Idem, pièce 0305, opinion from the Chief Public Prosecutor, 22 November 1935.

15 Artuso 2013, 53-58.

16 Artuso 2013, 53-58.

17 *Note des anciens membres de la Commission administrative sur leur attitude dans la question de la VdB* [Note by the former members of the Administrative Commission on their attitude regarding the VdB issue], ANLux, EPU 104, documents 77-82.

possibility of moving its seat for a long period of time.[18] The Administrative Commission did not consider itself as the representative of the government-in-exile, but, rather, as its successor; it was not an interim body acting in a purely administrative capacity, but a *de facto* government.[19] After the signing of the Franco-German armistice, this government developed its own strategy towards Germany: to submit to the new National-Socialist order in return for a guarantee of the country's sovereignty.

The collaboration between the Administrative Commission and the occupying authorities remained cordial for as long as Luxembourg was under military administration. On 21 July 1940, however, Gauleiter Gustav Simon, a National-Socialist official, was appointed Chief of the German civil administration in Luxembourg (*Chef der Zivilverwaltung in Luxemburg*, CdZ). In his function as CdZ, Simon answered solely to Adolf Hitler. His mission was to bring Luxembourg and its population, considered to be 'racially' German, back into the Reich (*Heim ins Reich*). Charged with annexing the country, Simon had no interest in the political collaboration offered by the Administrative Commission, but the docility of the *de facto* government allowed him to smoothly take control of the Luxembourg State apparatus.[20]

The Gauleiter's first measure was to ban the use of the French language in public and to make German the sole official language in the traditionally bilingual Grand Duchy – a decision that was in complete contradiction to Article 43 of the Hague Convention. On 13 August 1940, Gauleiter Simon announced that the Luxembourg Constitution had ceased to exist, since the government and the Grand Duchess had left the country. The oath of loyalty sworn to the Grand Duchess by the civil servants was declared null and void. Two days later, Simon declared himself chief of the Luxembourg administration. Being invested with the power to appoint or dismiss civil servants, he appointed German Commissioners (*Kommissare*) to the head

18 The exact, complete text of this Article 109, still in force, is: 'La ville de Luxembourg est la capitale du Grand-Duché et le siège du Gouvernement. – Le siège du Gouvernement ne peut être déplacé que momentanément pour des raisons graves.' Constitution du Grand-Duché de Luxembourg, available at: www.legilux.public.lu.

19 According to the Luxembourg constitution, the head of state was responsible for appointing the members of the government (art. 77). However, the members of the Administrative Commission had been mandated by the Chamber of Deputies. From mid-June to mid-August, the Administrative Commission therefore tried to obtain permission from the Germans to send a delegation to the Grand Duchess, who was then in exile in Lisbon. All these attempts failed.

20 Reduced to a role of intermediary, passing on the CdZ's orders, the Administrative Commission was severely affected by the arrest of its President, Albert Wehrer, on 24 October 1940 and formally disbanded two months later.

of Luxembourg's administrating authorities during the second half of August 1940.[21]

This was the context in which Luxembourg's judicial system was 'nazified'. On 15 August 1940, a German judge, Bergmann, President of the Higher Regional Court of Appeal (*Oberlandsgericht*) in Cologne, was appointed Commissioner for the administration of justice in Luxembourg (*Kommissar für die Justizverwaltung in Luxemburg*), replacing Frédéric Gilissen, President of the CSJ, as the head of Luxembourg's courts. On 11 November 1940, Luxembourg's courts were compelled to adopt the names of their German counterparts; the already downgraded CSJ was split into different chambers, which functioned independently of one another under the name of Appellate Court Senates (*Oberlandesgerichtliche Senate*). Four days later, Gauleiter Simon enacted an ordinance allowing those authorized to exercise judicial office under German law to exercise it in Luxembourg as well.[22]

A further step towards the complete annihilation of the once independent judicial system was taken by the end of the first winter of occupation. On 3 March 1941, Henri Nocké (a former Vice-President of the CSJ), as well as the judges Faber and Hansen (who presided over the District Tribunals of Luxembourg and Diekirch respectively), were summoned to a meeting during which Lütcke, Bergmann's deputy, announced the upcoming introduction of German civil law. He also told them that only members of the pro-German political movement *Volksdeutsche Bewegung* (VdB) would be kept in place.[23] On 18 July 1941, the Luxembourg judicial system was aligned with the German one by ordinance. From then on, justice was to be spoken "in the name of the German people". The German criminal code was introduced in Luxembourg on 15 March 1942. By then, the boundary between the two countries seemed to have completely vanished, even if appeals against decisions of the Appellate Court Senates to courts in Germany were not permitted. The Gauleiter wanted to avoid interventions from German institutions he could not control.[24]

The first reaction from within the Luxembourg judicial system came from Paul Faber, President of the Luxembourg District Tribunal. On 12 August 1940,

21 Artuso 2015, 123-131.

22 Dostert 1985, 193-196.

23 The *Volksdeutsche Bewegung* or 'Movement of Ethnic Germans' was founded on 13 July 1940, when the country was still under German military administration, by Luxembourgers favourable to the annexation by the Third Reich. By September 1940, it was the only authorized political movement in the country and, by the end of October, a campaign was launched to force a majority of adults – especially civil servants – to join it.

24 Dostert 1985, 193-196.

he publicly expressed his disapproval of the ordinance making German the sole official language in court – adding, however, that he had to point out that the measure was a violation of international law if he was to enforce it.[25] On 3 March 1941, during the meeting with Lütcke, the members of the Luxembourg delegation had also argued that the obligation to join the VdB not only jarred with their conscience but was also contrary to the Hague Convention. These were points over which the German authorities would not fret.

On 16 April 1941, another meeting with Bergmann and Lütcke took place, this time in the presence of all of the Luxembourg magistrates. On this occasion, Lütcke asserted that the Grand Duchy had ceased to exist as an independent state. The oath sworn to Grand Duchess Charlotte having lost its validity, all magistrates who wished to remain in office had to pledge fidelity to Hitler. Faber once again stepped forward and asked on what grounds Luxembourg citizens were to be treated like German civil servants, as there had been no peace treaty. Lütcke retorted that this was just a matter of mere formality, and that the annexation was an accomplished fact.[26]

Three months later, judges Kolbach and Calteux, both of the former CSJ, protested against the introduction of the formula "in the name of the German people".[27] In September 1942, ten magistrates sent back their VdB membership cards to protest against the forced mobilization of Luxembourgers in the German armed forces. This was probably the most sizeable movement of dissent that came from the ranks of the magistracy. But, in the face of events, it was merely symbolic as those magistrates expressly stated that they wished to remain in office. Even those who contested some of the Gauleiter's decisions were not ready break with his regime.

4 National-Socialist Judges

After the crucial meeting of April 1941, four out of fourteen members of the CSJ retired, two were arrested and deported, one was removed from office by a German court martial, and three others were removed from office and mobilized in the German army. Four remained in office, thus accepting to become German *and* National-Socialist judges.[28] The most prominent of

25 Michielsen 2004, 98.
26 Michielsen 2004, 109-110.
27 Michielsen 2004, 113.
28 Michielsen 2004, 117.

these was former Vice-President Nocké. Two others, Counsellors Aloyse Müller and Paul Goetzinger, had both shown sympathies towards the Reich prior to the war. In an enquiry led by the German SD in September 1940 to find out which Luxembourgian civil servants would be fit to serve the new regime,[29] it was noted that Goetzinger was 'said to be very pro-German'[30] and that Müller "had the reputation among his colleagues to be a 'Prussian' and that 'he would be an appropriate intermediary'."[31]

Over the next four years, Müller showed that this reputation was not misplaced. On 27 May 1941, he replaced Faber as head of the District Tribunal of Luxembourg, although several lawyers and a magistrate had been sent to Germany for forced labour, right before his nomination. He also witnessed the dismissal of two former colleagues of the CSJ without flinching. The fact that Müller adhered to the National-Socialist regime was finally illustrated by his attitude outside court. He requested NSDAP membership and was nominated as council member for Luxembourg City. When the American troops approached in early September 1944, he fled to Germany with his family.[32]

The fourth former CSJ magistrate who remained in office until the liberation was Counsellor Joseph Kolbach. In July 1941, he had protested against the formula "in the name of the German people", but, by the end of the month, he was appointed provisional Director of the District Tribunal of Luxembourg (*kommissarischer Landgerichtsdirektor bei dem Landgericht in Luxemburg*) by the German authorities.[33] On 21 April 1942, Kolbach annulled a marriage on the grounds that the wife was "Non-Aryan" – a decision that was the equivalent of a death sentence at that stage of the war. He had passed it with a former colleague at the CSJ, Jules Salentiny.[34] Yet the fates of both judges would be very different after the fall of the National-Socialist regime.

Salentiny was one of the ten magistrates who sent back their VdB membership cards in September 1942. Even though they had specified that they nevertheless wished to remain in office, they were immediately dismissed and arrested. Salentiny spent four days in prison.[35] After the war, this gesture of the ten magistrates was seen as an act of resistance; those who had kept

29 The SD (*Sicherheitsdienst* – Security Service) was the intelligence service of the Nazi Party.

30 ANLux EPU 95, GÖTZINGER, Paul.

31 ANLux EPU 95, MÜLLER, Aloys.

32 Wingerter, 2021, pp. 92-93.

33 ANLux Jt-128, 'Affaire Kolbach'.

34 *Ibidem*.

35 Bosseler & Steichen 1952, 190.

on working for the occupier until the end had to justify themselves. Like all civil servants, their attitude during the war was scrutinized within the framework of the 'administrative inquiry'.

On 13 November 1944, two months after the country had been liberated, the most compromised Luxembourgian magistrates – among them Nocké and Kolbach – submitted a collective letter to the Minister of Justice.[36] In it, they threatened the government, who had just returned from a four-year exile and was trying to impose its authority, as much as they pleaded their own cause. The magistrates implicitly accused the Grand Duchess and the Ministers of having caused the harm that had befallen the country, since their sudden flight had allowed the Germans to absorb Luxembourg's administrative machinery. After that clarification, the magistrates addressed the most sensitive question:

> Some might argue that the magistrates could have chosen to resign collectively. They forget that, with a few rare exceptions, they would not have been able to support their families until the end of a war which the British Prime Minister had already predicted to be long, very long, in September 1940. Moreover, a collective resignation would have had no other result than provoking the occupier to take drastic retaliatory measures.[37]

On 15 January 1945, Kolbach also handed a memorandum of his own to the Minister of Justice.[38] To justify his actions, he pointed out that his colleagues had not been more courageous and, once again, pleaded the necessity of taking care of his family:

> I admit that we should have resisted, although I am under the impression that this point might have been slightly exaggerated. I was then a member of the first Chamber of the Court and noted the absence of collective spirit with some bitterness. In these conditions, I didn't dare to stand out. I also think that the property and family situations should be taken into

36 ANLux Jt-128.

37 *Idem*: [Peut-être dira-t-on que les magistrats auraient dû se démettre en bloc de leurs fonctions. On oublie que sauf quelques rares exceptions ils n'auraient pas été à même d'entretenir leurs familles jusqu'à la fin de la guerre, dont le Chef du gouvernement anglais avait prédit, dès septembre 40, qu'elle serait longue, très longue, et surtout qu'une démission collective n'aurait eu d'autre résultat que de provoquer des représailles draconiennes de la part de l'occupant.]

38 ANLux Jt-128.

account when assessing the duty to resist. In that respect, I think it is fair to say that my duty was first and foremost to take care of my family.[39]

Concerning the introduction of German laws, he alleged that:

> [T]he threats made by President Bergmann on this occasion had the quality – this is odd coming from a personality who was apparently distinguished with an international reputation – of extreme savageness.[40]

Of course, like some other magistrates, he could have shown his discontent by sending back his VdB membership card in September 1942, but his German colleague Gaerner had advised him otherwise – he was already seen as a "ringleader" [*Rädelsführer*]. At the end of the procedure, the four judges that had remained in office until the end of the German occupation were either pensioned or removed.

5 The Collapse of the State

The CSJ was the supreme court of the Grand Duchy of Luxembourg and, as such, was one of the pillars of its sovereignty. Yet, when the country was *de facto* annexed in complete violation of international law, its institutions abolished and its state apparatus subsumed into the Gauleiter's administration, it did not react. Whenever criticism was expressed, it was expressed on an individual basis – the most outspoken magistrate was not even a member of the CSJ, but the President of the Luxembourg District Tribunal. Furthermore, their recriminations, such as they were, cannot be seen as acts of resistance or even opposition. In the end, they did not, strictly speaking, protest against the introduction of German as the sole official language in court, the obligation to join the VdB, or the formula "in the name of the German people". What bothered them most was that those decisions had been taken in absence of a proper peace treaty.

None of the magistrates of the CSJ resigned. Even those who went as far as to send back their VdB membership cards did not want to be removed. What

39 *Idem*: [Dans ces conditions, je n'osais pas me singulariser. J'estime d'autre part que dans l'appréciation du devoir de résistance, il faut tenir compte de la situation de famille et de fortune. Envisagé sous cet angle de vue, je crois pouvoir dire que ce devoir m'appelait parmi les derniers.]

40 *Idem*: [Les menaces que le Président Bergmann nous avait à cette occasion adressées revêtaient – chose étrange chez un personnage apparemment distingué d'une réputation internationale – un caractère d'une sauvagerie extrême.]

could explain this attitude, considering that there was no legal obligation for Luxembourg judges to stay in office? The willingness to protect their compatriots from harsher, German judges who would have replaced them? This would have been an excellent reason. But none of the members of the CSJ magistrates invoked it during the 'administrative inquiry'. What is evidenced in post-war sources is that they rather submitted to the new regime for personal, prosaic reasons: They did not want to lose their jobs.

The end of any form of collegiality within the CSJ, the tendency of its members to revert to individual strategies, was a direct consequence of the Luxembourg state collapse, which happened on the day of invasion. The magistrates, like most of Luxembourg's state officials, agreed that the government had ceased to exist once it had crossed the border. The scale of the catastrophe in the spring of 1940, as well as the apparent supremacy of Germany, led them to believe that there was no alternative to submission. The Grand Duchy was condemned to disappear and they were ready to become fully German. And if some of the CSJ magistrates complained about the improper way in which the annexation was realized, none of them expressed reluctance to enforce National-Socialist legislation. The legal vocabulary and concepts of the Third Reich were of course not entirely new to some Luxembourgian magistrates; they had already acclimatized parts of it before the war.

References

Artuso, Vincent, *La Collaboration au Grand-Duché de Luxembourg durant la Seconde Guerre mondiale (1940-1945). Accommodation, Adaptation, Assimilation*, Préface de Pascal Ory, Frankfurt/Main: Peter Lang 2013.

Artuso, Vincent, *La « Question juive » au Luxembourg (1933-1941). L'État luxembourgeois face aux persécutions antisémites nazies*, Rapport final avec une préface de Serge Klarsfeld, Luxembourg: Éditions forum 2015.

Bosseler, Nicolas & Raymond Steichen, *Livre d'or de la Résistance luxembourgeoise de 1940-1945*, Esch-sur-Alzette: Imprimerie-Reliure H. Ney-Eicher, 1952.

Dostert, Paul, *Luxemburg zwischen Selbstbehauptung und nationaler Selbstaufgabe. Die deutsche Besatzungspolitik und die Volksdeutsche Bewegung*, Luxembourg: Saint-Paul 1985;

Haag, Emile/Krier, Emile, *La Grande-Duchesse et son gouvernement durant La Seconde Guerre mondiale. 1940, l'année du dilemme*, Luxembourg: RTL Edition 1987.

Majerus, Pierre, *Le Luxembourg pendant La Seconde Guerre mondiale*, Luxembourg: Saint-Paul 1980

Michielsen, Joeri, *The "nazification and denazification" of the courts in Belgium, Luxembourg and the Netherlands*, Maastricht: Universitaire Pers Maastricht 2004.

Trausch, Gilbert (dir.), *Histoire du Luxembourg. Le destin européen d'un « petit pays »*, Toulouse: Privat 2003.

Weber, Paul, *Geschichte Luxemburgs im Zweiten Weltkrieg*, Luxembourg: Buck 1946;

Wingerter, Elisabeth, *Law, Order and Postwar Purges in the Grand-Duchy of Luxembourg 1944-1955. Transitional Justice and Redistribution through the Example of Justice, Gendarmerie and Police*, PhD diss, Université du Luxembourg, 2021.

About the Author

Vincent Artuso is a historian specialised in the history of collaboration in occupied countries during WWII. He is currently working as a research fellow at the Centre for Contemporary and Digital History of the University of Luxembourg.

12 The Italian Supreme Court Between Fascism and German Occupation (1943-45)

Antonio Grilli

Abstract

This chapter deals with the Italian *Corte di cassazione* during the German occupation in World War II. It is explained how the creation of the puppet state of the Italian Social Republic in 1943 – a reaction to the allied advances in the south – necessitated the relocation of the court from Rome to northern Italy. The influence of Nazism and fascism on its case law and the issue of its political reliability are considered, as well as the role of Justice minister Pisenti.

Keywords: German occupation of Italy in World War II; Italian Social Republic; Italian Corte di Cassazione; Piero Pisenti.

1 Introduction

Munich, 16 September 1943: Benito Mussolini is liberated from captivity by an SS commando.[1] His new plan is to create a totally new fascist regime in that part of Italy then under German control (all the north and the central part down to Naples; the southernmost part of the peninsula, including Sicily and Sardinia, being occupied by the Allies).

Fascist Italy had been a close ally of Nazi Germany since 1938,[2] and had also declared war on France and Great Britain in June 1940. But, three years

1 On Mussolini's liberation: Patricelli 2002; Götzel 1980.

2 Knox 2000; De Felice 1981.

Venema, D. (ed.), *Supreme Courts Under Nazi Occupation*. Taylor & Francis Group 2022
DOI: 10.5117/9789463720496_CH12

later, it had collapsed under the enormous burden of its military defeats.[3] On the night of 25 July 1943, Mussolini himself had been disavowed by the most prominent personalities of the regime,[4] gathered in the Great Council of Fascism: he resigned and was later arrested by order of King Victor Emanuel III. On 8 September, when the Anglo-American forces had already succeeded in taking control over Sicily and part of southern Italy, King Victor Emanuel III and the new Prime Minister, Pietro Badoglio, decided to abandon the Axis with Germany and sign an armistice with the Allies – even if a large part of Italy was then under German occupation.[5] In fact, the Third Reich had grown increasingly suspicious of the 'loyalty' of its ally after the fall of Mussolini, but its occupation of northern Italy, which took place as a form or retaliation motivated by strategic reason, did not always encounter tough resistance from the Italian army. The King, government, and all of the military leadership had fled to the south on 9 September. It was an ignominious escape, which left the Italian people and army in disarray.

Thus, from September 1943 until the final act of the liberation in April 1945, Italy experienced the drama of being a battleground not only between the Germans and Allies, but also between Mussolini's collaborationist regime in the North (the so-called 'Italian Social Republic',[6] calling upon all Italians to wash their hands clean of the dishonour of the 'treason'[7]) and the legitimate Italian government in the South, which had been placed under allied protection and was soon contributing to the efforts to liberate the country.[8] The very last fascist government (sometimes called, though not entirely justifiably, a 'puppet government'[9]), which did not take Rome for its capital, but was ranged around Lake Garda in the North, thus lived six hundred tormented days between German mistrust and the escalation of the Italian armed Resistance.[10]

It is well-known that the fascist regime in Italy had been (maybe with Lenin's Soviet Union) the first experiment of a fully totalitarian regime.[11]

3 Adams 1982; Morgan 2007; De Felice 1974a.

4 Bianchi 1963.

5 Rossi 2006; De Felice 1996.

6 Bocca 1994; Lepre 2000; Quartermaine 2000.

7 Tompkins 1966. About the supposed Italian 'treason': Kuby 1982.

8 About the so called 'Italian civil war', see primarily De Felice 2008; Lamb 1993; but first, in Italian, Pavone 1991.

9 Moseley 2004.

10 A few titles about the Italian 'Resistenza' among a vast literature: De Blasio Wilhelm 2014; Gobetti 2014; Peli 2015.

11 See in this framework Bosworth 2007; Gentile 2008.

Fascism had been in power in Italy between 1922 and 1943.[12] By 1926, the process of elimination of any political opposition was almost complete. A dictatorship was created, a secret police (the *Organizzazione per la Vigilanza e la Repressione dell'Antifascismo*, OVRA) was put in place, and a Special Tribunal for the Defence of the State had been charged, since its creation in 1926, with severely repressing any political opposition.[13]

Yet, the life of the ordinary law and daily judicial activity only slightly suffered from this rough climate. Lawyers, generally speaking, vindicated the neutral character of their profession: neutrality seemed to become their slogan, implicitly supported not only by the judges of the Supreme Court (*Corte di cassazione*), but even by one of its most significant members, the former Minister of Justice, Alfredo Rocco.

By 1930, a new penal code entered into force, strengthening the severity of repression and reintroducing the death penalty for ordinary crimes. Similarly, in 1942, a new civil code was adopted, which still exists in modern-day Italy (although it has been partially amended to eliminate any reference to fascist ideology, for example the concept of 'corporatism').

The *Corte di cassazione* became unique in Italy in 1925. Nearly twenty years later, in September 1943, it still had its seat in Rome and, consequently, submitted to the authority of the Italian collaborationist regime and that of the German occupier. All of its members (more than 120 at the time of the Italian armistice on 8 September) had, therefore, to accommodate themselves to the constraints of this new situation, which demanded fidelity to a new regime they surely disliked.

In the past, all judges had taken their oath of allegiance to the state at the beginning of their career, and nearly all of them were obliged to become members of the National Fascist Party (PNF) during the fascist dictatorship. But now the situation had changed: they had to face the reality of a foreign military occupation combined with the presence of a collaborationist regime that they regarded as fully illegitimate, even if it was headed by a former head of government.

The life of the *Corte di cassazione* – the very top of the judicial system – during the period of Nazi occupation and fascism collaborationism can thus be considered from a double point of view: the influence of Nazi-fascism on its case law and the issue of its political reliability.

12 About the origins of fascism: Mack Smith 1997; De Felice 1974b.

13 Recently: Franzinelli 2017; Dal Pont et al. 1961.

2 The Influence of Nazi-fascism on Case Law

As far as the first point is concerned, we know that the legal office of the German Plenipotentiary in Italy, SS-General Karl Wolff, regularly monitored the decisions of Italian courts, especially in criminal matters. We also know that the German legal office in 1944 strongly insisted that the Italian Justice Minister, Piero Pisenti, annul criminal judgments, which seemed to be too 'mild' or 'indulgent'. Then, in May 1944, the Germans asked the Ministry of Justice to obtain a list of all sensitive cases treated by the Italian judges up until that point. This request was perceived as an interference; Pisenti's rough answer was that such sensitive cases fell within the competence of the special courts, which did not normally communicate their judgments.[14]

This statement did not correspond to reality. In fact, we know that the Italian justice system experienced a steady competence confusion between 1943 and 1945. Thus, a criminal case could often be decided by the court that 'arrived first'.

Even ordinary judges could sometimes 'arrive first' (especially when they could rely on the police, which was not always the case!). In those cases, they were able to treat sensitive criminal cases, for example, abduction or hiding of goods, thefts against Italian and German armed forces, homicides, listening to enemy radio broadcasts, and so on. Their approach was indulgent, tied to the principles of the rule of law – and far from any purposes of deterrence. For this reason, they were very unpopular amongst German controllers and members of the fascist Republic. We have some reason to believe that such a mild attitude represented, in a certain sense, a form of implied resistance by many of the Italian ordinary judges.[15]

Besides those regular judges, and competing with them, there was a variety of special jurisdictions that existed: from the Special Tribunal for the Defence of the State (recreated in December 1943) to military and extraordinary courts, often illegally and arbitrarily established by local fascist authorities. Then there was also often the absence of justice: the enormous escalation of killings of suspects, who were shot by German units, as well as by units of the Italian "Republican Guard", police, and armed forces without any judgment – very often in retaliation to the Resistance. Those executions became more and more frequent after the liberation of Rome in June 1944.[16]

14 Grilli 2017, 131.

15 Grilli 2017, 228.

16 Many archival sources lead to such a conclusion. See for example: Central Archives of the State (CAS), Rome, collection 'Italian Social Republic. Ministry of Justice', vol. VI.

On the other hand, no significant role had been played by the German occupier or fascist authorities in terms of interfering with adjudication in the Italian Supreme Court between 1943 and 1945. In civil matters, the judgments of the *Corte di cassazione* retained their validity and remained in force after the end of the war; criminal judgments did not experience any external attempt to overturn them. For example, the Supreme Court's point of view, expressed in 1942, that a defendant who was in need when robbing or hiding goods should be acquitted, was not reversed. Most judges relied on this mild opinion, notwithstanding the fact that Minister Pisenti and Mussolini himself had recommended the utmost severity in repressing black-market trading, which they considered extremely harmful to a wartime economy.[17]

3 Political Reliability

As far as the political reliability of the Supreme Court is concerned, it is almost certain that most of its members who happened to find themselves in occupied Italy deeply disliked the new fascist republic of Mussolini and the Third Reich. They were monarchists, had taken their oath to the King (not to fascism), and believed in the neutrality of the law. They were sometimes depicted by fascists as enemies. On 27 January 1944, Vice-Minister Francesco Barracu accused Antonino Cordova and Giuseppe Messina – both judges in the Supreme Court – of being "freemasons and supporters of the Badoglio government".[18] However, such accusations did not have any impact – perhaps because of minister Pisenti's protection (he was a fascist committed to legality) and the extreme difficulty that would be involved in replacing them. It is possible that Barracu and the leadership of the Republican Fascist Party (*Partito Fascista Repubblicano*, PRF), including secretary Alessandro Pavolini, wished to replace most judges; they did not trust ordinary judges whom they felt to be politically unreliable, and they did not miss any occasion to express their views to Pisenti.

Yet, replacing unreliable judges, as has already been said, proved to be a challenge. The Supreme Court was protected by Pisenti himself, who believed that the prestige of the judicial system was the best way to legitimate, and

17 CAS, 'Italian Social Republic. Ministry of Justice', vol. V, Mussolini's letter of 12th December 1944 to all ministers.

18 CAS, 'Italian Social Republic. Presidency of the Council', vol. III, Barracu's letter to minister Pisenti of 27 January 1944.

lend credibility to, the fascist republic. In his opinion, the Supreme Court had to remain the authoritative centre of the entire judicial system – despite the war and notwithstanding all of the exceptional jurisdictions, including the German war tribunals arising from the military occupation.[19]

Therefore, when the Third Reich created for strategic reasons, in early September 1943, the so-called 'operations zones' of the Alps and the Adriatic Coast,[20] and removed them from any Italian jurisdiction, Pisenti firmly opposed the German point of view and the opinion of the local *Gauleiter*. Pisenti maintained that the Supreme Court in Rome retained full competence to decide on any appeal from courts located in these areas, namely those of Trento, Trieste, Belluno, and Bolzano. Although he was unable to change the German position on this issue, he repeatedly encouraged the Trieste Court of Appeal to join him in his fight to keep justice "in Italian hands".[21]

Pisenti succeeded in preventing judges from having to take a new oath of allegiance to the Italian Social Republic, officially claiming that this 'political' act was inappropriate during wartime; it would have to be postponed until the end of the war and the creation of new institutions (many Italian magistrates who were not purged in the post-war period on the grounds of collaborationism owe him a debt of gratitude for that!).[22]

Despite such protection, one major event proved right, once again, the mistrust with which the Italian judges regarded the dominant Nazi-fascist regime as a whole: the transfer of part of the Supreme Court to northern Italy. The Supreme Court at that time still resided in Rome; the city had been declared 'open', even though it was, in fact, controlled by the German army as an immediate hinterland of the war front. However, Rome was too far from northern Italy. War, bombardments, and lack of transportation made it extremely difficult to reach. Besides, how long would the eternal city still be in German hands? The possibility of appealing to the Supreme Court was at risk. Thus, Pisenti decided, by an act of 29 March 1944, to move three sections of the *Corte di cassazione* to Brescia; two sections specialized exclusively in criminal and civil matters respectively, whereas the third heard both.

Very soon, he had to face a form of resistance that he had not expected: most high judges declined the invitation to move, invoking every kind of pretext, such as age, family ties, the detrimental effects of the weather of the foggy north as compared with the more clement weather of Rome. A

19 See in this regard Pisenti's memoirs: Pisenti 1977, 81.

20 Wedekind 2003.

21 CAS, 'Pisenti Papers', vol. III (Pisenti's letter to the German 'Gauleiter' Reiner of 3 August 1944).

22 Grilli 2007, 46.

bundle of medical certificates sent from Rome reached the Ministry of Justice in Cremona. Judge Filippo Profeta argued that such a change in his life would surely provoke the breakdown of his family, whereas Judge Domenico Cortesani wrote to Pisenti in these terms, on 27 March 1944:

> I am 64 and I have 42 years of service, I am married, with two sons and one of them, an officer in the army has been missing since 8 September. I suffer from heavy impairment, hernia and arthritis: the transfer to a cold and humid location would be very harmful for me.[23]

The transfer to the north turned out to be a tough task. Nearly fifty judges (that is, more than half of those who were requested to leave) refused. These were retired. Though, thanks to Pisenti, they at least avoided every further sanction proposed by Pavolini and most of the fascist party. The latter regarded them as a kind of saboteurs and had proposed severe measures, such as loss of pension rights and even actions by the German police. In fact, Pisenti succeeded, after a long quarrel, in having his point of view accepted, according to which judges belonged to a separate corps and could not be treated as simple civil servants who could be submitted to disciplinary measures.[24]

The positions vacated by those Supreme Court judges who refused to move to northern Italy were taken by younger colleagues, eager to progress so quickly and so high in the judiciary. They could not really be defined as long-time fascists, or strongly pro-German and anti-Semitic oriented magistrates. There is no strong ideological motivation to be found in their selection, which was perhaps rather determined both by individuals' desire to boost their careers and by a common feeling that this highest and most sensitive degree of the judiciary could not be left ineffective in northern Italy. Thus, in the spring of 1944 (and maybe never again in this full-scale!), a very particular form of 'forced' mobility took place among the Italian Supreme Court judges.

On 19 May 1944, Pisenti could celebrate the opening session of the three new sections of the Supreme Court that had been established in Brescia. He considered the transfer to Brescia as a personal success and declared that the unity of the court was not affected so far. On the contrary, he claimed

23 CAS, 'Italian Social Republic. Ministry of Justice', vol. X, Cortesani's letter to minister Pisenti, 27 March 1944.

24 CAS, 'Italian Social Republic. Ministry of Justice', vol. VI, Pisenti's note to Alessandro Pavolini, 14 September 1944.

that, through this transfer, the existence of the fascist republic itself would be legitimated thanks to a more efficient rule of law.[25]

His vision soon proved too optimistic. It is true that the new segment of the *Corte di cassazione*, which had moved to the north, was able to render a considerable number of judgments – many of which, especially in civil matters, retained their force after the war. However, Pisenti's aim to legitimate Mussolini's state turned out to be a chimera, which evaporated totally when the civil war in Italy between fascism and anti-fascism escalated tremendously in the last year of the Second World War.

References

Adams, Henry Hitch, *Italy at war. World War II*, Alexandria: Time Life Books 1982.

Bianchi, Gianfranco, *25 luglio, crollo di un regime*, Milan: Murcia 1963.

Bocca, Giorgio, *La Repubblica di Mussolini*, Milano: Mondadori 1994.

Bosworth, R.J.B., *Mussolini's Italy: Life Under the Fascist Dictatorship, 1915-1945*, London: Penguin Books 2007.

Dal Pont, A., A. Leonetti, F. Maiello & L. Zocchi, *Aula IV. Tutti i processi del Tribunale speciale fascista*, Rome: ANPPIA 1961.

De Blasio Wilhelm, Maria, *The Other Italy: The Italian Resistance in World War II*, New York: Ishi Press 2014.

De Felice, Rienzo, *Mussolini. L'alleato. 1. Dalla guerra «breve» alla guerra lunga. L'Italia in guerra (1940-1943)*, Turin: Einaudi 1974a.

De Felice, Renzo, *Mussolini. Il fascista. 1. I. La conquista del potere. 1921-1925*, Turin: Einaudi 1974b.

De Felice, Renzo, *Mussolini. Il Duce II. Lo stato totalitario 1936-1940*, Turin: Einaudi 1981.

De Felice, Renzo, *Mussolini. L'Alleato. L'Italia in guerra II: Crisi e agonia del regime*, Turin: Einaudi 1996.

De Felice, Renzo, *Mussolini. L'Alleato. 2: La Guerra Civile*, 3rd ed., Turin: Einaudi 2008.

Franzinelli, Mimmo, *Il tribunale del Duce. La giustizia fascista e le sue vittime*, Milan: Mondadori 2017.

Ganapini, Luigi, *La repubblica delle camicie nere. I combattenti, i politici, i socializzatori, gli amministratori*, Milan: Garzanti 1999.

Gentile, Emilio, *La via italiana al totalitarismo. Il partito e lo Stato nel regime fascista*, Rome: Carocci 2008.

25 Grilli 2007, 41-43. Some more meaningful parts of Pisenti's speech of 19 May 1944 can be also found in Ganapini 1999, 255-256.

Gobetti, Ada, *Partisan Diary: A Woman's Life in the Italian Resistance*, Oxford University Press 2014.

Götzel, H., *Kurt Student und seine Fallschirmjäger*, Friedberg: Podzan Pallas 1980.

Grilli, Antonio, *Tra fronda e collaborazione. Magistrati nell'Italia occupata (1943-1945)*, Rome: Aracne 2017.

Knox, MacGregor, *Common Destiny: Dictatorship, Foreign Policy, and War in Fascist Italy and Nazi Germany*, Cambridge University Press 2000.

Kuby, Erich, *Verrat auf deutsch. Wie das Dritte Reich Italien ruinierte*, Hamburg: Hoffmann und Campe 1982.

Lamb, Richard, *War in Italy, 1943-1945: A Brutal Story*, London: Murray 1993.

Lepre, Aurelio, *La storia della Repubblica di Mussolini*, Milan: Mondadoni 2000.

Mack Smith, Denis, *Modern Italy: A Political History*, Yale University Press 1997.

Morgan, Phillip, *The Fall of Mussolini: Italy, the Italians, and the Second World War*, Oxford University Press 2007.

Moseley Ray, *Mussolini: The Last 600 Days of Il Duce*, Lanham: Taylor Trade 2004.

Patricelli, Marco, *Liberate il Duce. Gran Sasso 1943: la vera storia dell'Operazione Quercia*, Milano: Mondadori 2002.

Pavone, Claudio, *Una Guerra civile. Saggio storico sulla moralità nella Resistenza*, Milan: Bollati Boringhieri 1991 (transl. in English as *A Civil War: A History of the Italian Resistance*, London: Verso Books 2013).

Peli, Santo, *Storia della Resistenza in Italia*, Turin: Einaudi 2015.

Pisenti, Piero, *Una Repubblica necessaria (RSI)*, Rome: G. Volpe 1977.

Quartermaine, Luisa, *Mussolini's Last Republic. Propaganda and Politics in the Italian Social Republic (R.S.I.) 1943-45*, Exeter: Intellect 2000.

Rossi, Elena Aga, *Una nazione allo sbando. 8 settembre 1943*, Bologna: Il Mulino 2006.

Tompkins, Peter, *Italy Betrayed*, London: Simon & Schuster 1966.

Wedekind, Michael, *Nationalsozialistische Besatzungs- und Annexionspolitik in Norditalien 1943 bis 1945. Die Operationszonen „Alpenvorland" und „Adriatisches Küstenland"*, München: Oldenbourg 2003 (orig. 1964).

About the Author

Antonio Grilli is a professor of legal history at the Open University of Como/Rome, having previously served as an EC Lawyer in Brussels (2000-2018). He has published widely on justice during Fascism, including *Between Revolt and Collaboration: Judges in Occupied Italy (1943-1945)* (2017). He is currently writing a book on Mussolini's special tribunal for the State defence.

13 Supreme Courts Dealing with Nazi Occupation: The Struggle for Order and Identity

Derk Venema

Abstract

This chapter discusses, first, the ways the Nazi German occupiers secured their power and handled the courts in the countries studied, and how much of the rule of law and democracy was broken down. Next, it gives an overview of how the supreme courts performed under enemy rule, what they did to preserve the rule of law and democracy, and how their actions and policies were judged after the war. Finally, conclusions are drawn about the role and the possibilities of the supreme courts and the law under the regime of the Nazi German occupier, and autocratic rule in general.

Keywords: Judicial collaboration; Judicial resistance; Moral hygiene; Rule of law; Mayor in wartime dilemma

1 Introduction

The clash between policies of the German occupiers and aims of the national administrations and judiciaries played out differently in each of the occupied countries. Nevertheless, many measures and reactions appeared in more than one place. For the realization of the occupier's aims – ruling over Europe, creating *Lebensraum*, and eliminating the Jews – two things were essential: power and identity. To consolidate their power, the Germans needed well organized occupation regimes, consisting of German supervision and cooperating local administrative bodies. Their identity was expressed through propaganda, laws and other policy measures, meant to emphasize

Venema, D. (ed.), *Supreme Courts Under Nazi Occupation*. Taylor & Francis Group 2022
DOI: 10.5117/9789463720496_CH13

that they were not just any kind of occupying power, but the leaders of the Germanic master race, Europe's *Führungsvolk*.[1] The supreme courts aimed to continue their traditional role: administer justice impartially for the benefit of society. In order to fulfil that role to the best of their abilities under the circumstances, they also needed power and identity. Their position as leaders of the judiciary – and in many cases the only remaining leading institution of the three branches of government – was their power base. And because people do not only need food, shelter, and social order, but also crave expression of their national identity, the courts' legitimacy partly rested on their identification with national values. In many ways, the power claims and identities of occupiers and occupied did not align. Nevertheless, they were condemned to cooperate in what was their common interest: maintaining public order, the framework of society, enabling people to keep living their lives as normally as possible. The resulting negotiations, protests, measures, reactions, and discussions are described in this book.

Because we do not have complete data on all the aspects of the behaviour of the supreme courts under the occupation, and because not all aspects were present in all occupations, statistical conclusions, such as: 'refusing to apply an occupation ordinance yielded a 30% chance of arrest with an 85% chance of reputation improvement' are impossible. Also, criticizing the supreme court of one country for not trying what was successful for another country's supreme court, is not the point of this chapter, for at least two reasons. First, the information available in the occupied countries about each other's situation was incomplete and often unreliable. For example: Dutch legal circles were in the dark about the fate of the Norwegian Høyesterett until after the war.[2] Secondly, a successful strategy in one country would not necessarily have been a success in another: it will remain undecided, for example, whether the assertive attitude of the Belgian *Cour de Cassation* would have availed the Protectorate's Supreme Administrative Court. Situations were too different, and there existed no general scheme ('*kein Schema!*') of occupation policy as a point of reference: it was more or less every occupation regime for itself.

We can, however, sketch some general patterns in the manoeuvring room the different courts had, or imagined they had, in securing the national legal order, aiding the population or specific citizens, and defending national identity – 'our Dutch world', as law professor Cleveringa put it in his discussion

1 A term coined by *Großraum* theorist Werner Best; see the introductory chapter to this volume.

2 Jansen & Venema 2011, 131, 217-218.

with *Hoge Raad* judge Losecaat Vermeer.[3] This will answer the question posed in the introduction: what can the head of the judiciary do to defend democracy, the rule of law, and the population against an antidemocratic occupier? It also gives an indication of what *not* to expect from the (supreme) courts of a formerly democratic country under an undemocratic oppressor.

Section 1 discusses the ways the Nazi German occupiers secured their power and handled the courts in the countries studied, and how much of the rule of law and democracy was broken down. In Section 2, I will give an overview of how the supreme courts performed under enemy rule, what they did to preserve the rule of law and democracy, and how their actions and policies were judged after the war. Finally, in Section 3, conclusions are drawn about the role and the possibilities of the supreme courts and the law under the regime of the Nazi German occupier, and autocratic rule in general.

2 Securing the Regime – Encapsulating the Courts

To continue the fight against Nazi Germany, and to save an important symbol of and claim to legitimate independent nationhood, several countries established governments in exile.[4] Some of these were the incumbent governments at the time of the attack (in the Netherlands, Luxembourg, Belgium, and Norway), some were comprised of adversaries of the local government (of France and Czechoslovakia), and another more informal one was set up later (Denmark's Freedom Council, 1943). The monarchs of the Netherlands, Luxembourg, and Norway also left their countries, while the Belgian king stayed behind, as did the Danish king, whose government remained intact until 1943.

While the exiled governments were organizing themselves in London, on the continent Nazi Germany took off on its honeymoon with multiple ravished brides.[5] The administrations and judiciaries of the conquered countries cooperated with the oppressor, partly because of his overwhelming power, partly because of the civility of the German administrative officials and their seeming respect for international law. In the absence of the ministers, in Belgium, the Netherlands, and in Denmark from 1943, the highest civil servants had to fill the positions

3 Venema et al. 2008, see introduction.

4 Cf. also Conway & Romijn 2008, 50-51, 153.

5 This metaphor has often been used for the first phase of these occupations. For example: Deák 2015, title of Chapter 3: 'Defeat and Submission: Europe's Honeymoon with Hitler, 1939–1941'.

of the former heads of the departments, and in the case of Norway, a collaborating new government was formed under Vidkun Quisling. In Luxembourg, the Administrative Commission formed by parliament saw itself as the successor, rather than the temporary replacement of the legitimate exiled government. In these countries, German officials were appointed as supervisors of the departments (*Kommissare*) and as agents monitoring the work of the departments and other government agencies. The German occupiers left most of the departments intact, because they needed the administrative infrastructure to rule the countries effectively and to maintain public order. In France, a collaborating government was formed in Vichy by Marshal Pétain, which gained much international recognition, and in Prague the former Czechoslovakian government became the puppet government of the Protectorate of Bohemia and Moravia. Italy's situation was different: in 1943, the government voted Mussolini out and switched sides to the allies, after which the Germans occupied the north and set up a puppet regime under Mussolini, the Italian Socialist Republic.

The Germans established different kinds of occupation regimes, according to their different aims: eliminating the French military threat (France), protection against the British military threat and conversion to National Socialism on the grounds of Germanic ethnicity and therefore assumed receptiveness to Nazism (the Netherlands, Norway, Denmark, and Belgium), and annexation to the German Reich after the war on the basis of presumed Germanness (Luxembourg and the Protectorate). Italy's puppet government was supervised by an ambassador-plenipotentiary together with military leaders. In the background of all occupations stood the general goal of a new European order after the war. The persecution of Jews was practised in all occupied areas, as was, from 1942, economic exploitation. Countries in the same group did not necessarily have the same kind of regime. There was no central coordinating body for all or even some of the occupations. Only Hitler himself oversaw them, but he did not take very much interest in detailed structuring, and was against any kind of unification of occupation regimes. Also, national differences in the structure of the administration partly determined the form of the occupation regime.[6]

While in most occupied democratic countries the legislature and the highest executive authorities were dissolved, absent, or Nazified, the highest judicial authorities were all left in place (although in the case of

6 Röhr 1997, 25-26, 31.

Luxembourg in a soon strongly Germanized form). The German conquerors understood that a functioning judiciary is the backbone of a functioning legal system, which in turn is an important pillar of a well-organized society. International law specialists had agreed even before 1914 that the judicial continuity was an important key to a successful occupation regime, as Bost shows in her chapter on Belgium under the first German occupation. This is also why the threat of a strike could be effective, as it was in Belgium in the Second World War, when the Germans probably remembered the actual judicial strike under the previous occupation. Moreover, in the terms used in the introduction,[7] the authority of 'representative organizations' (government administration) depends to an important extent on 'legitimation from below', making it unwise to replace the 'native elites' in the administration at once with 'loyal elites' (Nazi sympathizers) or Germans. That is why existing representative organizations with their native elites were preferably used as 'control organizations'. Even in fascist Italy, Justice Minister Pisenti believed in judicial independence and protected the *Corte di Cassazione* (whose members were royalists rather that fascists) against undue influence by the executive. And the Germans accepted it. All in all, the German occupiers took care to secure the continuity of the administration, including the judiciary. This had been done in Germany itself as well, although especially Hitler and the SS kept complaining about the independent and non-revolutionary attitude of the German courts.

An outlier here is all but formally annexed Luxembourg: unlike the other countries, it was small and German enough for the Nazi occupier to replace much of the native elite with loyal elite and Germans. Its highest court, the *Cour Supérieur de Justice*, was effectively beheaded and quartered, when a German judge was appointment director of the judiciary and the court was dissolved into separate appeal court senates and integrated into the German court system.

2.1 New Courts

Although the supreme courts were necessary for social order, the Germans were careful not to leave their competence wholly intact. Many different types of new courts were introduced in the occupied territories to maintain public order and to further German policies.[8] In the countries

7 Borrowed from Lammers 1995.
8 See Graver 2015, 47-49, for application of this instrument in other cases.

more intensively administered by the occupier, more types of cases were tried by German or other special courts, thus shielding them off from regular domestic judicial scrutiny.[9] As is usual in wars and occupations, and active in all territories where the Nazi German army was present, were court martials dealing with offences by the occupation troops. These courts, however, could also try nationals of the occupied country who were suspected of acts against the occupation army. Additionally, in Norway, the Netherlands, and the Protectorate, SS and police courts were established. These were competent in cases concerning, in a broad sense, actions against German SS and police forces. In the Netherlands and the Protectorate, a German non-military criminal court was also introduced which could try Germans and others in cases concerning Germans or German interests. In these countries, the occupation regime leaders could remove cases from the regular courts and have them decided by German instances if deemed necessary. Finally, in the Protectorate, where the German take-over was one of the most far-reaching, a German court system for civil cases was set up, to complete the first step in the Germanization of the administration of justice, a prelude to annexation. None of the decisions of these German courts could be challenged before regular national courts, thus also excluding the supreme courts.

Along with this limitation of their jurisdiction, the Protectorate's Supreme Administrative Court was also forced to hand over thousands of cases not only to the German courts, but also to the judiciary of the new Germany-allied Slovak republic. The most drastic case in this respect, however, was again Luxembourg: not because of the introduction of new German courts, but because the Luxembourg courts themselves were *turned into* German courts, and German civil and criminal law was introduced.[10]

In addition to German courts, special political criminal courts were set up within the national court systems of the Netherlands, Norway, the Protectorate, and France, as had been in done in Germany itself. Their decisions mostly could not be reviewed by the regular supreme courts either. In sum, even without directly changing the existing competencies of the supreme courts, their jurisdictions were restricted by the introduction of all these new courts.

9 See also Best 1941, 65, table: the bottom line indicates the types of German courts in each country.

10 The fact that Luxembourg wasn't included in Best's overview may be due to its relative insignificance, but maybe Best regarded it as essentially German and virtually already incorporated in the *Reich*.

2.2 Symbols of Power and Loyalty

Symbols can be very powerful in constituting an associative connection between persons and groups or ideas, such as political affiliations. In terms of the concerns for material consequences and identity affirmation, as distinguished in the introduction, the use of symbols is meant to promote the latter.

Judicial oaths are rituals with a high symbolic value, expressing loyalty to the law, and sometimes to the executive power.[11] Although they generally do not have the status of a legal contract, they do have a certain psychological effect.[12] That effect is not equal for everyone taking an oath, however, but together with its symbolic value, it supports and expresses the hope that it is an essential tool which 'constitutes, underwrites, and guarantees this active willingness and commitment to perform one's official duties […].'[13] In several countries, existing judicial oaths were adapted, or they were supplemented by loyalty statements. In Germany, of course, judges swore an oath to Hitler, and in the Protectorate and Luxembourg, a similar oath to the Führer was introduced – illegally according to international law,[14] but in accordance with Germany's plans with these occupied territories.[15] In occupied Belgium in WWI and in the occupied Netherlands, a statement of loyalty to the occupier and his laws had to be signed, additionally to the original oaths. The Dutch *Hoge Raad* judges were sworn in by *Reichskommissar* Seyss-Inquart himself. On top of that, the Nazi judges from the new political criminal courts took their oaths with the president of the *Hoge Raad*, which lent them some legitimacy, even though the president was a war-time appointee loyal to the Germans. The judges of the French *Cour de Cassation*, perceived by the Germans as a symbol of their ideological enemy, the French Revolution, had to pledge allegiance to the Vichy government. Their colleagues of the *Conseil d'Etat* were obliged to swear the oath to Pétain in person. Remarkably, Italian Justice Minister Pisenti (a longstanding, loyal but critical fascist party member) prevented the introduction of a new judicial oath to the Italian Socialist Republic, because he preferred a more independent judiciary which, in his view, served as a better legitimization of the state.

11 Condren 2006, esp. Chapter 11. See also Schlesinger 2008.

12 Schwartz et al. 2019.

13 Aroney 2018, 197.

14 Oppenheim/Lauterpacht 1935, § 171, p. 355.

15 See also Mazower 2008, 109-111.

Another symbolic way to suggest loyalty to the occupier and dissociation from the former or exiled government, was to alter the executory formula of court decisions. In Belgium and the Netherlands, there was some controversy over the wording. In Belgium, it was the exiled government who in May 1940 unsuccessfully demanded the formula 'in the name of the King' be changed to 'in the name of the Belgian people', because of a break between them and the King, who had remained in the country and wanted to appoint new ministers to negotiate with the Germans. There was no German pressure for an alternative formula. In the Netherlands, however, Seyss-Inquart in his very first ordinance replaced the formula 'in the name of the Queen' with the more neutral 'in the name of the law', which was criticized by some, but legal according to international law. In Luxembourg, another foreshadowing of Germany's post-war intentions appeared in the new formula 'in the name of the German people'.

Additional measures with a strong symbolic value, but which were not *merely* symbolic, were taken in the countries to be incorporated into the German Reich directly after the war: in the Protectorate, judges had to take German language exams and all forms became bilingual. In the Supreme Administrative Court's courtroom, moved to a former shelter for the poor, national symbols were replaced with a portrait of the *Führer*. And in Luxembourg, the French language was banned from the courts, which were renamed in the German nomenclature. Awarding German judges competency in Luxembourg courts clearly prepared the formally still occupied country for inclusion into the *Reich*.

A more subtle use of symbolism is found in the provenance of laws. In Belgium and the Netherlands, the occupier aimed for greater acceptance of unpopular measures by having them formally issued by the national authorities. In Prague, the *Reichsprotektor* determined which laws were to be issued through the façade of the Protectorate government.

2.3 Personnel Policy

The occupiers realised that it was much harder to replace *judges* with loyal elites than to fill vacancies in government departments or at the local administrative level.[16] The reason for that was that deciding cases at law is a highly specialized profession, which requires years of training and experience, especially in the highest instance. This meant that among legal professionals, there were not many eligible candidates who were also at

16 Cf. van Goethem, De Wever & Wouters 2006.

least sympathetic to the 'New Order': the occupier was stuck with mostly native elites. The occupation regimes nevertheless succeeded in appointing some loyal elites to some of the supreme courts after dismissing Jews and judges deemed politically unreliable – as Hitler had done in Germany from 1933 with his 'Law for the Restoration of the Professional Civil Service'.[17] Norway's justice minister, for instance, worked hard to fill the vacancies left by the judges who had collectively resigned from the *Høyesterett*. Initially, less than half of the positions could be filled, and the court didn't regain full strength until after the war. In the Netherlands, the secretary-general for Justice was a Nazi party member, but like his Norwegian colleague took care not to appoint Nazi fanatics to the courts if it could be avoided. This made his task of filling open positions in the lower courts even more difficult, as it was hard to convince non-Nazis to accept an appointment from the current regime, especially in 'tainted' positions left vacant by the dismissal of Jewish judges. He had to put quite some pressure on two jurists from his Dutch East-Indies network, who were Nazi sympathizers but not party members, to accept an appointment to the *Hoge Raad* by the *Reichskommissar*. The newly appointed president had no experience as a judge and had to be 'managed' by one of the other judges.

In the Netherlands, the Protectorate and in France, Jewish judges were dismissed from the supreme courts. Politically unreliable judges were removed from the highest courts of Belgium (under the first and the second German occupation), Germany, the Protectorate, and Luxembourg. No German influence was exerted on personnel policy in Denmark. The Protectorate also lost some judges to Germany and Slovakia because of their nationality, along with many court cases pertaining to German or Slovak persons or issues. In the Netherlands and in Norway, the age limit was lowered from 70 to 65 to make room for political appointments of loyal elite. Norway's *Høyesterett* resigned before this measure could take effect, but in the Dutch *Hoge Raad* it created four vacancies between 1941 and 1943. In Luxembourg, ten out of fourteen judges in the *Cour Supérieure de Justice* retired or were removed after a crucial meeting in April 1941 with the new German leaders of the judiciary, who announced that Luxembourg had ceased to exist. Only six of the judges were replaced, not with Luxembourgian collaborationists, but with German judges.[18] This was made possible by awarding all German judges competence in Luxembourg's germanized courts, which was, together with the introduction of German law, an obvious preparation for annexation.

17 Cf. Graver 2015, 45-46 for other cases of oppressive regimes purging and packing courts.

18 See also Michielsen 2004, 102.

In Belgium, under neither German occupation were any appointments to the *Cour de Cassation* made. Under the first occupation many appointments in the courts could be prevented by using substitutes and postponing retirements, but eventually some Flemish activists succeeded in acquiring judicial posts, though not in the highest instance.[19] In Germany, the Protectorate, the Netherlands, France, and Italy, politically more reliable judges were appointed by the occupier, while in Norway a whole new supreme court had to be assembled. Most of the new loyal appointees, however, did not turn out to be rabid fanatics in their office – they were no Roland Freislers – although they weren't always fully competent either.

In Italy, the personnel problem had a different cause: many judges refused to move north to the new seat of the *Corte di Cassazione*, which forced minister Pisenti to appoint relatively young and inexperienced new judges.

2.4 Conclusion

The function of courts in a democracy with rule of law, as defined in the introduction, was impeded and restricted by the establishment and maintenance of antidemocratic occupation regimes. The occupiers in many ways followed examples from Nazi Germany, such as when they introduced new oaths, competence restrictions, political appointments and dismissals, and special courts. Moreover, the various German authorities relied increasingly on extra-legal measures, creating a so-called dual state: a state of unregulated measures alongside a state governed by norms.[20] Three major developments greatly reduced the democratic rule-of-law character of the occupied countries. First, the independence of the supreme courts was negatively affected by several measures. The new state executive powers in the occupied territories assumed the right to dismiss and appoint judges in disregard of the usual co-optation, thus threatening sitting judges into regime-friendly behaviour. The newly appointed loyal elites did not necessarily consider themselves as politically independent as their colleagues, although this did not have major effects on the way they decided cases. New oaths, new executive formulas and linguistic measures were symbolic ways to enlist the courts to the occupier's cause. Secondly, the other state powers, executive and legislative, were conflated under the belligerent occupier, who in addition set up new courts outside the supreme courts' jurisdiction. This tipped the power balance in

19 See also Bost & Peters 2016, 239-243.

20 Fraenkel 2017.

huge favour of the usurpers and took away an important guarantee for the rule of law: the executive's attitude of deference to the law and the courts. Thirdly, the more laws the occupying powers enacted, the less democratic the law as a whole became, because many of the occupier's ordinances were discriminatory and couldn't be successfully challenged in court. They regulated, among other things, food distribution, forced labour programmes, bans on political opposition, disenfranchisement and persecution of Jews, changes in the public administration, higher penalties for several types of offences, and simplifications in procedural law to speed up the handling of cases. While the democratic collective nature of decisions affecting the people was already lost by the abolishment of many parliaments and the absorption of the legislative power by the executive, democracy was weakened further by the content of the new laws that in many cases restricted liberty and denied equality.[21] Most cases involving politically sensitive legislative measures, however, were kept away from the regular domestic courts, and consequently could not be reviewed by the supreme courts.

In the next section, I will summarize what the judges in the supreme courts under these circumstances did to save what could be saved of the legal system and the rule of law, how they cooperated with the occupying regimes, and how they resisted and protested.

3 Judging under Enemy Rule

The following sections deal with what is the core of the country studies in this book: what did the supreme court judges do in the face of war and Nazi occupation? First, we will look at the initial stage of the occupation, when some supreme courts were involved in reorganizing the executive power. Then, the legal relation between occupier and courts is discussed with regard to its culmination point in the question of judicial review, as a special case of judicial conduct in relation to the occupier. The subsequent summary of the other ways in which the judges cooperated, collaborated, protested, and resisted shows how the administration of justice continued under an oppressive regime, and the final section presents an overview of national assessments of the supreme courts' courses of action in the immediate post-war period.

21 Cf. Whelan 2019, 36.

3.1 Administrative Continuity

The judges in the supreme courts, as all higher civil servants, felt responsible for the continuity of their country's administration, in order to preserve public order and prevent chaos. In two countries, supreme court judges played an important role in realizing administrative continuity after the ministers had fled. In Norway, *Høyesterett* president Paal Berg was a pivotal figure in attempts to ensure the continuity of the national administration by setting up an Administrative Council for the government of those regions that were occupied in the first weeks after the German attack. Berg irritated some of his colleagues by his autonomous attitude, partly overstepping the mandate from the court in his negotiations with the occupier.[22] The Belgian authorities had learned from their recent experience with belligerent occupation that it would yield significant benefits for the position of the remaining government officials when a formal delegation of powers to subordinate functionaries was introduced for the event that their superiors would be unable to execute their office. A retired judge of the *Cour de Cassation* drew up the bill. The court soon became directly involved in the forming of the war-time government by playing a decisive role in the discussions on the scope and nature of the powers delegated to the secretaries-general. On strong advice of the court's president and two attorney-generals, it was decided and laid down in the 'Protocol', an agreement between the Belgian administration and the occupier, that the decrees of the secretaries-general would have force of law. The court remained the leading actor in negotiations with the occupier concerning this topic. These actions at the start of the occupations show how some judges gave up their independent position vis à vis the executive, to do what was urgently necessary in a chaotic situation.

3.2 Judicial Review

In the context of the relation between courts and occupiers, the most interesting type of case is the one where a court renders judgment on acts of the occupying power, especially when those acts are particularly unreasonable and harmful. The interesting aspect is that in those cases, judges use their official capacity to scrutinize the occupier's policy, in other words: the law is explicitly presented as the boundary of the occupation regime's powers. This formal culmination point of the relation between the occupying forces and

22 See also Graver 2019, 26; Sandmo 2005, Ch. 8, esp. 250-272, 282-284.

the administrative institutions of the occupied territory is the only formal, legal, and public check on the occupier's measures. In theory, courts generally have four options: validation, invalidation, resignation, and declaring it a non-justiciable political question.[23] In his reaction to such court rulings (or non-rulings), the occupier reveals his position on the rule of law and its extent, which calibrates the power balance between the executive and the adjudicative branches in the current occupation. Some judiciaries in this study were competent to review legislative and other acts of the occupation regime, either against national law or against Hague Regulations article 43.[24] Others used the Hague Regulations not as applicable law in a case, but as an argument against certain measures of the occupier.

During the German occupation in the First World War, some Belgian courts made use of this right until the *Cour de Cassation* denied it to them in 1916. In the next war, in the Netherlands and Norway the controversy over judicial review was an important aspect of the relation between the occupier and (what was left of) the national government institutions. In Norway, the *Høyesterett* took a principled stand against the German demand not to use their power of judicial review. The unyielding attitude of the occupier led to the resignation of the judges in protest before Christmas 1940, before judicial review could be exercised in a court case. Its collaborating successor in a case from 1941 denied the Norwegian court the power to review the *necessity* of an ordinance, one of the two criteria of Hague Regulations article 43.[25] The same year, the ministry of justice published the decision in a pamphlet, with an introduction by one of the judges. This in turn was reviewed in Werner Best's pet project, the journal *Reich – Volksordnung – Lebensraum*.[26] Remarkably, the court did leave room for the review of ordinances that obviously transcended 'the bounds of a reasonable observation of [executive] duties'. With that decision, the court had left open the possibility of review against the other criterion of HR article 43, regarding the *nature* of the ordinance: whether it (reasonably) concerns public order in the first place. In 1943, a district court used that room to review a law, in addition claiming the right of judicial review of both the necessity *and* the nature of the ordinance,

23 Mahmud 1994, 100.

24 'The authority of the legitimate power having in fact passed into the hands of the occupier, the latter shall take all the measures in his power to restore, and ensure, as far as possible, public order and civil life, while respecting, unless absolutely prevented, the laws in force in the country.' See the introduction for some background to this treaty article.

25 Graver 2019, 35; the decision was published in *Zeitschrift für ausländisches öffentliches Recht und Völkerrecht* 1942/43, p. 599-610, directly following the Dutch Judicial Review Case.

26 Vasbotten 1941; Sch. 1942. See Sandmo 2005, 309-314.

and assuming explicitly and provocatively that this did not contradict the commissarial *Høyesterett's* decision.[27]

Concerning judicial review, the *Hoge Raad* of the Netherlands chose the path of accommodation, like their Belgian counterpart. It denied Dutch courts the right to review, leaving it somewhat unclear, however, whether that applied to all types of occupation ordinances. As in Norway, in a later stage of the occupation, Dutch district courts did start to review ordinances. The allied operations in Western Europe prevented the prosecution from taking the cases to the *Hoge Raad*. Nevertheless, the *Hoge Raad* did use the Hague Regulations in discussions with the occupier to enforce their argument against forced labour and a proposed divorce law amendment. Some of Luxembourg's highest judges referred to the Hague Regulations in their protest against the obligatory membership of the *Volksdeutsche Bund* and against the decision to make German the sole language of the courts.

In Belgium and Denmark, the question of review against *national* law arose. Under the second German occupation of Belgium, the constitutional review of decrees issued by the secretaries-general had been made possible by the wording of the 'Protocol', which the Germans had nevertheless agreed to. The rejection by a lower court of such a decree in relation to food distribution, however, led to the suspension of the judge. Only the threat of a strike by the *Cour de Cassation* succeeded in lifting the suspension. Although the judiciary, along with the Belgian authorities, tried to accommodate the Germans, they were reluctant to give up the power to review the legality of laws enacted during the occupation, giving rise to long discussions on the status of the secretaries-general's ordinances. The Germans on the other hand were anxious to retain the semblance of legality and legitimacy through, amongst other things, banning and preventing any public criticism by government institutions. Judicial scrutiny of their measures was therefore not tolerated. The president of the Danish *Højesteret* carried out a special case of judicial review: not only did he, on his own initiative and without knowledge of the court, advise on and contribute to a law criminalizing communist activities, he also wrote an article about that law stating that it fell outside the scope of the constitution, and was therefore not unconstitutional. This led to his isolation within the court, but the rest of the court did not have a very different policy. A municipal court agreed with the supreme court president that the law was not unconstitutional, after reviewing it against unwritten emergency law. But when the case came to the *Højesteret*, it merely declared

27 Graver 2019, 155-158; District Court of Aker, 25 August 1943 (Øverland's Case), *Annual Digest of Public International Law Cases* 1943-1945, case 156.

that raising the question of constitutionality lacked sufficient grounds. Like the Dutch *Hoge Raad*, the court solved the question of judicial review by evading it.

The Czech constitutional court was one of the world's oldest institutions with the specific power of constitutional review. Unfortunately, it did not get the chance to scrutinize decrees by the German authorities, who had explicitly made their legislative products immune to any kind of review and informally abolished the court in the summer of 1939. In France, the power of judicial review was officially introduced in 2008.

The cases of and discussions about the review of the occupation regime's measures show two things: the actual power relation between the courts and the executive, and the symbolic importance of outward appearances: who is perceived as having the power to determine what is allowed and what is not? The German occupiers did not accept public criticism, and did not want to be framed as violators of international law. They simply did not want the issue of the legality of their legislation to be raised at all. The Hague Regulations could be used as an argument effectively only in non-public communication. At the same time, and more so as the war progressed, they simply cast aside the Hague Regulations as irrelevant and impotent law from a bygone age. The dual state became more and more of a state of measures to the detriment of the state of norms.

In terms of the judicial virtues and values discussed in the introduction, one could say that by invoking the Hague Regulations, the courts asserted their independence, while by not reviewing, judges to a certain extent gave up their independent attitude. Their integrity, in the sense of scrupulous respect for the law and community standards, could become compromised in the eyes of the public, insofar as community standards demanded public rejection of the German occupier. In fact, as we shall see, to all forms of cooperation and non-cooperation a corresponding level of perceived integrity can be attached. In Section 3, we will discuss how dirtying one's hands, causing an integrity compromise, might nevertheless have been worth it. We will now take a look at other ways the supreme courts cooperated, resisted and collaborated under Nazi occupation.

3.3 Judicial Cooperation

The natural thing to do for members of the national administrations was to make the best of a bad situation. For the time being, the Germans had won the war with immense military superiority and were not likely to leave any time soon. So, like almost all civil servants, the judges of the supreme courts remained in function to maintain public order and the general organization of society. As all government departments, agencies and functions in a democratic rule-of-law state, the courts are ultimately meant to be there for the good of the people. If they function normally, it can be presumed, therefore, that their judges perceive the performance of their duties to be in the general interest, whether they view themselves more as an independent state power checking the executive, as in Belgium and other occupied countries, or more as loyal civil servants, as in Denmark. In both cases, impartially serving justice in the general interest is likely to be the well-meaning judge's general default motive, as it has been for ages.[28] This is also apparent from the wartime correspondence between the Dutch judge and law professor I have been quoting from: they did not disagree on *whether* the *Hoge Raad* should serve the people's general interests, but on *how* they should do that.[29] The neutral, objective, impersonal, and impartial nature of the bureaucratic civil service, including the courts, sustains the normal functioning of the state and of society.[30] Besides serving their country, there were more mundane motives for remaining in function like status, professional interest, and acquiring an income.

Securing administrative continuity was the lesson learned from Belgium's earlier experience with German occupation. This had led the governments of Belgium and the Netherlands to leave their civil servants, including judges, clear instructions to remain in office as long as possible for the benefit of the people, just as the Belgian government had done in 1914. The supreme courts took these instructions to heart. After its own resignation in December 1940, the Norwegian *Høyesterett* strongly advised the judges from the lower courts *not* to follow their example, because they could serve the Norwegian people better in their judicial capacity. Interestingly, the new collaborating *Høyesterett* also contributed to maintaining legal normality, acting for the most part as a normal court – in Graver's assessment: much as the resigned legitimate *Høyesterett* would have done. Its judges strived for continuity, did not adjudicate politically, and even treated Jewish defendants the same as everyone else. This shows that even political alignment with the Nazi occupier did not necessarily entail partiality in deciding cases. It seems that the judicial virtues of impartiality and

28 Cf. Den Tonkelaar & Den Tonkelaar 2014; see the introductory chapter to this volume.

29 Venema et al. 2008. This traditional judicial attitude is also apparent, for example, in research from the 1980s: De Groot-van Leeuwen 1991, 169-184.

30 Morgan 2018, 155.

equality are so engrained in the self-understanding of judges that even an extremist political persuasion favoured by an extremist regime often did not diminish them.

The argument of the proverbial mayor in wartime was used in support of remaining in function, as opposed to resigning at some point, by the supreme judges of Belgium, the Netherlands, Norway, and Denmark. They all argued for the importance of keeping the judiciary in their own national hands, a pragmatic choice for the lesser evil, which they presumed served the population best. All officials not supportive of German annexation sought to maintain their national administration, be it (formerly) democratic, as in most occupied countries in this book, or non-democratic, as in Vichy-France or Italy. The most important reasons for staying in function, and thus working with the enemy, were keeping the administration in national hands and in so doing being able to prevent chaos and mitigate the occupier's measures. This confirms fascism expert Philip Morgan's general assessment of occupier-occupied relations.[31] The population's well-being was the motive behind the efforts of the Belgian judges to find a *modus vivendi*, and to solve the judicial crises, choosing the lesser evil of cooperation rather than the greater evil of more repression. They particularly wanted to avoid the dire consequences of the judicial strike of 1918 when German courts were introduced. The Dutch and Czech judges provided information on their ethnic descent in the spirit of cooperation at the start of the occupation, in order not to provoke the occupier, who seemed at that early stage relatively benevolent and moderate. In Denmark, the judges' self-image as loyal civil servants instead of an independent check on the executive, together with their legalistic attitude led them to refrain from any protest, and accept and apply anti-sabotage laws that were introduced under German pressure. Interestingly, the Luxembourg supreme court judges did *not* use the common good as a reason for their remaining in function after the near total Nazification of the Luxembourg state.

Some peculiar double functions in two countries added to an image of obedience or even collaborationism. In the Protectorate, the president of the inactive Constitutional Court, Jaroslav Krejčí, was also Minister of Justice and Prime Minister. The much more important Supreme Administrative Court (SAC) also had a politically active president: Emile Hácha, who had presided over the court since 1925 and had been the country's president since 1938. He continued to combine these functions in the Protectorate's puppet

31 Cf. Morgan 2018, 196, 205-206, 208-210.

government, where SAC judge Josef Kliment was his personal secretary. Nazi-allied French Chief of State Philippe Pétain tried to create such a double role in the executive and adjudicative branches as well. He awarded Charles Frémicourt, president of the *Cour de Cassation* since 1937, the additional post of Minister of Justice, thus contributing to further conflation of state powers. But Frémicourt, surprised and displeased by this appointment, gave up his cabinet post within a few weeks. The other highest French court, the *Conseil d'Etat*, was already an ambiguous institution in terms of separation of powers, because it was also an important advisory body for the executive, hence its epithet 'the administration judging itself'. On top of this, after the dissolution of parliament in Pétain's 'National Revolution', it also acquired part of the third of the three state functions: legislative power. The Council, however, hardly used it but for enlarging its own role in the new administration.

Remaining in function also had an identity motive: it presupposed that national law is in better hands with native elites, because they are better in protecting the national character of the legal system against Germanization and Nazification. In the words of law professor Cleveringa: 'The judge must be independent, though not independent from the sense of justice or the conscience [...] of the people he belongs to.'[32] This connects the judicial virtue of an attitude of independence from the executive with that of integrity, in the sense of public alignment with public morality, and therefore with public trust.[33] In this case, that would entail public opposition to the occupier's policies. But even when the court's integrity as public *appearance* is tainted, the judges may very well have retained their publicly non-visible integrity, in the sense of honestly striving towards the best results for the people.[34] Nevertheless, as Cleveringa also made clear, remaining in function could at the same time have the negative consequence of legitimizing the occupier's power.

Section 3 further discusses the problematic ambiguities of remaining in function under the Nazi occupier. I will now, first, summarize how supreme court judges went further in their cooperation by actively collaborating with the Nazis. Subsequently, I will discuss what judges did in and outside of their office to oppose or criticize the occupier or to help citizens. Then the post-war evaluations of the supreme courts are reviewed.

32 Venema et al. 2008, 85. Cleveringa here quotes the words of an unnamed person he apparently agrees with.

33 Cf. Soeharno 2009, 40-43.

34 Cf. Soeharno 2009, 48-75.

3.4 Judicial Collaborationism

In the judiciary, the stereotypical collaborator might be imagined as an ardent Nazi taking or forcing pro-occupier decisions. This happened in Germany, where one *Reichsgericht* judge interpreted the term 'normality' in marriage law as 'fertility'. The court's president blocked the emigration of a former member to Luxembourg because he was a Jew. Judges in general were reactionary and anti-democratic but many were not Nazis. Nevertheless, almost all remained in function, applied Nazi laws, and gradually became deeply involved in the Nazi regime.

Luxembourg judges had willingly applied anti-Semitic laws and treated Jews as a legal category already before the war, and in France, the highest courts actively took part in the Nazi-friendly anti-Semitic policies of the Vichy regime, which surprised the Germans in its great willingness to collaborate. The Vichy regime and its highest courts did not need any encouragement to cleanse themselves of Jewish personnel, and the *Conseil d'Etat* interpreted anti-Jewish measures in their case law more harshly than necessary.

In Norway, Luxembourg, and the Netherlands, pro-Nazi and German-friendly judges were members of the highest courts, although very few fit the sketched stereotype. Moreover, in Norway and the Netherlands, politically sensitive cases were kept from the regular courts, so even pro-German judges hardly got the chance to promote the occupier's interests by their decisions, nor did they always strive to. In one rare example, in a decision from 1943, the Dutch *Hoge Raad* ensured a wide application of the '*Kultuurkamer*' (Culture Chamber) ordinance, requiring membership of that Nazi organization for dealing in art objects. A senate consisting of two collaborationists and three other members, decided against the lower courts that mass-produced paintings should also be considered 'art', widening the scope of the *Kultuurkamer* membership obligation.

The Danish *Højesteret* also handed down a judgment that went further than necessary in determining the scope of an occupation ordinance. To appease the Germans and not to encourage troublesome resistance, it applied a law against public subversive speech to a non-public lecture, because the intentions of the speaker were judged more important than the lecture's private nature. Above, I mentioned the autonomous actions of the *Højesteret* president with regard to the creation of German-desired anti-communist legislation. Although his intention was to provide a sound legal foundation for the government's measures concerning the detention of communists, he was heavily criticized for doing so, and for not consulting with his colleagues.

None of the Belgian members of the *Cour de Cassation* collaborated with the Germans, nor did the court as a whole. Two factors were probably crucial in this respect. Unlike for example in the neighbouring Netherlands, no judges were appointed to the court by the occupation regime, and differently from its other neighbour France, there was no collaborationist national administration. There are no reports of active collaborationism from the Protectorate either.

This overview suggests that the Nazification policies regarding the judiciaries, which weren't their main focus, did not cause a significant change in adjudication by the regular (supreme) courts. The introduction of new courts did, however, reduce the scope of their jurisdiction. The Luxembourg judiciary is an exception to this rule, as their highest court was split up and integrated into the German court structure, making German judges competent in Luxembourg.

Collaborationism by definition implies a less independent attitude towards the executive power. To what extent the public integrity of collaborationist judges was impaired depends on public morality: in France, for example, popular support for Pétain's collaborationist government was greater than support for Nazi party Nasjonal Samling and its leader, Quisling, was in Norway.

3.5 Judicial Non-cooperation

As has become clear, outright acts of resistance or protest by supreme courts were rare. I will first discuss collective protests of the courts and protest actions of individual judges, before mentioning several acts by judges as private persons. The Norwegian *Høyesterett* showed, as the only supreme court, how a very strong public protest signal could be given: by resigning collectively. Interestingly though, their collaborating successor court also resisted some Nazi policies: it advised, in response to a request by justice minister Riisnaes, to keep parliament in function. This was not the advice the minister was looking for, however, whereupon he withdrew his request. The collaborating court also treated Jewish litigants the same as any other – as did the German *Reichsgericht* until 1942.

During the first German occupation of Belgium, the vote on protest against German policies was repeatedly won by the reluctant majority of 9 to 8, and only once by the advocates of protest. Under the second German occupation of Belgium, the highest court was one of the most active of all courts in negotiating with the Germans on their policies, culminating in a strike threat and the publication of a letter of protest against the forced labour scheme. Nevertheless, it stuck to the same policy as 25 years before: remain in office to protect Belgian interests *as a court*. In the Netherlands *Hoge Raad*, there was never a majority in favour of public protest. Unlike the Belgian court, however, it had been decapitated early on by the suspension of its Jewish president, and further limited in its influence by the appointment of a Nazi as Secretary-General of Justice. Also, it didn't have a prominent and tireless mediator like the Belgian Attorneys-General Terlinden and Termicourt (during the first and second German occupation, respectively). It did resist in other ways. It prevented the introduction of a new divorce law based on Nazi ideology proposed by the occupier by stalling its advice, and finally delivering a negative opinion based on Hague Rules article 43. At least one judge was active in lobbying for the closing of an infamous detention camp, to which I will return in Section 3.

Although judicial resistance in Luxembourg was also minimal, the judges did criticize the new executive formula 'In the name of the German people' and protested against the compulsory membership of the *Volkdeutsche Bund*, appealing to their conscience and the Hague Rules. Some of them returned their membership cards in protest against the forced mobilization, but requested to remain in function, because they feared that resigning would only provoke the Germans to retaliate and cause the loss of the family income (although the latter was for many aristocratic supreme court judges not a very serious risk). The French *Conseil d'Etat* reversed some dismissals of civil servants, who had been ousted as Jews or political unreliables. The mitigation of sentences for small black market traders by the French *Cour de Cassation* rested, according to Millon, predominantly on considerations of public relations and post-war exoneration purposes. In the Protectorate, Supreme Administrative Court president Kliment decided to accept a German order of merit in the name of the entire court. In doing so, he ignored the German demand to point out specific judges deserving of the honour, and spared them the personal stain of Nazi approval. Although Italian minister Pisenti, like the German authorities, wanted strict punishment of black market crimes, he did not interfere when the *Corte di Cassazione* in an important precedent decision acquitted persons who had robbed or hidden goods because they were in dire need, going against the intention of the lawgiver. Even in Germany itself, the judiciary, which was on the whole not unsympathetic to Nazism, protested against incursions on their independence. *Reichsgericht* president

Bumke wanted to protest against the application to the court of the law that allowed dismissal of 'non-Aryans' from the civil service, but he was outvoted. A vice-president of the court resigned in 1939 because he did not want to become a member of the NSDAP.

Private non-cooperative actions have been reported from several countries, not excluding Germany. A famous case is *Reichsgericht* judge Dohnanyi, who was dismissed in 1941 and took part in an attack on Hitler in 1943, for which he was executed. In the occupied countries, several judges also acted as private persons against the interests of the German Nazis. A member of the Belgian *Cour de Cassation* in World War I anonymously criticized his own court's decision not to review occupation law in the underground press. *Høyesterett* president Paal Berg and two of his colleagues became active as leaders of the Norwegian resistance,[35] but by then they were no longer active as judges. Dutch *Hoge Raad* judge Donner, who was involved in church resistance activities, wrote on his diligently filled out and returned 'Aryan Declaration' (the non-Jewish lineage form obligatory for every member of the public administration), that the provided information should 'not in the least be regarded as cooperation' with any ensuing measures. Its symbolic nature and the fact that the form later found its way back to the *Hoge Raad* archive suggest a (post-war) exoneration function rather than the intention to cause any real effect at the time. The French *Cour de Cassation* judge who refused at gunpoint to salute a militia flag, on the other hand, made a direct public statement and took a big risk. A colleague from the same court gave advice to the underground ministry of Justice, and yet another edited a resistance paper. Perhaps surprisingly, the collaborationist Dutch *Hoge Raad* president Van Loon privately helped Jewish citizens. There are several other reports from Belgium and the Netherlands of judges helping colleagues and others in need. Although biographical details of most of the supreme court judges from other countries on this point are lacking, more of them probably helped fellow citizens privately.

Judicial activism, protest and resistance reveal an independent attitude, which may generate popular appreciation, but may also backfire. When it plays out well, it will be interpreted by the public as a display of integrity, as in the Norwegian case. When the result is not so unambiguous, as in the Belgian case, public reactions will be mixed. Non-visible resistance, of course, does not influence the public's perception of the court's integrity.

35 See also Graver 2019, 33.

3.6 Purges and Praises

Leading up to the general conclusions in Section 4 of this chapter, we will take a look at some earlier conclusions drawn on the supreme courts' war records: the post-war legal, political, and historiographical evaluations of the supreme courts' behaviour in their own countries.[36] After World War I, no external purge was deemed necessary in Belgium, because the judicial strike served as a strong symbol of resistance. Also, there was the court's public protest against the deportation of workers. Especially the former completely overshadowed the much-criticized decision of 1916 not to review German decrees, the introduction of German courts after the strike, and the overall pragmatic policy of cooperation. Under the second German occupation the rather activist court again protested against the deportation of workers, and again fought to retain the right to judicial review. It yielded the president an official decoration. The press, however, was critical of the pragmatic choices that had been made in the same general spirit as 25 years before. This resulted in a decades-long taboo on any public discussion of the court's wartime history.

In Norway, the effect of the war on the image of the supreme court was the greatest of all Nazi occupied countries: resigning in 1940 had turned the *Høyesterett* from elite clique into resistance heroes overnight. The successor commissarial *Høyesterett*, however, received a very different treatment: a strict moral quarantine was applied after the members were tried and convicted by the restored *Høyesterett*. The indictment included accepting their appointment under the occupation, their support of the Quisling government, and their denial of the power of judicial review. Only the last of these charges was not used as grounds for their conviction. The collaborating court was erased from legal and general history; their cases are not quoted, nor have they been published in any collection. Legal historian Erling Sandmo experienced heavy resistance from the 21st century *Høyesterett* when he disclosed his intention to include a chapter on the wartime court in the history of the *Høyesterett*.

After the Dutch wartime appointees in the *Hoge Raad* were dismissed and some prosecuted, there remained a stalemate between the returned government and the remaining pre-war appointees. The government wanted the judges to resign because of their lack of public protest during the occupation. The judges, however, would not give up their appointments for life and maintained that they had done the best they could have in the situation,

36 Venema 2012 compares the Netherlands, Belgium, and Norway.

which the ministers could not have assessed properly from their London exile. To resolve the situation, Jan Donner, the only judge who had escaped the odium of collaboration, was appointed president. As was the case with the Norwegian commissarial supreme court and the Belgian *Cour de Cassation*, the war history of the *Hoge Raad* was ostracized until the end of the 20th century. Instead of the *Hoge Raad*, a newly erected special supreme court dealt with cases against collaborators in the highest instance. But in a legal practical sense, there has been continuity: important war-time cases are still mentioned in handbooks today, and have been quoted in cases for decades.

In France, like in the Netherlands, a special court was created for the trials of collaborators, the *Haute Cour de Justice*. Its president, however, had been appointed in the *Cour de Cassation* by the Vichy regime. Both highest courts in France practiced self-exoneration by personnel policy: from the *Cour de Cassation* some wartime judges were dismissed, and many dismissed by Vichy were reappointed. Wartime President Frémicourt was appointed first honorary president of the court by decree of 9 June, 1954. In the *Conseil d'Etat*, the Jewish lawyer René Cassin (a founding member of general De Gaulle's Free French) was appointed vice-president, by which the court regained some legitimacy, just as Donner's appointment did for the Dutch *Hoge Raad*. The court purged itself and wrote its own history. Members appointed in the last phase of the occupation did, upon their deaths, not receive the usual commemoration speech in the court, which fits the general decades-long omertà surrounding the war history of the French supreme courts.

The Luxembourg supreme judges who had stayed on after the Nazification of the judiciary were removed or pensioned but not prosecuted. All war-time decisions were struck from legal history (already by Grand Ducal Decree of 22 April 1941) and never mentioned in any legal document or publication.[37] Except for the purge records, many Luxembourg archives have remained closed for a long time and research was not promoted by the government until recently.[38] Luxembourg is the only country where the moral quarantine of the occupation period is largely maintained to this day.

The Supreme Administrative Court in the Protectorate was criticized for the double roles of several members, and it was purged. Serious post-war criticism was also directed at the Danish *Højesterett* for its lack of a

37 Michielsen 2004, 235.

38 The Ministry of Justice recently funded the research project 'The history of justice in Luxembourg – HISTJUST', which yielded Wingerter 2021 and Fritz, Scuto & Wingerter 2022. See https://www.c2dh.uni.lu/projects/history-justice-luxembourg.

critical attitude. Nevertheless, the Danish courts purged themselves, and the supreme court could be left intact, because its president – who had made himself impossible after his autonomous involvement with anti-communist legislation – had already retired in 1944. The ordinary courts also tried collaborators, after the resistance had had the opportunity to vote out 'unfit' judges – which were only a few.

Although there is no room here to review all the reactions in the post-liberation press and subsequent historiography, we note that praise and blame for the same judicial actions stem from the ambiguity of the courts' positions under enemy occupation. Judicial cooperation by remaining in office was ambiguous between good and bad, and has been viewed by outsiders as motivated by either collaboration: 'they willingly legitimized the Nazi regime!', common interest: 'they tirelessly struggled to uphold the legal order!', or resistance 'they bravely prevented the occupier from appointing loyal elites!'. Leaving office in protest could likewise be differently evaluated, namely as heroic: 'they took a stand against the oppressor!', cowardly: 'they didn't have the guts to negotiate with the enemy!', or rational: 'they decided to follow their conscience.' Section 3 treats these ambiguities in the anthropological, sociological and ethical context sketched in the introduction to this volume.

4 General Conclusions

In this section, I will focus on three important aspects of this study. First, I will summarize the reasons for supreme court judges to remain in office under the occupier, and the general results of that choice, considering the possibilities and limits of their position. Then I will show how moral hygiene[39] played a role not only in the courts' and judges' actions but also in the ways others viewed them. Finally, I will argue how, in the light of the results of this study, a fair assessment of the supreme courts' courses of action under Nazi occupation can be made, in other words, how the Big Question can be answered: how did they do?

4.1 Considerations and Achievements of the Wartime Judge

Like mayors in wartime, judges faced the dilemma between remaining in office and resigning. The most important reasons for continuing their

39 See introduction and below for an explanation of this concept.

function were maintaining public order by keeping the justice system in national and non-collaborationist hands, thus being able to mitigate measures, negotiate with the occupier, and help people in need. The main reasons for leaving office were showing public disapproval with the occupier's policies and not morally compromising oneself by working with the enemy (observing moral hygiene). What could be achieved by the one choice could not be had with the other. Moreover, there were disadvantages connected to both options. Remaining in office meant having to work with the enemy, thereby getting dirty hands (failing in moral hygiene), which yielded the risk of being associated or even identified with the enemy. Those who resigned, however, could no longer use their office for the good of the people, lost their income, risked retaliation, and, even worse, made room for the appointment of collaborationists, thus compromising the image of the court and its pre-war appointees (affecting the court's moral hygiene) and the capacity of the court for organizing negotiations and resistance.[40]

To continue their work in the supreme courts meant to support the normal function of the law and the legal professions: maintain the societal status quo by enforcing legal rules, keep 'law and order.'[41] Under an enemy regime with transformational ambitions, this tendency in the judiciary works in two directions. It protects the status quo against interference, but at the same time it limits judges to their constitutional role, the sphere of adjudication. Many interventions by the occupier take place outside the jurisdiction of the courts: extra-legal measures, dismissals and new appointments, and the introduction of new legislation which is often made immune to judicial review. Against these, the courts have little defence, except careful negotiations and mitigated application. The courts' political neutrality lends at least some legitimization to the government that happens to be in power. Even in Nazi Germany itself, as Löhnig has shown, the *Reichsgericht* strove to provide 'legal normality', and did not consist of fanatics pushing the Nazi agenda. This had the double effect just described: keeping the pre-Nazi legal system functioning, while at the same time also enforcing new Nazi laws. The same goes for collaborationist commissarial *Høyesterett* in Norway, and the German-friendly Dutch *Hoge Raad* president Van Loon, who wished their courts would on the one hand continue business as usual, while on the other hand support the new regime. Although the Nazi regimes in

40 These considerations are very similar to the ones listed by Mahmud (1994, 128-129) in his study of high courts' responses to thirteen successful coups d'état in common law countries between 1958 and 1989.

41 Cf. Dyzenhaus 2010, 293.

Germany and in the occupied countries in varying degrees created a dual state, many loyal Nazis in the local judiciaries still remained true jurists, applying the law unbiased in a non-political way. This had a tempering effect on oppressive policy. Even the Italian Justice minister Pisenti, as mentioned before, endeavoured to maintain a neutral judiciary, because he was convinced that this would legitimize the fascist administration better than courts filled with fascist fanatics. Dutch law professor Cleveringa, however, deplores political neutrality of war-time judges in one of his letters from 1943 to *Hoge Raad* judge Losecaat Vermeer: 'While otherwise silent impassivity is a laudable virtue [of the *Hoge Raad*], it is currently a deplorable deficiency.'[42] But strong protests like the resignation of the Norwegian *Høyesterett* can only be made once.

What did the judges achieve by their actions? In all the countries studied, the judiciary as an institution, including the supreme courts, was left functioning by the occupier. In all cases, the supreme courts and their judges contributed to maintaining public order and civil life and the prevention of chaos. Even in Norway after the resignation of the *Høyesterett*, and in Luxembourg after the dissolution of the *Cour Supérieure de Justice*, the newly appointed collaborationist judges played their role in keeping the legal system functioning as the framework of civil life.

On the whole, we can conclude that most supreme court judges chose to perform their adjudicative function for the same bona fide reasons that most other government functionaries had for cooperating with the occupier: as 'a way of avoiding, or mitigating, not a hypothetical but an actual or imminent national catastrophe.'[43] The judges chose their lines of action, according to a utilitarian calculation, in the face of very real dangers, although in many cases the 'greater evil' that could be avoided for some time, eventually occurred anyway.[44] Judges did not, and could not, overthrow the occupier's regime and win the war. Graver's assessment in his study on courts faced with autocratic rulers applies to the cases studied in this book: 'both the judicial role and basic power relations contribute to the fact that courts seldom challenge the core interests of the regime such as its basic legality and main instruments of power.'[45] Or in the words of David Dyzenhaus: 'Judges are not revolutionaries.'[46] Making a utilitarian calculation which

42 Venema et al. 2008, p. 81.

43 Morgan 2018, 329.

44 Morgan 2018, 330.

45 Graver 2015, 59.

46 As he concludes from his studies into the South African judiciary under apartheid in Dyzenhaus 2010, 293.

results in remaining in office is very different from being indifferent. It is following sense with a heavy heart. For supreme court judges, like for private citizens, it was 'quite possible to support the policy of cooperation, hate the Germans and sympathize with the resistance movement, all at the same time.'[47] What was 'opposed politically', was 'in practice [...] accepted.'[48] We will now say more about the precarious position of the supreme court judges between an enemy ruler and a frustrated and suffering population, before discussing how to judge the judges.

4.2 Moral Hygiene

In the introduction, I defined moral hygiene as 'the practice of keeping one's own identity distinct from that of the enemy, as well as the assessment by others of the successfulness of that practice.' I will apply this concept, as developed in the introduction, to several aspects of the country studies and use two cases from the country studies for a more detailed application.

The risk of contamination with the evil identity of the Nazi occupier was present for all judges (and other government functionaries) who remained in function under the enemy. That more or less automatically made their hands dirty. The Belgian expression and practice of the 'lesser evil' illustrates this: notwithstanding their tough negotiating, the judges were forced to comply with German measures in the end. Because the outcome was ambiguous – some successes, many compromises, and some defeats – it did not yield a spotless moral reputation, which explains the mixed press after the war. One way of practising moral hygiene is by avoiding contact with representatives of the enemy. In the Netherlands, for example, loyal elite appointees in the *Hoge Raad* were actively isolated by the non-collaborationists who held separate meetings and only met with the collaborationist president in unavoidable professional situations. The Norwegian bar association tried to dissuade their members from handling cases before the new collaborating *Høyesterett*, and in Denmark, the *Højesterett* president was shunned by his colleagues after his autonomous active support of the anti-communist legislation pressured by the Germans. Administrative moral hygiene is another way to reaffirm distinction between oneself and the enemy, Examples are: the Dutch judge Donner writing a protest on his Aryan declaration form (which he did return), Luxembourg judges sending back their *Volksdeutsche Bund* membership cards (while requesting to remain in function), and French

47 Holbraad 2017, 216.

48 As Graver notes in his chapter on the Norwegian *Høyesterett*.

judges becoming more lenient on black marketeers towards the end of the war, hoping to create more distance between the German measures and themselves. In the midst of the war and German occupying powers, they strove to somehow keep their identity, their integrity, their national values, pride and honour. In the private and the professional spheres, this was less dangerous, but also less convincing, than in the public sphere.

The post-war period was a time of re-establishing moral and political order by sorting people in moral categories, and settling scores. After the liberation from the Nazi occupier, the threat of contamination and the blurring of the category boundaries between Nazism and national identity apparently still made itself felt, as it is felt even today. The mere existence of former collaborationists in post-war society was experienced as a possible source of pollution, threatening to destabilize the newly restored moral order. This motivated the ultimate maintenance of moral hygiene: the elimination of the sources of evil (by lynchings and formal death sentences) so that they could no longer infect others or society as a whole.[49] Hannah Arendt expresses this sentiment in her book on the trial of Adolf Eichmann, where she addresses the defendant in a rephrasing of the court's sentence: '[...] as you supported and carried out a policy of not wanting to share the earth with the Jewish people [...] no one [...] can be expected to want to share the earth with you. This is the reason, and the only reason, you must hang.'[50]

After liberation, the (reconstructed) supreme courts upheld their institutional integrity – which is in the eye of the beholder – by insisting on a moral quarantine: the war-time histories of many of the supreme courts remained a taboo subject (for the courts themselves, as well as for historians) until the end of the century. In Luxembourg and Norway, this took the form of the elimination from legal history of all war-time decisions of the *Cour Supérieure de Justice* and the commissarial *Høyesterett*, irrespective of their content. In 2017, French president Emmanuel Macron found it necessary to insist on breaking the moral quarantine the Vichy regime was apparently still kept in: 'It is convenient to see the Vichy regime as born of nothingness, returned to nothingness. Yes, it's convenient, but it is false. We cannot build pride upon a lie.'[51]

The 'convenient' view of Vichy, cited by Macron, was also applied in Norway to the collaborationist commissarial *Høyesterett*: it was treated as a blank page in Norwegian legal history. In this view, contamination is

49 See Venema 2019, 967-976.

50 Arendt 2006, 279.

51 'France organised this' 2017.

impossible and it keeps the post-war Norwegian justice system free from association with the former enemy. Even when in the early twenty-first century, the history of the *Høyesterett* was written, the court tried to block the inclusion of a 'chapter on villains' (their collaborationist predecessors) in a 'book on heroes', thus keeping its history clean.[52] That heroic history was created by the judges of the pre-war *Høyesterett* who had gloriously succeeded in maintaining moral hygiene, by resigning in protest early on, in December 1940. Their moral purity, however, was gained and kept only by *giving up* their status as judges, leaving the maintenance of social order through the legal system to the care of others. They probably sensed the risk of chaos or repression that lay in other judges following their example, so they urged them all to remain in function, knowing also that they would be getting their hands dirty. On the positive side, the influx of collaborationists, sources of moral pollution, could be limited to the *Høyesterett* itself. Thereby, the perfect scapegoat was created: one that did not do the legal order any serious harm, because its contagiousness was relatively well contained. Therefore, after liberation, it could be safely sent into the desert, carrying with it the bulk of the blame for judicial cooperation with the German occupier. This created the edifying and lasting opposition between heroes and villains which completely outshone the more ambiguous and untidy reality.[53]

An interesting case of moral hygiene in the Netherlands concerns the moral status of the *Hoge Raad* as opposed to that of one of the appeal courts. The *Hoge Raad*'s cooperation with the occupier, its acceptance of German-friendly appointees, and its lack of public protest earned it a weak and unpatriotic reputation. Although the judges themselves practised moral hygiene professionally and privately, they failed to make that known to the general public, in whose eyes the court had not emphasized its Dutch, non-Nazi identity strongly enough. The court had its reasons: the expected negative results of a public moral distancing – deterioration of relations with the occupier, more repression – weighed heavier in their considerations than the expected positive results – hope and inspiration for the people by making an anti-German statement. What the public then did not know, was that the *Hoge Raad* had protested on a number of occasions, carefully and discreetly, with some success. Notwithstanding present knowledge of these positive achievements and the valid reasons for remaining in function, the current

52 See also Sandmo 2007.

53 An interesting example is the controversial character of *Høyesterett* president Paal Berg, during and after the war. Hem 2012.

Hoge Raad prefers to preserve its negative war-image, being 'deeply saddened and overwhelmed with regret',[54] calling the period a 'black page' in which judges had acted 'wrongly', which should 'never again' be repeated.[55] Along with deploring the *Hoge Raad*'s war record, a decision by an appeal court from 1943 was then, and still is, celebrated for its mentioning of 'conscience' as grounds for not sending the condemned to a terrible detention camp. The judges are considered as 'role models'[56] and their ruling as a 'beacon.'[57] With that decision, the appeal court practised moral hygiene publicly, which to this day is hailed as an example of what the *Hoge Raad* should have done, celebrated with a book in 2003, and in 2018 with a conference and a play.[58] That the decision, by enraging the Germans, endangered reaching the goal it aimed for – the closure of the detention camp – is often ignored, along with the fact that the *Hoge Raad* lent essential support to the careful lobby that did lead to the camp's termination.

These two examples underline the attractive force of moral hygiene. They illustrate how World War II still functions as a source of morally pure characters to identify with and morally corrupted and evil characters to disassociate oneself from. These are, however, inevitably oversimplified versions of the uncomfortably ambiguous and messy reality, as the difference between being categorized as right or as wrong could lie in a single action of symbolic moral distancing, or in the absence of such an act. Whether such an act – such as resigning at the right time, or adding one significant word to the grounds of a decision – had any positive or negative effect on the material wellbeing of the people, is not relevant in a moral hygiene perspective.

4.3 Answering the Big Question: How Did the Courts Do?

Should the need for historical examples of morally right and wrong, of heroes and villains, influence our assessment of real people and their actions? Should supreme court judges have focused more on their people's need for a

54 On the *Hoge Raad* website: Corstens 2011. This is a speech by the *Hoge Raad* president at the launch of a book on its war history (Jansen & Venema 2011), which was presented to a granddaughter of L.E. Visser, the Jewish Hoge Raad president who was dismissed by the Nazis, and a daughter of law professor Cleveringa.

55 On the Dutch judiciary website: 'Rechtspraak, oorlog en vrijheid' 2020.

56 'Rechtspraak, oorlog en vrijheid' 2020.

57 In the Dutch Judges' Association journal and available on its website: Buruma 2018.

58 Hermans 2003; *Trema* 2018-3 (Dutch Judges' Association journal). https://trema.nvvr.org/editie/2018-03. https://watwedoen.nl/project/om-des-gewetens-wille/.

clear moral stance against the German occupier's policies than on keeping adjudication in their own hands? Can we expect that from supreme court judges, and if not, what *can* we expect from them?

If we judge solely from a moral hygiene point of view, the inescapability of dirty hands when remaining in function can only lead to one right choice: in order not to 'dirty your hands,'[59] you need to retreat into total moral quarantine and withdraw 'from public life altogether,' which Hannah Arendt, the champion of moral hygiene, consistently demanded as the only way to 'avoid legal and moral responsibility.'[60] From this perspective, any utilitarian argument for remaining in office, resting on expected material benefits such as public order and policy mitigation, is a mere self-serving hypocritical justification for keeping a job and an income.[61] Because any of your mitigating actions as an official under a Nazi regime are per definition futile,[62] the only aspect of your behaviour which is relevant for a moral judgment, is the extent to which you succeed in distancing and disassociating yourself from the Nazis, so Arendt's argument goes. Only the Norwegian court, by resigning in December 1940, 'washed its hands of what was going on,'[63] and lived up to this criterion of complete moral hygiene. All other judges of the supreme courts under Nazi occupation, except maybe those few who also resigned early on, have failed to act correctly in this strict moral hygiene perspective. In this line of thinking, arguments from moral hygiene and utilitarian arguments are totally incommensurable. This is apparent in Arendt's rhetorical statement that 'those who choose the lesser evil forget very quickly that they chose evil.'[64] But the expression 'lesser evil' merely meant 'the least negative consequences,' when choosing staying over quitting.[65] Consequently and ironically, the right choice from a moral hygiene point of view would be the 'greater evil.' Such a harsh judgment as Arendt's is understandable coming from someone who, as a Jew, had experienced Nazi oppression first hand. It is closely related to Professor Cleveringa's standpoint, condemned by *Hoge Raad* judge Losecaat Vermeer as *fiat iustitia, pereat mundus* (let justice be done, though the world perish).[66]

59 Arendt 2003a, 36.
60 Arendt 2003a, 34.
61 Arendt 2003b, 147-158, at 156.
62 Arendt 2003a, 45.
63 Arendt's expression, 2003a, 45.
64 Arendt 2003a, 36.
65 See the chapters on Belgium by Bost and Muller & Peters in this volume.
66 Venema et al. 2008, 83.

Philosopher David Luban discusses Arendt's position, supplementing a more relaxed moral identity perspective with utilitarian arguments. He proves her factual supposition – that staying on the job under the Nazis is always futile – to be simply untenable. He describes how two German officials, one Nazi and one anti-Nazi, saved lives by remaining in function, just like the famous Oskar Schindler[67] and Hans Calmeyer.[68] Between saving face and saving lives, they chose the latter – and their face was saved in the end by the outcome of the war. For them, their mayor-in-wartime problem was much clearer, because it demonstrably involved the lives of large numbers of (partly) identifiable individuals. The supreme court judges did not have that luxury: the benefits of their staying on the job were more abstract. Luban comes to a much more nuanced conclusion than Arendt, mixing moral hygiene terms with utilitarian considerations: 'Sometimes quitting is the right thing to do; but when there is *Spielraum* [manoeuvring room], and a genuine prospect of mitigating evil, staying at the desk can be the righteous path.'[69] But is this criterion better applicable to the judges and situations in occupied Europe? When is the mitigation prospect 'genuine'? Could the Belgian judges know what the prospects were when they protested against the forced labour programme? And how does a judge assess the *Spielraum* he has? *Some Spielraum* is a requisite of any workable occupation administration.[70] Did the Danish judges have more *Spielraum* concerning the anti-communist legislation than they thought? Should they have tried to find out?[71] Was it wise for the Norwegian judges to use up all their *Spielraum* at once by resigning? Didn't they reduce the *Spielraum* of other judges by doing that? Is *Spielraum* a clear and measurable entity, or is it unpredictable and changing every time it is tested? Did the Dutch *Hoge Raad* retain important *Spielraum* by disallowing judicial review, or did it rather diminish its own *Spielraum* and that of other courts? How will we know when we can't go back and try something different? The burden of hindsight, together with the speculative nature of what-if histories, makes a fair moral assessment of judges' actions in an unclear and unpredictable situation very difficult, whether limited to strict moral hygiene or expanded with a utilitarian perspective.

Instead of a moral assessment, it makes more sense to look at what could be expected from supreme courts under Nazi occupation. By now,

67 E.g. as depicted in Steven Spielberg, *Schindler's List* (United Pictures 1993).

68 E.g. Middelberg 2005.

69 Luban 2021, 664.

70 Lammers 1995, 9 & 18.

71 Cf. Morgan 2018, 209-210 on the obscurity of manoeuvring room.

it is clear what to expect from civil servants and judges under an enemy occupation: the overwhelming majority will remain in function, '[c]hoosing between bad and worse,'[72] and 'averting the "worst case scenario."'[73] In some countries, the government had explicitly instructed civil servants and judges to stay in their office for the benefit of the people. Soon, many of them, including supreme court judges, learned that they were caught in an ambiguous place, serving both sides, functioning on the boundary between their national identity and German Nazism, between good and evil. Still, many saw it as their moral duty to stay on the job, make their hands dirty, and brave the contamination and public moral criticism, for the benefit of society.[74] Few expressed this attitude better than Belgian prosecutor-general at the *Cour de Cassation* Georges Terlinden, the main negotiator with the Germans in the First World War: 'patriotism is *not* insurrection against the occupying forces; it consists in keeping our fatherland and cities safe from evils that can be avoided.'[75] If leaving office (and disregarding material consequences) is heroic from a moral hygiene point of view, remaining (and suffering moral contamination) is heroic from a utilitarian standpoint.

From the studies in this volume, we can learn that remaining in office is not the easy option. Though neither is quitting. The precarious and unresolvable ambiguity of their position under Nazi occupation confronted the judges with irreconcilable demands. We can conclude judges cannot deliver on both demands at the same time: practice unambiguous moral hygiene *and* make all possible efforts to mitigate the occupier's policies. Only a complacent hindsight perspective of strict moral hygiene can make those efforts look foolishly futile and morally insignificant.

References

Arendt, Hannah, 'Personal Responsibility Under Dictatorship', in: Hannah Arendt & Jerome Kohn (Ed), *Responsibility and Judgment*, New York: Schocken Books 2003a, 17-48.

Arendt, Hannah, 'Collective Responsibility', in: Hannah Arendt & Jerome Kohn (Ed), *Responsibility and Judgment*, New York: Schocken Books 2003b, 147-158.

72 The subtitle of Morgan 2018.

73 Morgan 2018, 90.

74 Lammers 1995, 14.

75 See Bost's contribution.

Arendt, Hannah, *Eichmann in Jerusalem. A Report on the Banality of Evil*, Penguin 2006.

Aroney, N., 'The rule of law, religious authority, and oaths of office', *Journal of Law, Religion and State* (6) 2018-2-3, 195-212.

Best, Werner, *Die deutschen Aufsichtsverwaltungen in Frankreich, Belgien, den Niederlanden, Norwegen, Dänemark und im Protektorat Böhmen und Mähren, vergleichende Übersicht*, Typescript 1941. https://www.delpher.nl/nl/boeken/view?coll=boeken&identifier=MMKB18B:056057000.

Bost, Mélanie and Kirsten Peters, 'Belgian Magistrates and German Occupiers, A Diachronic Comparison (1914-1918/1940-1944)', in: Annie Hondeghem, Xavier Rousseaux and Frédéric Schoenaers (Eds), *Modernization of the Criminal Justice System and the Judicial System. New insights on trust, cooperation and human capital*, Springer 2016, 233-260.

Buruma, Ybo, 'Het geweten, de rechtspraak en de Rule of Law', *Trema* 2018-3. https://trema.nvvr.org/editie/2018-03/het-geweten-de-rechtspraak-en-de-rule-of-law.

Condren, Conal, *Argument and Authority in Early Modern England. The Presupposition of Oaths and Offices*, Cambridge University Press 2006.

Conway, Martin & Peter Romijn (Eds), *The War for Legitimacy in Politics and Culture 1936-1946*, Oxford: Berg 2008.

Corstens, Geert, 'De Hoge Raad en de Tweede Wereldoorlog. Toespraak mr. Corstens van 17 november 2011 tijdens de presentatie van het boek "De Hoge Raad en de Tweede Wereldoorlog,"' 2011. https://www.hogeraad.nl/geschiedenis-hoge-raad/.

Deák, István, *Europe on Trial. The Story of Collaboration, Resistance, and Retribution During World War II*, Westview Press 2015.

De Groot-van Leeuwen, L.E., *De rechterlijke macht in Nederland. Samenstelling en denkbeelden van de zittende en staande magistratuur*, Arnhem: Gouda Quint 1991.

Den Tonkelaar J.D.A. & E.S.F. den Tonkelaar (Eds), *Thronus Iustitiae. 400 jaar inspiratie voor rechters*, Deventer: Kluwer, 2nd Ed. 2014.

Dyzenhaus, David, *Hard Cases in Wicked Legal Systems. Pathologies of Legality*, 2nd Ed, Oxford University Press 2010.

Fraenkel, Ernst, *The Dual State. A Contribution to the Theory of Dictatorship*, New York: Oxford University Press 2017 (orig. 1941).

'"France organised this." Macron denounces state role in Holocaust atrocity', *The Guardian*, 17 July 2017. https://www.theguardian.com/world/2017/jul/17/france-macron-denounces-state-role-holocaust-atrocity-paris-1942.

Fritz, Vera, Denis Scuto & Elisabeth Wingerter (Eds), *Histoire de la Justice au Luxembourg (1795 à nos jours) Institutions – Organisation – Acteurs* (Studien zur transnationalen Zeitgeschichte Luxemburgs Vol 1), Berlin: De Gruyter Oldenbourg 2022.

Graver, Hans Petter, *Judges Against Justice. On Judges When the Rule of Law is Under Attack*, Heidelberg: Springer 2015.

Graver, Hans Petter, *Krieg der Richter. Die deutsche Besatzung 1940-1945 und der norwegische Rechtsstaat*, Baden-Baden: Nomos 2019.

Hem, Per E., *Megleren. Paal Berg 1873-1968*, Ashehoug 2012.

Hermans, H.L.C., *Om des gewetens wille. De geschiedenis van een arrest in oorlogstijd*, Leeuwarden 2003.

Holbraad, Carsten, *Danish Reactions to German Occupation. History and Historiography*, ULC Press 2017.

Jansen, Corjo, in collaboration with Derk Venema, *De Hoge Raad en de Tweede Wereldoorlog. Recht en rechtsbeoefening in de jaren 1930-1950*, Amsterdam: Boom 2011.

Lammers, Cornelis J., 'Levels of collaboration: A comparative study of German occupation regimes during the Second World War', *The Netherlands' Journal of Social Sciences* (31) 1995, 3-31.

Luban, David, 'Complicity and Lesser Evils: A Tale of Two Lawyers', *Georgetown Journal of Legal Ethics* (34) 2021-3, 613-664. https://papers.ssrn.com/sol3/papers.cfm?abstract_id=3817495

Mahmud, Tayyab, 'Jurisprudence of successful treason: Coup d'Etat and common law', *Cornell International Law Journal* (27) 1994, 49-140.

Mazower, Mark, *Hitler's Empire. How the Nazi's Rules Europe*, New York: The Penguin Press 2008.

Michielsen, J.N.M.E., *The 'Nazification' and 'Denazification' of the courts in Belgium, Luxembourg and the Netherlands, The Belgian, Luxembourg and Netherlands. Courts and their Reactions to Occupation Measures and Measures from their Governments Returning from Exile* (PhD Diss Maastricht), Maastricht: Universitaire Pers Maastricht 2004.

Middelberg, Mathias, *Judenrecht, Judenpolitik und der Jurist Hans Calmeyer in den besetzten Niederlanden 1940-1945*, Göttingen: V&R Unipress 2005.

Morgan, Philip, *Hitler's Collaborators. Choosing between bad and worse in Nazi-occupied Western Europe*, Oxford: Oxford University Press 2018.

Oppenheim, L. & H. Lauterpacht, *International Law, A Treatise*, Vol. II: *Disputes, War and Neutrality*, London: Longmans, Green & Co. 5th Ed, 1935.

'Rechtspraak, oorlog en vrijheid', 2020. https://www.rechtspraak.nl/Themas/rechtspraak-oorlog-vrijheid.

Röhr, Werner, 'System oder organisiertes Chaos? Fragen einer Typologie der deutschen Okkupationsregime im zweiten Weltkrieg', in: Robert Bohn, *Die deutsche Herrschaft in den „germanischen" Ländern 1940-1945*, Stuttgart: Franz Steiner Verlag 1997, 11-45.

Sandmo, Erling, *Siste ord: Høyesterett i norsk historie*, Vol. 2: 1905-1965, Oslo: J.W. Capellen 2005.

Sandmo, Erling, "Just Past: on Historical and Legal History", in Kenneth Johansson and Marie Lindstedt Cronberg (red.), *Vänskap över gränser. En festskrift til Eva Österberg*, Lund: Studentlitteratur AB 2007, 113-128.

Schlesinger, Herbert J., *Promises, Oaths, and Vows. On the Psychology of Promising*, Analytic Press 2008.

Sch.[neider], H., 'Høiesterett avsier en dom av historisk betydning (Der Oberste Gerichtshof erläßt ein Urteil von geschichtlicher Bedeutung), udgitt av Justisdepartementet, Stenersens Forlag, Oslo, 1941', *Reich – Volksordnung – Lebensraum*, Vol. II, 1942, p. 487-488.

Schwartz, S., Spires, E. & Young, R., 'Why do people keep their promises? A further investigation', *Experimental Economics* (22) 2019, 530–551.

Soeharno, Jonathan, *The Integrity of the Judge. A Philosophical Inquiry*, Ashgate 2009.

Van Goethem H., B. De Wever & N. Wouters (Eds), *Local Government in Occupied Europe*, Antwerp, University Press, 2006.

Vasbotten, Per, *Høiesterett avsier en dom av historisk betydning*, Oslo: Stenersens Forlag 1941.

Venema, Derk, 'The Judge, the Occupier, His Laws, and Their Validity. Judicial review by the Supreme Courts of occupied Belgium, Norway, and the Netherlands 1940-1945 in the context of their professional conduct and the consequences for their public image', in: Margo De Koster, Hervé Leuwers, Dirk Luyten & Xavier Rousseaux (Ed), *Justice in Wartime and Revolutions*, Brussels: State Archives 2012, 193-213.

Venema, Derk, 'A Perilous Puppet. The Trial of Dutch Nazi Leader Anton Mussert', in: Andreas Raffeiner (Ed), *Auf der Klaviatur der Rechtsgeschichte. Festgabe für Kurt Ebert zum 75. Geburtstag* (Rechtsgeschichtliche Studien, Band 84), Hamburg: Verlag Dr. Kovač 2019, 967-976.

Venema, Derk, Leny de Groot-van Leeuwen & Thomas Mertens (Eds), *Onder de huidige omstandigheden, De Hoge Raad en het Toetsingsarrest 1942*, Den Haag: Boom Juridische uitgevers 2008.

Whelan, Frederick G., *Democracy in Theory and Practice*, Routledge 2019.

Wingerter, Elisabeth, *Law, Order and Postwar Purge in the Grand Duchy of Luxembourg (1944 – 1955): Transitional Justice and Redistribution through the example of Justice, Gendarmerie and Police*, (PhD Diss.) 2021.

https://trema.nvvr.org/editie/2018-03

https://watwedoen.nl/project/om-des-gewetens-wille/

About the Author

Derk Venema is assistant professor at the Law Faculty of the Open University in the Netherlands. He has published on the Dutch judiciary in WWII and transitional justice theory, amongst other subjects. He teaches professional ethics at the Training Centre for the Judiciary SSR, and is an associated researcher at CegeSoma, Brussels.

References

Aalders, Gerard, *Niets was wat het leek, Prins Bernhard*, Amsterdam: Boom 2014.

Adamová, Karolina, Karel Schelle, Jaromír Tauchen and Antonín Lojek, *Velké dějiny zemí Koruny české. Tematická řada. Stát*, Praha: Paseka 2015.

Adamová, Karolina, Karel Schelle, Jaromír Tauchen and Antonín Lojek, *Velké dějiny zemí Koruny české. Tematická řada. Právo*, Praha: Paseka 2017.

Adams, Henry Hitch, *Italy at war. World War II*, Alexandria: Life Time Books 1982.

Alibert, J., *Treize années noires (1933-1946), Souvernirs et réflexions*, Paris: L'Harmattan 2001.

Alkil, Niels (Ed), *Besættelsestidens Fakta* Vol I-II, Copenhagen: J.H. Schulz 1945.

Amara, Michael, *Des Belges à l'épreuve de l'exil: les réfugiés de la Première Guerre mondiale: France, Grande-Bretagne, Pays-Bas*, Brussels: Éditions de l'Université de Bruxelles 2008.

Andenæs, Johs, Magne Skodvin and Olav Riste, *Norway and the Second World War*, Oslo: Aschehoug 1966.

Arendt, Hannah, 'Personal Responsibility Under Dictatorship', in: Hannah Arendt & Jerome Kohn (Ed), *Responsibility and Judgment*, New York: Schocken Books 2003, 17-48.

Arendt, Hannah, 'Collective Responsibility', in: Hannah Arendt & Jerome Kohn (Ed), *Responsibility and Judgment*, New York: Schocken Books 2003, 147-158.

Arendt, Hannah, *Eichmann in Jerusalem. A Report on the Banality of Evil*, Penguin 2006.

Aroney, N., 'The rule of law, religious authority, and oaths of office', *Journal of Law, Religion and State* (6) 2018-2-3, 195-212.

Artuso, Vincent, *La Collaboration au Grand-Duché de Luxembourg durant la Seconde Guerre mondiale (1940-1945). Accommodation, Adaptation, Assimilation*, Préface de Pascal Ory, Frankfurt/Main: Peter Lang 2013.

Artuso, Vincent, *La « Question juive » au Luxembourg (1933-1941). L'État luxembourgeois face aux persécutions antisémites nazies*, Rapport final avec une préface de Serge Klarsfeld, Luxembourg: Éditions forum 2015.

Aubusson de Cavarlay, B., Marie-Sylvie Huré & Marie-Lys Pottier, *La justice pénale en France. Résultats statistiques (1934-1954)* (Les cahiers de l'Institut d'histoire du temps present, Série Justice 23) 1993.

Bancaud, A., *Une exception ordinaire, La magistrature en France, 1930-1950*, Paris: Gallimard 2002.

Bancaud, A. & R. Badinter, *Les ministres devant la justice*, Paris: Actes sud 1997.

Barak, Aharon, *The Judge in a Democracy*, Princeton University Press 2006.

Barendsen, Jan, & Derk Venema, *De rechtbank Arnhem en de Duitse bezetting*, Nijmegen: Wolf Legal Publishers 2004.

Barthélemy, Joseph, *Ministre de la justice, Vichy 1941-1943. Mémoires*, Paris: Pygmalion, 1989.

Baruch, Marc Olivier, *Servir l'État français. L'administration en France de 1940 à 1944*, Paris: Fayard, 1997.

Baruch, Marc Olivier, 'Changing Things so Everything Stays the Same: The Impossible "épuration" of French Society, 1945–2000', in: Nico Wouters (Ed), *Transitional Justice and Memory in Europe (1945-2013)*, Cambridge, Intersentia, Series on Transitional Justice, Vol 17, 2014, 63-94.

Baruch, Marc Olivier (Ed), *Faire des choix? Les fonctionnaires dans l'Europe des dictatures*, La documentation française, 2014.

Baxter, Richard R., 'The Duty of Obedience to the Belligerent Occupant', *The British Yearbook of International Law* 1950, 235-266.

Bayot, J., 'Eloge funèbre de M. le procureur général vicomte Hayoit de Termicourt', *Journal des tribunaux* 4729, 1971, 79-81.

Berger, Olivier, 'Des questions de justice dans l'occupation allemande de 1870-1871. Essai sur le fonctionnement particulier de la justice civile française et de la justice militaire allemande', in: Marie Houllemare and Philippe Nivet (Eds), *Justice et guerre de l'Antiquité à la Première Guerre mondiale. Actes du colloque (Amiens, 18-20 novembre 2009)*, Amiens: Encrage 2011, 173-182.

Bernard, J. J., *Le camp de la mort lente, Compiègne 1941-42*, Paris: Albin Michel 1944.

Best, G., 'Peace conferences and the century of total war: the 1899 Hague Conference and what came after', *International affairs* (75) 1999, p. 619-634.

Best, Werner, 'Grundfragen einer deutschen Großraum-Verwaltung', in: *Festgabe für Heinrich Himmler*, Darmstadt: L.C. Wittig Verlag 1941, 33-60.

Best, Werner, *Die deutschen Aufsichtsverwaltungen in Frankreich, Belgien, den Niederlanden, Norwegen, Dänemark und im Protektorat Böhmen und Mähren, vergleichende Übersicht*, Typescript 1941, https://www.delpher.nl/nl/boeken/view?coll=boeken&identifier=MMKB18B:056057000.

Bianchi, Gianfranco, *25 luglio, crollo di un regime*, Milan: Murcia 1963.

Birnbaum, P., *Les fous de la République, Histoire politique des juifs d'état de Gambetta à Vichy*, Paris: Fayard 1992.

Blom, J.C.H., et. al. (Eds), *A.E. Cohen als geschiedschrijver van zijn tijd*, Amsterdam: Boom 2005.

Boberach, Heinz, *Richterbriefe. Dokumente zur Beeinflussung der deutschen Rechtsprechung 1942–1944*, Koblenz: Bundesarchiv 1975.

Bocca, Giorgio, *La Repubblica di Mussolini*, Milano: Mondadori 1994.

Bohn, Robert, *Reichskommissariat Norwegen: "Nationalsozialistische Neuordnung" und Kriegswirtschaft*, München: Oldenburg Wissenschaftsverlag 2000.

Bonfils, Henri, *Manuel de droit international public (droit des gens)*, 5ème éd., Paris: Rousseau, 1908.

Bost, Mélanie, *Traverser l'occupation 1914–1918. Du modus vivendi à la grève, la magistrature belge face aux occupants allemands*, unpublished PhD thesis, Louvain: Université catholique de Louvain, 2013.

Bost, Mélanie, 'Judges, Lawyers, "Vultures' and 'Butchers": Actors and Stakes of the Rental Crisis in Occupied Brussels, 1914–1918', in: Mélanie Bost and Toon Vrints (Eds), *Doing Justice In Wartime: Multiple Interplays between Justice and Populations during the Two World Wars*, Studies in the History of Law and Justice 19, Switzerland: Springer 2021, 11-24.

Bost, Mélanie, and Jérôme De Brouwer, 'Le Barreau de Bruxelles face à l'Occupant au cours du Premier conflit mondial', *SIHPA* 2018-13.

Bost, Mélanie, and Aurore François, 'La grève de la magistrature belge (février à novembre 1918). Un haut fait de la résistance nationale à l'épreuve des archives judiciaires', in: Dirk Heirbaut, Xavier Rousseaux and Alain Wijffels (Eds), *Histoire du droit et de la justice: une nouvelle génération de recherches/Justitie-en rechtsgeschiedenis: een nieuwe onderzoeksgeneratie*, Louvain-la-Neuve: Presses universitaires de Louvain 2009, 19-44.

Bost, Mélanie and Kirsten Peters, 'Belgian Magistrates and German Occupiers, A Diachronic Comparison (1914-1918/1940-1944)', in: Annie Hondeghem, Xavier Rousseaux and Frédéric Schoenaers (Eds), *Modernization of the Criminal Justice System and the Judicial System. New insights on trust, cooperation and human capital*, Springer 2016, 233-260.

Bost, Mélanie, and Jan Julia Zurné, 'Excluding the wrongdoers: the use of judicial discipline as a purging tool of the Belgian magistracy after the two German occupations', in: Marc Bergère et al. (Eds), *Pour une Histoire connectée et transnationale des épurations en Europe au sortir de la Seconde Guerre mondiale*, Brussels: Peter Lang 2019, 117-133.

Bosworth, R.J.B., *Mussolini's Italy: Life Under the Fascist Dictatorship, 1915-1945*, London: Penguin Books 2007.

Boudens, Robrecht, *Kardinaal Van Roey en de Tweede Wereldoorlog*, Averbode: Altiora 1996.

Bouffandeau, Tony, 'La continuité et la sauvegarde des principes du droit public français entre le 16 juin 1940 et l'entrée en vigueur de la nouvelle Constitution', *Études et documents du Conseil d'État*, 1947, 23-27.

Broszat, Martin, 'Das weltanschauliche und gesellschaftliche Kräftefeld', in: Martin Broszat & Norbert Frei (Eds), *Das Dritte Reich, Ursprünge, Ereignisse, Wirkungen*, Freiburg: Ploetz 1983, 158-168.

Brown, R., *Group Processes. Dynamics within and between groups*, (2nd Ed) Malden: Blackwell Publishers 2000.

Brüggenmann, K., 'Foreign Rule and Collaboration in the Baltic Countries, 1860-1920. New Directions in Research', *Journal of Baltic Studies* (37) 2006-2, 155-162.

Bruland, Bjarte, *Holocaust i Norge. Registrering, deportasjon, tilintetgjørelse*, Oslo: Dreyers forlag 2017.

Burrin, Philippe, *France under the Germans. Collaboration and Compromise*, The New Press 1997 (French edition: *La France à l'heure allemande*, Paris: Seuil, 1995).

Burrin, Philippe, 'Les élites dans l'Europe nazie', in: Marc Olivier Baruch & Vincent Guigueno (Eds), *Le choix des X; l'École polytechnique et les polytechniciens 1939-1945*, Paris: Fayard, 2000, 79-95.

Burrin, Philippe, 'Faire l'histoire des occupations militaires', in: *La France sous Vichy. Autour de Robert O. Paxton*, Paris: Complexe 2004, 91-104. Benvenisti, Eyal, *The International Law of Occupation*, Princeton: Princeton University Press (2nd Ed) 2004.

Buruma, Ybo, 'Het geweten, de rechtspraak en de Rule of Law', *Trema* 2018-3. https://trema.nvvr.org/editie/2018-03/het-geweten-de-rechtspraak-en-de-rule-of-law.

Buschmann, Arno, *Das Reichsgericht – Ein Höchstgericht im Wandel der Zeiten*, in: Bernd-Rüdiger Kern & Adrian Schmidt-Recla (Eds), *125 Jahre Reichsgericht*, Duncker & Humblot 2006, 41-76.

Carlton, Eric, *Occupation. The Policies and Practices of Military Conquerors*, London: Routledge 1992.

Carp, J.H., *Een half jaar rechtspraak van het Vredegerechtshof*, Utrecht: Nenasu 1942.

Cassese, A., 'The Martens Clause. Half a Loaf or Simply Pie in the Sky?', *European Journal of International Law* (11) 2000/1, 187-216.

Černý, Bohuslav, 'Tvorba ceny v našem řízeném hospodářství', *Obzor národohospodářský*, (45) 1940, 374-384.

Chapoutot, Johann, *La loi du sang. Penser et agir en nazi*, Gallimard 2014.

Chapoutot, Johann, '"Volk" and "Justice" under the Third Reich', in: Émilie Delivré, Emmanuel Berger & Martin Löhnig (Eds), *Popular justice in times of transition (19th and 20th century Europe)*, 2017, 149-154.

Charle, C., 'Les spécificités de la magistrature française en Europe (XIXe-XXe siècles)', *Crises* (4) 1994 (Les juges contre la République?), 61-68.

Charles, Jean-Léon and Philippe Dasnoy, *Les secrétaires généraux face à l'occupant – Procès-verbaux des réunions du comité des secrétaires généraux (1940-1944)*, Brussels: Arts & Travel, 1974.

Charpentier, J., *Au service de la liberté*, Paris: Fayard 1949.

Charvin, R., *Justice et politique et évolution de leurs rapports*, Paris: Librairie générale de droit et de jurisprudence 1968.

Chomienne, C., 'Juger sous Vichy', *Le Genre humain*, (28) 1994, I, 117-131.

Chowaniec, Elisabeth, *Der ‚Fall Dohnanyi' 1943–1945. Widerstand, Militärjustiz, SS-Willkür*, Oldenbourg Wissenschaftsverlag 1991.

Cleveringa, R.P., [Protest speech], https://www.universiteitleiden.nl/dossiers/de-universiteit-en-de-oorlog/cleveringas-biografie.

Coady, C.A.J., 'The Problem of Dirty Hands', in: Edward N. Zalta (Ed), *The Stanford Encyclopedia of Philosophy* (Fall 2018 Edition), https://plato.stanford.edu/archives/fall2018/entries/dirty-hands/.

Codaccioni, Vanessa, *Justice d'exception. L'État face aux crimes politiques et terroristes*, Paris: CNRS Éditions 2015.

Cohen, A.E., 'Opmerkingen over de notitie van dr. de Paterover het doel van het Duitse civiele bestuur in Nederland', in: A.H. Paape, *Studies over Nederland in oorlogstijd*, Den Haag: Nijhoff 1972, 48-58.

Cointet, J. P., *Expier Vichy, L'épuration en France, 1943-1958*, Paris: Perrin 2008.

Colignon, Alain, 'C.N.A.A., L'agriculture en rangs d'oignon', *Jours de Guerre* (9) 1993, 49-93.

Condren, Conal, *Argument and Authority in Early Modern England. The Presupposition of Oaths and Offices*, Cambridge University Press 2006.

Conway, Martin & Peter Romijn (Eds), *The War for Legitimacy in Politics and Culture 1936-1946*, Oxford: Berg 2008.

Conway, Martin & Peter Romijn, 'Political Legitimacy in Mid-Twentieth-Century Europe. An Introduction, in: Martin Conway & Peter Romijn (Eds), *The War for Legitimacy in Politics and Culture 1936-1946*, Oxford: Berg 2008, 1-27.

Cornil, Léon, 'La Cour de cassation. Mercuriale prononcée par M. Léon Cornil, procureur général, à l'audience solennelle de rentrée de la Cour de cassation le 15 septembre 1948', *Journal des Tribunaux* 3778, 1948, 453-461.

Cornil, Léon, 'La Cour de cassation. Considérations sur sa mission. Discours prononcé par M. le Procureur général Cornil à l'audience solennelle de rentrée de la Cour de cassation le 15 septembre 1950', *Journal des Tribunaux* 3863, 1950, 489-498.

Corstens, Geert, 'De Hoge Raad en de Tweede Wereldoorlog. Toespraak mr. Corstens van 17 november 2011 tijdens de presentatie van het boek "De Hoge Raad en de Tweede Wereldoorlog."' https://www.hogeraad.nl/geschiedenis-hoge-raad/.

Cotillon, J., *Raphaël Alibert, Juriste engagé et homme d'influence à Vichy*, Paris: Economica 2009.

Cybichowski, Sigmund, 'Die Besetzung Lembergs im Kriege 1914/15' *Zeitschrift für Internationales Recht* (26) 1916, 427-478.

Dal Pont, A., A. Leonetti, F. Maiello & L. Zocchi, *Aula IV. Tutti i processi del Tribunale speciale fascista*, Rome: ANPPIA 1961.

Dantoing, Antoine, 'Le cardinal Van Roey de la neutralité à la présence', *Jours de Guerre* (5) 1991, 55-67.

Deák, István, *Europe on Trial. The Story of Collaboration, Resistance, and Retribution During World War II*, Westview Press 2015.

De Blasio Wilhelm, Maria, *The Other Italy: The Italian Resistance in World War II*, New York: Ishi Press 2014.

De Felice, Rienzo, *Mussolini. L'alleato. 1. Dalla guerra «breve» alla guerra lunga. L'Italia in guerra (1940-1943)*, Turin: Einaudi 1974.

De Felice, Renzo, *Mussolini. Il fascista. 1. I. La conquista del potere. 1921-1925*, Turin: Einaudi 1974.

De Felice, Renzo, *Mussolini. Il Duce II. Lo stato totalitario 1936-1940*, Turin: Einaudi 1981.

De Felice, Renzo, *Mussolini. L'Alleato. L'Italia in guerra II: Crisi e agonia del regime*, Turin: Einaudi 1996.

De Felice, Renzo, *Mussolini. L'Alleato. 2: La Guerra Civile*, 3rd ed., Turin: Einaudi 2008.

De Groot-van Leeuwen, L.E., *De rechterlijke macht in Nederland. Samenstelling en denkbeelden van de zittende en staande magistratuur*, Arnhem: Gouda Quint 1991.

[de Haene, Joseph], *Les lettres d'un provincial ou les propos du Conseiller Eudoxe. Nouvelle édition vendue au profit des mutilés de la guerre*, Bruxelles-Paris: J. Van Oest 1919.

De Huberich, Charles Henry, and Alexander Nicol-Speyer, *Législation allemande pour le territoire belge occupé (textes officiels)*, 21 Vols, La Haye: Martinus Nijhoff 1914-1918.

Deiseroth, Dieter, 'Der Reichstagsbrand-Prozess – ein rechtsstaatliches Verfahren?', *Kritische Justiz* Vol. 42 2009, 303-316.

De Jong, L., *Het Koninkrijk der Nederlanden in de Tweede Wereldoorlog, deel 4, Mei '40 – Maart '41*, Den Haag: Martinus Nijhoff 1972.

De Jong, L., *Het Koninkrijk der Nederlanden in de Tweede Wereldoorlog, deel 6, Juli '42 – Mei '43*, Den Haag: Martinus Nijhoff 1975.

De Jonghe, Albert, *Hitler en het politieke lot van België (1940-1944): de vestiging van een Zivilverwaltung in België en Noord-Frankrijk*, Antwerpen: Nederlandsche Boekhandel 1972.

De Jonghe, Albert, 'La lutte Himmler-Reeder pour la nomination d'un HSSPF à Bruxelles (1942-1944)' (Part I-IV), *Cahiers d'Histoire de la Seconde Guerre Mondiale* (3-8) 1974-1984.

Delforge, Paul, *La Wallonie et la Première Guerre mondiale: pour une histoire de la séparation administrative*, Namur: Institut Destrée 2008.

de Louvain, Albert [Émile Kebers, lawyer], 'Lettre ouverte à Monsieur Edmond Picard', *L'Âme belge* 1917, 120-126.

Deltour, Pol, 'Het weinig heroïsch pragmatisme van de Belgische oorlogsmagistratuur (1940-1944)', *Panopticon* 1995, 153-161.

Den Tonkelaar J.D.A. & E.S.F. den Tonkelaar (Eds), *Thronus Iustitiae. 400 jaar inspiratie voor rechters*, Deventer: Kluwer, 2nd Ed. 2014.

De Pater, J.C.H., 'Doel van het Duitse civiele bestuur in Nederland', in: A.H. Paape, *Studies over Nederland in oorlogstijd*, Den Haag: Nijhoff 1972, 39-47.

De Ruiter, J., *Jan Donner jurist*, Amsterdam: Boom 2003.

De Schaepdrijver, Sophie, *De Groote Oorlog. Het Koninkrijk België tijdens de Eerste Wereldoorlog*, Antwerpen: Atlas 1997.

Dinstein, Yoram, *The International Law of Belligerent Occupation*, Cambridge: Cambridge University Press 2009.

Donner, J., *Plaats en taak van de Hoge Raad der Nederlanden*, Calvinistische Juristen Vereniging 1962.

Dostert, Paul, *Luxemburg zwischen Selbstbehauptung und nationaler Selbstaufgabe. Die deutsche Besatzungspolitik und die Volksdeutsche Bewegung*, Luxembourg: Saint-Paul 1985.

Douglas, M., *Purity and Danger. An Analysis of the Concepts of Pollution and Taboo*, London, ARK Paperbacks, 1984 (orig. 1966).

Dyzenhaus, David, *Hard Cases in Wicked Legal Systems. Pathologies of Legality*, 2nd Ed, Oxford University Press 2010.

'Ein bißchen Bibel und viel Unrecht', *Der Spiegel* 40/1979.

Enquêtecommissie Regeringsbeleid 1940 – 1945. Verslag houdende de uitkomsten van het onderzoek, Vol 7c Leiding en voorlichting aan ambtenaren en burgers in de bezette gebieden – het contact met en de politiek ten aanzien van de verzetsbeweging in Nederland (punten G en H van het enquêtebesluit) Verhoren, 's-Gravenhage: Staatsdrukkerij- en Uitgeverijbedrijf: 1955.

Essers, Peter, *Belast verleden. Het Nederlandse belastingrecht onder nationaalsocialistisch regime*, Kluwer 2012.

Fabre, Philippe, *Le Conseil d'État et Vichy: le contentieux de l'antisémitisme*, éditions de la Sorbonne 2001.

Faider, Charles, 'La Cour de cassation. Discours prononcé par M. Ch. Faider, procureur général, à l'audience solennelle d'installation de M. le Conseiller Lelièvre le 7 décembre 1885 et dont la Cour a ordonné l'impression', *Bulletin des arrêts de la Cour de cassation de Belgique* 1886, 1569-1575.

Fasseur, Cees, *Juliana & Bernhard. Verhaal van een huwelijk. De jaren 1936-1956*, Balans 2009.

Fleuren, J.W.A., *Een ieder verbindende bepalingen van verdragen*, Boom Juridische uitgevers 2004.

Foyer, Jean 'Les juridictions administratives, une spécificité française', http://www.vie-publique.fr/decouverte-institutions/institutions/approfondissements/juridictions-administratives-specificite-francaise.html

Fraenkel, Ernst, *Der Doppelstaat* (2nd Ed), Europäische Verlagsanstalt 2012.

Fraenkel, Ernst, *The Dual State. A Contribution to the Theory of Dictatorship*, New York: Oxford University Press 2017 (orig. 1941).

'"France organised this." Macron denounces state role in Holocaust atrocity', *The Guardian*, 17 July 2017. https://www.theguardian.com/world/2017/jul/17/france-macron-denounces-state-role-holocaust-atrocity-paris-1942.

François, J.P.A., *Handboek van het volkenrecht, Tweede deel*, Zwolle: W.E.J. Tjeenk Willink 1933.

Frank, Hans (Ed), *Nationalsozialistische Leitsätze für ein neues deutsches Strafrecht*, Teil 1, 3rd ed., Berlin: Deutsche Rechts- und Wirtschaftswissenschaft Verlags-Ges. 1935.

Frantz, Constantin, *Die Nationalliberale Rechtseinheit und das Reichsgericht*, Augsburg 1873.

Franzinelli, Mimmo, *Il tribunale del Duce. La giustizia fascista e le sue vittime*, Milan: Mondadori 2017.

Freeman, Alwyn V., 'War crimes by Enemy Nationals Administering Justice in Occupied Territory', *The American Journal of International Law* XLI 1947-3, 579-610.

Freisler, Roland et al., *Grundzüge eines Allge meinen deutschen Strafrechts. Denkschrift des Zentralausschusses der Strafrechtsabteilung der Akademie für deutsches Recht über die Grundzüge eines Allgemeinen Deutschen Strafrechts*, Berlin: R. v. Decker's Verlag 1934 (= *Schriften der Akademie für Deutsches Recht*, Heft 1).

Fritz, Vera, Denis Scuto & Elisabeth Wingerter (Eds), *Histoire de la Justice au Luxembourg (1795 à nos jours) Institutions – Organisation – Acteurs* (Studien zur transnationalen Zeitgeschichte Luxemburgs Vol 1), Berlin: De Gruyter Oldenbourg 2022.

Fruin, *De Nederlandsche wetboeken*, 's-Gravenhage: Martinus Nijhoff 1940.

Gabolde, M., 'Le problème judiciaire pendant l'occupation', in: *La vie de la France sous l'occupation*, Fondation Hoover, Paris: Plon 1957, II, 619-642.

Ganapini, Luigi, *La repubblica delle camicie nere. I combattenti, i politici, i socializzatori, gli amministratori*, Milan: Garzanti 1999.

Ganshof van der Meersch, Walter, 'Eloge funèbre de M. le procureur général vicomte Hayoit de Termicourt', *Journal des Tribunaux* (4729) 1971, 81-84.

Garner, James Wilford, *International Law and the World War*, London: Longmans, Green and Co. 1920.

Garnot, B., *Histoire de la justice, France, XVIe-XXIe siècle*, Paris: Folio histoire, Gallimard 2009.

Gellner, Ernest, *Nations and Nationalism*, Oxford, Blackwell, 1983.

Gentile, Emilio, *La via italiana al totalitarismo. Il partito e lo Stato nel regime fascista*, Rome: Carocci 2008.

Gérard-Libois, Jules and José Gotovitch, *L'an 40, La Belgique occupée*, Brussels: CRISP 1971.

Gids voor de rechterlijke macht 1943.

Gille, Louis, Alphonse Ooms and Paul Delandsheere, *Cinquante mois d'occupation allemande*, Brussels: Dewit, 1919.

Gobetti, Ada, *Partisan Diary: A Woman's Life in the Italian Resistance*, Oxford University Press 2014.

Görtemaker, Manfred & Christoph Safferling (Eds), *Die Akte Rosenburg: Das Bundesministerium der Justiz und die NS-Zeit*, C.H. Beck 2016.

Gotovitch, José, *Note relative à la magistrature sous l'occupation*, Brussels: C.R.E.H.S.G.M. 1972.

Götzel, H., *Kurt Student und seine Fallschirmjäger*, Friedberg: Podzan Pallas 1980.

'Gouvernement de Londres,' in: Paul Aron and José Gotovitch (Eds), *Dictionnaire de la Seconde Guerre mondiale en Belgique*, Brussels: Versailles 2008.

Graditzky, Thomas, 'Les expériences d'occupation autour de la Grande Guerre: quelle mobilisation du Règlement de La Haye?', in: James Connolly, Emmanuel Debruyne, Élise Julien and Matthias Meirlaen (Eds), *En territoire ennemi 1914-1949. Expériences d'occupation, transferts, héritages*, ed. by, Villeneuve d'Ascq: Septentrion 2018, 153-164.

Graver, Hans Petter, *Judges Against Justice. On Judges When the Rule of Law is Under Attack*, Heidelberg: Springer 2015.

Graver, Hans Petter, *Dommernes krig. Den tyske okkupasjonen 1940–1945 og den norske rettsstaten*, Oslo: Pax forlag 2015.

Graver, 'Judging without Impunity: On the Criminal Responsibility of Authoritarian Judges', *Bergen Journal of Criminal Law and Criminal Justice* (4) 2016-1, 125-149.

Graver, Hans Petter, 'Judicial Independence Under Authoritarian Rule: An Institutional Approach to the Legal Tradition of the West', *Hague Journal on the Rule of Law*, 2018, https://doi.org/10.1007/s40803-018-0071-8

Graver, Hans Petter, *Okkupasjonstidens Høyesterett*, Oslo 2019.

Graver, Hans Petter, *Der Krieg der Richter Die deutsche Besatzung 1940-1945 und der norwegische Rechtsstaat*, Baden-Baden: Nomos 2019.

Grilli, Antonio, *Tra fronda e collaborazione. Magistrati nell'Italia occupata (1943-1945)*, Rome: Aracne 2017.

Gruchmann, Lothar, *Justiz im Dritten Reich 1933-1940. Anpassung und Unterwerfung in der Ära Gürtner*, Oldenbourg Wissenschaftsverlag 2009.

Gründer, Horst, *Walter Simons als Staatsmann, Jurist und Kirchenpolitiker*, Mocker & Jahn, 1975.

Haag, Emile/Krier, Emile, *La Grande-Duchesse et son gouvernement durant La Seconde Guerre mondiale. 1940, l'année du dilemme*, Luxembourg: RTL Edition 1987.

Hácha, Emil, 'Gedanken eines ehemaligen Verwaltungsrichters', *Prager Archiv für Recht, Verwaltung und Wirtschaft* (25) 1943, 165-168.

Haferkamp, Hans-Peter, *Die heutige Rechtsmissbrauchslehre: Ergebnis nationalsozialistischen Rechtsdenkens?*, Berlin: Verlag Spitz, 1995.

Haferkamp, Hans-Peter, "Österreichisches', 'Deutsches' und 'Nationalsozialistisches' in der Rechtsprechung des Reichsgerichts zum ABGB zwischen 1939 und 1945', in: Barbara Dölemeyer & Heinz Mohnhaupt (Eds), *200 Jahre ABGB. (1811-2011) Die österreichische Kodifikation im internationalen Kontext*, 2012, 159-175.

Haffner, Sebastian, *Von Bismarck zu Hitler. En Rückblick*, Kindler Verlag 1993.

Hanquet, René, *Les pouvoirs des secrétaires généraux pendant l'occupation*, Brussels: Goemaere 1946.

Hansen, Nicolas, *Un haut magistrat belge face à l'occupation. Joseph Jamar, Premier président de la Cour de cassation de 1940-1944* (unpublished history M.A. dissertation), Louvain-la-Neuve 2008).Farcy, J.-C., *L'histoire de la justice française de la Révolution à nos jours*, Paris: Presses Universitaires de France 2001.

Hartung, Fritz, *Jurist unter vier Reichen*, Carl Heymanns Verlag 1971.

Hattenhauer, Hans, 'Das NS-Volksgesetzbuch', in: Arno Buschmann et al. (Eds), *Festschrift Rudolf Gmür zum 70. Geburtstag*, Bielefeld 1983, 255-297.

Hechter, M., 'Alien Rule and Its Discontents'. *American Behavioral Scientist* (53) 2009-3, 289-310.

Heck, Philipp, *Grundriss des Schuldrechts*, Scientia Verlag 1994.

Hedemann, Justus Wilhelm, *Die Flucht in die Generalklauseln*, Tübingen: Mohr 1933.

Hem, Per E., *Megleren Paal Berg 1873-1968*, Oslo: Aschehoug 2012.

Herbert, Ulrich, *Best. Biographische Studien über Radikalismus, Weltanschauung und Vernunft*, Bonn: Dietz 1996.

Hermans, H.L.C., *Om des gewetens wille. De geschiedenis van een arrest in oorlogstijd*, Leeuwarden 2003.

Hermans, H.L.C., *Een ambitieuze jurist in gevaarlijk vaarwater. Johannes van Loon, President van de Hoge Raad in oorlogstijd*, Den Haag 2008.

Het proces Mussert (NIOD Bronnenpublicaties, Vol. 4), Amsterdam: Sijthoff 2nd edition, 1987.

Hitler, Adolf, *Mein Kampf*, München: Zentralverlag der NSDAP 1942.

Hochberger, Ernst, 'Die deutsche Gerichtsbarkeit im Protektorat Böhmen und Mähren', *Zeitschrift für osteuropäisches Recht*, (6) 1939-1940, 121.

'Hohle Nuß', *Der Spiegel* 05/1992.

Holbraad, Carsten, *Danish Reactions to German Occupation. History and Historiography*, ULC Press 2017.

Hooykaas, J.P., 'Toepasselijkheid van wettelijke strafbepalingen', *Nederlands Juristenblad* (19) 1944-1, 13-14.

Howard, R. M., & Carey, H. F., 'Is an independent judiciary necessary for democracy?', *Judicature* (87) 2004-6, 284-291.

Hull, William I., *The Two Hague Conferences and their Contributions to International Law*, Boston: Ginn & Company 1908.

Innstilling fra undersøkelseskommisjonen av 1945, Oslo: Aschehoug 1946.

Israel, L., *Robes noires, années sombres*, Paris: Fayard 2005.

Jäckel, Eberhard, *Frankreich in Hitlers Europa; Die deutsche Frankreichpolitik im Zweiten Weltkrieg*, Deutsche Verlag-Anstalg GmbH, Stuttgart: Deutsche Verlag-Anstalg, 1966.

Jäckel, E., *La France dans l'Europe de Hitler*, Paris: Fayard 1968.

Jacobson, Arthur J. and Bernhard Schlink (Eds), *Weimar A Jurisprudence of Crisis*, University of California Press Berkeley 2000.

Janečková, Eva, *Státoprávní uspořádání Protektorátu Čechy a Morava (1939-1945)*, Plzeň: Vydavatelství a nakladatelství Aleš Čeněk 2013.

Jansen, Corjo, 'De opstelling van de Nederlandse rechters en raadsheren tijdens de bezetting', *Trema* 2018-3, https://trema.nvvr.org/editie/2018-03/de-opstelling-van-de-nederlandse-rechters-en-raadsheren-tijdens-de-bezetting.

Jansen, Corjo, in collaboration with Derk Venema, *De Hoge Raad en de Tweede Wereldoorlog. Recht en rechtsbeoefening in de jaren 1930-1950*, Amsterdam: Boom 2011.

Jasch, Hans-Christian, 'Das Ringen um die Verwaltungsgerichtsbarkeit. Verwaltungsgerichtsbarkeit als Instrument der Rechtsvereinheitlichung im Dritten Reich', *Die Verwaltung* (38) 2005, 546-576.

'Jean Servais', *Annales du notariat et de l'enregistrement*, December 1946.

Joachim, Václav, *Nový zákon o Nejvyšším správním soudě ze dne 16. června 1937 č. 164 Sb. z. a n.*, Praha: V. Joachim 1937.

Jørgensen, Troels G., 'En dansk lov mod kommunismen', *Juristen* 1941, 497-504.

Jugnot, G., *Histoire de la justice française de l'époque franque à nos jours*, Paris: Ellipses 2011.

Justitsministeriet og retshåndhævelsen under besættelsen: beretning (afgivet paa grundlag af foreliggende danske dokumenter) (Den Parlamentariske Kommissions Betænkning: Beretning til Folketinget afgivet af den af Tinget under 15. Juni 1945, 19. December 1945, 8. Januar 1948 og 25. Oktober 1950 nedsatte Kommission i Henhold til Grundlovens Paragraf 45: Bilag 12, Vol VII), 1950.

Kern, Bernd-Rüdiger & Klaus-Peter Schroeder (Eds), *Eduard von Simson (1810–1899): „Chorführer der Deutschen" und erster Präsident des Reichsgerichts*, Baden-Baden: Nomos 2001.

Kershaw, Ian, *The Nazi Dictatorship. Problems & Perspectives of Interpretation* (4th Ed), London: Arnold 2000.

Kershaw, Ian, *Hitler 1889-1936: Hubris*, New York: W.W. Norton 2000.

Kershaw, Ian, *Hitler 1936-1945: Nemesis*, New York: W.W. Norton 2000.

Kirchheimer, Otto, *Political Justice: The Use of Legal Procedure for Political Ends*, Princeton: Princeton University Press 1961.

Kirchner, Carl, 'Reichsgericht und Bundesgerichtshof. Berufsherkunft, Alterszusammensetzung und Schicksal seiner Mitglieder', *Deutsche Richterzeitung* 1959, 107.

Klarsfeld, Serge, *Le calendrier de la persécution des Juifs de France 1940-1944*, Les Fils et Filles des Déportés Juifs de France & The Beate Klarsfeld Foundation, 1993.

Klemann, H.A.M., *Nederland 1938-1948, economie en samenleving in jaren van oorlog en bezetting*, Amsterdam: Boom 2002.

Kliment, Josef, *Zákon o nejvyšším správním soudě a jeho jednací řád*, Praha: Čin 1937.

Knapp, Viktor, *Problém nacistické právní filosofie*, Dobrá Voda: Vydavatelství a nakladatelství Aleš Čeněk 2002.

Knox, MacGregor, *Common Destiny: Dictatorship, Foreign Policy, and War in Fascist Italy and Nazi Germany*, Cambridge University Press 2000.

Kolbe, Dieter, *Reichsgerichtspräsident Dr. Erwin Bumke: Studien zum Niedergang des Reichsgerichts und der deutschen Rechtspflege*, C.F. Müller 1975.

Koppen, J.P. van & J. ten Kate, *De Hoge Raad in persoon. Benoemingen in de Hoge Raad der Nederlanden 1838-2002*, Deventer: Kluwer 2003.

Kossmann, Richard, 'Das Arbeitsgebiet der Gruppe Qu 2', in: Elisabeth Wagner (Ed), *Der Generalquartiermeister. Briefe und Tagebuchaufzeichnungen des Generalquartiermeisters des Heeres General der Artillerie Eduard Wagner*, Munich: Olzog 1963, 302-312.

Krieser, Helmut, 'Die deutsche Gerichtsbarkeit im Protektorat Böhmen und Mähren – Ausübung und Umfang', *Deutsches Recht* (10) 1940, 1745-1754.

Kroener, Bernhard R., Rolf-Dieter Müller & Hans Umbreit (Eds), *Germany and the Second World War, Vol. V/1 Organization and Mobilization of the German Sphere of Power*, Oxford: Clarendon Press 2000.

Krois, 'Die Verwaltung des Reichskommissars', *Reich – Volksordnung – Lebensraum* (II) 1942, 15-52.

Kuby, Erich, *Verrat auf Deutsch. Wie das Dritte Reich Italien ruinierte*, Hamburg: Hoffmann und Campe 1982.

Lamb, Richard, *War in Italy, 1943-1945: A Brutal Story*, London: Murray 1993.

Lammers, C.J., 'The Interorganizational Control of an Occupied Country', *Administrative Science Quarterly* (33) 1988, 438-457.

Lammers, Cornelis J., 'Levels of collaboration: A comparative study of German occupation regimes during the Second World War', *The Netherlands' Journal of Social Sciences* (31) 1995, 3-31.

Lammers, C.J., 'Occupation Regimes Alike and Unlike: British, Dutch and French Patterns of Inter-Organisational Control of Foreign Territories', *Organisation Studies*, 2003, 24(9), 1379-1403.

Lammers, C.J., *Vreemde overheersing, Bezetten en bezetting in sociologisch perspectief*, Amsterdam: Bakker 2005.

Langášek, Tomáš, *Ústavní soud Československé republiky a jeho osudy v letech 1920-1948*, Plzeň: Vydavatelství a nakladatelství Aleš Čeněk 2011.

Leclercq, Paul, 'Du pouvoir judiciaire. Discours prononcé par M. Paul Leclercq avocat général à l'audience solennelle de rentrée de la Cour d'appel de Bruxelles le 2 octobre 1911', *Belgique Judiciaire* (72) 1911, 1137-1153.

Leclercq, Pierre, 'L'interprétation de la loi du 10 mai 1940', *Journal des Tribunaux* (3671) 1946, 65-70.

Le Cocq, V. & A. S. Poiroux, *Les notaires sous l'occupation (1940-1945), acteurs de la spoliation des Juifs*, Paris: Nouveau monde éditions 2015.

Lemkin, Rapheal, *Axis Rule in Occupied Europe Law of Occupation, Analysis of Government, Proposals for Redress*, second edition, Clark: The Lawbook Exchange 2008 (Orig. 1944).

Lepre, Aurelio, *La storia della Repubblica di Mussolini*, Milan: Mondadori 2000.

Lepsius, Oliver, 'Personengebundene oder strukturorientierte Bewertungskriterien für juristisches Verhalten im Nationalsozialismus', in: Hermann Nehlsen & Georg Brun (Eds), *Münchener rechtshistorische Studien zum Nationalsozialismus*, Frankfurt/Main: Peter Lang 1996, 63-102.

Leuchtenburg, William E., *The Supreme Court Reborn. The Constitutional Revolution in the Age of Roosevelt*, Oxford: Oxford University Press, 1995.

Linzer, D. A., & Staton, J. K., 'Global measure of judicial independence, 1948-2012' *Journal of Law and Courts* (3) 2015-2, 223-256.

Lobe, Adolf, *50 Jahre Reichsgericht*, Berlin/Leipzig: Walter de Gruyter 1929.

Lochack, D., 'La doctrine sous Vichy ou les mésaventures du positivisme', in *Les usages sociaux du droit*, Paris: PUF, 1989, 252-285.

Loening, Edgar, 'L'administration du gouvernement-général de l'Alsace durant la guerre de 1870-1871. Deuxième article', *Revue de droit international et de législation comparée* V (1873), 94-99.

Löhnig, Martin, 'Ehelichkeitsanfechtung durch den Staatsanwalt (1938 – 1961)', *Zeitschrift der Savigny Stiftung für Rechtsgeschichte – Germanistische Abteilung* (124) 2007, 323-346.

Löhnig, Martin, *Neue Zeiten – Altes Recht. Die Anwendung von NS-Gesetzen durch deutsche Gerichte nach 1945*, Berlin: de Gruyter 2016.

Löhnig, Martin, 'Generalklauseln in der Rechtsprechung der österreichischen Senate des Reichsgerichts 1939-1945: Eine Studie auf Grundlage der Wiener Reichsgerichtsakten', in: *Beiträge zur Rechtsgeschichte Österreichs* (7) 2017-2, 181-203.

Lokin, J.H.A. & C.J.H. Jansen, *Tussen droom en daad. De Nederlandse Juristen-Vereniging 1870-1995*, Zwolle: W.E.J. Tjeenk Willink 1995.

Lorenz, Max, 'Die Neuregelung der Strafgerichtsbarkeit im Protektorat Böhmen und Mähren', *Deutsche Justiz* 1939, 177.

Louveaux, Charles, 'La magistrature dans la tourmente des années 1940-1944', *Revue de Droit pénal et de Criminologie* (7) 1981.Kaul, Friedrich Karl, *Geschichte des Reichsgerichts*, Vol 4: *1933 – 1945*, Akademie 1971, 620-665.

Luban, David, 'Complicity and Lesser Evils: A Tale of Two Lawyers', *Georgetown Journal of Legal Ethics* (34) 2021-3, 613-664. https://papers.ssrn.com/sol3/papers.cfm?abstract_id=3817495

Lüth & Wesel, 'Freymuth, Grossmann, Orgler: Drei Richter für die Republik', in: Redaktion Kritische Justiz (Eds), *Streitbare Juristen. Eine andere Tradition*, Baden-Baden: Nomos 1988, 204-218.

Luyten, Dirk, 'Introduction', in: Margo De Koster, Hervé Leuwers, Dirk Luyten and Xavier Rousseaux (Eds),*Justice in Wartime and Revolutions. Europe, 1795-1950, Justice and Society VI*, Brussels: AGR 2012, 5-13.

Mach, Zdzisław, *Symbols, Conflict, and Identity. Essays in Political Anthropology*, Albany: State University of New York Press 1993.

Mack Smith, Denis, *Modern Italy: A Political History*, Yale University Press 1997.

Mahmud, Tayyab, 'Jurisprudence of successful treason: Coup d'Etat and common law', *Cornell International Law Journal* (27) 1994, 49-140.

Majerus, Pierre, *Le Luxembourg pendant La Seconde Guerre mondiale*, Luxembourg: Saint-Paul 1980.

Majerus, Benoît: 'Von Falkenhausen zu Falkenhausen. Die deutsche Verwaltung Belgiens in den zwei Weltkriegen', in: Günther Kronenbitter, Markus Pöhlmann & Dierk Walter (Eds), *Besatzung. Funktion und Gestalt militärischer Fremdherrschaft von der Antike bis zum 20. Jahrhundert*, Paderborn: Ferdinand Schöningh 2006, 131-145.

Maleville, Georges, *Conseiller d'État, Témoignage*, Paris: Litec, 1977.

Mandl, Vladimír, *Právní soustava Německé říše*, Praha: V. Linhart 1939.

Maršálek, Pavel, *Veřejná správa Protektorátu Čechy a Morava v letech 1939-1945*, Praha: Vodnář 1999.

Maršálek, Pavel, *Protektorát Čechy a Morava: státoprávní a politické aspekty nacistického okupačního režimu v českých zemích 1939-1945*, Praha: Karolinum 2002.

Maršálek, Pavel, *Pod ochranou hákového kříže: nacistický okupační režim v českých zemích 1939-1945*, Praha: Auditorium 2012.

Massot, Jean, 'Le Conseil d'État et le régime de Vichy', *Vingtième siècle, revue d'histoire* (58) 1998-2, 83-99.

Mazel, P.E., *In naam van het recht..., De Hoge Raad en de Tweede Wereldoorlog*, Arnhem: Gouda Quint 1984.

Mazower, Mark, *Hitler's Empire. How the Nazi's Rules Europe*, New York: The Penguin Press 2008.

Meihuizen, J., *Noodzakelijk kwaad, De bestraffing van economische collaboratie in Nederland na de Tweede Wereldoorlog* (PhD Diss), Amsterdam: Boom 2003.

Meihuizen, Joggli, *Smalle marges. De Nederlandse advocatuur in de Tweede Wereldoorlog*, Amsterdam 2010.

Meyer, Ahlrich, 'Großraumpolitik und Kollaboration im Westen Werner Best, die Zeitschrift 'Reich-Volksordnung-Lebensraum' und die deutsche Militärverwaltung in Frankreich', *Beiträge zur nationalsozialistischen Gesundheits- und Sozialpolitik* (10) 1992, 29-76.

Meyers, Armand, 'La Magistrature et l'Occupation. Discours prononcé à l'audience solennelle de rentrée du 1er octobre 1919 de la cour d'appel de Liège', *Journal des Tribunaux*, 1919, col. 542.

Michielsen, J.N.M.E., *The 'Nazification' and 'Denazification' of the courts in Belgium, Luxembourg and the Netherlands, The Belgian, Luxembourg and Netherlands. Courts and their Reactions to Occupation Measures and Measures from their Governments Returning from Exile* (PhD Diss Maastricht), Maastricht: Universitaire Pers Maastricht 2004.

Middelberg, Mathias, *Judenrecht, Judenpolitik und der Jurist Hans Calmeyer in den besetzten Niederlanden 1940-1945*, Göttingen: V&R Unipress 2005.

Mill, John Stuart, *Utilitarianism*, orig. 1861, many editions.

Millon, C., Les *droits de la puissance occupante sur la justice judiciaire française, 1940-1944*, Paris, Dalloz Nouvelle bibliothèque de Thèses 2011.

Miosge, 'So begann 1933 der Zugriff auf das Reichsgericht', *Recht und Politik* (44), 2008, 226-230.

Miřička, August and Vladimír Solnař, *Nová úprava trestního soudnictví v Protektorátu Čechy a Morava*, Praha: Melantrich 1939.

Moll, Martin & Heinz P. Wassermann: 'Reich, Volksordnung, Lebensraum', in: Michael Fahlbusch, Ingo Haar & Alexander Pinwinkler (Eds.), *Handbuch der völkischen Wissenschaften: Akteure, Netzwerke, Forschungsprogramme*, De Gruyter 2017, 2118–2124.

Moravčík, Ctibor, *Organizace soudnictví Protektorátu Čechy a Morava*, Brno: Masarykova univerzita, 1993.

Morgan, Phillip, *The Fall of Mussolini: Italy, the Italians, and the Second World War*, Oxford University Press 2007.

Morgan, Philip, *Hitler's Collaborators. Choosing between bad and worse in Nazi-occupied Western Europe*, Oxford: Oxford University Press 2018.

Moritz, G., *Gerichtsbarkeit in den von Deutschland besetzten Gebieten 1939-1945*, (*Studien des Instituts für Besatzungsfragen* Vol 7), Tübingen: Institut für Besatzungsfragen 1955.

Mornet, A., *Quatre ans à rayer de notre histoire*, Paris: Self 1949.

Moseley Ray, *Mussolini: The Last 600 Days of Il Duce*, Lanham: Taylor Trade 2004.

Motive zu dem Entwurfe eines Bürgerlichen Gesetzbuches für das Deutsche Reich (Band 1, Allgemeiner Theil), Berlin/Leipzig: Guttentag 1896.

Mouffe, Chantal, *The Democratic Paradox*, London: Verso, 2000.

Muller, Françoise, *La Cour de cassation belge à l'aune des rapports entre pouvoirs: de sa naissance dans le modèle classique de la séparation des pouvoirs à l'aube d'une extension de la fonction juridictionnelle (1832-1914/1936)*, Bruges: La Charte 2011.

Nabulsi, Karma, *Traditions of war, Occupation, resistance, and the law*, Oxford: Oxford University Press 2007.

Nahmmacher, Kathrin, *Die Rechtsprechung des Reichsgerichts und der Hamburger Gerichte zum Scheidungsgrund des § 55 des EheG 1938 in den Jahren 1938 bis 1945*, Berlin: Peter Lang 1999.

Nationaal-socialistisch jaarboek 1942.

Nationaal-socialistische almanak 1943-1944.

Nationaal-socialistische (fascistische) staatsleer (NSB brochure 3), 1933.

Nestler, L., *Die faschistische Okkupationspolitik in Belgien, Luxemburg und den Niederlanden (1940-1945)*, (*Europa unterm Hakenkreuz*, Vol 4), Berlijn: Deutscher Verlag der Wissenschaften 1990.

Neuman, H.J., *Arthur Seyss-Inquart. Het leven van een Duits onderkoning in Nederland*, Utrecht: Veen 2nd edition 1989.

Niksch, Dieter, *Die sittliche Rechtfertigung des Widerspruchs gegen die Scheidung der zerrütteten Ehe in den Jahren 1938-1944*, Köln 1990.

Nissen, Henrik S., *1940 Studier i forhandlingspolitikken og samarbejdspolitikken*, Copenhagen: Gyldendal 1973.

Nissen, Gunnar, 'Krigstid og Landssvikoppgjør i ettertid, i Gunder Egge', in: Gunnar Nissen & Johannes Dannevig, *Den dømmende makt. Domstolenes organisasjon og virksomhet*, Oslo: Universitetsforlaget 1983.

Novotný, Josef, 'Nejvyšší správní soud: (historické poohlédnutí na naše správní soudnictví, jeho přítomnost a nutnost neodkladných změn.). I. část', *Správní právo* (32) 1999, 73-92.

Nüßlein, Franz, 'Die deutsche Gerichtsbarkeit im Protektorat Böhmen und Mähren – Strafrechtspflege', *Deutsches Recht* 1940, 2085-2091.

Nýdl, Bohumil, 'Základy nacionálně-socialistické nauky právní', *Právník*, (78) 1939, 1-20.

Ockrent, Roger, *Les crises constitutionnelles du pouvoir législatif en Belgique. Les pouvoirs des Secrétaires généraux sous l'occupation ennemie, suivie de: Délégation du Pouvoir législatif au Roi, Avant-projet de réforme constitutionnelle*, Brussels: Office de Publicité 1944.

Ondruš, Radek, *Vybraná rozhodnutí Nejvyššího správního soudu ve věcech administrativních 1918-1948 a jejich využití v současné aplikační praxi*, Praha: Linde 2001.

Ondruš, Radek, 'Nejvyšší správní soud 1918-1952 a jeho odkaz pro současnost', *Justiční praxe* (1) 2002, 91-99.

Oppenheim, L. & H. Lauterpacht, *International Law, A Treatise*, Vol. II: *Disputes, War and Neutrality*, London: Longmans, Green & Co. 5th Ed, 1935.

Osterkamp, Jana, *Verfassungsgerichtsbarkeit in der Tschechoslowakei (1920-1939): Verfassungsidee, Demokratieverständnis, Nationalitätenproblem*, Frankfurt am Main: Klostermann 2009.

Oudemans, Th.C.W. & A.P.M.H. Lardinois, *Tragic Ambiguity. Anthropology, Philosophy and Sophocles' Antigone*. Leiden, E.J. Brill, 1987.

Pasák, Tomáš, *Pod ochranou říše*, Praha: Práh 1998.

Passelecq, Fernand, *La magistrature belge contre le despotisme allemand*, Paris-Nancy: Librairie militaire 1918.

Patricelli, Marco, *Liberate il Duce. Gran Sasso 1943: la vera storia dell'Operazione Quercia*, Milano: Mondadori 2002.

Pauli, Gerhard, *Die Rechtsprechung des Reichsgerichts in Strafsachen zwischen 1933 und 1945 und ihre Fortwirkung in der Rechtsprechung des Bundesgerichtshofes*, De Gruyter 1992.

Pavone, Claudio, *Una Guerra civile. Saggio storico sulla moralità nella Resistenza*, Milan: Bollati Boringhieri 1991 (transl. in English as *A Civil War: A History of the Italian Resistance*, London: Verso Books 2013).

Paxton, R. O., *La France de Vichy, 1940-1944*, Paris: Le Seuil 1973.

Peli, Santo, *Storia della Resistenza in Italia*, Turin: Einaudi 2015.

Peters, Kirsten, 'Les abandons de poste dans la magistrature lors de la Seconde Guerre mondiale', *Cahiers d'histoire du temps présent* (24) 2011, 163-186.

Petersen, Georg, 'Die Tradition des Reichsgerichts', in: Albert Kistner (Ed), *Festschrift zur Eröffnung des Bundesgerichtshofes*, C.F. Müller 1950, 25-37.

Pfeiffer, Gerd, 'Das Reichsgericht und seine Rechtsprechung', in: *Deutsche Richterzeitung* 1979, 325-332.

Pirenne, Jacques, et Marcel Vauthier, *La législation et l'administration allemandes en Belgique*, Paris – New Haven: Presses universitaires de France 1925.

Pisenti, Piero, *Una Repubblica necessaria (RSI)*, Rome: G. Volpe 1977.

Planiol, Marcel, George Ripert & Jean Boulanger, *Traité élémentaire de Droit Civil*, Paris 1943.

Plum, Günter, 'Staatspolizei und Innere Verwaltung 1934-1936', *Vierteljahrshefte für Zeitgeschichte* 13 (1965), p. 191-224.

Poulsson, Erik T., 'Den Norske Sakførerforening juli 1941-mai 1945', in: Christophersen, Rolf (Ed), *Den Norske Sakførerforening 1933–1958*, Oslo: Den Norske Sakførerforening 1958, 91-121.

Pradier-Fodéré, Paul, *Traité de droit international public européen et américain suivant les progrès de la science et de la pratique contemporaines*, Paris:

G. Pedine-Lauriel 1897.Petersen, Harald & Jens Herfeldt, *Retsvæsen og Politi under Besættelsen* (*Danmark under Verdenskrig og Besættelse* Vol III), Copenhagen 1948.

Princ, Michal, *Soudnictví v českých zemích v letech 1848-1938: (soudy, soudní osoby, dobové problémy)*, Praha: Wolters Kluwer 2015.

Quartermaine, Luisa, *Mussolini's Last Republic. Propaganda and Politics in the Italian Social Republic (R.S.I.) 1943-45*, Exeter: Intellect 2000.

Rabl, Kurt, 'Das Reichskommissariat', in: Du Prel & Janke, *Die Niederlande im Umbruch der Zeiten* 1941, 83-90.

Rádl, Zdeněk, *Nejvyšší správní soud*, Praha: Nákladem Československého Kompasu 1933.

Raïssac, G., *De la Marine à la justice. L'orage d'une fin d'été. Un magistrat témoigne*, Paris: Albin Michel 1972.

'Rechtspraak, oorlog en vrijheid', 2020. https://www.rechtspraak.nl/Themas/rechtspraak-oorlog-vrijheid.

Redor, Marie-Joëlle, *De l'État légal à l'État de droit; l'évolution des conceptions de la doctrine publiciste française, 1879-1914*, Paris: Économica/Presses universitaires d'Aix-Marseille, 1992.

Remy, D., *Les lois de Vichy, Actes dits « lois » de l'autorité de fait se prétendant « gouvernement de l'Etatfrançais*, Paris: Romillat 1992.

Rentrop, Wilhelm, 'Preise im Protektorat', *Prager Archiv für Gesetzgebung und Rechtsprechung*, (21) 1939, 235-242.

Ricoeur, P., 'La Symbolique du mal', in: P. Ricoeur, *Finitude et culpabilité*, Paris, Aubier, 1960.

Röhr, Werner, 'System oder organisiertes Chaos? Fragen einer Typologie der deutschen Okkupationsregime im zweiten Weltkrieg', in: Robert Bohn, *Die deutsche Herrschaft in den „germanischen" Ländern 1940-1945*, Stuttgart: Franz Steiner Verlag 1997, 11-45.

Rolin, Henri, 'Procédure en cassation', in: *Réforme de la procédure*, Vol III, Brussels: Centre d'études pour la réforme de l'État 1938, 229-344.

Romijn, Peter, '"Restoration of confidence": The Purge of Local Government in the Netherlands As a Problem of Postwar Reconstruction', in: *The Politics of Retribution in Europe* 2000, 173-193.

Romijn, Peter, *Snel, streng en rechtvaardig. De afrekening met 'foute' Nederlanders*, Olympus 2002.

Romijn, Peter, *Burgemeesters in oorlogstijd*, Amsterdam: Balans 2006.

Romijn, P., 'Ambitions and dilemmas of local authorities in the German-occupied Netherlands, 1940-1945', in: H. van Goethem, B. De Wever & N. Wouters (eds.) *Local Government in Occupied Europe*, Antwerp, University Press, 2006, 33-36.

Romijn, Peter, *Der lange Krieg der Niederlande. Besatzung, Gewalt und Neuorientierung in den vierziger Jahren*, Wallstein Verlag 2017.

Rosendaal, Joost, *Nijmegen '44. Verwoesting, verdriet en verwerking*, Nijmegen: Vantilt 2009.

Rossi, Elena Aga, *Una nazione allo sbando. 8 settembre 1943*, Bologna: Il Mulino 2006.

Rousselet, M., *Histoire de la magistrature française: des origines à nos jours*, Paris: Plon 1957.

Roxin, Claus, *Täterschaft und Tatherrschaft*, 10th Ed, De Gruyter 2019.

Royer, J. P., *Histoire de la Justice en France*, Paris: Presses Universitaires de France 1996.

Rudelle, Odile, 'Constitutionnaliser la Déclaration des droits de l'Homme?', in: Marc-Olivier Baruch & Vincent Duclert (Eds), *Justice, politique et République de l'affaire Dreyfus à la guerre d'Algérie*, Bruxelles, Complexe, 2002, 125-143.

Rüthers, B., *Die unbegrenzte Auslegung, Wandel der Privatrechtsordnung im Nationalsozialismus*, Heidelberg: C.F. Müller Verlag (5th Ed), 1997.

Rüthers, Bernd, *Die unbegrenzte Auslegung*, Mohr Siebeck 2012.

Sandmo, Erling, *Siste ord: Høyesterett i norsk historie*, Vol. 2: 1905-1965, Oslo: J.W. Capellen 2005.

Sandmo, E., 'Just past: on historical and legal history', in: K. Johansson & M. Linstedt Cronberg (Eds), *Vånskap over gränser. En Festskrift till Eva Osterberg*, Lund 2007, 113-128.

Sansico, V., *La justice déshonorée*, Paris: Tallandier 1995.

Sauvé, Jean-Marc, 'Le Conseil d'État et la protection des droits fondamentaux', lecture at Nagoya University, 27 October 2016.

Scavenius, Erik, *Forhandlingspolitiken under besættelsen*, Copenhagen: Hasselbalch 1948.

Schädler, Sarah, *Justizkrise und Justizreform im Nationalsozialismus. Das Reichsjustizministerium unter Reichsjustizminister Thierack (1942-1945)*, Mohr Siebeck 2009.

Schelle, Karel and Jaromír Tauchen, *Recht und Verwaltung im Protektorat Böhmen und Mähren*, München: Dr. Hut 2009.

Schelle, Karel and Jaromír Tauchen et al., *Demokratiserung der tschechischen Rechtsordnung (1989-2009)*, München: Dr. Hut 2009.

Schelle, Karel and Jaromír Tauchen et al., *Protektorát Čechy a Morava – jedna z nejtragičtějších kapitol českých novodobých dějin (vybrané problémy)*, Brno: The European Society for History of Law 2010.

Schlesinger, Herbert J., *Promises, Oaths, and Vows. On the Psychology of Promising*, Analytic Press 2008.

Schmidt, 'Deutsche Strafgerichtsbarkeit im Protektorat Böhmen und Mähren', in: *Prager Archiv für Gesetzgebung und Rechtsprechung*, 1939, 1099 ff.

Schmitt, Carl, *Völkerrechtliche Großraumordnung: mit Interventionsverbot für raumfremde Mächte. Ein Beitrag zum Reichsbegriff im Völkerrecht*, Berlin: Deutscher Rechtsverlag 1939.

Schmitt, Carl, *Der Begriff des Politischen*, Berlin: Duncker und Humblot 2002 (orig. 1932).

Schmoeckel, Mathias, 'Der maßgebliche Zeitpunkt zur Bestimmung der Sittenwidrigkeit nach § 138 BGB', in: *Archiv für die civilistische Praxis* (197) 1997-1/2, 1-197.

Sch.[neider], H., 'Høiesterett avsier en dom av historisk betydning (Der Oberste Gerichtshof erläßt ein Urteil von geschichtlicher Bedeutung), udgitt av Justisdepartementet, Stenersens Forlag, Oslo, 1941', *Reich – Volksordnung – Lebensraum*, Vol. II, 1942, p. 487-488.

Schreiber, Otto (Ed), *Die Reichsgerichtspraxis im deutschen Rechtsleben. Festgabe der juristischen Fakultäten zum 50jährigen Bestehen des Reichsgerichts (1. Oktober 1929)*, Berlin, de Gruyter 1929.

Schröder, Jan, 'Gab es eine (Privat-) Rechtstheorie der Weimarer Republik?', in: Martin Löhnig & Mareike Preisner (Eds), *Weimarer Zivilrechtswissenschaft*, Mohr Siebeck 2014, 151-174.

Schubert, Werner, *Die Deutsche Gerichtsverfassung 1869-1877*, Vittorio Klostermann 1981.

Schubert, Werner (Ed), *Volksgesetzbuch. Teilentwürfe, Arbeitsberichte und sonstige Materialien*, Berlin: De Gruyter 1988.

Schubert, Werner, Peter Rieß & Jürgen Regge (Eds), *Quellen zur Reform des Straf- und Strafprozeßrechts, Abt. II: NS-Zeit (1933-1939) Strafgesetzbuch, Vol 1 & 2*, Berlin: De Gruyter 1989.

Schuyt, Kees, *R.P. Cleveringa. Recht, onrecht en de vlam der gerechtigheid*, Amsterdam: Boom 2018.

Schwartz, S., Spires, E. & Young, R., 'Why do people keep their promises? A further investigation', *Experimental Economics* (22) 2019, 530–551.

Seyss-Inquart, Arthur, 'Aus Anlass der Übernahme der Regierungsgewalt', Den Haag, May 29th 1940, in: Reichsminister Seyss-Inquart, *Vier Jahre in den Niederlanden. Gesammelte Reden*, Amsterdam: Volk und Reich Verlag 1944, p. 7-12.

Seyss-Inquart, A., 'Die politische Aufgabe des Reichskommissars', *Reich – Volksordnung – Lebensraum* (II) 1942, 9-14.

Siebert, Wolfgang, *Verwirkung und unzulässige Rechtsausübung*, Marburg 1934.

Sikkes, J.H., *... In geval van een vijandelijken inval. Ambtelijk gedrag in bezettingstijd en de daarvoor geldende aanwijzingen*, Deventer: Kluwer 1985.

Simons, Walter, '7 Jahre Reichsgerichtspräsident', in: *Deutsche Juristenzeitung* 1929, 1249ff.

Soeharno, Jonathan, *The Integrity of the Judge. A Philosophical Inquiry*, Farnham: Ashgate 2009.

Soulez-Larivière, D., *Les juges dans la balance*, Paris: Ramsay 1987.

Stengers, Jean, *L'action du Roi en Belgique depuis 1831, Pouvoir et influence*, Paris: Duculot 1992.

Stern, Elisabeth & Sifton, Fritz, *Keine gewöhnlichen Männer, Dietrich Bonhoeffer und Hans von Dohnanyi im Widerstand gegen Hitler*, C.H. Beck 2013.

Stirk, P., 'Carl Schmitt's "Völkerrechtliche Grossraumordnung"', *History of Political Thought* (20) 1999-2, 357-374.

Stirk, Peter, *The Politics of Military Occupation*, Edinburgh: Edinburgh University Press 2009.

Strauß, Walter, 'Reichsgericht und Bundesgerichtshof', in: Bundesminister der Justiz (Ed), *Festgabe 75 Jahre Reichsjustizgesetze*, 1954, 51-55.

Tamm, Ditlev, *Retsopgøret under besættelsen*, Copenhagen: Gyldendal 1984.

Tauchen, Jaromír, 'Prameny práva v nacistickém Německu', in: *Dny práva 2009 – Days of Law 2009*, Brno: Masarykova univerzita 2009, 2757-2773.

Tauchen, Jaromír, 'Právní řád a publikace právních předpisů v Protektorátu Čechy a Morava', in: *Dny práva 2012 – Days of Law 2012*, Brno: Masarykova univerzita 2013, 701-716.

Tauchen, Jaromír, 'Legislation on the Disposal of Jewish Property in the Protectorate of Bohemia and Moravia', in Martina Fiamová (Ed), *Anti-Semitic Legislation in Slovakia and in Europe*, Bratislava: Ústav pamäti národa 2015, 110-124.

Tauchen, Jaromír, 'Das Protektorat Böhmen und Mähren und seine Rechtsordnung (1939–1945)', *Beiträge zur Rechtsgeschichte Österreichs* (10) 2020-2, 260-268.

Telders, B.M., *Verzamelde geschriften*, Vol IV, Den Haag: Nijhoff.

Telders, C.S., 'Ben', in: C.S. Telders et al. (Eds), *Levensbeschrijving van prof. mr. B. M. Telders*, 's-Gravenhage: Martinus Nijhoff 1972, 11-54.

Terlinden, Georges, *La magistrature belge sous l'occupation allemande: souvenirs de guerre, août 1914 – octobre 1918, discours prononcé devant la Cour de Cassation de Belgique*, Bruxelles: Bruylant 1919.

Thiessen, Jan, 'Gute Sitten und „gesundes Volksempfinden': Vor-, Miss- und Nachklänge in und um RGZ 150, 1', in: Arndt Kiehnle, Bernd Mertens & Gottfried Schiemann (Eds), *Festschrift für Jan Schröder zum 70. Geburtstag*, Tübingen: Mohr Siebeck 2013, 187-219.

Thiessen, Jan, '"Anschluss" an die "Arisierung": Drei wirtschaftsrechtliche Reichsgerichtsfälle aus Österreich', in: *Beiträge zur Rechtsgeschichte Österreichs* 2017, 204-215.

Thiessen, Jan, *Der Ausschluss aus der GmbH als „praktische Durchführung einer verbrecherischen Irrlehre' – eine Rechtsfortbildungsgeschichte*, Mohr Siebeck 2022.

Thoma, Richard, 'Das Reich als Demokratie', in Richard Thoma & Gerhard Anschütz (Eds) *Handbuch des deutschen Staatsrechts*, Vol 1, Tübingen: Mohr 1930-32, 186-200.

Thonissen, Jean-Joseph, *La Constitution belge annotée offrant sous chaque article l'état de la doctrine, de la jurisprudence et de la législation*, 2nd Ed, Brussels: Bruylant 1876.

Tompkins, Peter, *Italy Betrayed*, London: Simon And Schuster 1966.

'Toujours debout', *Justice libre, affilié au Front de l'Indépendance* (3) May 1945.

Trausch, Gilbert (Ed), *Histoire du Luxembourg. Le destin européen d'un « petit pays »*, Toulouse: Privat 2003.

United Nations Office on Drugs and Crime (Ed), *Commentary on The Bangalore Principles of Judicial Conduct*, 2007, 147-159. https://www.unodc.org/documents/nigeria/publications/Otherpublications/Commentry_on_the_Bangalore_principles_of_Judicial_Conduct.pdf.

'Un point d'Histoire', *Justice Libre* [clandestine], November 1942.

Van den Dries, N.C.M.A., *De Hooge Raad der Nederlanden tijdens de bezetting*, Leiden: Brill 1945 (partly published in Venema et al. 2008).

Van den Wijngaert, Mark, *Het beleid van het comité van de Secretarissen-generaal in België tijdens de duitse bezetting 1940-1944*, Brussels: Paleis der Academiën 1975.

Van Goethem, Herman, 'La convention de La Haye, la collaboration administrative en Belgique et la persécution des Juifs à Anvers', *Cahiers d'Histoire du Temps Présent* (17) 2006, 117-197.

Van Goethem H., B. De Wever & N. Wouters (Eds) *Local Government in Occupied Europe*, Antwerp, University Press, 2006.

Vasbotten, Per, *Høiesterett avsier en dom av historisk betydning*, Oslo: Stenersens Forlag 1941.

Venema, Derk, *Rechters in oorlogstijd, De confrontatie van de Nederlandse rechterlijke macht met nationaal-socialisme en bezetting*, Den Haag: Boom Juridische uitgevers 2007, http://repository.ubn.ru.nl/handle/2066/37572.

Venema, D., 'Transitional Shortcuts to Justice and National Identity', *Ratio Juris* (24) 2011-1, 88-108.

Venema, Derk, 'The Judge, the Occupier, His Laws, and Their Validity. Judicial review by the Supreme Courts of occupied Belgium, Norway, and the Netherlands 1940-1945 in the context of their professional conduct and the consequences for their public image', in: Margo De Koster, Hervé Leuwers, Dirk Luyten & Xavier Rousseaux (Ed), *Justice in Wartime and Revolutions*, Brussels: State Archives 2012, 193-213.

Venema, Derk, 'Een levensgevaarlijke marionet. De terdoodveroordeling van Anton Mussert', in: R. Baas et al. (Eds.), *Rechtspleging en rechtsbescherming. Liber amicorum voor prof. dr. Leny E. de Groot-van Leeuwen*, Deventer: Kluwer 2015, p. 293-306.

Venema, Derk, 'Judiciaries and Foreign Rule. Legal anthropological reflections on three Belgian cases', in: Annie Hondeghem, Xavier Rousseaux & Frédéric Schoenaers, (Eds.), *Modernisation of the Criminal Justice Chain and the Judicial System. New Insights on Trust, Cooperation and Human Capital*, Dordrecht: Springer 2016 (*Ius Gentium: Comparative Perspectives on Law and Justice*, Vol. 50), 266-275.

Venema, Derk, 'The Netherlands', in: Lavinia Stan & Nadya Nedelsky (Eds), *The Encyclopedia of Transitional Justice. Vol. 2: Country Studies*, Cambridge: Cambridge University Press, 2nd Edition 2019.

Venema, Derk, 'A Perilous Puppet. The Trial of Dutch Nazi Leader Anton Mussert', in: Andreas Raffeiner (Ed), *Auf der Klaviatur der Rechtsgeschichte. Festgabe für Kurt Ebert zum 75. Geburtstag* (Rechtsgeschichtliche Studien, Band 84), Hamburg: Verlag Dr. Kovač 2019, 967-976.

Venema, Derk, Leny de Groot-van Leeuwen & Thomas Mertens (Eds), *Onder de huidige omstandigheden, De Hoge Raad en het Toetsingsarrest 1942,* Den Haag: Boom Juridische uitgevers 2008.

Verburg, M.E., *Geschiedenis van het Ministerie van Justitie. Deel II: 1898-1940*, Den Haag: Sdu Uitgevers 2001.

Verburg, M.E., *De procureurs-generaal in vergadering bijeen, Grepen uit de notulen van 60 jaar,* Den Haag: Sdu Uitgevers 2005.

Verburg, Marcel, *Geschiedenis van het Ministerie van Justitie 1940-1945. Een departement in oorlogstijd*, Amsterdam: Boom 2016.

Vergez-Chaignon, B., *Histoire de l'épuration*, Paris: Bibliothèque historique Larousse 2010.

Verhoeyen, Etienne, 'La lettre pastorale du Cardinal van Roey sur la capitulation du 28 mai 1940 – Le rôle du barreau et de la magistrature', *Cahiers d'Histoire de la Seconde guerre mondiale* (5) 1978, 221-242.

Verwaest, Rik, *Van Den Haag tot Genève: België en het internationale oorlogsrecht (1874-1950)* (Justice and Society II), Brugge: De Keure 2011.

Veselá, Jarmila and Jaroslav Lepšík, *Německé trestní řízení. Německé vojenské trestní řízení*, Praha: Českomoravský kompas, 1939.

Vlček, Eduard, *Dějiny trestního práva v českých zemích a v Československu*, Brno: Masarykova univerzita 2006.

Vogel, J. & P. Schulten, 'Het dwaalspoor van een praktisch staatsrecht, Jaap Schrieke (1884-1976)', in: P.J. Knegtmans, P. Schulten & J. Vogel (Eds), *Collaborateurs van niveau, opkomst en val van de hoogleraren Schrieke, Snijder en Van Dam*, Amsterdam: Vossiuspers AUP 1996, 30-154.

Vollprecht, Hans, 'Das Reichsverwaltungsgericht und die Aufsichtsführung in Kriegsschädensachen', *Deutsche Verwaltung* (19) 1943, 426-428.

Von Frijtag Drabbe Künzel, G., *Het recht van de sterkste, Duitse strafrechtspleging in bezet Nederland*, Amsterdam: Bert Bakker 1999.

Wadle, Elmar, 'Das Reichsgericht im Widerschein denkwürdiger Tage', in: Wadle, Elmar (Ed), *Verfassung und Recht, Wegmarken ihrer Geschichte*, Böhlau 2008, 277-290.

Walzer, Michael, *Just and Unjust Wars*, New York: Basic Books 1992.

Weber, M., *Wirtschaft und Gesellschaft*, Tübingen, Mohr, 1922.

Weber, Paul, *Geschichte Luxemburgs im Zweiten Weltkrieg*, Luxembourg: Buck 1946.

Wedekind, Michael, *Nationalsozialistische Besatzungs- und Annexionspolitik in Norditalien 1943 bis 1945. Die Operationszonen „Alpenvorland" und „Adriatisches Küstenland"*, München: Oldenbourg 2003 (orig. 1964).

Weil, P. & D. Pouyaud, *Le droit administratif*, Paris: Presses Universitaires de France 2010.

Weinkauff, H., 'Die deutsche Justiz und der Nationalsozialismus. Ein Überblick', in: *Die deutsche Justiz und der Nationalsozialismus*, Vol. 1, Stuttgart: Deutsche Verlags-Anstalt 1968, 17-188.

Weisberg, R., *Vichy, la justice et les Juifs*, Paris: Editions des archives contemporaines 1998.

Weitjens, W.M.A., *Hoor en wederhoor*, 1946.

Whelan, Frederick G., *Democracy in Theory and Practice*, Routledge 2019.

Wils, Lode, *Flamenpolitik en aktivisme: Vlaanderen tegenover België in de Eerste Wereldoorlog*, Leuven: Davidsfonds 1974.

Wingerter, Elisabeth, *Law, Order and Postwar Purge in the Grand Duchy of Luxembourg (1944 – 1955): Transitional Justice and Redistribution through the example of Justice, Gendarmerie and Police*, (unpublished PhD Diss.), University of Luxembourg 2021.

Wnuck, Felix Tilman, 'Rechtspraxis im Protektorat Böhmen und Mähren. Eine Mikrogeschichte des Amtsgerichts in Brünn im Jahre 1942', *Journal on European History of Law* (9) 2018-2, 50-58.

Wunderlich, Georg, *Der belgische Justizstreik, insbesondere die deutschen Staatsanwaltschaften in Belgien (Zugleich eine Studie zum Rechte der Okkupation)*, Berlin: Heymann 1930.

X., 'Occupatio bellica', *Frankfurter Zeitung*, 4 August 1940, 3.

Zarusky, Jürgen, 'Recht und Justiz in der NS-Diktatur. Neue Literatur', *Zeitschrift für Neuere Rechtsgeschichte* (28) 2006, 409-432.

Zurné, Jan Julia, *Tussen twee vuren. Gerecht en verzet tijdens de Tweede Wereldoorlog*, Tielt: Lannoo 2017.

https://trema.nvvr.org/editie/2018-03

https://watwedoen.nl/project/om-des-gewetens-wille/

https://www.conseil-etat.fr/actualites/discours-et-interventions/le-conseil-d-etat-et-la-protection-des-droits-fondamentaux

https://www.courdecassation.fr/agenda-evenementiel/

Index[1]

1 Made with the assistance of Carolus Grütters.

Made in the USA
Monee, IL
13 September 2026

63176219R00188